International Perspectives: Integration and Inclusion

International Perspectives: Integration and Inclusion

Edited by
James Frideres
John Biles

Queen's Policy Studies Series
School of Policy Studies, Queen's University
McGill-Queen's University Press
Montreal & Kingston • London • Ithaca

X

SCHOOL OF
Policy Studies
Publications Unit
Robert Sutherland Hall
138 Union Street
Kingston, ON, Canada
K7L 3N6
www.queensu.ca/sps/

The preferred citation for this book is:
Frideres, J. and J. Biles, eds. 2012. *International Perspectives: Integration and Inclusion*. Montreal and Kingston: Queen's Policy Studies Series, McGill-Queen's University Press.

Library and Archives Canada Cataloguing in Publication

International perspectives : integration and inclusion / edited by James Frideres, John Biles.

(Queen's policy studies series)
Co-published by: McGill-Queen's University Press.
Includes bibliographical references.
ISBN 978-1-55339-317-7

1. Emigration and immigration—Social aspects. 2. Immigrants—Social conditions. 3. Social integration. 4. Emigration and immigration—Government policy. I. Frideres, James S., 1943- II. Biles, John, 1971-III. Queen's University (Kingston, Ont.). School of Policy Studies IV. Series: Queen's policy studies series

JV6225.I58 2012   304.8   C2012-900452-9

CONTENTS

Part 2   Beyond Politics: Infrastructure and Policy

ACKNOWLEDGEMENTS

International comparisons are not always as valued as they need to be in the world of policy-makers, practitioners, and researchers. Too often, opportunities for engaging one's peers on questions of mutual concern are deemed to be junkets that should quickly be jettisoned in difficult economic times. While this common sense approach is certainly common, it is not necessarily sensible. In the world of social policy, experiments are rare and fraught with ethical challenges; thus, a reliance on examining what others have attempted and what they learned from the experience becomes indispensible.

The annual International Metropolis Conferences have been a space for these global conversations on integration and migration for the past 15 years. Without them and many of the core figures that have animated them, this volume would not have been possible. We owe a debt of gratitude to Meyer Burstein, Rinus Penninx, Jan Rath, Paul Spoonley, and Erin Tolley, to name but a few.

In Canada we are indebted to Rachelle Leroux and Jodi Peterson of the Citizenship and Immigration Canada library, who helped us locate references in the wide and eclectic universe of global academic journals. We are equally indebted to Mark Howes, Valerie Jarus, and Maureen Garvie at the Queen's School of Policy Studies for the professional manner in which they ably stick-handled this volume through the multiple stages of production. Arthur Sweetman's initial idea to develop this series and Howard Duncan's agreement to devote some of the Metropolis Project's resources to this and related volumes must be noted.

The time and intellectual energy required to complete this project were stolen from that allotted to various important people in our lives, including Carol, Adelaide, Mary-Lee, and Deborah Tunis. We appreciate your support and tolerance of our poor time management skills.

Finally, we would like to acknowledge the tremendous work undertaken by those tasked with developing and implementing integration and inclusion policies around the world. The work is difficult, particularly in the present fiscal environment, and often seems thankless, with critics decrying the limitations to the integration and inclusion flowing from the policies, and yet others asserting that the same policies are undermining societal cohesion and should be eliminated. We admire your ability to constantly seek to find the balance between going too far and not going far enough. This is the work of nation building, and you are the architects. We hope that we may have aided you in this important endeavour.

INTRODUCTION

JOHN BILES* AND JAMES FRIDERES

Current indicators reveal that migration patterns will continue until the end of the twenty-first century, driven by demographic trends: an aging population and negative population replacement rates in high income countries – for example, birth rates less than 2.1. A few illustrations will demonstrate how demographic trends will influence high and low income countries in the future. Today there are about 214 million international migrants worldwide, of which 60 percent live in developed countries and 59 percent originate in developing countries. While the number of immigrants in the world only represents 3 percent of the world's population, numerically they are the largest number in recorded history (International Organization for Migration 2011). Most of them have moved permanently, with only small but stable return flows back to their countries of origin (Zlotnik 2010).

Push factors in countries of origin, including labour force growth and natural disasters along with the pull factors including better labour market opportunities and demographic contractions in developed nations, seem likely to ensure the overwhelming South-North flow of immigrants. In the inflows to major immigrant receiving countries, the percentage of immigrants from developing countries varies from a low of around 40 percent in Germany and the United States, 80 percent in Australia and Canada, and 90 percent in Spain and the United Kingdom (Simmons 2011). Between 1975 and 2005, the immigrants' share of the receiving societies'

---

*The opinions expressed in this chapter are those of the authors and do not necessarily reflect those of Citizenship and Immigration Canada or the Government of Canada.

International Perspectives: Integration and Inclusion, ed. J. Frideres and J. Biles. Montreal and Kingston: Queen's Policy Studies Series, McGill-Queen's University Press. © 2012 The School of Policy Studies, Queen's University at Kingston. All rights reserved.

populations in the more developed world has doubled from 5 to 10 percent (IOM 2011), thus diversifying both sides of the integration equation – the "host societies"[1] and the newcomers themselves. This population flow is destined to continue, as projections reveal that there will be a significant growth in the labour force in developing countries from 2.4 billion in 2005 to 3.6 billion in 2040 (McDonald and Kippen 2001). Others maintain that climate change will induce disasters likely to result in additional migration flows of refugees (Collett 2010; United Nations 2000). The ramifications for the kinds of integration and inclusion strategies necessary to obtain positive sum outcomes are profound.

NUMBERS, GEOGRAPHY, AND CAPITAL

All of the figures above point to the need for policy-makers in receiving and sending nations to focus on the process of integration as these migrants attempt to establish themselves in their new homes. To ensure a cohesive and inclusive society, receiving societies need policies and programs that will be most effective and efficient in integrating newcomers. As many developed countries have chosen to make immigration part of their solution to meet their economic and demographic needs, immigrants and their children are important components in a country's economic, social, cultural, and political development, including the country's overall level of well-being.

Given the diversity of the world's national labour markets, existing immigration stocks, and historical migration patterns, it is not surprising that governments diverge in terms of their migration policies (Collett 2010). Countries with long histories of immigration tend to focus more on placing conditions upon immigrants and/or restricting immigration flows. These countries are not developing migration policies for the first time but rather are revising and reforming them on the basis of their experiences (Simmons 2010). A similar process of revising integration strategies is taking place in explicit recognition that previous policies have not been as successful as hoped or as capable of adjusting to a diversification of both newcomers and receiving communities. In addition, over the past quarter-century an increasing number of "new immigration" nations have already introduced (and others are poised to do so) immigration reforms designed to attract highly skilled newcomers, while sending countries actively develop strategies designed to maximize benefits to their citizens (MIPEX 2011).

At the same time, there is increasing recognition that migrants may be both an asset and liability for both sending and receiving countries. For the receiving nations, the mobility of people can reduce labour market imbalances, promote the exchange of expertise and ideas, and result in the availability of experts to train younger generations, particularly in the skilled trades. In countries of origin, migrant remittances can improve the standard of living of the families left behind, and their collective remittances may support various forms of economic and social development. With an estimated $316 billion sent home in 2009, the impact on the economic resilience of those countries has been substantial. Some researchers also hypothesize that allowing out-migration of those with high levels of human capital encourages a wider range of their compatriots to acquire higher levels of human capital. Since many of these individuals will not migrate, the result is a rise in overall levels of human capital in sending countries (Stark, Helmenstein, and Prskawetz 1998).

However, liabilities of migration can also be found on both sides of the equation. For receiving societies, the easy assumptions of portability of credentials and experience controlled through an appropriately calibrated selection regime have been debunked, and the real limits of selection's ability to reduce transaction costs of immigration and integration is increasingly apparent. For sending societies, the impact of brain drain, particularly in the health professions, continue to garner attention.

It is important to confront the challenges and fears that opponents to migration have exploited. For example, if we needlessly constrain legal means for migration, it will take place through unsafe and irregular channels, ultimately undermining the confidence in the ability of governments to govern. We must work to understand the demands of an increasingly diverse society so that the end result is social cohesion and integration (Ki-moon 2008). We must also specify that social cohesion and integration, while often conflated in public discourse, remain two separate, albeit linked, processes. Social cohesion is the process by which a society seeks to generate sufficient centripetal force to exist and flourish as a harmonious community; it is concerned with the inclusion/exclusion of all citizens, not just the foreign born. Integration, on the other hand, is the process (or end goal) by which immigrants become accepted into society, both as individuals and as groups. This integration of newcomers is often defined as a reciprocal process whereby both newcomers and host societies adapt to one another to create an evolving social cohesion that ties all citizens together in mutual obligations, responsibilities, and respect. In short, the integration of newcomers is only one of the many axes of concern for those interested in social cohesion. In this volume we will deal almost exclusively with the integration and inclusion of newcomers; broader conceptions of social cohesion are tackled in a companion volume edited by Spoonley and Tolley (2011).

INTEGRATION AND INCLUSION

Integration and inclusion have long been the subjects of considerable research in classic countries of immigration such as Australia, Canada,

New Zealand, and the United States (Adelman et al. 1994; Biles, Burstein, and Frideres 2008; Hawkins 1991; Hendersen et al. 1997; Reitz and Breton 1994; Bloemraad 2006). In the past two decades, these countries have increasingly been joined by a wide range of European nations that have seen themselves shift from nations of emigration to nations of a hybrid of immigration/emigration or predominantly of immigration. These countries run the gamut from those with long-standing experience such as the United Kingdom to those such as Austria, Finland, and Spain, whose contemporary experience with migration is more limited. An additional array of countries have also emerged, including Israel, China, and Japan, that have quite specific, if not unique, experiences with migration (Noam 1994; Weiner 1997). The result has been an astonishing amount of research published in this period (Baldwin-Edwards and Shain 1994; Penninx, Spencer, and Van Hear 2008).

It has become quite commonplace for various bilateral comparisons to be undertaken, such as Canada-Australia (Adelman et al. 1994; Hawkins 1991) and Canada-United States (Schmidt Sr 2007; Bloemraad 2006; Strum and Biette 2005). Multilateral comparisons, often principally based in Europe, have become more common as well (Collett 2011; Hammar 2010; IOM 2011; Bertelsmann Stiftung and MPI 2010; Ersanilli and Koopmans 2010; Joppke 1999, 2007; Givens 2007; Van Tubergen, Maas, and Flap 2004; Kogan 2006; Kesler 2006; Favell 2003). Most of these comparative studies focus on specific aspects of integration, usually labour market participation or civic engagement. By contrast, this volume seeks to tackle a broader approach to integration and so has brought together contributors from all of these groupings of nations. It seeks to glean comparisons and contrast approaches across 11 nations: Australia, Austria, Canada, China, Finland, Israel, Japan, Spain, Sweden, the United Kingdom, and the United States. In addition, it contains chapters comparing public opinion as well as formal legislative approaches to immigration as measured by the MIPEX index now in its third iteration.

CROSS-NATIONAL COMPARISONS

The difficulties in detailed cross-national comparisons are legion, although comparisons within a broad framework are both possible and invaluable to those tasked with implementing policy and programs as well as those who study immigration, integration, and inclusion (Ersanilli and Koopmans 2011). We should be clear that we have not asked the authors to describe the integration and inclusion "models" of the countries they cover. We agree with the misgivings of Duyvendak and Scholten (2011) in terms of how models tend to obscure more than they reveal and tend to result in path dependency or resistance to change. With this in mind, we have asked all of the authors to contribute country case studies that address six different aspects: 1) the historical context of immigration and related demographics; 2) the broad definition or approach or evolution of approaches to integration and inclusion underpinning policies; 3) the policies and programs designed to foster integration and inclusion; 4) an empirically grounded critical assessment of those policies and programs; 5) any best practices that emerge from this analysis; and finally, 6) the challenges that have either been successfully tackled or remain to be effectively addressed.

Each of these components is worth some discussion before launching into the volume itself. A better understanding of the limitations and peculiarities of each component will allow readers to approach each case study critically and to harvest relevant knowledge for themselves. Perhaps the most problematic issue raised when comparisons are made relates to those critiques that deny the very possibility of comparisons, a position usually premised upon claims of contextual specificity. In the context of immigration, this issue is most commonly a question of the overall size of the flows of migrants, the characteristics of where they hail from, and the kinds of communities in which they settle, as well as the human and financial capital that newcomers import. The critiques are certainly pertinent to the countries we have included in this volume: it is hard to imagine more disparate contexts than those we have incorporated here.

However, rather than a failing, we see this breadth as a virtue of this volume. The major countries of immigration are prone to a certain group-think and path dependency ("but we've always done it this way"), so the illustration that there are, in fact, significant variations on what can and has been done to facilitate attraction and retention is an important lesson that is missed when only the most similar cases are included in the analysis. This variation in case studies is also useful to countries with less pronounced immigration histories, as it provides examples from other parts of the world and does not just rest comfortably within the confines of the pan-European comparisons that are so common. In short, in this volume, we have sought to broaden the policy solution set.

Despite the difficulties inherent in international comparisons, policy-makers also remain focused on examining impacts of selection regimes, settlement delivery mechanisms, and means to utilize fully the capital (human and financial) that newcomers bring with them. For example, the connections between selection regimes and integration programming are becoming increasingly clear in all major immigrant receiving countries. In particular, there is increasing recognition that all categories of newcomers are selected, whether by themselves, by others, or through various mechanisms to match newcomers to labour market needs. (See box, "Examples of Immigration Categories," which identifies the various categories currently employed by immigrant receiving countries.)

Accordingly, with each category of newcomers, host societies have options available to minimize settlement and integration programming needs and therefore expenses incurred. Learning from the experiences of others enables a wider view than would otherwise be the case for policy-makers, practitioners, and researchers, all of whom are extremely interested in selection models and associated integration outcomes.

In a related fashion, the division between major urban and smaller centres where newcomers settle, as well as rural areas with less recent experiences with migration, has also become a focus of international comparisons. In particular, host societies are interested in how different delivery models for settlement services, including the role of municipalities, effects integration outcomes. The scale of most settlement and integration programs does not lend itself to rapid change, so once again cross-jurisdictional comparisons are invaluable.

Examples of Immigration Categories

- Immigrant
- Economic immigrant
- Skilled worker
- Business class immigrant
- Investor, entrepreneur, self-employed immigrant
- Family class immigrant
- Principal applicant
- Dependant
- Undocumented worker
- Temporary foreign worker
- Domestic worker
- Live-in caregiver
- International student
- Provincial nominee
- Refugee
- Sponsored refugee
- Government-assisted refugee
- Convention refugee
- Asylum refugee
- Protected person
- Unaccompanied refugee children

Finally, how to most effectively harness the human and financial capital of newcomers continues to bedevil most immigrant receiving states. The most common problems surround the recognition of foreign credentials as well as the effective implementation of investor and entrepreneur programs that do not fall prey to those with a more flexible conception of the rule of law. In all cases, a better understanding of diverse approaches attempted around the world leads to more informed policy discussions.

FRAMING DISCOURSE: DEFINITION AND APPROACH TO INTEGRATION AND INCLUSION

In recent years it has become clear that definitions and approaches to integration and inclusion vary considerably. Most recently, the retreat from multiculturalism exemplified by political speeches in the United

Kingdom, the Netherlands, Germany, and France, to name a few, has obscured more than it has clarified. Informed observers are well aware that the development of the "pillars" approach utilized in the Netherlands bears little connection to the republican model of France, or to the integrationist approach of Canada (Duyvendak and Scholten 2011; Winter 2010). Despite these differences, it is possible to categorize these approaches along a more discerning continuum of approaches, which can then inform policy debates in all of the countries in question.

Integration

Integration is defined as the process (or end goal) by which immigrants become accepted into society, both as individuals and as groups, and are able to fully participate in the social, cultural, political and economic structures of their society. By definition, integration is a two-way process involving both immigrants and the host society. Moreover, it takes place at both the individual and collective level (IOM 2010).

Increasingly, as Huddleston suggests (2010), both newcomers and host communities will diversify with continuing immigration. Immigrants will take permanent residency, and new generations will be born into the host country; they will form part of their receiving society and shape its future through their contributions in the many aspects of public life. This evolution of the host population obviously has ramifications for both integration and social cohesion as it fundamentally alters what newcomers are trying to integrate into. This is particularly true of the myriad ways in which immigrants are influenced with regard to their level of social, political, cultural, and economic integration.

Policies and Programs

There is general agreement by governments that policies help shape the flow of migrants. However, the precise role of these policies and their interactions has not been systematically studied. Interestingly, in the sparse literature, one study even suggests that the impact of policy is minimal, although this may be an artifact of the study design (Ersanilli and Koopmans 2011). Despite the paucity of evidence, policy analysts and public discourse appear to agree that the general features of admission and settlement policies have profound impacts (good or bad) on the integration of immigrants and the subsequent relations with native born residents.

Policy-makers and practitioners are particularly interested in comparisons that inform their daily work. Unfortunately, there is relatively little comparative work that achieves this end. Instead, policy-makers retreat to closed-door, invitation-only discussions like the Intergovernmental Consultations on Asylum, Refugee, and Migration Policies (IGC), which meets regularly to discuss policy and program issues and usually features a roundtable discussion. The IGC is an informal, non-decision-making forum for intergovernmental information exchange and policy debate on issues of relevance to the management of international migratory flows. It brings together 17 participating states, UNHCR, IOM, and the European Commission. IGC activities are informal and flexible and structured around three clusters of issues (admission, control, and enforcement; asylum and refugees; immigration and integration) and two cross-cutting activities (technology and country of origin information). These consultations tend to focus on very precise programmatic issues and feature presentations by policy-makers tasked with those issues. There is very little in the way of joint critical comparative analysis; instead, each country is left to develop the analysis it requires for its own policy processes.

While aspects of policy and programming inevitably differ across countries, thus thwarting systemic analysis, there are some fairly standard components. These include information and orientation; language and skills; labour market access; mainstreaming services/welcoming communities programming; and, increasingly, an emphasis on planning and performance measurement. Furthermore, there is a contemporary international conversation among policy-makers as to where on the immigration continuum these services should be available, how they should be provided, and who should pay for them. For these conversations to be informed, more robust international comparisons are essential.

CRITICAL ASSESSMENT

Similar to policies and programs, little comparative research is framed by solid performance measurement or evaluation data and instead tends to rely on broad societal level indicators. A possible exception may be the Migrant Integration Policy Index (MIPEX), which assesses how European countries (and Canada and the United States) provide opportunities for immigrants to participate in society through assessing each government's commitment to integration. The index measures the extent to which immigrants can live with their family, have a secure residence status, have access to employment and education, and benefit from general services as well as from special measures addressing their specific needs. It also measures whether immigrants enjoy civic rights, are entitled to participate in public life, can acquire citizenship, and are protected against discrimination.

The index falls prey to the normative value ascriptions as outlined by Wallace-Goodman (2010). For example, one indicator pertains to "engaging with affected communities." In this index, maximum points are awarded to countries having formal consultative bodies, and minimum points for countries having less formal interactions, although they may include more robust engagements of civil society. Nevertheless, the index provides a broad overview of the integration efforts of each country. Empirically based assessments of the relative successes (or failures) of settlement and integration programs and policies are vitally important to informed policy debates around the world. Nevertheless, those seeking isomorphic relations between policy on the one hand and practice and empirical research on the other are cautioned that policy decisions are often made in contested political environments, thus limiting the extent to which the comparisons are congruent with policy outcomes.

Best Practices

Somewhat ironically, while critical assessments are few and far between, there is a greater literature on best practices that can be gleaned from around the world. Indeed, any number of networks around the world purport to fulfill this mandate, e.g., Metropolis, the International Migration, Integration and Social Cohesion Organization (IMISCOE), the Centre on Migration, Policy and Society (COMPAS), and the Migration Policy Institute (MPI). What is lacking in this literature is generally a sense of any intellectual rigour that would be brought to bear on what constitutes a best practice and therefore give the reader confidence that the selected practices were indeed those worthy of emulation rather than simply those with which the author(s) were familiar. The perfect criteria are not nearly as badly needed as some criteria to better inform discussions occurring globally as investments in settlement and integration come under increasing scrutiny by governments seeking to rebalance their budgets in the wake of economic recession.

Challenges: Vanquished and Contemporary

Finally, while it is certainly possible to compile lists of challenges, it is rather more difficult to identify those that may have been effectively addressed. Generally, as in the media, little research attention is accorded to planes that land safely. Given the flurry of immigration, integration, and inclusion policies that have characterized the last decade as well as the enormous quantity of resources that nations have provided, it would be surprising if some challenges have not been overcome. This sense that success can be obtained is critical to the work of those in the field and to attracting and maintaining political commitment (Bertelsmann Stiftung and MPI 2009). For example, the new model of viewing homelessness, which has shifted global approaches away from shelters and towards addressing core housing need, is instructive as to how shifts in paradigms will lead to successes. International comparisons have the power to shift paradigms and to encourage greater expenditures when success can be defined and international experiences suggests it can be obtained.

This volume is divided into two sections. Part 1 focuses on specific countries and their history, policies, and programs related to immigration and integration. We have included countries with well-established immigration/integration policies which have dealt with migration issues for long periods of time. In other cases, we have included "insular" countries such as Japan. We have also included China in our country-specific case studies; while the authors have not addressed the issue of international immigration, their focus is upon internal migration from various regions within the country. Part 2 focuses on infrastructure and policy. It includes comparative chapters on integration focusing on Europe and Canada, and a Canada-Sweden comparison on economic returns to citizenship. A third chapter looks at public opinion in several countries regarding immigration.

The chapters in Part 1 outline the historical context of immigration as well as the population changes over time. This section will provide the reader with a broad understanding of the early immigration policies and their attempts at integration or assimilation. Given the variable understanding of concepts, we also have asked the contributing authors to incorporate, as best as possible, how their state defines integration and whether or not the definition has changed over time. Next, each chapter identifies the policies and programs that have been put into place to promote immigrant integration and discusses how and why policies have evolved. Each chapter also provides a contemporary profile of immigrants in that country and current integration policies and programs for various dimensions of integration.

Authors were then tasked with evaluating the policies and programs and providing a critical assessment of policies, using existing empirical evidence. Their assessments will provide readers with a basis of a comparison of the diversity of policies and an identification of "best practices." The authors have attempted to identify the main challenges (current and future) facing the integration of immigrants in their country and how these issues might be germane for other states.

This is not to argue that we have produced the perfect internationally comparative volume. Rather, we have tasked the individual authors with highlighting the components of a comparative frame most relevant to their context. In addition, their varying academic backgrounds and interests act as a prism through which their chapters have emerged. In our conclusion to this volume, we present our analysis of what we perceive to be the most interesting themes. Readers are cautioned, however, that the value of international comparisons, like beauty, is best captured in the eyes of the beholder. We trust that you will find much of value to you in this volume whether you are a researcher, a practitioner, or a policy-maker, and regardless of the country in which you find yourself situated.

NOTE

1.   "Host society" is a commonly used to term to denote the society that receives immigrants and into which those immigrants integrate. We prefer it to "receiving society," which is the other commonly used term, and one which we feel lends itself more to discussion of immigration than integration. "Host" at least implies some level of hospitality and reciprocity. However, we feel it falls short of the mark in terms of the depth of reciprocity and power sharing necessary for integration to work effectively (Biles and Ibrahim 2005). Nevertheless, owing to the wide currency of "receiving society" within the field of immigration studies and "host society" within integration studies, we have opted to use them as short-hand throughout this chapter.

REFERENCES

Adelman, H., A. Borowski, M. Burstein, and L. Foster, eds. 1994. *Immigration and Refugee Policy: Australia and Canada Compared*. Toronto: University of Toronto Press.

Baldwin-Edwards, M. and M.A. Schain, eds. 1994. *The Politics of Immigration in Western Europe*. Ilford, Essex: Frank Cass.

Bertelsmann Stiftung and Migration Policy Institute. 2009. *Migration, Public Opinion and Politics*. Gutersloh: Verlag Bertelsmann Stiftung.

—2010. *Prioritizing Integration*. Gutersloh: Verlag Bertelsmann Stiftung.

Biles, J., M. Burstein, and J. Frideres, eds. 2008. *Immigration and Integration in Canada in the Twenty-First Century*. Montreal and Kingston: McGill-Queen's University Press.

Biles, J., and H. Ibrahim. 2005. "Religion and Public Policy: Immigration, Citizenship, and Multiculturalism – Guess Who's Coming to Dinner?" In *Religion and Ethnicity in Canada*, ed. P. Bramadat and D. Seljak, 154-77. Toronto: Pearson.

Bloemraad, I. 2006. *Becoming a Citizen: Incorporating Immigrants and Refugees in the United States and Canada*. Berkeley: University of California Press.

Collett, E. 2010. *The Future of European Migration: Policy Options for the European Union and Its Member States*. Migration Policy Institute, Switzerland, International Organization for Migration.

—2011. "Immigrant Integration in Europe in a Time of Austerity." Migration Policy Institute. At http://www.migrationpolicy.org/pubs/TCM-integration.pdf (accessed 9 May 2011).

Duyvendak, J.W. and P.W.A. Scholten. 2011. "Beyond the Dutch 'Multicultural Model': The Coproduction of Integration Policy Frames in the Netherlands." *International Migration and Integration* (12):331-48.

Ersanilli, E. and R. Koopmans. 2010. "Rewarding Integration? Citizenship Regulations and Socio-Cultural Integration of Immigrants in the Netherlands, France and Germany." *Journal of Ethnic and Migration Studies* 36(5):773-91.

—2011. "Do Immigrant Integration Policies Matter? A Three-Country Comparison among Turkish Immigrants." *West European Politics* 34(2):208-34.

Favell, A. 2003. "Integration Nations: The Nation-State and Research on Immigrants in Western Europe." *Comparative Social Research* (22):13-42.

Givens, T.E. 2007. "Immigrant Integration in Europe: Empirical Research." *Annual Review of Political Science* (10):67-83.

Hammar, T. 2010. "Introduction to European Policy: A Comparative Study." In *Selected Studies in International Migration and Immigrant Incorporation*, ed. M. Martiniello and J. Rath, 45-58. Amsterdam: University of Amsterdam Press.

Hawkins, F. 1991. *Critical Years in Immigration: Canada and Australia Compared*. Montreal and Kingston: McGill-Queen's University Press.

Henderson, A., A. Trlin, R. Pernice, and N. North. 1997. "English Language Requirements and Immigration Policy in New Zealand, 1986–1997." *New Zealand Population Review* 23:19-44.

Huddleston, T. 2010. *The Future of Integration Policy*. Migration Policy Group, Geneva, International Organization for Migration.

International Organization for Migration (IOM). 2010. *World Migration Report: The Future of Migration, Building Capacities for Change*. Migration Policy Group. Geneva: IOM.

—2011. "Input to the Ninth Coordination Meeting on International Migration." New York, February 17-18. Department of Economic and Social Affairs, United Nations Secretariat.

Joppke, C. 1999. *Immigration and the Nation-State: The United States, Germany and Great Britain*. Toronto: Oxford University Press.

—2007. "Transformation of Immigrant Integration: Civic Integration and Antidiscrimination in the Netherlands, France and Germany." *World Politics* 59(2):243-73.

Kesler, C. 2006. "Social Policy and Immigrant Joblessness in Britain, Germany and Sweden." *Social Forces* 85(2):743-70.

Ki-moon, H.E. Ban. 2008. "Address to the Second Global Forum on Migration and Development." 29 October, Manila.

Kogan, I. 2006. "Labor Markets and Economic Incorporation among Recent Immigrants in Europe." *Social Forces* 85(2):697-721.

McDonald, P. and R. Kippen. 2001. "Labour Supply Prospects in Sixteen Developed Countries, 2000–2050." *Population and Development Review* 27(1):1-32.

MIPEX. 2011. *Migrant Integration Policy Index III*. Brussels: British Council and Migration Policy Group.

Noam, G., ed. 1994. *Immigrant Absorption in Israel*. Jerusalem: JDC-Brookdale Institute.

Penninx, R., D. Spencer, and N. Van Hear. 2008. "Migration and Integration in Europe: The State of Research." Report commissioned by the Economic and Social Research Council for NORFACE. At http://www.norface.org/files/migration-COMPAS-report.pdf (accessed 4 July 2011).

Reitz, J. and R. Breton. 1994. *The Illusion of Difference: Realities of Ethnicity in Canada and the United States.* C.D. Howe Institute.

Schmidt, R. Sr. 2007. "Comparing Federal Government Immigrant Settlement Policies in Canada and the United States." *American Review of Canadian Studies* 37(1):103-22.

Simmons, A.B. 2010. *Immigration and Canada: Global and Transnational Perspectives.* Toronto: Canadian Scholars' Press.

—2011. "Population Growth: From Fast Growth to Possible Decline." In *The Changing Canadian Population*, ed. B. Edmonston and E. Fong, 23-40. Montreal and Kingston: McGill-Queen's University Press.

Spoonley, P. and E. Tolley, eds. 2011. *Diverse Nations, Diverse Responses: Approaches to Social Cohesion in Immigrant Societies.* Montreal and Kingston: McGill-Queen's University Press.

Stark, O., C. Helmenstein, and A. Prskawetz. 1998. "Human Capital Depletion, Human Capital Formation, and Migration: A Blessing or a 'Curse?'" *Economic Letters* 60:363-7.

Strum, P. and D. Biette, eds. 2005. *Education and Immigrant Integration in the United States and Canada.* Proceedings of a conference held 25 April. Washington, DC: Woodrow Wilson International Centre for Scholars. At http://www.wilsoncenter.org/topics/pubs/DUSS_us_canada_final.pdf (accessed 9 May 2011).

United Nations. 2000. "Replacement Migration: Is It a Solution to Declining and Ageing Populations?" United Nations Population Division. At http://www.un.org/esa/population/publications/migration/execsum.htm (accessed 9 May 2011).

Van Tubergen, F., I. Maas, and H. Flap. 2004. "The Economic Incorporation in Eighteen Western Societies: Origin, Destination, and Community Effects." *American Sociological Review* 69(5):704-27.

Wallace-Goodman, S. 2010. "Integration Requirements for Integration's Sake? Identifying, Categorizing and Comparing Civic Integration Policies." *Journal of Ethnic and Migration Studies* 36(5):753-72.

Weiner, M., ed. 1997. *Japan's Minorities: The Illusion of Homogeneity.* New York: Routledge.

Winter, E. 2010. "Trajectories of Multiculturalism in Germany, the Netherlands and Canada: In Search of Common Patterns." *Government and Opposition* 45(2):166-86.

Zlotnik, H. 2010. "Globalization and Interdependence." 27 October, United Nations, New York.

PART 1

IMMIGRATION IN THE INTERNATIONAL ARENA

CHAPTER 1

INTEGRATION AND INCLUSION OF IMMIGRANTS IN AUSTRALIA

JOCK COLLINS

Australia, with the United States, Canada, and New Zealand, is one of the few Western countries to have actively pursued a settler immigration policy over the six decades following the end of World War II. About one million migrants arrived in each of the four decades following 1950: 1.6 million between October 1945 and June 1960, about 1.3 million in the 1960s, about 960,000 in the 1970s, about 1.1 million in the 1980s, and 900,000 in the 1990s. In the past decade Australian immigration intakes increased significantly to reach record postwar levels in 2008, falling after the global financial crisis. By the 2006 Australian census, about 22.2 percent (DIAC 2008, 1) of the Australian population were first generation immigrants, exceeding that relative immigrant population of United States, Canada, and New Zealand, as it had done for many decades. In the post-1945 period, about 6.4 million immigrants have arrived in Australia, with immigrants now a major component of the Australian population increase from 7 million to 22.4 million people today. In Australia's major cities such as Sydney, Melbourne, and Perth, more than half of the population are first or second generation immigrants. Immigration has contributed about half of Australia's population growth (Australian Productivity Commission 2006, xv-xvi).

Since the end of the White Australia Policy in the early 1970s, Australia's immigration net has trawled all corners of the globe. One of the outcomes of immigration has been the emergence of a society characterized by a great degree of cultural, religious, linguistic, and ethnic diversity, particularly in Australia's largest cities, given the urban destination of most immigrants. The result is that Australia today is one of the world's most

International Perspectives: Integration and Inclusion, ed. J. Frideres and J. Biles. Montreal and Kingston: Queen's Policy Studies Series, McGill-Queen's University Press. © 2012 The School of Policy Studies, Queen's University at Kingston. All rights reserved.

cosmopolitan nations. This chapter critically investigates how the state has responded to the settlement needs of this large, diverse immigrant community and attempts to answer the following questions: What has been the content of programs and services to address the needs of new immigrants in Australia? How has the programmatic and philosophical content of Australian multiculturalism changed over time? What has happened to Australia's immigrants? Are they included or excluded from economic, political, social, and cultural activities of daily Australian life? What do they think of life in Australia, and what do non-immigrant Australians think of them?

The aim of this chapter is thus to investigate the extent to which immigrants have been included in, and integrated into, Australian society. The term *integration* has some conceptual limitations and aspects that are country specific. To take the latter first, Australia introduced a settlement policy of integration in the brief interregnum between the end of assimilation and the emergence of multiculturalism in the late 1960s and early 1970s, but the policy was not clearly defined or distinguished from those that preceded or followed (Lopez 2000). The term *integration* lacked currency in Australian policy debates about immigrant settlement until the last years of the Howard government (1996–2007); it was then floated as a possible alternative to multiculturalism, which appeared to also interest the Labor opposition. But the elements of an integration settlement policy have never been clearly defined, nor has there been any attempt to specify how different this would be from Australian multiculturalism policy. Indeed, the terms *assimilation* and *integration* are largely synonymous in the Australian context, as they appear to be in the European and US context (Schneider and Crul 2010, 1145). The concept of *social inclusion* also has some conceptual limitations – ironically, because of its breadth – and aspects that are country specific. Social inclusion embraces a wide range of economic, political, social, and cultural domains and has objective/subjective and formal/substantive aspects. It is synonymous with, though not identical to, the concepts of social cohesion, social justice, social order, and social harmony (Jupp 2007, 11-14). It is sometimes defined in terms of its opposite, social exclusion, just as social cohesion is often defined in juxtaposition to social conflict (Collins 2007a). Other binaries often investigated include belonging/isolation, participation/non-involvement, recognition/rejection, and equality/inequality. Subjective issues of identity, belonging, place attachment, values and solidarity, and concepts of social capital and friendship networks are also key elements when attempting to evaluate immigrant social inclusion in Australia (Markus and Kirpitchenko 2007, 23). Racism, racial discrimination, and racialization, as well as social class, are also central to an evaluation of the settlement story of Australia's immigrants (Collins 1991, 2000; Hage 1998).

While social exclusion had wide usage in a conceptual and operational sense in the UK under the Blair Labour government, and other countries, social inclusion was not embraced in Australia until the Rudd Labor government introduced a Social Inclusion Board in May 2008. However, immigrant minorities and ethnic diversity are not central to the Social Inclusion Board's activities and are not identified in the board's six priorities (Social Inclusion Board 2008). It is also important to note at the outset that Australian multiculturalism policy is very different to that in other countries (Castles 2000, 145-54). Moreover, multiculturalism in Australia has undergone significant change since its introduction over three decades ago. As Delanty (2009, 140) has argued, "Multiculturalism can mean quite different things depending on the conception of diversity that is invoked." While the notion was borrowed from, and is most similar to, Canadian multiculturalism, it is not established in legislation like its Canadian counterpart. Moreover, unlike British multiculturalism, which is often viewed as a conservative alternative to anti-racism policy, Australian multiculturalism embraces (albeit inadequately) anti-racism elements and has been accompanied by the introduction of a range of programs and services that extend beyond the cultural sphere to the economic, social, and political sphere. However, in the past two decades, many of these multicultural programs and services have been diluted or eliminated as the political construction of Australian diversity has been re-engineered to suit a post-9/11 climate where minority immigrants have been increasingly positioned as a threat to the nation.

With these conceptual points of departure in mind, this chapter critically evaluates the strengths and weaknesses of Australian multiculturalism from the point of view of Australia's immigrants themselves. The next section traces the policy responses to immigrant settlement in Australia from assimilation to integration to multiculturalism. The chapter then looks at the (contradictory) evidence across many different objective and subjective dimensions of immigrant social inclusion, social integration, and social cohesion in economic, social, political, and cultural life in Australia today. The final section draws these arguments together, highlighting the key stumbling blocks for immigrant settlement in Australia in the coming decades, suggesting key strengths and weaknesses of Australian multiculturalism, and raising the possibility of introducing a more cosmopolitan Australian multiculturalism to address these strengths and weaknesses.

From Assimilation to Multiculturalism

Assimilation was introduced by the first Australian immigration minister, Arthur Calwell, in 1947 who promised that a large-scale settler immigration program would not change the British character of Australian society. The principle was simple: immigrants had to become identical to other Australians and had to be treated in the same way as any other

Australians, except in regard to citizenship, which required a period of residency before it too was available to all immigrants. The assimilation policy was thus based on the central assumption that new immigrants should shed their difference (cultural, linguistic, religious, dress, food) and become the same as Australians (Castles et al. 1988; Collins 1991). The roots of assimilation policy were to found in the same prejudice and xenophobia that informed White Australia immigration policy. Under assimilation, there were no policy initiatives introduced to respond to different immigrant needs in the areas of education, health, welfare, the law, and the labour market (Collins 1991, 228-30). Assimilation resulted in significantly poorer socio-economic outcomes for immigrants from a non-English speaking background in schools, the labour market, hospitals, law courts, and broader society. Ethnic communities and their supporters mobilized to end assimilation: the contradictions of the assimilation model in attracting immigrant minorities but condemning them and their children to social exclusion led to its eventual replacement. After a brief interregnum of *integration* policy – which shifted the emphasis to meeting specific migrant community needs rather than "Anglo-conformity" (Levey 2008) – *multiculturalism* was introduced in the mid-1970s and remains the official policy and philosophy of immigrant settlement in Australian today.

The Whitlam Labor Government (1972–75) and its immigration minister, Al Grassby, rejected the assimilation philosophy that compelled new immigrants to leave their cultural baggage at the Australian customs control. He was looking for a more inclusive philosophy of immigrant settlement that would be accepting of, and responding positively to, religious, cultural, and linguistic difference (Grassby 1973). This was a landmark change in Australian settlement policy. But it was the conservative Fraser government (1975–83) that entrenched multiculturalism in Australia, borrowing the term and many policy approaches from the Canadian experience. Under multiculturalism, the cultural backgrounds of Australia's immigrant communities became a point of celebration, not shame. Moreover, multiculturalism took as a point of departure the fact that immigrants have different needs to non-immigrants and these different needs required migrant specific programs and services if immigrant minorities were to overcome the disadvantages that emerged particularly because of their poor English-language abilities (Collins 1991, 234-6). A wide range of programs and services for new immigrants – including SBS Television and Radio and child and adult migrant education programs – were introduced by the Fraser government, following the Galbally Report (Galbally 1978). Castles et al. (1988, 70) describe the report as institutionalizing an "ethnicity model" of disadvantage in which questions of social structure were ignored or mystified while ethnic community organizations were mobilized to deliver a wide range of programs and services. Thus an ethnic community-based welfare system was introduced as the backbone of multiculturalism, with ethnic community's leaders – mainly older males – providing a framework of political patronage with the peak body, the Federation of Ethnic Communities Councils of Australia (FECCA), holding a key position in federal government development of, and deliberations about, ethnic affairs policy.

The Hawke government later redefined multiculturalism as for *all* Australians and endorsed the three dimensions of multicultural policy proposed by the 1989 National Agenda for a Multicultural Society. These dimensions were cultural identity (the rights to maintain cultural religious and linguistic freedom in Australia), social justice (the right of all Australians to equality), and economic efficiency (the economic advantages that immigration and cultural diversity bring if this productive diversity is recognized and rewarded) (Office of Multicultural Affairs 1989). Hawke (1986) defined multiculturalism in 1986 as being "essentially equality of opportunity for everyone in this country from whatever cultural background they might come." The Office of Multicultural Affairs (OMA) was established in the Department of Prime Minister and Cabinet, reflecting the importance of ethnic affairs policy and multicultural program and services, while the Bureau of Immigration, Multicultural and Populating Research (BIMPR) was established to fund research on immigration and multiculturalism and to disseminate the results. The Keating Labor government (1991–96) was also a strong supporter of multiculturalism, but it introduced the six-months waiting period that made new non-humanitarian immigrant arrivals wait for half a year before they could access welfare and other services (Collins 1995). This policy change took away support for new immigrants at the very stage that their settlement needs were greatest and was introduced in the belief that migrants were "ripping off" welfare payments, a belief that was not supported by research then or later.

The conservative Howard government (1996–2007) had an attitude to multiculturalism that was at best lukewarm and at worst hostile. In office the Howard government retreated from multiculturalism. John Howard hardly used the word in his first term of office. Immigration was viewed through the prism of economic rationalism: the Howard government continued the economic emphasis on "productive diversity" and on the value of the "dividends of diversity" for the wider society (Howard 1996). Via its immigration minister, Phillip Ruddock, the Howard government stripped funding from many of the policies and programs established by previous Australian governments to support new immigrant settlement. It axed the OMA and BIMPR and cut funding to a range of migrant programs and services, including labour market programs and English language programs. It also introduced a two-year waiting period for non-humanitarian immigrant arrivals to access welfare payments. Migrant community service organizations such as the Migrant Resource Centres were marginalized with threats to cut funding if they were critical of government policy. The Howard government also introduced a citizenship test for new immigrants and introduced a set Australian values as part of a redefining of Australian national identity. The Australian Citizenship Council proclaimed in its report, *Australian Citizenship for a New Century* (2000), that "public acceptance of diversity" and abstract civil values were what united Australian citizens.

The roots of the Howard government's attitude to multiculturalism can be seen in the 1988 bicentennial immigration debate, when Howard, then the leader of the federal opposition, played the "prejudice card" by abandoning a long-held bipartisan stance and turning immigration and multiculturalism into a political issue by promising to reduce Asian immigration and abandon multiculturalism. He again played the "race card" in the 2001 federal election by sending the Australian navy to block the arrival on Australian shores of boats carrying unauthorized arrivals seeking asylum in Australia and introduced the "Pacific solution," whereby Pacific Island nations were paid to accommodate Australia's boat people – a stand that turned out to be decisive in his re-election (Marr and Wilkinson 2003). The Howard government also introduced mandatory detention for boat people – including children – in remote camps, even though the vast majority were eventually granted refugee status under the 1956 UN Convention on Refugees. Many of these policies mimicked the policies of One Nation, the anti-immigration party established by Pauline Hanson. This political opportunism was a form of "dog whistle politics" that gave the prime minister's and Conservative government's imprimatur to the racist concerns about minority immigration, particularly boat people (Poynting et al. 2004).

The Rudd Labor government (2007–10) made some cautious moves towards establishing the centrality of multiculturalism, though without great enthusiasm or major changes to its programmatic content, possibly because of a view within the Labor government that multiculturalism was not a vote winner among swinging voters. It revived the Australian Multicultural Advisory Council in 2008, and the prime minister has emphasized Australia's multicultural character in responses to violent attacks upon Indian overseas tertiary education students (O'Malley and Drape 2009). The re-establishment of the council was justified by the benefits to Australia of cultural diversity, justice for minorities, protection against racism, and equal economic opportunity (Ferguson 2008). Moreover, the Rudd government has explicitly included Indigenous peoples in the public discourse of diversity. Indeed, Rudd's 2008 "Apology to Australia's Indigenous Peoples" embodied elements of both the social justice and cultural recognition arguments that characterize multiculturalism as civic pluralism. However, the Rudd government did little to restore multiculturalism to the position of priority and influence that it had in the Fraser and Hawke governments. Ethnic community organizations and their leaders continued to be ignored by government, which appeared to think that there were few votes in multiculturalism.

IMMIGRANT SOCIAL INTEGRATION AND INCLUSION

Much of the debate about Australian immigration and multicultural- ism is framed from the viewpoint of whether the majority host culture gains gain or loses out as a consequence in terms of standard of living and lifestyle. This section looks at a different question: How successful have Australian immigration and multiculturalism been in the eyes of the immigrants themselves? Consistent with the argument presented in the introductory section about the concepts of social inclusion and integration, the evidence presented relates to a wide range of economic, social, political, and cultural dimensions of immigrant life in Australia. In addition, research is canvassed on racist attitudes and practices, im- migrant social and friendship networks, and the identities, aspirations, and belonging of immigrant youth.

Many international (Huntington 1997, 2004) and Australian (Blainey, 1984; Sheehan 1998, 2006) conservative commentators have argued that an immigration program that delivers immigrants from a great diversity of national, ethnic, religious, linguistic, and cultural backgrounds – such as Australia has experienced – is a recipe for social division and conflict. These critics have argued that multiculturalism in Australia and other countries will divide the nation into a number of competing and con- flicting tribes living parallel lives from the mainstream majority culture (Schneider and Crul 2010, 1144). This critique has been sharpened when immigrants of Muslim faith are included among immigrant settlers. The main problem with this argument, addressed below, is that the Australian evidence does not support it.

In addition, multiculturalism has many critics from the left. Here the concern is that multicultural policies are based on essentialized, stereo- typical, homogenizing notions of ethnicity that do not reflect the diversity of ethnic communities and the fluidity of ethnic identities, particularly of immigrant youth. In this view, multiculturalism in Australia (Hage 1998, 2002) is a policy of conservative containment for managing immigrant minorities by conceding peripheral and superficial cultural and religious rights (the 5 Ds of dance, diet, dress, dialect, and devotion) while exclud- ing them from economic, social, cultural, and political power, which remains the preserve of the white "mainstream." In this view, ethnicities are "caged," paraded as exotic performers for the host society, and always banished to its margins. In this critique, multiculturalism is viewed as a clever way that the capitalist state contains and constrains immigrant minorities, getting the benefits of the economic returns of migrant labour and immigrant entrepreneurs while maintaining their marginalization.

The main problems with this argument are threefold. First, it ignores the important gains and space, embodied in the 5 Ds, that multicultural- ism provided for immigrant minorities that were denied to them under assimilation policy. Second, it ignores the fact that the emergence of multi- culturalism, at least in Australia, was not the result of a conspiracy theory of the capitalist state but the result of immigrant *agency*, as immigrant communities – in alliance with progressive mainstream organizations and individuals such as the Teachers Federations – fought against the constraints of assimilation to provide a more central place and greater opportunity for minority immigrants and their children in Australian society (Martin 1978). Third, it ignores the fact that immigrant minorities in Australia have made significant inroads into the economic and political realms of Australian life. This is not to say that there are not contradic- tions or limitations within Australian multiculturalism. These have been identified in the previous section and will be revisited in the conclusion. Rather, the argument is that the evidence highlights the extent to which immigrant minorities have penetrated most aspects and dimensions of Australian life. Granted, this progress is not universal; a key contradic- tion of multiculturalism is its bi-modal nature – that is, the coexistence of achievement and under-achievement of immigrants from the same national, ethnic, cultural, or religious background.

Social Inclusion

The social exclusion framework shifts the focus away from the role of resource constraints (important though these often are) onto the other factors that can prevent people from participating in various forms of social, economic, and political activity. It shares with deprivation the idea that disadvantage is often multi-faceted and can only be adequately captured within a multi-dimensional framework (Saunders and Wong 2009, 11). To quote Levitas et al. (2007, 9): "Social exclusion is a complex and multi-dimensional process. It involves the lack or denial of resources, rights, goods and services, and the inability to participate in the normal relationships and activities, available to the majority of people in society, whether in economic, social, cultural, or political arenas. It affects both the quality of life of individuals and the equity and cohesion of society as a whole." The next section presents the evidence of immigrant social inclusion across a wide range of indicators.

Inclusion in the Economic Domain

The economic domain is critical to the life-chances of immigrants in Australia. Analysis of the industrial and occupational distribution of immigrant men and women in the Australian labour market in the 1960s and 1970s showed a highly gender-segmented labour market with immigrants from the UK, Ireland, and other English-speaking countries exhibiting similar – or better – labour market profiles to their non-immigrant counterparts, while minority immigrants were over-concentrated into menial, low-paying jobs. However, the end of the White Australia policy and a shift in the last three decades towards skilled migration have seen the arrival of many highly skilled immigrants from Asian countries. Patterns of labour market segmentation have thus been diluted as Asian immigrants moved into the primary labour market to take professional, managerial, and highly skilled jobs in finance, media, and other service sector industries (Collins 2006). Despite this trend, the immigrant profile in the Australian labour market is still bi-modal. Over half (51.7 percent) of non-OECD born immigrants in Australia hold tertiary education qualifications, compared to 32.4 percent of the native born. Only in Canada are non-OECD born immigrants more likely to hold tertiary education qualifications (63.6 percent). In all other OECD countries, the rate of non-OECD born immigrants who hold tertiary education qualifications is about one-third or less (OECD 2009, 97). On the other hand, in 2007 immigrants comprised nearly half (43 percent) of all employment in low-skilled occupations while immigrants, irrespective of the year of arrival in Australia, and comprised about one in three unskilled workers. Most of these immigrants were born in non-English-speaking countries (Collins 2011).

Nevertheless, racial discrimination in the labour market constrains the employment and promotion opportunities of immigrant minorities. Hawthorne (1994) demonstrated the discrimination in Australia faced by engineers born in the Middle East when compared to similarly qualified British born engineers. More recently, Booth, Leigh, and Varganova (2009) sent out job applications with similar CVs but distinctively different Anglo-Saxon, Indigenous, Italian, Chinese, and Middle Eastern names. They found statistically significant differences in callback rates, suggesting that ethnic minority candidates would need to apply for more jobs in order to receive the same number of interviews. These differences varied systematically across groups, with Italians (a more established migrant group) suffering less discrimination than Chinese and Middle Easterners (who have typically arrived more recently). Both studies demonstrate the resilience of racial discrimination that constrains the inclusion of immigrant minorities in the labour market at levels commensurate with their human capital.

The rate of immigrant unemployment is another important measure of social inclusion, since having a job impacts on income and well-being. On average, unemployment rates for immigrants are only slightly higher than for non-immigrants (Australian Productivity Commission 2006). But it is important to disaggregate this data. Unemployment data for 2004 show that immigrants on skilled visas in Australia had lower unemployment rates (4.3 percent) than the Australian born (4.9 percent). Those on temporary visas had a higher unemployment rate (6.4 percent) but not as high as permanent entrants under the family stream (8.8 percent); however, both these immigrant categories suffered less unemployment than the humanitarian intake, whose unemployment rate was 16.9 percent, more than three times that of the Australian born and about two and a half times greater than the average unemployment rate for immigrants in all categories of entry (ibid., 64).

The 2006 national census data, for a year that was at the height of the second postwar Australian boom, show that immigrant Australians with ancestry linked to Lebanon, Vietnam, the Pacific Islands, and African nations had much higher unemployment rates than immigrants of other ancestry and those with Australian ancestry. First and second generation immigrants of Lebanese/Middle Eastern, Vietnamese, and North African ancestries had rates of unemployment two to three times higher than average, with 22 percent of the Vietnamese second generation and 15 percent of the North African/Middle East second generation unemployed at a time when the Australian economy was generally regarded as fully employed. The presistence of disproportionately high unemployment rates for Vietnamese and Lebanese over decades indicates a problem of social exclusion for them, particularly for the second generation (Collins 2011).

Figure 1, based on labour force survey data for 2008–09, shows that although Australia escaped economic recession following the global financial crisis, immigrant minorities were hit hardest by the rise in unemployment that followed the economic downturn induced in the country's economy by the crisis.

Figure 2 shows that immigrants born in Northern Africa and the Middle East and in Oceania (New Zealand and the Pacific Islands) were hit hardest by the rise in unemployment rates. Data from the 2006 census also show that at a time when national unemployment rates were around 5 percent, unemployment rates for first and second generation immigrants who are Muslims were much higher than for immigrants of other religious background. Second generation Muslim males had a much higher rate of unemployment (18.1 percent) than first generation Muslim males (13.6 percent) and second generation Muslim females (12.5 percent) (Collins 2011).

Income and wealth, or lack of it, make up one measure of immigrant inclusion/exclusion. Ethnic origin or immigrant background is not a key axis of disadvantage in Australia, according to Saunders (2005) and Wilkins (2007). Nevertheless, immigrant minorities seem to be disproportionately concentrated at both ends of the income and wealth spectrum. The landmark Henderson National Poverty Inquiry (1975) found that immigrants from a non-English-speaking background (NESB immigrants) were significantly overrepresented among the Australian poor. Reviewing the poverty data more than two decades later, Williams and Batrouney

FIGURE 1
Unemployment Rate vs Country of Birth, Australia, October 2008 to October 2009

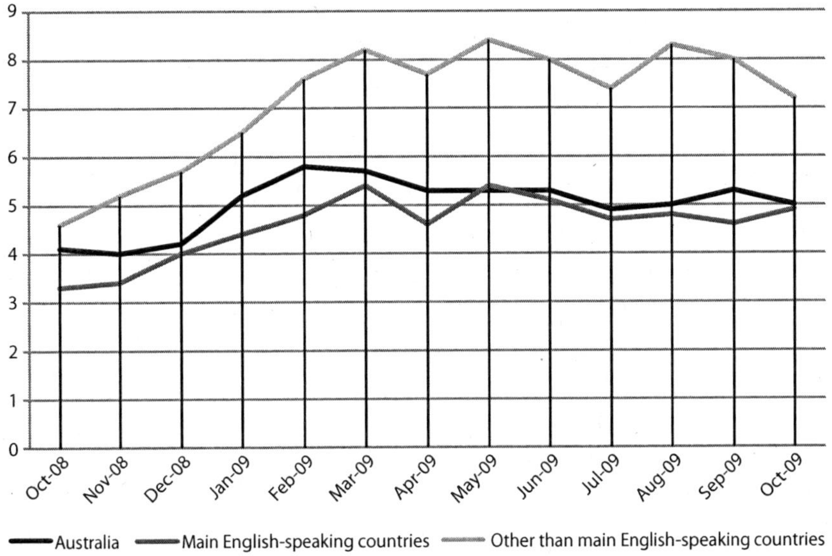

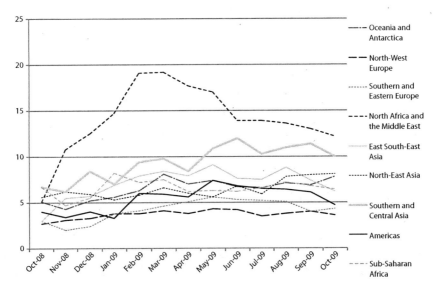

━━Australia ━━Main English-speaking countries ━━Other than main English-speaking countries

Source: Author's compilation from Labour Force Survey 2008–09, Australian Bureau of Statistics.

FIGURE 2
Unemployment Rate vs Country of Birth (Male and Female), All Age Range, All States, Australia

Source: Author's compilation from Labour Force Survey 2008–09, Australian Bureau of Statistics.

(1998, 263-5) reported that over the period 1981–82 to 1985–86, the poverty of immigrants increased by 50 percent, while for those born in Australia, it increased by 16 percent. Fincher and Wulff (1998) demonstrate that the suburbs of high concentration of minority immigrants – the western suburbs of Sydney and Melbourne in particular – are also the neighbourhoods of greatest urban poverty in Australia. Studies of income distribution also suggest that recently arrived immigrants, particularly those of a minority background, are "more heavily concentrated in the lower reaches of the distribution than other immigrants or the Australian-born" (Saunders and King 1994, 90).

At the other end of the wealth spectrum, a disproportionately large number of minority immigrants have made considerable fortunes in Australia. Each year the magazine *Business Review Weekly* publishes its list of the wealthiest 200 Australians. In its latest list (2010) the wealthiest Australian – worth $A5.04 billion – is Czechoslovakia born Frank Lowy, while the third wealthiest is Anthony Pratt, son of recently deceased Polish born immigrant Richard Pratt. The wealthiest new entrant is Chinese born Australian citizen Chau Chak Wing, who entered the list at number 35 with $920 million. Overall, 18 of the wealthiest 57 families in Australia are of minority immigrant background, as are at least 35 of the wealthiest 200 individuals. Australia's postwar immigrants are spread across all social classes, which is itself a measure of the inclusion of Australia's immigrants.

Inclusion in the Political Domain

Immigrant minorities have had a significant impact on political life in Australia at the local, state, and federal levels. The Federal Finance minister, Penny Wong, is of Chinese ancestry. In the past decade Victoria had a premier (Steve Bracks) of Lebanese background, while NSW had a premier (Maurice Iemma) of Italian background. In NSW, the key power brokers in the previous Labor government have been Eddie Obeid, of Lebanese background, and Joe Tripodi, of Italian background, with a number of ministers (Costa, Della Bosca) of Greek and Italian background. Similarly, former Melbourne City Council's lord mayor, Wellington Lee, is of ethnic Chinese background, as is former deputy lord mayor of Sydney, Henry Tsang. There are also a large number of local government mayors, such as Nick Lallich in Fairfield, one of Australia's most ethnically diverse LGAs.

Identity and Belonging

It is also important to consider subjective dimensions of immigrant inclusion in Australian society. Key issues here include national identity, feelings of belonging, aspirations, friendship networks, values, and trust. Two recent research projects involving minority immigrant youth provide interesting insights in this regard. The first was a 2007 survey of 340 young people aged 13–18 living in western or southwestern Sydney suburbs (hereafter the Sydney survey) designed so that 80 percent of respondents were of minority background (Collins and Reid 2009). The second was a research project involving a survey of 392 young Muslims living mainly in Sydney and focus groups of Muslim youth in Sydney, Melbourne, and Darwin (hereafter the Muslim survey) (Jakubowicz, Collins, and Chafic 2012). Both surveys provide evidence to suggest that first and second generation immigrant youth feel included in Australian society and are confident of their future in Australia. However, they are less certain about their identity as Australians.

Parekh (2000, 341) has argued that "a multicultural society cannot be stable and last long without developing a common sense of belonging among its citizens." The young respondents to the Sydney survey felt good about living in Australia: two in three young people reported to "often feeling good about living in Australia" and another one in four reported to "sometimes feeling good about living in Australia." They had strong aspirations and hopes for the future and also liked living in their suburb, felt "ownership" of their local places and spaces and felt that they "belong" in local neighbourhoods. Moreover, minority youth surveyed had friendship networks that extended beyond their ethnic or religious group, so that they did not live their lives parallel to and disconnected from other minority youth or youth from the majority. The Muslim survey also found social connectedness, with only 16 percent of the youth surveyed reporting that they had only Muslim friends.

The issue of national identity among minority youth in Australian multicultural society has long been a contentious issue (Castles et al., 1988; Sheehan 1998; Hage 1998; Castles 2000). As Parekh (2008, 4) has put it, "national identity raises difficult issues in multicultural societies." Only one-third of the informants in the Sydney survey identified themselves as "Australian," even though two-thirds were born in Australia. One in 20 "rarely" felt Australian, and about the same proportion did not really feel Australian at all. On the other hand, when asked if the Australian flag was important to them, approximately two-thirds of the youths thought the flag was important "often or sometimes." This result supports the argument that minority youth in Sydney have diverse and multiple identities; Butcher and Thomas (2003), who also interviewed young people in western Sydney, found that they forged hybrid, fluid identities that incorporate their migrant identity with elements of "being Australian." This position is consistent with the argument of Parekh (2008, 15) that "while some social identities are common to most societies, others vary." And even in the same society, identities are in a state of constant change. The young informants in the Muslim survey were very concerned with being "marginalized" within Australian society. Yet they do not ascribe to themselves a "minority" status, but rather see themselves as part and parcel of the Australian community. Indeed, they were more likely to identify as "Australian" than youth from the Sydney survey. Four out of every ten (41.58 percent) Muslim youth surveyed self-identified as "Australian" while another one in three (33.67 percent) gave their identity as "Muslim Australian." The vast majority (eight out of ten) of Muslim youth surveyed also "felt good about living in Australia."

SOCIAL COHESION

One important data base for evaluating social cohesion in Australia comes from two surveys conducted in 2007 and 2009 and funded by the Scanlon Foundation. The 2009 survey reported responses from 3,800 Australians aged over 18 years, 2,000 drawn nationally and 1,800 drawn from six areas of high immigrant minority concentration (Markus 2009). Both surveys asked questions across a range of social, economic, and political variables, including belonging, social justice and equity, participation, acceptance and rejection, and worth. The 2007 survey provided evidence of a high level of social cohesion, fostering a sense of belonging, social justice, and worth, a finding that continued to hold true in the 2009 survey (ibid., 3). However, the surveys also found that a minority – one in ten – of Australians hold strongly negative views on issues related to immigration and cultural diversity (ibid.). The 2009 survey found that in areas with high immigrant concentration, there was a greater reported experience of discrimination, while social cohesion was more difficult to maintain in these areas: "If sense of threat and lack of trust thwart the building of links between neighbours, there is the risk of escalating conflict should tensions arise. In such environments attitudes can develop which target and blame ethnic groups as the cause of socio-economic problems" (Markus 2009, 3).

Social Conflict

Social cohesion is, as we have seen, multi-faceted and thus hard to define and study. Its opposite is social conflict. But all societies exhibit conflict between different groups over time, oscillating between moments of cohesion and conflict. How much or what kind of conflict shifts a society from cohesive to divisive? In making this judgment, it is also important to acknowledge that social conflict in not necessarily a bad thing. The Chicago school of sociology saw conflict by ethnic groups as a necessary stage in the path to successful immigrant assimilation. In Robert Park's (2000) early theory of a "race relations cycle," ethnic conflict is an inevitable but intermediate stage that all new ethnic groups traverse on the way to assimilation in a Western metropolis. Max Weber (1970) saw ethnic conflict as a rational behaviour of ethnic groups designed to maximize their power in the marketplace, while Karl Marx saw class conflict as the driving force of capitalist society. There are many instances of ethnic or racial conflict in Europe and North America, many involving minority youth (Collins and Reid 2009). Indeed, critics of immigration to, and of multiculturalism in, Western societies argue that social conflict inevitably accompanies the settlement of cultural and religious minorities (cf. Blainey 1984; Huntington 1997, 2004).

How can the Australian experience of a non-discriminatory immigration policy be judged from the standpoint of conflict involving ethnic or religious minorities? A high point of ethnic conflict in Australia was the Sydney Cronulla Beach riots in December 2005, when thousands of mainly drunk white males chased and bashed men and women of "Middle Eastern appearance," and a retaliatory gang of males of "Middle Eastern appearance" sought revenge in a smash, bash, and flee raid in their cars on the suburbs surrounding Cronulla a few days later. The seriousness of the events at Cronulla Beach and the sentiments that propelled it should not be denied. In many ways, the riots were a wake-up call to Australian society, particularly in its cosmopolitan metropolises. They exposed the ever-present tensions between tolerance and prejudice, racism and multi-culturalism, and cohesion and conflict, and were a rather crude reminder of the responsibilities that go with non-discriminatory immigration policy at a time when globalization is increasing the size and diversity of immigration flows around the world. However, the riots were not the darkest of Australia's recent experiences with ethnic conflict, a badge worn by Australia's Islamic or "Middle Eastern appearance" community in the post-9/11 years (Collins 2007b). In recent years there has also been considerable conflict in Sydney related to opposition to proposed developments of new mosques and Islamic schools (Dunn 1990, 2001).

The Cronulla beach riots did not occur in the "front-line" suburbs of diverse, immigrant minority settlement, such as the southwestern Sydney suburbs of Lakemba or Fairfield or Liverpool, but in a white enclave of Cronulla Beach in the Sutherland shire. No one died, though there was personal injury and property damage as well as much undermining of Sydney's international reputation. Set against the history of ethnic relations and ethnic conflict in Australia and other Western countries, the conclusion is that social conflict is the aberration and social cohesion the norm (Collins 2007a).

Racism

The Cronulla Beach riots did remind Australians, and the world, of the persistent, ugly underbelly of racism and prejudice in Australia. Legacies of the White Australia policy – Australia's explicitly racist policy of immigrant selection for seven decades of the twentieth century (Markus 2001) – still echo in some Australians nearly four decades after it was dismantled. Dunn and his colleagues have conducted extensive telephone polling on Australian attitudes to immigrant minorities to find that 44 percent of Australians agree that there are ethnic or cultural groups who don't fit into Australian society; 42 percent of Australians agree that Australia is weakened by those groups, while 85 percent think that there is racial prejudice in Australia. On the other hand, they conclude that 87 percent of Australians think that diversity is a good thing (Dunn and Forrest 2008: Forrest and Dunn 2006). Muslim Australians are particular targets of racist attitudes (Dunn, Klocker, and Salabay 2007) and racist actions (Human Rights and Equal Opportunity Commission 1991, 2004). This result is not surprising, given a very negative, stereotyping construction of Muslims that persists in many organs of the Australia print and electronic media (Manning 2004, 2006), particularly in discourses about Middle Eastern crime and Muslim terrorists (Poynting et al. 2004). One of the most recent instances of racism in Australia was a series of attacks on Indian overseas students in Sydney and Melbourne in 2009. Indian students mobilized in large numbers to protest these incidents. Widely reported in Australian and Indian media, the occurrences have led to a reduction in Indian students enrolling in Australian universities – despite visits to India by the deputy prime minster and federal education minister and the Victorian premier – threatening the viability of Australia's second largest export industry, worth some $17 billion. Such events are reminders of both the resilience of racism and prejudice in Australian society and of the economic and social costs of racism in a multicultural society.

CONCLUSION

This chapter argues that Australia's immigrants are a very heterogeneous, diversified group, within and between ethnic groups, with linguistic, cultural, religious, human capital, and spatial and social class dimensions fracturing the immigrant experience, making it impossible to discuss *the* migrant experience of inclusion and cohesion in Australian society. Moreover, terms such as *social integration, social inclusion* and *social cohesion* are resonant with local, regional, and national nuance, just as policies such as multiculturalism are. The outcomes are contradictory. Immigrants are overrepresented among the wealthiest Australian billionaires and overrepresented among the poor, the unemployed, and the self-employed. Some are highly paid professionals, others concentrated in manual, low-paid jobs. Some immigrants have moved to the top of political life in Australia, while others are marginalized and disenfranchised. Most immigrants identify strongly with Australia, are very positive about their future in Australia, feel a sense of belonging in their local neighbour-hood, and yet are reluctant to identify as Australians. Most of the time, Australian suburbs and towns are characterized by social cohesion, yet as Sydney's Cronulla Beach riots of December 2005 attest, social conflict occasionally rears its ugly head. Everyday life in multicultural Australia is generally harmonious, yet racism persists, as in the attacks on foreign Indian students in Melbourne and Sydney in the past few years, threaten-ing Australia's largest export industry, education.

Australian multiculturalism policy, though largely gutted of program-matic content and enthusiasm since the mid-1990s, has served Australia's achievements in terms of social cohesion and social inclusion relatively well, as the evidence presented above suggests. However, its weaknesses must be addressed in order to ensure that new immigrants arriving in Australia in coming decades are included in the country's economic social, political, and cultural life, and in order to reduce the size and composition of the bi-modal minority of immigrants who experience social exclusion. First, Australian multiculturalism must be re-energized, refocused, and reshaped to meet the changing character and composition of global im-migration dynamics in general and Australian immigration intakes in particular (Castles and Miller 2009). A new Galbally Report is needed to review the adequacy of migrant programs and services in contemporary Australian society and to refresh and recommit Australian governments at all levels to the goals of immigrant social inclusion. Second, Australian multiculturalism must move from the static, stereotyped, and essentialist notions of ethnicity that have characterized its philosophy and practice in the past and instead recognize the fluidity and global connectedness, the transnational identities of contemporary immigrant communities in Australia, particularly of first and second generation youth. A *cosmopolitan multiculturalism*, marrying the commitments of programs and services of multiculturalism to improve migrant social inclusion with a more globally oriented understanding of identity and belonging of cosmopolitanism (Delanty 2009, 132-56) consistent with a globalized nation, would be more relevant to Australia's ethnic and cultural diversity in the twenty-first century. Cosmopolitan multiculturalism could also assist in overcoming one of Australian multiculturalism's key contradictions: that it has not sufficiently engaged the mainstream, dominant Anglo-Australian com-munity. The focus of Australian multiculturalism would shift from be-ing concerned only with ethnic minorities to being concerned with all Australians living in an increasing globalized world. This shift would also assist in valuing the globalized, fluid, hybrid identities of immigrant youth, shoring up their subjective inclusion in the nation and in the com-munities where they live their daily lives.

Third, Australian multiculturalism has always had a problem with the place of its Indigenous population in the multicultural nation, a problem also indentified in the Canadian case (Kymlicka 1995). The Rudd Labor government's apology to Australia's Indigenous people makes it now possible to develop a cosmopolitan multiculturalism inclusive of all Australians and permits new bridges in inclusion to be built between Indigenous, minority immigrant, and majority anglo-Australian communities. As Delanty (2009, 156) argues, "instead of presupposing discrete cultural groups, as in liberal multiculturalism, a cosmopolitan perspective requires the internal transformation of all groups in a process of ongoing deliberation and interpretation." Fourth, racism is the cancer of culturally diverse societies. While Australian multiculturalism has been more effective than the British version in embracing anti-racist elements, racism is persistent and enduring in Australia and other Western countries, with Indigenous and immigrant minorities the main casualties and social exclusion in everyday life the main consequence. Since cosmopolitanism "is not merely about the plurality of cultures but more about the embracing of difference and the search for an alternative political order" (ibid., 150), a cosmopolitan multiculturalism moves the political community from a liberal notion of tolerance and harmony – which both exaggerates and stereotypes cultural differences and sweeps racism under the carpet – to a cosmopolitan political culture that can more directly address, and track, racism and racial discrimination.

References

Australian Citizenship Council. 2000. *Australian Citizenship for a New Century*. Canberra: The Council.

Australian Productivity Commission. 2006. *Economic Impacts of Migration and Population Growth*. Final report, April. Australian Government Productivity Commission, Canberra.

Blainey, G. 1984. *All for Australia*. North Ryde, NSW: Methuen Haynes.

Booth, A., A. Leigh, and E. Varganova. 2009. "Does Racial and Ethnic Discrimination Vary across Minority Groups? Evidence from a Field Experiment." At http://people.anu.edu.au/andrew.leigh/pdf/AuditDiscrimination.pdf (accessed 28 July 2010).

Butcher, M. and M. Thomas, eds. 2003. *Ingenious: Emerging Youth Cultures in Urban Australia*. Sydney: Pluto Press.

Business Review Weekly. 2010. "The Rich List: The 200 Wealthiest Australians." May 2010.

Castles, S. 2000. *Ethnicity and Globalisation: From Migrant Worker to Transnational Citizen*. London: Sage.

Castles, S. and M. Miller. 2009. *The Age of Migration*. 4th ed. London: Macmillan.

Castles, S., M. Kalantzis, B. Cope, and M. Morrissey. 1988. *Mistaken Identity: Multiculturalism and the Demise of Nationalism in Australia*. Sydney and London: Pluto Press.

Collins, J. 1991. *Migrant Hands in a Distant Land: Australia's Post-war Immigration*, 2nd ed. Sydney and London: Pluto Press.

—1995. "Immigration and the Keating Government." In *Equity and Citizenship under Keating*, ed. M. Hogan and K. Dempsey, 88-116. Sydney: Public Affairs Research Centre, University of Sydney.

—2000. "Immigration and Immigrants: Ethnic Inequality and Social Cohesion." In *The Politics of Australian Society: Political Issues for the New Century*, ed. P. Boreham, G. Stokes, and R. Hall, 302-16. Sydney: Longman.

—2006. "The Changing Political Economy of Australia Immigration." *TESG Tijdshrift* 97(1):7-16.

—2007a. "The Landmark of Cronulla." In *Social Cohesion in Australia*, ed. James Jupp and John Nieuwenhuysen, 61-9. Cambridge and Melbourne: Cambridge University Press.

—2007b. "Immigrants as Victims of Crime in Australia." Special issue, *International Review of Victimology* 14:57-79.

—2011. "The Global Financial Crisis, Immigration and Immigrant Unemployment, and Social Inclusion in Australia." In *Immigration and the Financial Crisis: The United States and Australia Compared*, ed. J. Higley, J. Nieuwenhuysen, and S. Neerup, 145-58. Monash Studies in Global Movements Series. Cheltnam, UK: Edward Elgar.

Collins, J. and C. Reid. 2009. "Minority Youth, Crime, Conflict and Belonging in Australia." Special issue on ethnic crime, *JIMI* 10(4):377-91.

Delanty, G. 2009. *The Cosmopolitan Imagination: The Renewal of Critical Social Theory.* Cambridge: Cambridge University Press.

Department of Immigration and Citizenship (DIAC). 2008. *The People of Australia: Statistics from the 2006 Census.* Canberra: Commonwealth of Australia.

Dunn, K. 1990, "Mosques and Islamic Centres in Sydney: Representations of Islam and Multiculturalism." UNSW. At http://www.bees.unsw.edu.au/school/staff/dunn/C00.pdf

—2001. "Representation of Islam in the Politics of Mosque Development in Sydney." *Journal of Economic and Social Geography* 92(3):291-308.

Dunn, K.M. and J. Forrest. 2008. "Contemporary Manifestations of Racism in Australia." In *Racisms in the New World Order: Realities of Culture, Colour and Identity*, ed. N. Gopalkrishnan and H. Babacan, 95-106. Newcastle: Cambridge Scholars Publishing.

Dunn, K.M., N. Klocker, and T. Salabay. 2007. "Contemporary Racism and Islamophobia in Australia: Racializing Religion." *Ethnicities* 7(4):564-89.

Ferguson, L. 2008. Interview with Affinity Intercultural Foundation. At http://www.affinity.org.au/index.php/news-and-media-releases/56-multiculturalism-is-here-to25stay.html?2c173a96a4dbdc369dded119d13f6d06=3c3ceec3f17bc01121b6aca0e1839905 (accessed 7 June 2010).

Fincher, R. and M. Wulff, M. 1998. "The Locations of Poverty and Disadvantage." In *Australian Poverty: Then and Now*, ed. R. Fincher and J. Nieuwenhuysen, 144-64. Melbourne: Melbourne University Press.

Forrest, J. and K.M. Dunn. 2006. "Racism and Intolerance in Eastern Australia: A Geographic Perspective." *Australian Geographer* 37(2):167-86.

Galbally, F. 1978. *Migrant Services and Programmes: Report of the Review of Post-Arrival Programmes and Services for Migrants.* Canberra: Australian Government Printing Service.

Grassby, A.J. 1973. "A Multi-Cultural Society for the Future." Canberra: Australian Government Publishing Service.

Hage, G. 1998. *White Nation: Fantasies of White Supremacy in a Multicultural Society*. Sydney: Pluto Press.

—2002. "Postcript: Arab-Australians Belonging after 'September 11.'" In *Arab-Australians Today: Citizenship and Belonging*, ed. Ghassan Hage, 241-8. Carlton South: Melbourne University Press.

Hawke, R.J. 1986. "Government's Position on Multiculturalism." *Ethnos* 53:7.

Hawthorne, L. 1994. *Labour Market Barriers for Immigrant Engineers in Australia*, Bureau of Immigration and Population Research. Canberra: Australian Government Publishing Service.

Howard, J. 1996. "Statement on Multiculturalism." Canberra, 3 December 1996. At http://www.multiculturalaustralia.edu.au/doc/howard_2.pdf (accessed 2 February 2010).

Human Rights and Equal Opportunity Commission. 1991. *Racist Violence: Report of the National Inquiry into Racist Violence in Australia*. Canberra: Australian Government Publishing Service.

—2004. *Ismae-Listen: National Consultations on Eliminating Prejudice against Arab and Muslim Australians*. Sydney: Human Rights and Equal Opportunity Commission.

Huntington, S.P. 1997. *The Clash of Civilisations and the Remaking of the World Order*. New York: Simon & Schuster.

—2004. *Who Are We? The Challenges to America's National Identity*. New York: Simon & Schuster.

Jakubowicz, A., J. Collins, and W. Chafic. 2012. "Young Australian Muslims: Social Ecology and Cultural Capital." In *Muslims in the West and the Challenges of Belonging*, ed. F. Mansouri and V. Marotta, 34-59. Melbourne: Melbourne University Press.

Jupp, J. 2007. In *Social Cohesion in Australia*, ed. J. Jupp and J. Nieuwenhuysen, 9-20. Cambridge and Melbourne: Cambridge University Press.

Kymlicka, W. 1995. *Multicultural Citizenship: A Liberal Theory of Minority Rights*. Oxford: Oxford University Press.

Levey, G.B. 2008. "Multicultural Thought in Australian Perspective." In *Political Theory and Australian Multiculturalism*, ed. G.B. Levey. New York: Berghahn.

Levitas, R., C. Pantazis, E. Fahmy, D. Gordon, E. Lloyd, and D. Patsios. 2007. *The Multi-Dimensional Analysis of Social Exclusion*. Department of Sociology and School for Social Policy, University of Bristol.

Lopez, M. 2000. *The Origins of Multiculturalism in Australian Politics, 1945–1975*. Melbourne: Melbourne University Press.

Manning, P. 2004. *Dog Whistle Politics and Journalism: Reporting Arabic and Muslim People in Sydney Newspapers*. Sydney: Australian Centre for Independent Journalism.

—2006. *Us and Them: A Journalist's Investigation of Media, Muslims and the Middle East*. Sydney: Random House Australia.

Markus, A. 2001. *Race: John Howard and the Remaking of Australia*. Crows Nest, NSW: Allen & Unwin.

—2009. *Mapping Social Cohesion 2009: The Scanlon Foundation Surveys*. Monash Institute for the Study of Global Movements. At http://www.apo.org.au/research/mapping-social-cohesion-2009-scanlon-foundation-surveys (accessed 29 July 2010).

Markus, A. and L. Kirpitchenko. 2007. "Conceptualising Social Cohesion." In *Social Cohesion in Australia*, ed. J. Jupp and J. Nieuwenhuysen, 21-32. Cambridge and Melbourne: Cambridge University Press,

Marr, D. and M. Wilkinson. 2003. *Dark Victory*. Sydney: Allen & Unwin.

Martin, J. 1978. *The Migrant Presence: Australian Responses, 1947–77*. Sydney: Allen & Unwin.

OECD. 2009. *International Migration Outlook, SOPEMI 2009*. Paris: OECD.

Office of Multicultural Affairs. 1989. *National Agenda for a Multicultural Australia*. Canberra: Australian Government Printing Service.

O'Malley, S. and J. Drape. 2009. "Australia Isn't Racist, Rudd tells India." *Sydney Morning Herald*, 1 June.

Parekh, B. 2000. *Rethinking Multiculturalism: Cultural Diversity and Political Theory*. Houndmills, Basingstoke: Macmillan.

—2008. *A New Politics of Identity*, Houndmills, Basingstoke: Palgrave Macmillan.

Park, R.E. 2000. "The Nature of Race Relations." In *Theories of Race and Racism: A Reader*, ed. L. Back and J. Solomos, 105-12. London: Routledge.

Poynting, S., Noble, G., Tabar, P. and Collins, J. 2004. *Bin Laden in the Suburbs: Criminalizing the Arab Other*. Sydney: Federation Press.

Rudd, K. 2008. "Apology to Australia's Indigenous Peoples." Speech to the Australian Parliament, 13 February. At http://www.pm.gov.au/node/5952 (accessed 8 February 2010).

Saunders, P. 2005. *The Poverty Wars: Reconnecting Research with Reality*. Sydney: UNSW Press.

Saunders, P. and A. King. 1994. *Immigration and the Distribution of Income*. Canberra: AGPS.

Saunders, P. and M. Wong. "Still Doing It Tough: An Update on Deprivation and Social Exclusion among Welfare Service Clients." Social Policy Research Centre, University of New South Wales, July 2009.

Schneider, J. and M. Crul. 2010. "New Insights into Assimilation and Integration Theory." Introduction to special issue, *Ethnic and Racial Studies* 33(7):1143-8.

Sheehan, P. 1998. *Among the Barbarians: The Dividing of Australia*. Sydney: Random House.

—2006. *Girls Like You*. Sydney: Macmillan.

Social Inclusion Board. 2008. At http://www.socialinclusion.gov.au/SIAgenda/Priorities/Pages/default.aspx (accessed 29 July 2010).

Weber, M. 1970. "Bureaucracy." In *From Max Weber: Essays in Sociology*, ed. H.H. Gerth and C.W. Mills, 196-244. London: Routledge.

Wilkins, R. 2007. "The Changing Socio-Demographic Composition of Poverty in Australia: 1982 to 2004." Working Paper No. 12/07, Melbourne Institute of Applied Economic and Social Research, University of Melbourne.

Williams, L. and T. Batrouney. 1998. "Immigrants and Poverty." In *Australian Poverty: Then and Now*, ed. Ruth Fincher and John Nieuwenhuysen, 258-75. South Carlton: Melbourne University Press.

CHAPTER 2

INTEGRATION POLICY IN AUSTRIA

JULIA MOURÃO PERMOSER AND SIEGLINDE ROSENBERGER

During the past decade, immigrant integration has become one of the most widely debated topics in Western Europe. Far right parties – which have been gaining influence in many European countries – are especially quick to capitalize on the widespread fears that the alleged "lack of integration" of certain immigrant populations is leading to the creation of "parallel societies" and to the rise of "religious extremism" (Howard 2009). In reaction, governments struggle to seize the issue for themselves, waging fierce political battles over the appropriate response to what is widely perceived as a major challenge facing European societies. Thus, integration has become a ubiquitous topic in the European media and political debates in general, and in Austria in particular. Consequently, in the academic literature, immigrant integration has attracted increased attention by sociologists, ethnographers, and political scientists alike (see Givens 2007 for a review).

Yet despite this intense engagement with the topic in the political and academic discourse, the concept of immigrant integration remains rather ambiguous and contested. For some observers, integration means equal treatment and equal access by migrant populations to the same rights and duties as native citizens; for others, it refers to migrants' adoption of the majority society's values and way of life (for a typology see Schiffauer 2008, 7-15). Therefore, before going on to analyze Austrian politics and policies of immigrant integration, it is imperative that we lay down our analytical framework. For the purposes of this paper, we build upon the conceptualization by Johan Wets (2006), who distinguishes between three dimensions of integration: social, cultural, and structural. *Social integration* refers in this case primarily to the degree of interaction and "contact" between immigrant and native population groups. Here the

International Perspectives: Integration and Inclusion, ed. J. Frideres and J. Biles. Montreal and Kingston: Queen's Policy Studies Series, McGill-Queen's University Press. © 2012 The School of Policy Studies, Queen's University at Kingston. All rights reserved.

whole debate on "parallel lives" and "social cohesion" comes into play (Cantle 2001; Vertovec 2006, 25-7). *Cultural integration* refers to the degree to which immigrant and native communities share values, norms, and preferences. *Structural integration,* in turn, refers to the socio-economic and political aspects of integration as represented by the degree of inclusion of, and participation by, migrant populations in the major institutions of society. Of particular relevance are the labour market, the welfare state, the educational system, the housing market, and the political system. Here it is important to note that this differentiation of the concept of integration into three dimensions is not meant normatively – we do not postulate a particular understating of what integration is or should be like. Rather, these are analytical distinctions that enable us to assess the character and the goals pursued by specific integration policies.

Against this background, the paper aims to find out *how* and *to what extent* the different dimensions of integration are addressed in Austrian politics. In order to do so, the following sections look into (1) patterns of immigration to Austria and evidence on the structural position of immigrant populations; (2) existing civic/cultural integration policies, as well as the political contexts in which they emerged; and (3) structural opportunities and barriers to integration conditioned by measures adopted in other policy fields. In our conclusion we sum up the main remaining challenges that Austria faces in the field of immigrant integration and propose avenues for future policy in this area.

Our main finding is that in Austria the politics of immigrant integration is primarily discursively constructed as pertaining to the cultural dimension. Whenever the topic is discussed and policies are enacted under the label of "integration," they tend to cover civic integration and focus on language acquisition and civic education, thus emphasizing the sharing of values and norms as well as the cultural aspect of the need to use a common language. Moreover, the discourse refers exclusively to the integration of third-country nationals, that is, of immigrants from outside the EU, even though 40 percent of all alien residents living in Austria come from other EU countries (Huddleston and Niessen 2011; Kraler 2011). This approach goes hand in hand with a restrictive immigration policy and citizenship regime as well as with a discursive self-understanding that has historically characterized Austrian politics and is only recently starting to change: of "not being" and "not wanting to be" a country of immigration (Bauböck and Perchinig 2006; Perchinig 2009). At the same time, the structural integration of foreign born population and their offspring (second and third generation) suffers from severe deficits, particularly with respect to educational attainment. To a certain extent the lack of policies addressing structural integration is mitigated by a strong welfare state. Within the framework of the Austrian welfare state, there are scattered policies that contribute to improving the socio-economic incorporation of immigrant populations. Nevertheless, it has to be noted that these policies are only available to immigrants who have acquired Austrian citizenship or possess certain types of residence permits. Other categories of immigrants – particularly temporary / seasonal workers and asylum seekers – have very restricted access to social rights and therefore do not benefit from the developed labour and welfare policies.

IMMIGRATION AND IMMIGRANT POPULATIONS IN AUSTRIA

Throughout its history, Austria has been a target country for international migration. During its imperial past, it was the centre of a multi-ethnic empire and as such received large influxes of populations from what is nowadays considered Eastern Europe and the Balkans. After World War II, there were two main waves of international migration, first in the 1960s and '70s and then in the 1990s, followed by continuous flows of family migration.

The first wave occurred within the regulated framework of the so-called *Gastarbeiter*[1] programs of the 1960s and early 1970s, whereby the Austrian government actively recruited temporary labour migrants for low-skilled jobs (see Bauböck 1996; Payer 2004). These migrants came from low-educated rural areas in less developed southern countries, especially Turkey and former Yugoslavia. The *Gastarbeiter* program was based on the premise that immigrant workers would return to their country of origin after working abroad for a certain time. As a consequence, there were no policies aimed at improving the educational and qualification level of these immigrants and their children and their integration into Austrian society (Perchinig 2009, 233). On the contrary, there were legal impediments to the integration of immigrants into society, such as curtailed rights and obstacles to the acquisition of permanent resident status and citizenship. Tellingly, immigrant children were often offered language courses in their mother tongues – Turkish and Serbo-Croatian – rather than in the language of the host country, so that they would be able to integrate into the country of origin of their parents.[2]

However, the envisaged return of these temporarily recruited labour migrants did not take place as planned. Many migrants decided to stay and in fact managed to acquire permanent status or even Austrian citizenship. The *Gastarbeiter* program ended in the 1970s, and since then the government has adopted a discourse of "zero immigration." In reality, however, immigration has continued to rise, although mainly under the rubric of family reunification. Thus, along with their permanent settlement in Austria, the previous *Gastarbeiter* began a new immigration pattern as they started to bring their families to Austria through family reunification.

A second wave of immigration took place in the 1990s, when large numbers of refugees fleeing the Yugoslav war sought refuge in this country. In total about 90,000 refugees from former Yugoslavia, primarily from Bosnia and Croatia, fled to Austria. They were initially given temporary protection status, but it eventually became clear that a speedy return would not be possible. Thus, the government recognized that these refugees had become residents and gave them permanent status (Bauböck 1996, 21-2).

In addition to these two main streams, there are also other channels of immigration to Austria. One of them is the freedom of movement within the European Union. Since Austria joined in 1995, there have been no restrictions on the entrance and settlement of EU citizens – who have a right of free movement – into the territory.[3] The main groups of immigrants from EU countries have been German, then Polish. Furthermore, the influx of temporary labour migrants into Austria has continued even after the adoption of the zero-immigration policy in the 1970s, although on a much smaller scale. In particular, since the legislative reform of 2002, Austrian legislation allows for a number of temporary workers to come into the country on short-term (in principle, also non-renewable) visas. The official possibility of recruiting temporary workers was foreseen by the 2002 law under the label of "seasonal workers," even though in reality a significant number of these workers are not employed in seasonal industries. In a sense, the political intention behind the recruitment of labour migrants under the legal category of "seasonal worker" represents an attempt to revive the *Gastarbeiter* regime under a different guise (Perchinig 2006, 296).

Currently, the main sources of immigration to Austria from "third-countries" are family reunification and asylum seekers. In the year 2007, of all the persons who were granted an entry permit for the first time, about 27 percent were asylum seekers, 22 percent were entitled to a permit due to family reunification, 20 percent were seasonal workers with a non-renewable visa, 16 percent were students, and 11 percent were qualified labour migrants (Österreichischer Integrationsfonds 2009, 28). Although only about one-third of applicants are granted refugee status, the decision process may take several years. Many asylum seekers thus live in Austria for a long time and are de facto immigrants during the waiting period of their asylum claim, although their rights and freedoms are extremely curtailed during this time.

The successive waves of labour migration and continuous influx of family immigrants and refugees have led to a relatively high number of persons of migration background within the population. As of 1 January 2011, Austria had a population of about 8.4 million, of which 18.6 percent had a migration background – meaning either themselves or both parents were born abroad[4] (Statistik Austria 2011, 20). First generation immigrants make up 15.7 percent of the population. Among the first generation, 40 percent possess Austrian citizenship and 60 percent remain foreign citizens (ibid.). Overall, 11 percent of the population do not have Austrian citizenship; of those, 64 percent have been living in Austria for longer than five years (ibid.). Of the foreign population, 60 percent is made up of third-country nationals, whereas 40 percent are citizens of other EU countries (ibid.).

The main ethnic groups of migrants have remained the same for the past few decades. About half of the new incoming migration to Austria are from EU countries, whereas the main groups of third-country nationals are persons from former Yugoslavia and Turkey. In 2007, for instance, 107,000 people immigrated to Austria, of which about half were citizens from a second EU country, mostly Germans, and 10 percent were returning Austrians. Incoming migration by third country nationals makes up only 37 percent of the total (Österreichischer Integrationsfonds 2009, 25).

TABLE 1
Average Net International Migration to Austria for the Years 2005, 2008, and 2010 by Citizenship

	2005	*2008*	*2010*
Austria	−3,863	−4,976	−4,163
Foreign citizens (total)	48,195	39,412	31,858
EU 26/EEA/Switzerland	18,958	25,633	22,443
Germany	8,639	10,544	7,779
Former Yugoslavia (without Slovenia)	11,156	3,160	3,631
Turkey	4,899	2,133	1,375

Source: Statistik Austria (2008a, 2010a).

Before analyzing the integration policies pursued in recent times, we would like to make a general assessment of the current social and economic situation of immigrants in Austria. As we shall see, third-country immigrants occupy a rather marginal position within the socio-economic structure, having lower education, higher unemployment rates, lower income, and higher poverty rates than the native population (see Fassmann 2007; Statistik Austria 2008b, 2008c; Österreichischer Integrationsfonds 2009). This situation attests to the precarious structural integration of immigrant communities and points to the necessity of adopting effective integration policies. Nevertheless, there are major differences between various groups of immigrants. In particular, there is a huge chasm between immigrants from EU and EEA (European Economic Area) countries on the one hand, and immigrants from third countries on the other hand, especially from Turkey and former Yugoslavia.

Although this discrepancy is present in all areas, it is particularly vivid in the field of education, which serves as an example of the broader phenomenon. The educational level of immigrants differs significantly from that of Austrian citizens, and there are also substantial differences between immigrant groups themselves. Whereas immigrants from EU / EEA countries tend to have higher educational levels than Austrian citizens, immigrants from traditional sending countries – Turkey and former Yugoslavia – have much lower levels. For instance, whereas in 2010 10.7 percent of Austrian citizens and 25.8 percent of citizens of other EU countries had a university degree, this level of education was only reached by 3.4 percent of citizens from former Yugoslavia and 2.4 percent of Turkish citizens. By contrast, in the same year, about 72.1 percent of Turkish citizens and 47.6 percent of citizens from former Yugoslavia had only compulsory school education,[5] whereas only 24.6 percent of the Austrian citizens and 14.1 percent of citizens from a second EU country were in a comparable situation (see Table 2). For the second generation the situation does not markedly differ. The educational system can therefore be characterized as ethnically segmented (Herzog-Punzenberger 2005). Socio-economic differences offer only a partial explanation; as a recent OECD report points out, even after accounting for socio-economic background, significant performance gaps remain between the performance of natives and third-country immigrants (or their children) in the educational system (Nusche, Shewbridge, and Rasmussen 2009).

TABLE 2
State of Education, Unemployment, and Poverty Rates 2010 by Nationality (data given in %)

	Education*			Unemployment**	Poverty***
	Compulsory School Education	Higher School Education	Tertiary Education	Unemployment Rate	At Risk of Poverty
Total	25.7	14.5	11.4	4.4	12
Austria	24.6	14.2	10.7	3.9	10‡
EU 27	14.1	23.1	25.8	6.2	15
Former Yugoslavia	47.6	11.8	3.4	8.6†	15†
Turkey	72.1	6.2	2.4	13.9	46
Other	29.4	17.5	37.6	11.6	57

† Excluding citizens from Slovenia.
‡ Only citizens by birth (excluding naturalized citizens).
Source: *Statistik Austria (2010b) (includes population aged older than 15 in private households). **Statistik Austria (2010b). ***Statistik Austria (2010c).

INTEGRATION AS A CONTESTED POLICY FIELD

Despite the long history of migration and the evident structural disadvantage suffered by persons with a migration background in access to education and upward mobility (see Table 2), integration has only very recently become a political priority for the Austrian government. In fact, immigrant integration was only institutionalized as an autonomous policy field in 2011 with the creation of a State Secretariat for Integration within the Ministry of Interior. The relatively late appearance of integration as a political field in Austrian politics can be partially explained by the predominance of an exclusionary discourse towards immigrants that translates into a national self-understanding of "not being a country of immigration" (see Valchars 2006; Kraler 2011). This "denial" is a defining moment of Austrian immigration discourse that has strongly influenced the way integration policy emerged as a political topic and the way it is approached in policy-making. Currently, however, the rise in political salience had much more to do with the negative approach to immigration by far-right parties than with a concerted political effort to tackle the institutional and structural obstacles that hamper the full incorporation of certain immigrant groups. This anti-immigration climate has created strong biases in the way in which integration is approached by political elites. The need for integration policies is mainly viewed within the context either of cultural adaption to the proclaimed Austrian value system or to the control and restriction of immigration to Austria. Nonetheless, recently a different dynamic has been sparked by the efforts of certain actors – especially some regional and local governments as well as industrial associations and economic interest groups – to recognize the importance of highly qualified labour migration and to tackle the issue of integration in a more proactive and welcoming way (Industriellevereinigung Wien 2009).

The issue of integration did not enter the political agenda until the 1990s, in a context of strong anti-immigrant sentiments. Three phenomena marked the 1990s as an unfavourable period for immigration and integration politics. Firstly, by this time it had become clear that some former *Gastarbeiter* were not going to return to their home countries, and that, on the contrary, they were increasingly acquiring Austrian citizenship and bringing their families to join them in their new homeland. It was also clear that this group was, for the most part, structurally disadvantaged in comparison to the majority population and culturally diverse. The combination of ethnic difference, cultural estrangement, and socio-economic marginalization reinforced anti-foreigner sentiments among the population and contributed to the perception that there was an "integration problem." Secondly, the 1990s saw the rapid rise of far-right parties in Europe, and in particular in Austria. The FPÖ (Freiheitliche Partei Österreichs), led by Jörg Haider, was highly successful in mobilizing latent xenophobic sentiments in the population by adopting strongly anti-foreigner slogans and campaigns (Wodak and Reisigl 2000). Thirdly, the 1990s were marked by a negative shift in the political perception of asylum. Whereas during the Iron Curtain period, refugees fleeing communist regimes were perceived as political heroes and received strong political support, by the 1990s the image of the refugee had changed completely. The strong influx of asylum seekers gave rise to claims that Austria had exhausted its receiving capacity. At the same time, the figure of the "bogus asylum seeker" or "economic refugee" came into being, so that asylum seekers were increasingly treated as illegal migrants in disguise and associated with welfare state abuse and criminality (Rosenberger and König 2011).

It was in this context that "integration" – actually the *failure* of integration – entered the political debate in Austria. As a consequence, in the political discourse integration has primarily negative connotations. For instance, integration has been used repeatedly to justify legislation aimed at restricting immigration, creating obstacles for potential asylum seekers, and curtailing rights of foreign citizens. As Ruth Wodak and Michael Krzyzanowski (2009) show through a discourse analysis of parliamentary debates, in two major reforms of the immigration and asylum laws in 1997 and 2002, integration was the buzzword used to justify more restrictive legislation. The same can be said of the major legislative reform of the immigration and integration laws, which took place in 2005 (Österreichisches Parlament 2005). That "integration" was used discursively as a justification to restrict immigration is also evident in the slogan "Integration vor Neuzuzug" (Integration before new immigration) of the right-wing government coalition between the centre-right party ÖVP and the far-right party FPÖ (later BZÖ),[6] in power between 2000 and 2006 (Regierungsprogramm der ÖVP-FPÖ Koalition 2000).

The allegation that certain communities are not well integrated is also often brought up in connection with religion, especially Islam. Even though Austria has an inclusive model of religious governance in which Islam is recognized as an official religion entitled to several rights and privileges (Mourão Permoser and Rosenberger 2009), Muslims are nevertheless often targeted by a rhetoric stressing that they will not comply with the Austrian value system, particularly in respect to gender equality. For example, the Interior Ministry of Austria commissioned a report about Muslims in Austria that became known as "the integration study" (Rohe 2006). The idea was to evaluate whether the Muslims community in Austria was "willing to integrate" or not. The study was based on a survey in which Muslims were asked questions about their religiosity and about their opinion on different topics. The author then classified the Muslim community into different groups according to their degree of religiosity and their attitudes. The conclusion reached was that there was a significantly large group of Muslims who were very religiously observant and conservative in their opinions. These were deemed to be "unwilling to integrate." A similar study was commissioned in 2009, this time encompassing all immigrants but with a special focus on the Turkish community (Ulram 2009).

THE CULTURAL DIMENSION OF INTEGRATION POLICIES

In accordance with the claims of failed cultural integration, the agencies responsible for enacting concrete integration measures focus their activities on the cultural dimension of integration. At the federal level, this responsibility lies primarily with the Ministry of Interior, either directly or through the Austrian Integration Fund, an external agency financed by the ministry.[7] The ministry also funds the so-called Austrian National Contact Point for Integration, located within the International Organization of Migration, in order to collect data, produce reports, and network with other EU countries.[8] Until 2003, the integration policy of the Ministry of Interior was focused exclusively on recognized refugees and aimed at assisting refugees organizationally, financially, and psychologically in the first years following their entitlement to refugee status. The Austrian Integration Fund was the agency responsible for carrying out this task by offering psychological counselling, helping refugees to find housing, organizing German language training, and so on (see Nationaler Kontaktpunkt Österreich 2005, 49-57).

In 2002 a major amendment of the immigration legislation (revised in 2005 and 2011) under the centre-right/far-right coalition brought a major change in the integration policy of the ministry. From then on, immigrants expecting to settle down in Austria were required to sign a so-called "integration agreement."[9] This agreement amounts to a piece of paper stating that the migrant must achieve a basic level of knowledge of the German language within a specific period of time – to be proven by passing a standardized exam – as a condition of being able to stay in the country (NAG 2005, paras. 14-16). Despite the focus on language acquisition, which under certain circumstances can be aimed at empowering immigrants, this policy was implemented within the context of a highly exclusionary discourse. The idea of introducing this mandatory language requirement originated from the far-right party FPÖ, which was very offensively waging an anti-immigrant campaign. The party heralded the introduction of this requirement in the law as a major achievement and as a further step in the consolidation of a restrictive immigration policy. Presenting the legislative package in which this requirement was included, the representative of the FPÖ, Peter Westenthaler, finished his speech: "With this law we make one thing clear: Austria is not an immigration country and we will make sure that it does not become one!"[10] (Österreichisches Parlament 2002, 55). When the law was revised in 2005 and 2011, the requirement was made progressively more stringent, and emphasis was put on security and the protection of native citizens against "abuse" of Austrian institutions by immigrants (Österreichisches Parlament 2005, 48-51). Thus we see how also this policy initiative was put forward with a discursive focus on cultural assimilation and immigration control rather than with a participatory aim.

The requirement affects third-country nationals who have applied for a residence permit since 1998, and the language level required has been progressively raised. In 2002, immigrants were required to prove a basic knowledge of German equivalent to the level A1 of the European Language Framework. Since 2005 this has been increased to the level A2. The ultimate time limit to complete the requirement became five years, after which deportation may follow; gradual financial penalties start after two years of non-completion. Since 2011, potential immigrants for family reunification are required to prove language knowledge at the level A1 already before entry into the territory, followed by level A2 after two years as a condition to stay and level B1 as a condition for the acquisition of permanent residence after five years. Exceptions are made for older and sick persons, as well as for children under nine years old and children who have completed their schooling in Austria. The possibility of an extension in special cases is foreseen by the law. Financial assistance (up to 50 percent) for taking specially designed language/integration courses is provided for certain groups of migrants, on the condition of timely fulfilment of the requirement within two years. Highly qualified migrants, temporary/seasonal migrants, and asylum seekers are excluded from the requirement and from the subsidies. A similar requirement was also introduced for those migrants who apply for Austrian citizenship (StbG 1985 [2006], para. 10). They must pass both a language test and a "civic education" test with questions about the history, geography, and culture of Austria and of the province where they live (Perchinig 2010).

Since these legislative developments have entered into force, the Ministry of Interior and the Austrian Integration Fund have been increasingly engaged in organizing, promoting, and enforcing these integration requirements of language acquisition and "civic education." Thus, although also these measures have been undertaken within the framework of a restrictive turn and by a government openly hostile to immigrants, it must be said that this is the first time that the government is promoting any type of measures explicitly aimed at the integration of immigrants beyond the confines of recognized refugees. In that sense it may be considered as a development in the direction of establishing integration as a policy field. However, this policy field is characterized by a unilateral focus on the migrant, not on structural change and adaptation on the part of the receiving society. Furthermore, sometimes the emphasis on integration seems to be more symbolic than substantial (Mourão Permoser 2012). For example, in March 2009 the Interior Ministry started a process of development of a "National Action Plan on Integration"[11] with the stated aim of bringing together different actors and stakeholders to devise a new comprehensive integration policy. Nevertheless, the conclusions presented in the interim report indicated that there would be no major change in the government's course of action (Bundesministerium für Inneres 2009). To the contrary, the path of restriction and focus on language requirements was reinforced in the latest legislative package.

Interestingly, EU citizens are not covered by integration measures, although for a totally different reason. EU legislation entitles European citizens to equal rights and access to all institutions on an equal basis as natives (EU Directive 2004/38/EC). Thus, in terms of structural integration, EU immigrants are given equal treatment the moment they set foot in Austria. As for cultural and social integration, EU citizens seem to be considered as "integrated" *a priori*, without the need for special policies in this respect. The same is true of highly qualified migrants, who are also exempted from the fulfilment of civic integration requirements. These two forms of special treatment – for EU citizens and highly qualified migrants – indicate that there are ethnic and economic undertones behind discourses that emphasize the need for cultural integration of immigrants.[12]

At the provincial and local levels, the situation is rather different from at the national. Some provinces have a much broader approach towards immigrant integration. A particularly striking contrast to the politics undertaken at the national level is the long-standing commitment of the City/Province of Vienna to a proactive policy in the area of immigrant integration.[13] In 1972 the City/Province of Vienna created an "Immigrant Fund"[14] with the objective of offering counselling and assistance to immigrants on legal and social issues.[15] In 1992 it created the Viennese Integration Fund.[16] From 1992 to 2004 the latter fund was responsible for counselling of migrants, conflict mediation, political consultancy, and lobby for migrants' interests. In 1996 a position within the local government (Integrationstadträtin) was created. In 2004, the Viennese Integration Fund was replaced by a full-fledged department inside the municipality administration in charge of integration and diversity issues.[17] In a 2007 report the municipality presented its overall approach to integration: "Integration is an asymmetrical and mutual process which aims at increasing equal access and participation by eliminating barriers, fighting discrimination, and promoting strategies of empowerment. At the same time, immigrants should be invited, encouraged and motivated to contribute to individual and social advancement by overcoming everyday difficulties despite their comparatively disadvantaged starting point" (Magistrat der Stadt Wien 2007, 11).[18]

Since 2006, a number of other provinces and cities have also started to become active in developing their own approach to integration in the form of *Integrationsleitbilder* ("mission statements" for integration policy).[19] In general, these have been formulated as the outcome of a consultation process involving several political and civil society actors. They reflect this diversity of interests and tend to portray integration as a cross-cutting issue. The mission statements include proposals for concrete measures to improve integration, and it remains to be seen whether these will yield a positive outcome. While it is still too early to assess the effectiveness of these enterprises, clearly these provincial and local governments are taking a more active stance on the issue of integration than their national counterpart. The same is true of the European Union, which, despite lacking explicit competence in integration, has been instrumental in making funds available to finance many grassroot projects through the EQUAL and INTI programs, and more recently, the European Integration Fund.[20]

THE STRUCTURAL DIMENSION OF INTEGRATION

The Ministry of Interior is responsible for setting the legal framework that determines immigrants' rights and therefore shapes the conditions for immigrants' structural integration into the main institutions of society. The legal framework in Austria distinguishes between two broad categories of immigrants: those with a residence permit and those without (immigrants on a temporary permit, asylum seekers, etc.). Here it is important to note that, from the point of view of the Ministry of Interior, only those categories of immigrants with a residence permit should be offered the possibility of becoming integrated (Nationaler Kontaktpunkt Österreich 2005, 39-46). The other categories are systematically excluded from integration activities and in many cases also legally blocked from participation in mainstream institutions such as the labour market and educational system. According to the Ministry of Interior, this is a logical consequence of the fact that these immigrants are not legally entitled to settle in Austria. In fact, for the ministry any exaggerated attempts by these immigrants to become integrated should be regarded with suspicion as possibly indicating a hidden intention to settle permanently in the country (ibid., 41).

As for those immigrants with a residence permit, the legal framework is structured in a way that permits increasing access to rights with increasing time of residence. In this context the European Union has also been an important actor, especially through the establishment of the EU-wide status of "long-term resident," which reinforces the principle that the length of stay should go hand in hand with the progressive acquisition of rights. According to Directive 2003/109/EC,[21] the status of long-term resident can be acquired after five years of lawful residence[22] and entitles the immigrant to equal treatment with EU nationals in a number of areas, including social security, social services (especially subsidized housing), education, and vocational training.

Another essential factor impacting the range of opportunities for immigrants is of course the citizenship regime. Traditionally, Austria's citizenship regime has been based on the concept of *jus sanguinis*, meaning that citizenship is acquired by descent rather than by birth in the territory. Access to citizenship by immigrants in Austria is limited and has been made increasingly difficult with every legislative amendment since the 1990s (Çinar 2009). The period of legal residence required for naturalization is ten years, while spouses of Austrian citizens have to wait for six years of residence and at least five of marriage. Children and grandchildren of non-Austrians who are born in the country do not immediately acquire Austrian nationality but may go through a facilitated nationalization process. Further requirements include the abdication of the previous citizenship and proof of regular and stable resources above a certain limit set at a relatively high level, which means that immigrants employed in low-wage jobs or in precarious employment are ineligible for naturalization (Stern 2011). In addition, as already mentioned, additional requirements have been put in place with the aim of reducing the number of naturalizations, such as language and civic education tests (König and Stadler 2003). These new requirements are not an Austrian specificity, but rather they reflect the emergence of a European-wide trend towards the introduction of coercive "civic integration" policies and the use of restrictive naturalization and integration criteria to curb immigration (Joppke 2007). Nevertheless, as recent efforts to create European-wide indexes of citizenship and integration policies have shown, Austria's citizenship regime ranks among the most restrictive in Europe (Niessen et al. 2007; Çinar 2009; Howard 2009).

In addition to the legal framework for the settlement of immigrants, there are a number of other policies which are not characterized as "integration policies" but do affect directly the capacity of immigrants to take part in social institutions. Austria has a well-developed welfare state and a number of redistributive policies that contribute to a better integration of society as a whole. Particularly important in this regard are labour market policies and unemployment benefits, subsidized housing, and welfare aid, all of which play an important role in mitigating the effects of income inequality (Guger et al. 2009). Considering that third-country immigrants are strongly overrepresented among the lower-income share of the population, these policies can be considered as beneficial for integration. In 2006, for instance, 25 percent of all welfare aid recipients were foreign citizens (ibid., 169). Similarly, the services of the Austrian Public Employment Service (AMS)[23] also contribute to the better inclusion of immigrants into the labour market. Nevertheless, the AMS does not officially have special programs for persons with migration background, even though certain initiatives are created with this group in mind (Arbeitsmarktservice Österreich 2008, 30). Rather, it follows a policy of treating equally native and migrant background populations with either Austrian citizenship or long-term residence permits (Nationaler Kontaktpunkt Österreich 2005, 68).

Another excellent example of policies that are not conceived of as integration policies but have integration effects is the recently accorded free kindergarten year for five-year-olds. Against the background that the educational system in Austria is highly selective and tends to reproduce social structures of inequality, a debate has recently emerged about the possibility of establishing a compulsory kindergarten year. Until now school attendance has been free and compulsory in Austria for all children between the age of six and fifteen. Children younger than six years old could additionally take advantage of public or privately organized kindergartens, but they were not obliged to do so. Since attending even a public kindergarten is not free of charge, and the number of places is scarce, the percentage of children attending kindergartens in Austria is rather low in comparison to other EU countries. Migrant children in particular tend to be taken care of by the family and to not attend kindergartens. This in turn has negative effects for these children's acquisition of German language skills and is therefore prejudicial to their performance when they enter the school system. The problem is an important one, considering that school children with a non-German mother tongue make up 16 percent of the overall student population in Austria and 21 percent of the students enrolled in primary schools (Nusche et al. 2009). Against this background, in May 2009 the government decided to introduce a free and compulsory half-day kindergarten year for five-year-old children. The measure affects all children and was not formulated as an integration measure; nevertheless, it was clearly intended to promote better integration of children from migrant origin, as the official statement of the vice-chancellor makes clear: "The free kindergarten year ensures that all children, *independent of origin* and income, will have the same starting point at the entrance into the Austrian school system." (Bundeskanzleramt Österreich 2009, emphasis added).

Interestingly, these policies at the national level are not conceived of as integration policies and are not part of a concerted effort to create a comprehensive integration policy. Rather, they are usually understood as belonging within a range of inclusionary and redistributive policies that characterize the Austrian welfare state. Moreover, these policies are not coordinated by a federal authority in charge of integration. On the contrary, they are dispersed initiatives by different actors which incidentally have a direct impact on immigrants and persons of migrant background. Here there is a discrepancy between the official understanding of integration falling primarily under the competence of the Ministry of Interior, and the reality of a multiplicity of actors involved in different aspects of policy-making that affect immigrants.

In general, therefore, at the national level one observes a dichotomy between two different kinds of policies. On the one hand, there are policies that are explicitly conceived of as "integration policies." At the national level, these policies are generally focused on cultural integration, in particular the acquisition of language skills. On the other hand, there are a number of social policy measures of universal character that benefit migrants and help their incorporation into mainstream institutions, especially subsidized housing, unemployment benefits, and welfare aid (i.e., direct transfers), which have a strong redistributive effect (Guger et al. 2009). These benefits are, however, only available to immigrants with a long-term resident visa and are usually not conceived of as pertaining to the field of integration measures but rather as universal social policies.

CONCLUSION

In sum, integration in Austria was for a long time largely ignored as a field of political action. When it did enter the political agenda, it was largely due to a negative politicization of the topic by anti-immigrant actors. Integration was used within a larger discursive strategy that sought to justify restrictive immigration policies by framing resident immigrant communities as a problem. In that context, integration was depicted primarily in its cultural dimension, with the allegation of "lack of integration" often being brought up in connection to the religion, values, and attitudes of immigrant communities. The same focus on the cultural dimension that exists at the discursive level also characterizes the policies undertaken at the national level explicitly under the label of integration. Since 2011, a new State Secretariat for Integration was created within the Ministry of Interior, signalling the intention to centralize efforts and launch new initiatives in the area of integration. Nevertheless, the competence to implement integration measures is still dispersed among different actors and levels of government. As we have seen, there are sometimes substantial differences in the way each of these actors/levels approaches to the integration issue.

This chapter has shown that in Austrian politics, immigrant integration is primarily addressed in its cultural dimension rather than in its social and structural dimensions. The predominance of the cultural dimension is particularly striking, given that the target immigrant population constitutes an economically deprived group. Moreover, it is also interesting to note that the emphasis on cultural assimilation in Austria has a predominantly exclusionary character. In that sense, it differs strongly from the emphasis on cultural assimilation present in other immigrant societies such as the United States, where the idea of the "melting pot" has historically served the inclusionary purpose of communicating a general willingness to incorporate persons of all origins into a common whole. By contrast, in Austria the emphasis on assimilation goes hand in hand with the ideology of not being a country of immigration. Assimilating into Austrian culture is conceived of as a unilateral requirement on the part of the immigrant, rather than as a two-way process involving adaptation on both sides.

Even so, the question of integration has only recently started to become an issue in Austrian politics, but it is set to stay a hot issue for a long time to come. For the future, the main challenge facing policy-makers will be to break the connection between ethnicity and social stratification. In this respect, two things will be instrumental. First, early access to socio-economic rights for foreign citizens on an equal footing with nationals is crucial in order to improve structural integration and to allow immigrants to benefit from the many social measures that mitigate income inequalities and diminish social stratification. Secondly, the educational system needs to be reformed in order to promote social mobility. At the moment the educational system works to reproduce inequalities rather than to fight them. In a context where immigrant communities are also socially deprived, this reinforces ethnically-marked social stratification. A further major challenge will be to improve the perception of immigration and of immigrants among the majority population. The level of xenophobia in Austria is very high (Friesl, Harnachers-Zuba, and Polak 2009) and the political discourse on immigration is strongly influenced by far-right parties that mobilize hostile sentiments against immigrants in their campaigns. Of course, to improve this situation would need a more proactive and inclusionary attitude on the part of the government, as well as a concerted effort to communicate the benefits of immigration to the majority population.

Notes

1. German for "guest-worker" or "foreign-worker."
2. Austria Wochenschau 14/1979, *Schulversuche in Wien: Gastarbeiterkinder lernen zweisprachig*, Filmarchiv Austria.
3. One exception are the nationals of the new member states that joined the European Union in its last enlargement. The citizens of these member states are subject to transitional agreements that block them from taking up work in other member states for a number of years. Nevertheless, once these agreements have expired, these citizens too will be able to enjoy a right to free movement and reside and work in any member state of the European Union under conditions of equal treatment with nationals.
4. Migration background is defined here as persons who migrated to Austria themselves (first generation), or who were born in Austria from parents who were both first generation immigrants to Austria (second generation). This is the official definition adopted by Statistik Austria. Data collected on the basis of this definition has only been available since 2008 because another definition was used before. See http://www.statistik.at/web_de/statistiken/bevoelkerung/bevoelkerungsstruktur/

bevoelkerung_nach_migrationshintergrund/index.html (accessed 3 December 2009).

5. In Austria, compulsory school education amounts to nine years: from six to 15 years of age.

6. In 2005 (during the ÖVP-FPÖ coalition government), a group of politicians around Jörg Haider split from the FPÖ and created a new far-right party under the name BZÖ (Bündnis Zukunft Österreichs). The newly founded splinter party, BZÖ, continued the coalition with the ÖVP, whereas those who decided to stay in the FPÖ went into opposition.

7. *Österreichischer Integrationsfonds*, http://www.integrationsfonds.at/.

8. *Nationaler Kontaktpunkt Österreich im Europäischen Migrationsnetzwerk*, http://www.iomvienna.at/index.php?module=Content&func=display&id=239&newlang=eng.

9. In German, *Integrationsvereinbarung*. The original legislative proposal foresaw an integration contract, *Integrationsvertrag*, but the name was later changed to integration agreement. Technically, neither "contract" nor "agreement" is correct, because both terms imply a voluntary act. In reality, what the law actually does is to unilaterally impose a requirement on the migrant (see the discussion in Rohsmann 2003, 76-80). The requirement has been in force since 1 January 2003.

10. Own translation. The words of the congressman in the original are: "Mit den heutigen Gesetz schaffen wir jedenfalls Klarheit: Österreich ist kein Einwanderungsland und wird auch keines werden. Dafür werden wir sorgen!"

11. "Nationaler Aktionsplan für Integration," http://www.bmi.gv.at/cms/BMI/_news/BMI.aspx?id=796272564D3853386665673D&page=8&view=1 (accessed 10 December 2009).

12. In fact any requirement for EU citizens to fulfill an integration agreement or the like would be incompatible with EU law. Nevertheless, there is no attempt to make EU citizens comply with such measures voluntarily or to offer them incentives to adapt culturally. There is also no political debate on an alleged "unwillingess" or "inability" to integrate on the part of EU nationals as there is for third-country nationals from poor countries.

13. As the capital, Vienna is both a province and a city.

14. Zuwanderer-Fonds.

15. Austria Wochenschau 7/1972, *Beratungsstellen für Gastarbeiter eingerichtet*, Filmarchiv Wien.

16. Wiener Integrationsfonds.

17. Magistratsabteilung für Integrations- und Diversitätsangelegenheiten (MA-17), http://www.wien.gv.at/integration/.

18. Own translation. The original reads: "Integration als asymmetrischer und wechselseitiger Prozess muss einerseits Teilhabe und Partizipation durch die Öffnung von Zugängen, Entgegenwirken von Diskriminierung und Strategien des Empowerments ermöglichen. Andererseits sind die ZuwanderInnen zu ermutigen, zu motivieren und aufzufordern, trotz ihrer vergleichsweise schwierigen Ausgangslage ihren Alltag bestmöglich zu bewältigen und somit ihren Beitrag für die individuelle wie auch gesellschaftliche Fortkommen zu leisten."

19. More specifically, the following provinces have developed mission statements in the years in brackets: Tirol (2006), Salzburg (2006), Upper Austria (2008), Lower Austria (2008), Voralberg (currently under work), and Steiermark (currently under work). Several cities have also developed their own mission statements, not listed here for reasons of space.
20. At http://www.bmi.gv.at/cms/BMI_Fonds/integrationsf/start.aspx (accessed 11 December 2009).
21. Council Directive 2003/109/EC of 25 November 2003; implemented into national legislation through the NAG 2005, which entered into force in 2006.
22. Under a renewable residence permit. Time spent on a student visa counts as half (art. 4, para.2).
23. At http://www.ams.at/english/14595.html.

REFERENCES

Arbeitsmarktservice Österreich. 2008. Geschäftsbericht 2008 Wien, AMS. At http://www.ams.at/_docs/001_EndversionGB2008.pdf

Bauböck, R. 1996. "'Nach Rasse und Sprache verschieden': Migrationspolitik in Österreich von der Monarchie bis heute." Vienna: Forschungsberichte des Instituts für Höhere Studien – Reihe Politikwissenschaft 31.

Bauböck, R., and B. Perchinig. 2006. "Migrations- und Integrationspolitik." In *Politik in Österreich: Das Handbuch*, ed. H. Dachs, P. Gerlich, H. Gottweis, H. Kramer, V. Lauber, W.C. Müller and E. Talos, 726-42. Wien: Manz.

Bundeskanzleramt Österreich. 2009. "Gratis-Kindergartenjahr fördert sprachliche und kreative Fähigkeit zum besten Zeitpunkt." At http://www.bka.gv.at/site/cob__34790/currentpage__7/6589/default.aspx (accessed 8 December 2009).

Bundesministerium für Inneres. 2009. Zwischenbericht zur Erstellung eines Nationalen Aktionsplans für Integration Wien. At http://www.integrationsfonds.at/fileadmin/Integrationsfond/NAP/Nationaler_Aktionsplan_Zwischenbericht.pdf

Cantle, T. 2001. *Community Cohesion Report*. London: UK Home Office.

Çinar, D. 2009. "EUDO Citizenship Observatory: Country Report on Austria." RSCA/EUDO-CIT-CR 2009/16. At http://eudo-citizenhip.eu

Fassmann, H., ed. 2007. 2. *Österreichischer Migrations- und Integrationsbericht 2001-2006: Rechtliche Rahmenbedingungen, demographische Entwicklungen, sozioökonomische Strukturen*. Klagenfurt/Celovic: Drava.

Friesl, C., U. Harnachers-Zuba, and R. Polak, eds. 2009. *Die Österreicher/-innen: Wertewandel 1990–2008*. Wien, Czernin Verlag.

Givens, T. 2007. "Immigrant Integration in Europe: Empirical Research." *Annual Review of Political Science* 10:67-83.

Guger, A., M. Agwi, A. Buxbaum, E. Festl, K. Knittler, V. Halsmayer, H. Pitlik, D. Sturn, and M. Wüger. 2009. "Umverteilung durch den Staat in Österreich Wien." Österreichisches Institut für Wirtschaftsforschung, September 2009.

Herzog-Punzenberger, B. 2005. "Schule und Arbeitsmarkt ethnisch segmentiert? Einige Bemerkungen zur 'Zweiten Generation' im österreichischen Bildungssystem." In *Heraus Forderung Migration*, ed. S. Binder, 191-211. Wien: Institut für Geographie und Regionalforschung der Universität Wien.

Howard, M.M. 2009. *The Politics of Citizenship in Europe*. Cambridge: Cambridge University Press.

Huddleston, T. and J. Niessen. 2011. *Index Integration und Migration III*. At www.mipex.eu (accessed 30 December 2011).

Industriellevereinigung Wien. 2009. Vielfalt als Chance und Wachstumsstrategie Vienna, November 2009.

Joppke, C. 2007. "Beyond National Models: Civic Integration Policies for Immigrants in Western Europe." *West European Politics* 30(1):1-22.

König, K. and B. Stadler. 2003. Entwicklungstendenzen im öffentlich-rechtlichen und demokratiepolitischen Bereich. In *Österreichischer Migrations- und Integrationsbericht*, ed. H. Fassmann and I. Stacher, 226-60. Wien: Drava Verlag.

Kraler, A. 2011. "Immigrant and Immigration Policy Making in Austria." In *Migratory Policy Making in Europe*, ed. G. Zincone, R. Penninx, and M. Borkert, 21-60. IMISCOE. Amsterdam: Amsterdam University Press.

Magistrat der Stadt Wien, MA 17. 2007. *Integration und Diversität in Wien 2007: Aufgaben und Tätigkeiten der MA 17*. Wien: Stadt Wien.

Mourão Permoser, J. 2012. "Civic Integration as Symbolic Politics? Insights from Austria." *European Journal of Migration and Law* (forthcoming).

Mourão Permoser, J. and S. Rosenberger. 2009. "Religious Citizenship versus Politics of Migrant Integration: The Case of Austria. In *International Migration and the Governance of Religious Diversity*, ed. P. Bramadat and M. Koenig, 259-92. Montreal and Kingston: McGill-Queen's University Press.

NAG (Niederlassungs- und Aufenthaltsgesetz) 2005. "Bundesgesetz über die Niederlassung und den Aufenthalt in Österreich." BGBl I 2005/100.

Nationaler Kontaktpunkt Österreich. 2005. "Integrationspraktiken in Österreich: Eine Landkarte über Integrationpraktiken und -philosophien von Bund, Ländern und Sozialpartnern, June 2005." At http://www.emn.at/modules/typetool/pnincludes/uploads/Integrationsbericht_Juni%202005_web.pdf

Niessen, J., T. Huddleston, L. Citron, A. Geddes, and D. Jacobs. 2007. *Migrant Integration Policy Index*. British Council and Migration Policy Group, September 2007. At www.integrationindex.eu

Nusche, D., C. Shewbridge, and C.L. Rasmussen. 2009. *OECD Reviews of Migrant Education, Austria*. Paris: Organisation for Economic Co-operation and Development.

Österreichischer Integrationsfonds. 2009. *Migration and Integration: Zahlen. Daten. Fakten*. Wien.

Österreichisches Parlament. 2002. Stenographisches Protokoll der 109. Sitzung der XXI. GP des Nationalrates, am 9 Juli 2002.

—2005. Stenographisches Protokoll der 116. Sitzung der XXII. GP des Nationalrates, am 7 Juli 2005.

Payer, P. 2004. ""Gehen Sie an die Arbeit." Zur Geschichte der "Gastarbeiter" in Wien 1964-1989." At http://www.stadt-forschung.at/downloads/Gastarbeiter.pdf

Perchinig, B. 2006. "Einwanderungs- und Integrationspolitik." In *Schwarz-Blau: Eine Bilanz des "Neu-Regierens,"* ed. E. Talós and M. Fink, 295-312. Wien: Lit Verlag.

—2009. "Von der Fremdarbeit zur Integration? (Arbeits) migrations- und Integrationspolitik in der Zweiten Republik." *Österreich in Geschichte und Literatur* 53(3):228-46.

—2010. "All You Need to Know to Become an Austrian: Naturalisation Policy and Citizenship Testing in Austria." In *A Redefinition of Belonging? Language and Integration Tests for Newcomers and Future Citizens*, ed. E. Ersbøll, D. Kostakopoulou, and R. van Oers, 25-50. Leiden/Boston: Martinus Nijhoff.

Regierungsprogramm der ÖVP-FPÖ Koalition. 2000. "Österreich neu Regieren."

Rohe, M. 2006. Perspektiven und Herausforderungen in der Integration muslimischer MitbürgerInnen in Österreich. Wien, Bundesministerium für Inneres, May 2006.

Rohsmann, K. 2003. "Die 'Integrationsvereinbarung' der Fremdengesetznovelle 2002: Integrationsförderung durch Sprach(kurs)zwang?" Diplomarbeit, Universität Wien, Wien.

Rosenberger, S. and A. König. 2011. "Welcoming the Unwelcome: Politics of Minimum Reception Standards for Asylum Seekers in Austria." *Journal of Refugee Studies* (9 December). doi 10.1093/jrs/fer051.

Schiffauer, W. 2008. *Parallelgesellschaften. Wie viel Wertekonsens braucht unsere Gesellschaft? Für eine kluge Politik der Differenz*. Bielefeld: Transcript Verlag.

Statistik Austria. 2008a. *Migration Statistics 2008*. At http://www.statistik.at/web_de/dynamic/services/publikationen/2/publdetail?id=2&listid=2&detail=542

—2008b. *Arbeitsmarktstatistik – Jahresergebnisse 2008*. Wien.

—2008c. "In Österreich leben 1,4 Mio. Menschen mit Migrationshintergrund." At http://www.statistik.at/web_de/presse/032181 (accessed 6 June 2008).

—2010a. *Migration Statistics 2010*. At http://www.statistik.at/web_de/services/publikationen/2/index.html?id=2&listid=2&detail=488

—2010b. *Microcencus – Labour Force Survey 2010*. At: http://www.statistik.at/web_de/dynamic/services/publikationen/3/publdetail?id=3&listid=3&detail=485

—2010c. *EU-SILC 2010*. At: http://www.statistik.at/web_de/frageboegen/private_haushalte/eu_silc/index.html

—2011. "Migration und Integration. Zahlen. Daten. Indikatoren 2011." At http://www.statistik.at/web_de/services/publikationen/2/index.html?id=2&listid=2&detail=621 (accessed 7 July 2011).

StbG (Staatsbürgerschaftsgesetz 1985 – StbG). 1985 [2006]. "Bundesgesetz über die österreichische Staatsbürgerschaft." BGBl. Nr. 311/1985 (WV) idF BGBl. I Nr. 37/2006.

Stern, J. 2011. "Ius Pecuniae – Staatsbürgerschaft zwischen ausreichendem Lebensunterhalt, Mindestsicherung und Menschenwürde." In *Migration und Integration*, ed. J. Dahlvik, H. Fassmann, and W. Sievers, 55-74. Vienna: V & R Unipress.

Ulram, P.A. 2009. Integration in Österreich: Einstellungen, Orientierungen, und Erfahrungen von MigrantInnen und Angehörigen der Mehrheitsbevölkerung. Wien, Bundesministerium für Inneres. At http://www.bmi.gv.at/cms/BMI_Service/Integrationsstudie.pdf

Valchars, G. 2006. *Defizitäre Demokratie, Staatsbürgerschaft und Wahlrecht im Einwanderungsland Österreich*. Wien: Studienreihe Konfliktforschung.

Vertovec, S. 2006. "The Emergence of Super-Diversity in Britain." COMPAS Working Paper WP-06-25, Oxford University.

Wets, J. 2006. "The Turkish Community in Austria and Belgium: The Challenge of Integration." *Turkish Studies* 7(1): 85-100.

Wodak, R. and M. Krzyzanowski. 2009. *The Politics of Exclusion: Debating Migration in Austria*. London: Transaction Publishers.

Wodak, R. and M. Reisigl. 2000. "'Austria First,' a Discourse: Historical Analysis of the Austrian 'Anti-Foreigner-Petition' in 1992 and 1993." In *The Semiotics of Racism: Approaches in Critical Discourse Analysis*, ed. M. Reisigl and R. Wodak, 269-304. Vienna: Passagen Verlag.

Chapter 3

Integrating Britain's Culturally Diverse Citizens

Varun Uberoi and Derek McGhee

In our ordinary language, "integration" can be understood in different ways, but one way of doing so is to see it as the means by which previously separate things become combined. This way of seeing integration is often applied to how governments approach their culturally diverse citizens. In doing so, what is being discussed is how governments combine these citizens so that they can not only live together peacefully but also feel like a community. This helps them to accept collectively binding decisions that are inconvenient, to pay taxes that provide public services that they may not use, to delay their demands so that the more urgent ones of other citizens can be met, and so on.[1] All these are normal facets of political life that involve some sacrifice and all of them could be achieved using the law. But when citizens feel they form a community, they are more willing to make such sacrifices, and legal coercion can thus be kept to a minimum. Governments therefore seek to integrate their culturally diverse citizens, and in this chapter we examine how successive British governments have attempted to do so.

Indeed, following Bhikhu Parekh (1998), we can identify five ideal types or approaches to integration that the British, or any government, might use. In practice, they overlap, but the first of them is *proceeduralism*. Advocates of this approach suggest that the state should be neutral between various cultural groups, as only then can it be fair to each of them. The state should be a purely formal institution that ensures that citizens obey the law and discharge their fair share of the burdens of collective life. As long as citizens do this, they should be free to adhere to whatever culture they wish, and thus a very thin form of community is sought. It is

International Perspectives: Integration and Inclusion, ed. J. Frideres and J. Biles. Montreal and Kingston: Queen's Policy Studies Series, McGill-Queen's University Press. © 2012 The School of Policy Studies, Queen's University at Kingston.

a community made stable through treating all citizens fairly, as doing so breeds affection for a society and institutions that are just (Rawls 1993).

Advocates of a second approach, *assimiliation*, suggest that the state cannot be culturally neutral. It usually reflects the beliefs, norms, and values of a cultural majority, and even if it did not, some cultural influence is unavoidable. After all, policy-makers have to decide what language to conduct their public affairs in, which public holidays to observe, and what history to teach children; none of these can be done without reference to a culture. Culture also provides a way of seeing the world that is inescapable when policy-makers decide what to do about controversial issues like euthanasia, divorce, abortion, sex education, polygymy, violent sports, capital punishment, homosexuality, gay marriage, and so on (Parekh 1998, 6). Short of policy-makers deciding not to take a position on such issues, culture cannot be set aside. Neutrality is impossible, and as the state reflects the culture of a majority, it should require minorities to assimilate and acquire the culture of the majority. This position will sustain a community akin to the nations that emerged from early modernity onwards (Scruton 1988).

Advocates of a third approach, *civic assimiliation*, accept the critique of proceeduralism but note that just because culture is inescapable, neutrality is impossible, and the majority's culture is reflected in the state, it does not follow that all cultural minorities should assimilate. Indeed, to expect assimilation is unreasonable as it is extremely difficult to abandon one's culture and acquire another; it is also a deep infringement of individual liberty. For civic assimilationists, the preferred approach is to assimilate *only* into the public culture, which is the beliefs, institutions, and practices that regulate the shared lives of all citizens. Such a public culture will be profoundly shaped by a cultural majority, but it can also be endorsed by those from many different cultural backgrounds. Hence, even though America's public culture is shaped by its Anglo-Protestant history, few of its minorities have difficulty identifying with the Constitution and Bill of Rights (Walzer 2001). If the public culture is thin and largely procedural, it matters little if it has been shaped by a cultural majority, as minorities can internalize it as their own and adhere to the rules of the community so as to be part of it (Habermas 1993).

Pluralists or multiculturalists note how, like assimilationists, civic assimilationists place all the emphasis on cultural minorities whose beliefs, norms, and practices are also excluded from the public culture, and yet as citizens they are entitled to be treated equally. The public culture also enjoys great prestige as it is the authority that all must submit to, and as it reflects the cultural majority, they too enjoy such prestige. But those who are excluded from the public culture do not; they are relegated to second-class status, which helps to legitimize discrimination and cultivate feelings of exclusion from a community dominated by a cultural majority whose status seems very different. Like the previous two approaches, civic assimilation also says little about the disproportionate levels of material inequality that cultural minorities often suffer compared to the cultural majority. Reinforcing notions that the latter group is superior, material inequality increases the allure of assimilation as a "way out" and further cultivates feelings of exclusion from a community that accepts disadvantage amongst cultural minorities. Dominated by the cultural majority, the community culturally and materially excludes cultural minorities. This situation is rectified by recasting the beliefs, norms, and practices that comprise the public culture to reflect not only the majority's culture but minority cultures as well. The material needs of minorities must also be recognized through special measures that focus on alleviating the disadvantage that specific groups suffer. In recognizing the cultural and material needs of all, integration is seen as a two-way process in which a majority and minorities compromise to build a community that is more inclusive (Modood 2005, 2007).

Radical pluralists, however, might suggest that pluralists do not go far enough, as all groups are defined significantly by their culture, which also gives them a great deal in life that they cherish. Such groups often require systems of self-government to reflect their group's cultural needs. Whether the demands are for separate civil or familial legal systems or devolving power to facilitate a level of self-determination, the state should respect the need for different degrees of minority self-governance. Not doing so fosters resentment against the state for not recognizing various groups' cultural needs; doing so fosters gratitude and thus an attachment to the state. Such attachment may be restricted to the state and need not extend to all citizens, but it is sufficient to sustain a thin sense of community to which all are committed because all get what their cultural group needs.

Examining the merits of these different forms of integration would require a very different chapter to what is relevant for a comparative public policy volume of this nature. However, we will show that many of these approaches can be found in Britain. Different approaches have risen, fallen, or combined with others, and we refrain here from arguing whether any of them have succeeded or failed. After all, to do so we would have to identify indicators of success and failure; and presenting arguments for the indicators we favour as opposed to those that we do not would require a chapter in itself. We would also have to ask if the data available reflect the indicators that are appropriate, and it is unclear if they do. Exploring the merits of these different approaches is thus not relevant to this chapter, and exploring their successes and failures is not possible within its confines. More modestly, we will show how four of the five approaches to integration that we have outlined above have been adopted by successive British governments since World War II.

We illustrate the presence of these approaches using various pieces of legislation, government archival records, publicly available government policy documents, and political speeches. Used as indicators of what approach to integration was adopted by successive British governments, these documents relate to the various areas of policy that are often used to integrate Britain's culturally diverse citizens and make them feel like a community. Hence we examine documents relating to immigration policy, because immigration can be restricted so as to preserve a homogenous community, or it can be liberalized to create a culturally diverse one. Likewise, we look at documents relating to race relations policy, because it can be used to punish those who treat others as if they were not part of the community and to create a more liberal form of community. Further, we examine documents relating to education policy, because governments can use it to inculcate in children a particular understanding of the community. Documents from these and other areas are relevant to showing what approach successive British governments have adopted towards integration, and we proceed in three stages to do so. We first examine how governments approached integration from World War II to the turn of the twenty-first century, showing how a proceeduralist approach grew into a pluralist one. We then examine how the last government approached integration and show how a civic assimilationist and a pluralist approach have combined, after which we conclude by briefly discussing whether the recently elected coalition government is abandoning this pluralist approach.

INTEGRATION IN BRITAIN, 1945–2000: FROM PROCEEDURALISM TO PLURALISM

Waves of immigration in the postwar period were much bigger than earlier ones, and they brought with them people of greater racial and cultural difference than in earlier eras. The 1948 *Nationality Act* gave Commonwealth migrants permission to enter, reside, work, and claim benefits in the United Kingdom, and many wanted to avail themselves of this opportunity. From 1948 to 1952, between 1,000 and 2,000 colonial immigrants arrived in Britain each year. In 1954, the number rose to 10,000. In 1960, 58,000 colonial immigrants arrived and by 1961 the inflow had reached 136,000 (Paul 1997, 132). As one official at the time put it, these people "do not belong in any real sense"; the 1958 riots in Nottingham and Notting Hill, caused by British whites attacking those of West Indian descent, created fear that Britain had a "race problem" (136). There were calls to restrict immigration, and in the Queen's Speech of 1961, the Conservative government announced its intention to do so. The 1962 *Commonwealth Immigration Act* was thus introduced, and the implicit message was that the cause of riots was the arrival of newcomers, not the racism of the cultural majority. In this milieu, two approaches to integration seemed dominant.

The first becomes clear when we note that many felt that the "state had a duty to be race neutral" (Rose 1969, 200). Indeed, such proceeduralism was how calls to legislate against the incitement of racial and religious hatred were rejected when Oswald Mosely's British Union of Fascists emerged. It was also the main argument that had been used by successive Conservative governments in the 1950s and early '60s. Hence, before the 1964 general election, the then leader of the Conservative Party, Sir Alec Douglas Home, said, "Those who ask for special legislation [dealing with racial discrimination] ignore the fact that at present, all British citizens, irrespective of race, creed or colour are equal under the law" (cited in Bleich 2003, 42). But proceeduralism may also have masked a less race-neutral and more assimilationist approach, as the government records surrounding the introduction of the 1962 *Commonwealth Immigration Act* illustrate. After all, the home secretary at the time, Richard (Rab) Butler, said in a cabinet memorandum, "We must recognise, that although the scheme [created by the act] purports to relate solely to employment and be non-discriminatory, its aim is primarily social and its restrictive effect is intended to, and would in fact, *operate on coloured people almost exclusively*" (Memorandum from Home Secretary to Cabinet, 6 November 1961, emphasis added). Likewise, Butler suggested that his preference was for assimilation, but this wasn't working:

> The Commonwealth Migrants Committee recognise that ... unrestricted Commonwealth immigration is on balance to our economic advantage; that control cannot at present be conclusively justified on the grounds of employment, health and public order and that its introduction would give rise to sharp criticism in some Commonwealth countries and fierce controversy in Parliament. *Nevertheless... since assimilation is not taking place to any significant extent while coloured immigration is likely to go on increasing, control should be accepted as a sad necessity.* (ibid., emphasis added)

Proceeduralism and assimilationism combined during this period, but were somewhat replaced with the election of a Labour government.

Despite supporting the passage of the 1962 *Commonwealth Immigration Act*, the new government wanted to introduce measures to protect cultural minorities from discrimination. Roy Hattersley, then a backbench MP, encapsulated the government's main argument for doing so: "Without integration limitation is inexcusable, without limitation, integration is impossible" (Bleich 2003, 47). Clearly the latter entailed at least some short-term acceptance of the cultural majority's prejudice, but the quid pro quo for many in the Parliamentary Labour Party for accepting the limitation of immigration in 1962 was improved integration through the 1965 *Race Relations Act* (ibid.). As Eric Bleich carefully shows, the act dealt specifically with "expressive" and "access based" racism. Written and spoken expressions that could be used to incite hate against others on the grounds of colour, race, or ethnic or national origins were prohibited, as was discrimination that prevented access to public places like bars and hotels. There were no measures relating to employment or housing discrimination; with regards to expressive racism, there was nothing about discrimination that was offensive but did not incite hate. The maximum punishment for expressive racism was a prison sentence of two years and a fine of £1,000, but the decision to prosecute had to be made by a state representative like the attorney general of England or Wales, or the lord advocate of Scotland (ibid., 58). It was more likely that the matter would be dealt with by the race relations boards that were introduced and designed at the local level to promote conciliation once a complaint was made. All of this seemed to be a move away from assimilation; after all, if discriminatory practices were to be punished, then it was more acceptable to be different. Indeed, Roy Jenkins, the home secretary who passed the act, said famously in 1966, "I do not think that we need in this country a melting pot which will turn everyone out in a common mould, as one of a series of carbon copies of someone's misplaced vision of a stereo-typed Englishman. I define integration ... not as a flattening process of uniformity, but cultural diversity coupled with equality of opportunity in an atmosphere of mutual tolerance" (quoted in Favell 1998, 104). But the act was not just a move away from assimilation – it was also a move away from proceeduralism. The *law* was no longer race neutral, as it gave racial minorities the protection they needed and was now being used to make *society* more race neutral.

It was, however, a weak act, and it was thus strengthened by the 1968 *Race Relations Act*, which extended the law against access racism to employment, housing, trade unions, employers organizations, banking, and elsewhere. Race relations boards were given the power to investigate racism and if necessary bring forward legal proceedings. The act thus confirmed that the law could not be race neutral and so further legitimated difference. But it was also seen as anti-assimilationist by those like Enoch Powell, who gave his infamous "Rivers of Blood" speech three days before the second reading of the legislation in Parliament. Powell endorsed reducing the numbers of immigrants allowed into the UK and repatriating many of those who had arrived, but he also suggested that the act would protect the wrong people as it made immigrants a "privileged or special class" and restricted the majority's "*right* to discriminate in the management of [their] own affairs." He also clearly identified the conception of integration that he favoured by saying, "to be integrated into a population means to become for all practical purposes indistinguishable from its members," and he thought that very few immigrants were prepared to integrate in this way (Powell 1968, emphasis added). Powell thought assimilation possible but not probable and the act decreased the likelihood of it even further. He was promptly dismissed from the shadow cabinet, but assimilationism remained popular amongst many, as the public's reaction to his speech might suggest (Hansen 2000, 186-7).

It would be difficult to definitively argue, however, that Powell's dismissal meant that assimilationism was dead amongst senior Conservative politicians, who upon returning to power in 1970 passed the 1971 *Immigration Act*. It aimed to *reduce* immigration from the New Commonwealth (countries like India and Pakistan) whilst *facilitating* immigration from the Old Commonwealth (countries like Australia and New Zealand). To reduce immigration from the former, the term "patrial" was introduced into British law. Patrials were British subjects or United Kingdom and Commonwealth citizens whose parents or grandparents had been born, adopted, naturalized, or registered in the United Kingdom or who had lived in the UK for more than five years. As patrials were, on the whole, those whose ancestors were born in the UK, they were unlikely to be immigrants from the New Commonwealth and thus unlikely to be racially or culturally too different (Paul 1997, 181). New immigrants from the New Commonwealth lost their right to enter, reside, work, and claim benefits in Britain, while old Commonwealth immigrants did not, suggesting a preference for those who were racially and culturally similar. This was not said explicitly, but the then Home Secretary who passed the act, Reginald Maudling, did later claim, "It is a simple fact of human nature that for the British people there is a great difference between Australians and New Zealanders for example, who come of British stock, and people from Africa, Caribbean and the Indian sub-continent who were equally subjects of the Queen and entitled to total equality before the law when established here, but who in appearance, habits, religion and culture, were totally different from us" (Maudling 1978, 158).

Such preference for those who are racially and culturally similar may then have resulted in at least some preference for an assimilationist understanding of integration, but Labour's return to power in the two elections of 1974 and Roy Jenkins's return to the Home Office facilitated a *modest* move towards a pluralist understanding of integration.

Although himself admitting that by the 1970s his "liberal instincts" needed "a little stimulation," Jenkins, under the influence of his special advisor Anthony (now Lord) Lester, passed the 1976 *Race Relations Act*. It expanded the definition of discrimination so that it no longer related solely to direct and intentional actions but also to indirect and unintentional ones. Treatment that is formally equal but in effect discriminates against a particular group was judged to be an indirect form of discrimination. For example, dress codes forbidding men from wearing a beard and compelling them to wear a helmet would be an indirect form of discrimination for religious Sikh men for whom a turban and a beard are religiously important. The act also introduced a very modest form of affirmative or "positive" action: "Training bodies, employers, or unions" could "allocate training resources to underrepresented racial groups" and encourage them to apply for certain jobs. Although no formal quotas were allowed, the emphasis was on enabling cultural minorities to compete effectively.

Victims of discrimination could go directly to the courts, but they would be aided as well by a new enforcement mechanism in the form of the Commission for Racial Equality, which would also advise the government, run anti-discrimination advertising, and promote "good relations between persons of different groups." That same year, turban-wearing Sikhs were made legally exempt from wearing motorcycle helmets. In 1979 slaughterhouses providing *halal* and *kosher* meat were made exempt from certain health and safety provisions. Stronger discrimination laws, limited affirmative action, and legal exemptions for minority religious practices signalled a modest move towards pluralism, as they suggested an attempt to improve the protection of minorities whilst recognizing their material and cultural needs.

Despite the election of a Conservative administration in 1979 that introduced no major race relations initiatives and brought in more restrictive immigration legislation, this modest move towards pluralism was not undone. Indeed, Thatcher's government, at least at some level, accepted the remaking of Britain's public culture by accepting the need to reshape Britain's education system in her government's reaction to the Swann Report. Advocating a form of "multicultural education," the report said, "We are not seeking to fit ethnic minorities into a mould which was originally cast for a society relatively homogenous in language, religion and culture, nor to break this mould completely ... We are instead looking to recast the mould into a form which retains the fundamental principles of the original *but within a broader pluralist conspectus* – diversity within unity" (Swann 1985, 8, emphasis added). The secretary of state for education, Keith Joseph, accepted the vast majority of the report's findings and said, "We want the schools to preserve and transmit our national values in a way which *accepts Britain's ethnic diversity* and promotes tolerance and racial harmony. Whether or not a school contains ethnic minority pupils, its ethos and curriculum should promote understanding and respect among all its pupils for the different ethnic groups which *now contribute to our national life*" (*Hansard*, 14 March 1985, emphasis added).

Such a statement from a Conservative secretary of state for education, who was also Thatcher's mentor, was significant. Indeed, later in his final statement as secretary of state for education, Joseph said:

> The concern of all of us must be to establish the educational policy that is right for our ethnically mixed society. *In the Government's view such a policy ... must strive to educate all our children and young people so that they are better prepared for adult life in an ethnically mixed Britain, in a way that will do full justice to the accumulated richness of this country's national culture. Some may ask are there not also Sikh, Hindu, Muslim and Caribbean cultures? Yes of course there are, just as there have long been Protestant and Catholic and Free Church and other Christian variants of Christian culture: and Jewish culture too. But all these can be cherished within the broad British culture* ... We need to develop within our children and

young people the capacity to respect the cultures and beliefs of the different groups that make up our society. (Joseph 1986, 7, emphasis added)

Joseph thus noted the diverse strains in Britain's national culture and suggested that the cultures of minorities could also be included in it, thus endorsing what Bhikhu Parekh would later call a "multiculturally constituted common culture." Similar arguments can be found in the later works of the most important and profound multiculturalists, but such ideas were already significant in the 1980s (Parekh 2000, 213). Indeed, Joseph was not alone; as the then Home Secretary Douglas Hurd claimed, amidst the difficulties and complexities that surrounded Salman Rushdie's publication of the *Satanic Verses*, "There are ... increasing signs of *black and Asian Britons* playing their full part in the mainstream of our national life. Whether you look at police officers, magistrates, local councillors or Parliamentary candidates, men and women from the ethnic minorities can now be seen in growing numbers. In both our economic *and our cultural life they are making a welcome and positive contribution to this nation*" (Hurd 1989, 10, emphasis added). Integration by the end of Thatcher's tenure was, at least in part, conceived in pluralist terms.

Perhaps realizing, as Shamit Saggar observes (2003), that in the 1992 and 1997 general elections, four out of five non-white voters voted Labour, this party could not afford to abandon a pluralist approach. Indeed, after Labour returned to power in 1997, it introduced the *Race Relations Amendment Act* in 2000 in response to Recommendation 11 of Lord Macpherson's inquiry into the death of a black teenager, Stephen Lawrence. Macpherson's report highlighted the significance of institutional racism, and the act thus extended the 1976 *Race Relations Act* to public authorities and compelled them to promote "equality of opportunity and good relations between persons of different racial groups." This period was what some have called the "multicultural moment" in Britain. Not only was this act passed but some non-Christian and non-Jewish faith schools were given government recognition and financial support. "The primary purpose rule," which had required spouses to prove that their marriage was not designed to get British residency, was abolished. And power was devolved to Britain's national minorities in Scotland and Wales (Meer and Modood 2009). In an often-quoted speech, Robin Cook, then foreign secretary, noted that "pluralism is not a burden we must reluctantly accept. It is an immense asset that contributes to the cultural and economic vitality of our nation" (Cook 2001). Indeed, even William Hague, leader of the Conservative Party and a Thatcherite, was making claims that suggested he favoured a pluralist understanding of integration: "America may have had its huddled masses but we have had our Celts, Picts, Saxons, Angles, Normans, Jews, Hugenots, Indians, Pakistanis, Afro Carribeans, Bengalis and countless others. These are all British people, all of them" (Hague 1999, 5). Illustrating that even

Conservatives on the right of their party were by this stage beginning to see how the British had to recognize their culturally diverse past, not ignore it, Hague also seemed to accept how this cultural diversity was reconfiguring Britain's public culture. Hence. just before the 2001 general election, he spoke of "the way in which Muslim values are being built into the edifice that is modern Britain" (2001, 6).

By the turn of the millennia, then, there was at least some broad consensus amongst the two leading political parties that the integration of Britain's culturally diverse citizens should be understood in pluralist terms. But in 2000 the Commission for Multi-Ethnic Britain (CMEB) published its report, which had taken nearly two years to write. It was written by a commission comprised of many leading intellectuals and chaired by Bhikhu Parekh. Controversially the report stated, "Britishness as much as Englishness, has systematic, largely unspoken, racial connotations. Whiteness nowhere features as an explicit condition of being British, but it is widely understood that Englishness, and, therefore, by extension Britishness is racially coded. 'There aint no black in the Union Jack,' it has been said" (CMEB 2000, 38). Advocating "re-imagining" what it means to be British, it suggested that Britain should be seen as a Habermasian "post nation" or a "community of communities."

The report was condemned in the right-wing press for being anti-British and for suggesting that "British" was a racist term (McLaughlin and Neal 2004). The home secretary, Jack Straw, implied that the section on "re-imagining what it means to be British" was inconsistent and seemed to disagree with the idea itself: "I'm in a sense sorry to say this ... that where I do strongly part company with the Commission is over the view that's expressed in chapter three of this document about Britishness" (Straw 2000). Straw's response was perhaps the first sign of a change: attacks on multiculturalism as a mode of integration by those on the right might be something to be expected, but, as Tariq Modood notes, by 2004 "there was a swathe of civil society fora and institutions of the *centre-left* or the *liberal-left* which held seminars or produced special publications with titles like 'Is Multiculturalism Dead?', 'Is Multiculturalism Over?', 'Beyond Multiculturalism,' etc." (2007, 11, emphasis added) There was a "crisis of multiculturalism," and opponents and proponents of multiculturalist modes of integration accepted its presence (Joppke 2004; Vasta 2007).

THE DECADE OF 2000–10: CIVIC ASSIMILATIONISM AND PLURALISM COMBINED

We move on now to examine whether what followed in the decade after the CMEB's report can really be understood as a retreat from pluralism or multiculturalism as a way of integrating Britain's culturally diverse citizens. But to do so, it is first necessary to understand how the government's approach to integration has changed during this decade. Indeed, it was a decade in which immigration became a major concern for the British public. IPSOS Mori's polling showed that "immigration and asylum" did not even feature as an issue that would help respondents decide who to vote for in the two years running up to the 1997 general election. But by 2008, for 52 percent of respondents, "immigration and asylum" was an issue that would help them to decide how to vote. Such concern had increased with the numbers of immigrants coming into Britain. Indeed, while postwar immigration was extensive, a net inflow of migrants (more coming in than going out) had only begun in the early 1990s. It rose to 171,000 in 2000, declined to 151, 000 in 2003, rose to 222,600 in 2004, and then rose even further after the new accession countries joined the EU (Vertovek 2007, 1028).

It was not just the numbers of immigrants that were creating concern, however (Uberoi and Saggar 2009). In 2001 the worst riots in a genera-tion tore through the northern towns of Oldham, Burnley, and Bradford. Provoked by far-right groups, young Muslims rioted. Shortly after, the attack of September 11 occurred. Civil unrest combined with terrorism to conjure an unnecessary fear across the political spectrum of Muslims engaging in extra-political activity (Uberoi and Modood 2010), and a Community Cohesion Review Team led by Ted Cantle was set up to re-view the causes of the riots. The team recommended fostering cohesion:

> We believe that there is an urgent need to promote community cohesion, based upon a greater knowledge of, contact between, and respect for, the various cultures that now make Great Britain such a rich and diverse na-tion. It is also essential to establish a greater sense of citizenship, based on (a few) common principles which are shared and observed by all sections of the community. This concept of citizenship would also place a higher value on cultural differences. (Home Office 2001, 10)

Contact and knowledge between different cultural groups had to be improved, but what was also necessary was a greater sense of citizenship. This position cohered well with the ambitions of then Home Secretary David Blunkett, as in his previous cabinet post he had made citizenship education a compulsory part of the national curriculum. Indeed, in his response to Cantle's report, Blunkett said, "The UK has had a relatively weak sense of what political citizenship should entail. Our values of individual freedom, the protection of liberty and respect for difference, have not been accompanied by a strong, shared understanding of the civic realm. This has to change" (Blunkett 2001, 2). He seemed to begin a process of reorienting integration in Britain towards a civic assimilation, illustrated in section 1 of the *Nationality Immigration and Asylum Act of 2002* (McGhee 2008, 47). The new section created citizenship ceremonies for those having recently become British citizens and made it necessary for "those that apply for naturalisation as a British citizen to have sufficient knowledge about life in the United Kingdom," described to new immigrants as follows:

> We respect the laws, the elected parliamentary and democratic political structures, traditional values of mutual tolerance, respect for equal rights and mutual concern ... To be British is to respect those overarching specific institutions, values, beliefs and traditions that bind us all, the different nations and cultures together in peace and in a legal order ... So to be British does not mean assimilation into a culture so that original identities are lost. (Home Office 2005a, 15)

Immigrants were required to become British to the extent that they respected the law, democratic structures, and various "overarching specific institutions" – though they were not required to assimilate and jettison their cultural particularities. What was required was that they assimilate into Britain's public culture; but Blunkett's civic assimilationism did not entail a purely liberal conception of citizenship in which citizens possess an array of legal, political, and social rights (Miller 2000). It entailed a conception of citizenship that was partly republican in nature, as citizens were not only required to be cognisant of and willing to claim their various rights but also to be cognisant of and willing to fulfil their obligations to one another and the state. Hence in Blunkett's 2004 consultation document, *Strength in Diversity*, he said:

> To build a successful integrated society we need to promote an inclusive concept of citizenship, which goes further than the strictly legal definition of nationality and articulates *the rights and responsibilities we share. Building this wider notion of active citizenship through participation, volunteering and civic action, underpinned by a sense of shared values, is one of the main ways in which we can strengthen the relationships and connections between communities.* (Home Office 2004, 6, emphasis added)

It is then an active sense of citizenship that is implied in this civic assimilationism, suggesting that citizens must not only internalize Britain's existing public culture but be willing to actively participate in it.

The consultation paper also acknowledged that experiencing a sense of community is more difficult when people are "becoming less alike in economic terms" (Gilroy 2004, 132). "People of all races and religions" were said to share experiences of "deprivation and disadvantage," but it was also stated that "we know that they affect particular groups more profoundly" (Home Office 2004, 13). Indeed, the government conceded that despite its "huge investments," the scale of disadvantage experienced in British ethnic minority communities appeared to have changed little (ibid.). Black, Pakistani, and Bangladeshi communities were singled out as being particularly disadvantaged and relatively untouched by public policy strategies. Whilst a more recent document is more sanguine, nonetheless it concedes that "some groups have been left behind and need extra help" (DCLG 2010, 11). As well as a civic assimilationist approach to integration, material disadvantage amongst certain communities was also seen as an important aspect of creating a more integrated Britain (McGhee 2008). Indeed, such disadvantage was viewed as cultivating extremism: "Structural inequalities and the legacy of discrimination have resulted in whole groups that are effectively left behind, with young people failing to share in the opportunities that should be available to all, which in turn fuels their disengagement from mainstream society and creates pathways to extremism" (Home Office 2004, 5).

The consultation paper eventually became a strategy document, its title signalling the importance of material inequality as it was called *Improving Opportunity, Strengthening Society: The Government's Strategy to Increase Race Equality and Community Cohesion* (Home Office 2005b).

This focus on material inequalities was construed by some as a distancing from multiculturalism, as a long-running critique of it suggests that it fails to take account of material inequality (Hobsbawm 1996; Fraser 2000). This charge is untrue, as the discussion of it above as an ideal type indicates; moreover, a quick look at systematic accounts of multiculturalist modes of integration in Britain indicates a clear appreciation for material and cultural issues and indeed their intimately related nature (Parekh 2008; CMEB 2000; Swann 1985). But civic assimilation was also described as a departure from a multiculturalist or pluralist mode of integration. Hence, in outlining his notion of active citizenship, Blunkett said, "An active concept of citizenship can articulate shared ground between diverse communities. It offers a shared identity based on membership of a political community, rather than forced assimilation into a monoculture, *or an unbridled multiculturalism which privileges difference over community cohesion*"(Blunkett 2002a, 6, emphasis added).

Blunkett's statement, viewed as a departure from multiculturalism, also illustrates how the policy was seen as divisive; others echoed the claim. Trevor Phillips, then chair of the Commission for Race Equality and now head of the Equality and Human Rights Commission, said that multiculturalism "suggests separateness" (*Times*, 3 April 2004). Multiculturalism was thus caricatured either as divisive – not a form of integration that fosters a sense of community – or as a form that is not pluralist but instead radically pluralist in nature as it institutionalizes separateness. Yet recall the Swann Report's desire for "diversity within unity" and the CMEB's desire to "re-imagine Britishness": neither was about separatism but about a more equitable integration in which immigrants and their descendants were given a role in remaking the community. Likewise, it is possible, as we described at the beginning of this chapter, for radically plural forms

of integration to cultivate a sense of community; however, this criticism
has perhaps stuck.

After the terrorist bomb attacks of 7/7 in London, the government announced a Commission on Integration and Community Cohesion (CICC),
which had a local government focus. With integration coming under the
control of the Department of Local Government and Communities, this
focus was somewhat inevitable. But while emphasizing the importance of
"strengthening rights and responsibilities," the CICC advocated a move
from a "one size fits all" integration model to a more varied approach.
Its head, Dara Singh, himself a local government chief executive, suggested that Britain needed "a new model of integration that can keep up
with the pace of change in our communities. And one that can be flexible
enough to accommodate differences in local experience" (Singh 2006, 1).
He also suggested that "settled communities" were worried about the
unfair allocation of public funds and services; in short, there was fear
that "immigrants and minorities were getting special treatment," and
this fear was cultivating division (CICC 2007, 33).[2] Crucially, hostility to
multiculturalism remained. Ruth Kelly, then secretary of state for Local
Government and Communities, announced, "We have moved from a period of uniform consensus on the value of multiculturalism, to one where
we can encourage that debate by questioning whether it is encouraging
separateness" (Kelly 2006, 2). Singh wanted to retire the term: "Our view
is that we need to update our language to meet the current climate. We
therefore intend to avoid using the term 'multiculturalism' in our report
because of its 'catch all' and confusing quality. Our focus is on what
practical policies we need to make our complex society work – where
race, faith and culture are important, but not the only, elements of that
complexity" (CICC 2007, 13).

This rhetorical position has certainly convinced many that there is a
"retreat" from multiculturalism in Britain (Joppke 2004; Vasta 2007). But
logic requires that in order for there to be a retreat, there must be evidence
of reversal of key policies. However, if anything, anti-discrimination provisions have been strengthened to deal with the incitement of religious
hatred (Meer 2008; Uberoi and Modood, forthcoming). Likewise, exemptions for minority religious practices remain, as do forms of multicultural
education (Uberoi 2008). Unlike in the Netherlands where dual citizenship
programs were abandoned, public broadcasting devoted to multicultural issues was cut, the burkha was banned in public spaces, and so on,
there has been no such a drastic shift in Britain (Meer and Modood 2009;
Entzinger 2003; Hansen 2007). Certainly, community and social cohesion
is emphasized by policy-makers, and it is easy to see why this leads many
to think that a pluralist or multiculturalist approach is being abandoned.
Ellie Vasta makes the point well: "Many, particularly those on the Left,
dislike and avoid the notion of cohesion due to an inherent meaning of
social order and social control that appears too similar to 'assimilation'"

(2007, 12). But to see all discussion of cohesion as anti-multiculturalist is to accept the false critique that multiculturalist or pluralist modes of integration are only about difference. As we saw earlier, this was not true of the Swann Report or the CMEB's report, both of which saw unity and diversity as vital. But we can go further, as those advocating civic assimilation and cohesion are not simply jettisoning a pluralist approach to integration.

As the extended quote below shows, Tony Blair in his valedictory lecture in 2006 simultaneously endorsed the civic assimilation that Blunkett had trumpeted along with a multicultural approach and suggested that the former was always accompanied by the latter:

> Integration ... is not about culture or lifestyle. It is about values. It is about integrating at the point of shared, common unifying British values. *It isn't about what defines us as people, but as citizens, the rights and duties that go with being a member of our society.* Christians, Jews, Muslims, Hindus, Sikhs and other faiths have a perfect right to their own identity and religion, to practice their faith and to conform to their culture. This is what multicultural, multi-faith Britain is about. That is what is legitimately distinctive. But when it comes to our essential values – belief in democracy, the rule of law, tolerance, equal treatment for all, respect for this country and its shared heritage – then that is where we come together, it is what we hold in common; it is what gives us the right to call ourselves British. At that point no distinctive culture or religion supercedes our duty to be part of an integrated United Kingdom ... *it is necessary to go back to what a multi-cultural Britain is all about. The whole point is that multicultural Britain was never supposed to be a celebration of division; but of diversity. The purpose was to allow people to live harmoniously together, despite their difference; not to make their difference an encouragement to discord. The values that nurtured it were those of solidarity, of coming together, of peaceful co-existence. The right to be in a multicultural society was always, always implicitly balanced by a duty to integrate, to be part of Britain, to be British and Asian, British and black, British and white.* Those whites who support the BNP's [British National Party's] policy of separate races and those Muslims who shun integration into British society both contradict the fundamental values that define Britain today: tolerance, solidarity across the racial and religious divide, equality for all and between all. So it is not that we need to dispense with multicultural Britain. *On the contrary we should continue celebrating it.* (Blair 2006, 3, emphasis added)

Blair thus certainly defined integration as civic assimilation, but he did not exhibit scepticism of multiculturalism. Nor did he accept the caricature that it was about separatism; instead, he wanted to "go back to what multicultural Britain was always about." In doing so, as Meer and Modood (2009) have shown, Blair suggested that multiculturalism was always accompanied by civic assimilationism, and that what he thought was necessary was not an abandonment of the former but added emphasis on the latter.

Likewise, Blunkett, a leading exponent of civic assimilation, also echoed the Commission for Multi-Ethnic Britain in claiming, "Britain is now a nation of nations and a community of diverse cultures and beliefs. We should take pride in this plurality and draw both common citizenship and political identity from it" (Blunkett 2002b, 152). Equally, Trevor Phillips does not just emphasize civic assimilationism; he does not just claim that people should "expect to share in how we make decisions" and "carry the responsibilities of making the society work." He also notes that "integration has to be *a two way street* in which settled communities accept that new people will bring change with them" (Phillips 2005, 6, emphasis added). Despite their criticism of multiculturalism, then, neither Blunkett nor Phillips has jettisoned multiculturalist ambitions. Policy-makers may thus make overt statements that are critical of multiculturalism, but not only do they simultaneously endorse multiculturalist ideas but the main approach of civic assimilationism that has been championed since Blunkett's arrival at the Home Office is conceptualized as *not* at odds with a pluralist approach but as accompanying it. Little wonder that the most prominent scholar to suggest that the country is retreating from multiculturalism has recently resiled from this claim by indicating that it would be "misleading to brand" what is occurring in Britain as a retreat from multiculturalism (Joppke 2008, 537).

CONCLUSION

A pluralist understanding of integration today thus combines with a civic assimilationist one, just as a proceeduralist understanding once combined with an assimilationist one. But this may change, because at the time of writing a Conservative Party-led coalition has taken office, and David Cameron, Britain's prime minister, has announced his intention to cut immigration down to tens of thousands and has criticized "state multiculturalism" (Cameron 2011, Uberoi 2011). Despite the best efforts of this new government, immigration continues to rise, but it is notable that the Conservative Party has long suggested that "multiculturalism, which should allow diversity to flourish within an overall framework of unity, is tending to foster difference for its own sake and demands for special treatment. This prevents integration" (Conservative Party 2007, 23). Echoing the way that Blunkett rhetorically cast multiculturalism as not being a form of integration, many Conservatives also suggest that multiculturalism engenders separatism. There are thus not only cross-party similarities in the way in which a multiculturalist mode of integration is attacked: there is also the possibility that in time it may be usurped. But is this possibility high?

It is difficult to say. A pluralist understanding of integration has certainly not been uprooted. Recall that perhaps the first sign of possible change was the government's reaction to the CMEB report, but more than a decade later, over 100 of their 127 recommendations have been accepted by the government (Modood 2010). Likewise, the commission's central and most controversial point was that Britishness needs to be reimagined, that people's national identities needed to be made more inclusive. If ever there was a pluralist ambition, that was it, and recall that Jack Straw seemed to disagree with it. But only a year later, John Denham, then minister with responsibility for community cohesion, advocated "positive action ... to be taken to build a shared vision and identity" (Denham 2001, 12). In 2004 Denham claimed, "While a modern British identity will ... draw heavily on the history of the White majority we cannot discover Britishness in that history alone; it will have to draw on *all* those who now make up our country" (Denham 2004, 2, emphasis added).

Likewise in their interim report on national security, the Conservative Party stated, "We need to rebuild Britishness in ways which do not breed shallow nationalism but do allow us to understand the contributions that all traditions, whether primarily ethnic or national have made and are making to our collective and shared identity" (Conservative Party 2007, 137). Further, even when criticizing "state multiculturalism," Cameron endorsed a multiculturalist idea by advocating "a clear sense of national identity open to everyone" (Cameron 2011). A pluralist type of integration may well have been challenged in the decade since the millennium, but some aspects of it remain and are even the focus of cross-party consensus (Uberoi and Modood, forthcoming).

NOTES

We are grateful to Tariq Modood and Jan Dobbernak for their helpful comments.

1. Bhikhu Parekh uses these examples to make a very similar but not identical point in Parekh 2002, 4.
2. The issue of "fairness" to all groups was trumpeted again by UK government ministers. See DCLG 2010; Denham 2010.

REFERENCES

Bleich, E. 2003. *Race Politics in Britain and France: Ideas and Policymaking since the 1960s.* Cambridge: Cambridge University Press.

Blunkett, D. 2001. "Blunkett Calls for Honest and Open Debate on Citizenship and Community." 10 Downing Street Newsroom. At http://www.number-10.gov.uk/news.asp?newsID=3255

—2002a. "Integration with Diversity: Globalization and the Renewal of Democracy and Civil Society." Foreign Policy Centre. At http://www.fpc.org.uk/articles/182

—2002b. *Politics and Progress: Renewing Democracy and Civil Society*. London: Politicos.

Blair, T. 2006. "The Duty to Integrate, Shared British Values." Speech, 8 December 2006.

Brown, G. 2008. "Security and Liberty Can Be Protected." Speech, 17 June. At http://www.number10.gov.uk/Page15786

Commission on Integration and Community Cohesion (CICC). 2007. *Our Shared Futures*.

Commission for Multi-Ethnic Britain (CMEB). 2000. *Commission for Multi-Ethnic Britain's Report*. London: Profile Books.

Conservative Party. 2007. "An Unquiet World." Submission to the Shadow Cabinet, National and International Security Policy Group.

Cook, R. 2001. Speech to the Social Market Foundation, 19 April 2001.

Denham, J. 2001. "Building Cohesive Communities: A Report of the Ministerial Group on Public Order and Community Cohesion." Home Office.

—2004. "Real and Imaginary Fears." *Prospect* 96 (March):2-3.

Department for Communities and Local Government (DCLG). 2010. "Tackling Race Equality: A Statement on Race." Department for Communities and Local Government.

Entzinger, H. 2003. "The Rise and Fall of Multiculturalism: The Case of the Netherlands." In *Toward Assimilation and Citizenship*, ed. C. Joppke and E. Morawska. Basingstoke: Palgrave Macmillan.

Favell, A. 1998. *Philosophies of Integration*. London: Macmillan.

Fraser, N. 2000. "Rethinking Recognition." *New Left Review* 3 (May).

Gilroy, P. 2004. *After Empire: Melancholia or Convivial Culture*. London and New York: Routledge.

Habermas, J. 1993. "Struggles for Recognition in Constitutional States." *European Journal of Philosophy* 1(2):1993.

Hague, W. 1999. Speech to the Centre for Policy Studies, 19 January 1999.

—2001. "Vote For What You Value." 1 June 2001.

Hansen, R. 2000. *Citizenship and Immigration in Postwar Britain*. London: Oxford University Press.

—"Diversity, Integration and the Turn from Multiculturalism in the United Kingdom." In *Diversity, Recognition and Shared Citizenship in Canada*, ed. K. Banting, T. Courchene, and F. Siedle. Montreal: Institute for Research and Public Policy.

Hobsbawm, E. 1996. "Identity Politics and the Left." *New Left Review* 217 (May): 38-47.

Home Office. 2001. *Report of the Independent Review Team*. Home Office.

—2004. *Strength in Diversity: Towards a Community Cohesion and Race Equality Strategy*. Home Office.

—2005a. *Life in the United Kingdom: A Journey to Citizenship*. Her Majesty's Stationery Office.

—2005b. *Improving Opportunity, Strengthening Society: The Government's Strategy to Increase Race Equality and Community Cohesion*. Home Office.

Hurd, D. 1989. Speech at Birmingham Central Mosque, 24 February 1989. *New Life* (3 March).

Joppke, C. 2004. "The Retreat of Multiculturalism in the Liberal State." *British Journal of Sociology* 55:2.

—2008. "Immigration and the Identity of Citizenship." *Citizenship Studies* 12:6.

Joseph, K. 1986. "Without Prejudice: Education for an Ethnically Mixed Society." *Multicultural Teaching* 4:3.

Kelly, R. 2006. "Britain: Our Values, Our Responsibilities." Speech to Muslim Organizations on Working Together to Tackle Extremism Together, 11 October. At http://www.communities.gov.uk/index.asp?id=1503690

Mauding, R. 1978. *Memoirs.* London: Sidgwick and Jackson.

McGhee, D. 2008. *The End of Multiculturalism? Terrorism, Integration and Human Rights.* Maidenhead: Open University Press.

—2010. *Security, Citizenship and Human Rights: Shared Values in Uncertain Times.* Basingstoke: Palgrave.

McLaughlin E., and S. Neal. 2004. "Misrepresenting the Multicultural Nation: The Policy Making Process, News Media Management and the Parekh Report." *Policy Studies* 25:3.

Meer, N. and T. Modood. 2009. "The Multicultural State We're In: Muslims, 'Multiculture,' and the Civic Re-Balancing of British Multiculturalism." *Political Studies* 56:3.

Memorandum to Cabinet. 1961. Memorandum from Home Secretary to the Cabinet, 6 October 1961, Macmillan Cabinet Papers. Available through Adam Matthew Publications. At http://www.ampltd.co.uk/

Miller, D. 2000. "Citizenship and Pluralism." In *Citizenship and National Identity,* ed. D. Miller. London: Polity Press.

Modood, T. 2005. *Multicultural Politics, Racism Ethnicity and Muslims in Britain.* Edinburgh: Edinburgh University Press.

—2007. *Multiculturalism.* Cambridge: Polity Press.

—2010. Talk at Misrecognition Conference, 22-23 January, Bristol.

Parekh, B. 1998. "Integrating Minorities." In *Race Relations in Britain,* ed. T. Blackstone, B. Parekh, and P. Sanders. London: Routledge.

—2000. *Rethinking Multiculturalism.* London: Macmillan.

—2004. "Common Belonging." In *Cohesion Community and Citizenship: Proceedings of the Runnymede Conference.* Runnymede.

—2008. *A New Politics of Identity.* Basingstoke: Palgrave Macmillan.

Paul, K. 1997. *Whitewashing Britain: Race and Citizenship in the Postwar Era.* Ithaca, NY: Cornell University Press.

Phillips, T. 2005. "Sleepwalking to Segregation." Speech, Manchester Council for Community Relations, 22 September. At http://www.humanities.manchester.ac.uk/socialchange/research/social-change/summer-workshops/documents/sleepwalking.pdf

Powell, E. 1968. Speech to the Conservative Association Meeting, Birmingham, 20 April.

Rawls, J. 1993. *Political Liberalism.* New York: Columbia University Press.

Rose, E.J.B. and associates. 1969. *Colour and Citizenship.* London: Oxford University Press.

Saggar, S. 2003. *Race and British Electoral Politics.* London: Routledge

Scruton, R. 1988. "In Defence of the Nation." *Salisbury Review* (December).

Singh, D. 2006. Speech by Darra Singh at the Launch of the Commission on Integration and Community Cohesion. At http://www.communities.gov.uk/index.asp?id=1502287

Straw, J. 2000. Speech at the Launch of the Future of Multi-Ethnic Britain Report, *Runnymede Quarterly Bulletin* (December).

Swann, M. 1985. *Education for All: The Report of the Committee of Inquiry into the Education of Children from Ethnic Minority Groups*. Her Majesty's Stationery Office.

Uberoi, V. 2008. "Do Policies of Multiculturalism Undermine National Identities?" *Political Quarterly* 79:3.

—2011. "Does Cameron Have Multiculturalist Ambitions?" *The Independent*, 8 February 2011.

Uberoi, V. and T. Modood. 2010. "'Who Doesn't Feel British?' Divisions over Muslims." *Parliamentary Affairs* 63:2.

—Forthcoming. "Inclusive Britishness: A Multiculturalist Advance." *Political Studies*.

Uberoi, V. and S. Saggar. 2009. "Extremism and Diversity." In *Options for a New Britain*, ed. V. Uberoi et al. Basingstoke: Palgrave Macmillan.

Vasta, E. 2007. "Accomodating Diversity: Why Current Critiques of Multiculturalism Miss the Point." Compass Working Paper No. 53.

Vertovek, S. 2007. "Super Diversity and Its Implications." *Ethnic and Racial Studies* 30:6.

Walzer, M. 2001. "Nation States and Immigrant Societies." In *Can Liberal Pluralism Be Exported?*, ed. W. Kymlick and M. Opalski. London: Oxford University Press.

CHAPTER 4

CANADA – FOSTERING AN INTEGRATED SOCIETY?

JOHN BILES, ANNIE CARROLL, RADOSTINA PAVLOVA, AND MARGARET SOKOL*

Every national government is concerned with establishing the centripetal forces that hold a nation state together. Given Canadian diversity, with the multiplicity of First Nations even at the outset of nationhood, with two major colonizing empires and subsequent immigration from around the globe, the Government of Canada is more practised at this endeavour than most. There are those who trace Canada's activity in this area back into the distant past (Dreisziger 1988; Joshee 1995; Biles and Panousos 1999; Day 2000), but for our purposes a quick recap from the late 1960s onwards will suffice.

National identity, national unity, social cohesion, shared citizenship, social capital, social inclusion, and an integrated society have all been dominant thematic terms utilized by successive national governments. However, strong commonalities cut across this 50-year span of public policy discourse: foci on balancing rights and responsibilities of citizenship, on shared values, and on connecting across differences. The subtexts or the problems to be solved have been twofold: concern with attachment and belonging on the one hand and with inclusion and exclusion on the other.

In all cases a strong role for the federal government has been articulated, most commonly with Canadian Heritage and its predecessor departments in the lead and Citizenship and Immigration Canada (CIC) in a

---

*The opinions expressed in this chapter are those of the authors and do not necessarily reflect those of Citizenship and Immigration Canada or the Government of Canada.

International Perspectives: Integration and Inclusion, ed. J. Frideres and J. Biles. Montreal and Kingston: Queen's Policy Studies Series, McGill-Queen's University Press. © 2012 The School of Policy Studies, Queen's University at Kingston. All rights reserved.

supporting role.[1] However, the arrival of the Multiculturalism Program at CIC in the fall of 2008 means that it now has a policy mandate to examine both how newcomers are faring in comparison to the Canadian born, and whether or not CIC should be striving to shift the Canadian born along the continuum towards a more integrated society, thus increasing the challenge for newcomers and thereby impacting settlement programming. In short, CIC must now focus on answering both the questions "Are newcomers integrating?" and "Integrating into what?" This requires a shift in perspective, from simply a Canadian born versus foreign born comparative approach to assessing successful immigrant integration to a more global view of Canadian society as a composition of a myriad of ethnic, religious, linguistic and other groups, and considering its ability to integrate newcomers and function cohesively as a polity (see Table 1).

The history of immigration to Canada has been well rehearsed (Knowles 1997; Kelley and Trebilcock 1998); however, a brief summary is essential to setting the scene. As these authors have described, immigration levels in Canada have fluctuated, and four distinct periods can be observed (Beaujot and Matthews 2000). First, in the post-Confederation period (1896–1914), immigration was considered part of national development policies. From 1896–1905, industrialization, urbanization, and settlement of Western Canada resulted in a large inflow of manual labourers, farmers, agricultural workers, and domestic servants from abroad. Canada welcomed its largest number of immigrants between 1908 and 1913, with over 400,000 immigrants arriving in 1913 alone. To preserve the British heritage of the nation, immigrant groups were limited to white Anglo-Saxon Protestants (Roy 2003; Ward 1990; Ferguson 1975). Restrictive policies such as the head tax imposed on Chinese immigrants were common to limit the entry of non-traditional groups (Li 1998). However, despite the government's efforts to preserve this British character, high demand for labour brought on by rapid economic development exceeded the supply from preferred groups. In the latter part of this period, labour was recruited from non-traditional countries of South and East Europe and Asia.

The outbreak of the First World War ended this period of high immigration (University of Calgary 2001). Economic hardship and xenophobia brought about 20 years of restrictive policies resulting in record low numbers of immigrants to Canada during the war years and the Great Depression (1914–45).

Postwar economic prosperity and political freedom once again attracted many foreigners to Canada. Immigration levels to Canada increased with the arrival in the 1950s of immigrants from war-torn Great Britain and European countries such as Poland and Italy. The postwar period (1945–89) can be considered a second wave of high immigration to Canada during which significant changes were made to the country's immigration system. In 1962, restrictive and discriminatory policies based on race, religion and national origin were lifted, and in 1967, the point system was introduced. From here on, skilled workers and business immigrants

TABLE 1
Dominant Terminology for the Government of Canada's Interests in the Centripetal Forces That Hold Canadians Together

Period	Dominant Centripetal Label/Approach	Components of Approach	Summary Statement
1960s–70s	National identity and national unity	Connecting across differences Articulating Canadian values	Prime Minister Pierre Trudeau: "National unity if it is to mean anything in the deeply personal sense, must be founded on confidence in one's own individual identity; out of this can grow respect for that of others and a willingness to share ideas, attitudes and assumptions. A vigorous policy of multiculturalism will help create this initial confidence. It can form the base of a society which is based on fair play for all" (1971).
1980s–early 1990s	National unity	Loyalty and commitment to Canada Rights and obligations	Secretary of State David Crombie's "Citizenship 87: Proud to Be Canadian" discussion paper : "The federal government regards citizenship as a cornerstone of national unity and is resolved to buttress it with new legislation."
1993–2001	Social cohesion	Values Hope Trust Reciprocity	Definition of social cohesion used by Policy Research Initiative's work in this area: "Social cohesion is the ongoing process of developing a community of shared values, shared challenges and equal opportunity in Canada based on a sense of hope, trust and reciprocity among Canadians" (Social Cohesion Network 1998)
2001–03	Shared citizenship	Contact Culture Values	Prime Minister Jean Chrétien's speech at the Progressive Governance Summit in Berlin, 2000, "The Canadian Way in the Twenty-First Century": "Canada has become a post-national, multicultural society. It contains the globe within its borders, and Canadians have learned that their two international languages and their diversity are a comparative advantage and a source of continuing creativity and innovation."

... continued

TABLE 1
(Continued)

Period	Dominant Centripetal Label/Approach	Components of Approach	Summary Statement
2003–06	Social inclusion Social capital	Values Connections	Prime Minister Paul Martin Jr in response to Speech from the Throne in 2004: "And you see the importance of national will in protecting the values that define and inspire us. Let us understand that within our Charter of Rights are enshrined our basic freedoms – and we as a nation of minorities must never allow these fundamental rights to be compromised if we are to protect our national character and our individual freedom. And let us understand that the pride we take in our diversity, our linguistic duality and our rich multicultural society, the satisfaction with which we present ourselves to the world as a country of inclusion, will ultimately erode and be lost if we are not vigilant, if we do not vigorously combat racism and exclusion, if we do not together stare into the face of hate and declare: This is not our Canada."
2006–	Integrated society	Values Rights and responsibilities Active, connected, productive citizens	CIC Minister Jason Kenney to Economic Club of Canada: "I want to see an integrated society based on active and engaged citizens, not a series of separated ethnocultural silos. I want Canadians, whether they've been here for a few months or all of their lives, to embrace our shared values, our shared history and institutions. I want newcomers to integrate into our proud and democratic Canadian society and I want us all to work together to invest in and help strengthen the prosperity of a country that continues to attract newcomers."

Source: Authors' compilation.

would be allocated points and admitted to Canada based on their skills, education, and training rather than ethnic or religious background. Not only did this policy eliminate the discriminatory nature of the previous selection system but it also met the demands of a growing postindustrial and service sector economy. Until the end of this period, economic immigration levels would be determined according to the state of the labour market. A "tap on–tap off policy" was in place: depending on high or low unemployment, immigration levels increased or decreased (Green and Green 1999; Triadafilopoulos 2012).

During the postwar period, the composition of Canada's immigrant population changed dramatically: Whereas in the nineteenth and early twentieth centuries the large majority of the immigrant population in Canada consisted of white Europeans and Americans, an increasing number of immigrants in the late twentieth century hailed from Asia, the Caribbean, Latin America, and Africa. The large number of immigrants from these regions can also be explained by Canada's increasing international humanitarian commitments. The resettlement of, for example, a large number of Hungarians (1956–57), Czechoslovakians (1968–69), Ugandan Asians (1972), Chileans (1973), Indochinese (1975–80), and Kosovars (1999) is illustrative (CIC 2009). In addition to its commitment to refugee resettlement, the humanitarian aspect of Canada's immigration policy is characterized by the liberalization of family reunification. This period saw an increase in the number of skilled immigrants sponsoring relatives.

Importantly, the Mulroney government also decoupled immigration levels from the business cycle. This change launched the contemporary period (mid-1980s–present), marked by sustained levels of relatively high immigration in the range of 200,000–250,000 newcomers a year over the last twenty years (ibid.). The objective of today's immigration program is to welcome permanent and temporary migrants who will contribute to Canada's economic, social, and cultural development, all while protecting the health, safety, and security of Canadians. In addition to this group, Canada is welcoming a growing number of temporary workers. For instance, in 2009, Canada welcomed over 900,000 foreign workers, foreign students, asylum seekers, and other visitors (ibid.). These sustained levels of high immigration, in combination with temporary workers, make for a heterogeneous Canadian immigrant population.

CONTEMPORARY PROFILE OF TODAY'S NEWCOMERS

The 2006 Census revealed that there were then over six million immigrants in Canada, representing one in five Canadians – the highest proportion in 75 years. Over time, the ethnic profile of Canada's newcomer population has changed from predominantly European to non-European ancestries. Today over 200 ethnic origins are represented within Canada's diverse mosaic. The majority (75 percent) of newcomers belong to a visible minority group[2] and report a mother tongue other than French or English, such as Chinese languages (18.6 percent), Italian (6.6 percent), Punjabi (5.9 percent), Spanish (5.8 percent), German (5.4 percent), Tagalog (4.8 percent), and Arabic (4.7 percent) (Statistics Canada 2009a). The top source countries of permanent residents include the People's Republic of China, India, Philippines, United States, and United Kingdom (CIC 2009) (see Figure 1).

FIGURE 1
Permanent Residents in Canada by Top Ten Source Countries, 2007–09

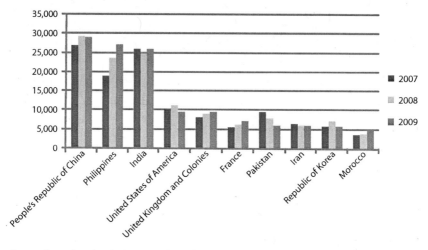

Source: Reproduced with the permission of the Minister of Public Works and Government Services Canada, 2012. CIC (2009).

The majority (86.8 percent) of newcomers settle in three Canadian provinces: Ontario, Quebec, and British Columbia. In fact, these provinces' large metropolitan centres of Toronto, Montreal, and Vancouver attract seven out of ten newcomers (Statistics Canada 2009a). While more recent trends indicate that newcomers are increasingly choosing other destinations – for example, the number of newcomers settling in Edmonton increased by 70.8 percent between 2006 and 2010, and by nearly 60 percent in Winnipeg for the same period, while it remained stable or slightly decreased in Canada's three largest cities (CIC 2009) – these are still the areas with highest concentrations of newcomers.

Many of Canada's newcomers are young. Nearly 60 percent are in the prime working age group of 25 to 54, compared to 42.3 percent of Canadian born. Moreover, many newcomers are highly educated (Statistics Canada 2009a). Among recent immigrants, 51 percent are university graduates, compared to 28 percent among previous cohorts and 20 percent of the Canadian population (Statistics Canada 2009b).

DEMOGRAPHIC PROJECTIONS

Like many other Western countries, Canada has an aging population. According to Statistics Canada, in 2051, seniors (65 years and older) will outnumber children (aged 0 to 14) by 1.85. Immigration is often thought of as a means to respond to the challenges of an aging population, and if the current immigration levels are sustained or are increased to address this problem, as some policy-makers have suggested, the composition and makeup of the Canadian population will shift[3] (Statistics Canada 2011).

Already, recent immigrants, those who landed between 2001 and 2006, represent 17.9 percent of the total foreign born population and 3.6 percent of the total Canadian population. In this five-year period, the foreign born population grew by 13.6 percent, four times higher than the growth of the Canadian born population, and growth of this kind is predicted to be maintained. Statistics Canada projects that by 2031 the foreign born population could represent 25-28 percent of the Canadian population, surpassing the high of 22 percent seen in the early twentieth century. In 2006, 39 percent of Canadians were either foreign born or had a foreign born parent, and experts project that by 2031, this figure could increase to 46 percent. Metropolitan areas would continue to be home to the majority of newcomers. The foreign born population would increase in Toronto (from 46 to 50 percent), Vancouver (40 to 44 percent) and Montreal (21 to 30 percent). The foreign born population in second-tier cities of immigration such as Calgary (30 percent), Ottawa (29 percent) and Kitchener (28 percent) is also projected to increase (Statistics Canada 2010c).

The increase in immigration will result in a large growth of Canada's visible minority population. By 2031, nearly three out of ten Canadians (between 29 and 32 percent) could belong to a visible minority group, almost doubling the proportion seen in 2006. South Asians and Chinese will remain the largest group, while the Arab and West Asian group are projected to grow fastest (see Figure 2).

Moreover, fewer than two out of three Canadians are likely to report affiliation with a Christian denomination. According to projections, the non-Christian population could more than double by from 2006 to 2031, rising from 8 percent in 2006 to 14 percent in 2031. The greatest increase would be seen among the Muslim population, which, due to the makeup of immigration source countries and higher fertility, could triple during this period and reach a 7.3 percent share of the total Canadian population by 2031 (ibid.).

In addition, between 29 and 32 percent of Canadians, compared to less than 10 percent in 1981, would have a mother tongue other than French or English (ibid.). In sum, with sustained levels of immigration, the ethno-cultural and religious diversity of the Canadian population will increase, resulting in myriad opportunities and as well as challenges for policy-makers on the road to fostering social integration.

Naturally these demographics have evolved in conjunction with legislative/constitutional and program changes that we feel are important to describe briefly here, as they define a unique Canadian approach to settlement, integration, and diversity in a multicultural society.

FIGURE 2
Canada's Population by Visible Minority Group, 2006 and 2031 Projection Scenarios

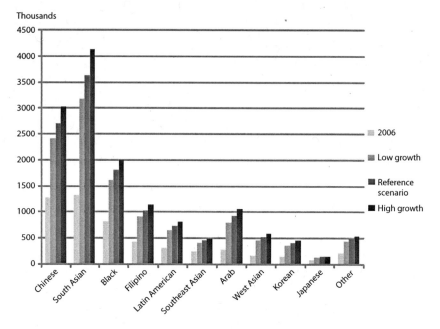

Note: Projection scenarios are based on low and high fertility, life expectancy, immigration, and internal migration. The reference scenario represents the scenario if the 2006 situation and trends were to continue.

Source: Adapted from Statistics Canada (2010c, Table 4, p. 23). Referenced April 2011.

Legislative / Constitutional Frame

Through the *Canadian Multiculturalism Act,* the *Immigration and Refugee Protection Act,* and the *Citizenship Act,* as well as a broader constitutional and legislative suite that includes the Charter of Rights and Freedoms, the *Human Rights Act,* the *Official Languages Act,* and the *Employment Equity Act* amongst others, the Government of Canada has committed itself to facilitating the full participation of all Canadians in the social, cultural, economic, and civic spheres of Canadian society. Accordingly, the focus of CIC programming is on operationalizing the "two-way street" approach reflected in this suite of legislation through assisting individuals to become active, connected, and productive citizens and through working with communities and Canadian institutions to aid individuals in accomplishing this objective. Working with a wide range of societal actors including other orders of government, voluntary sector and community partners, employers, school boards, and other stakeholders, CIC seeks to minimize income disparities and strengthen social integration by assisting in the removal of barriers and enabling individuals to participate in the labour market, encouraging social and cultural connections amongst people of different backgrounds and identities, encouraging inter-cultural and inter-faith understanding and civic knowledge and participation, and inculcating a sense of the rights and responsibilities of Canadian citizenship and the value of diversity. Importantly, the Canadian approach to multicultural-ism, as opposed to most European variants, has always focused upon the reciprocal obligations of newcomers and the larger Canadian community to adapt to one another to foster an integrated society – the "two-way street" of integration (Biles and Winnemore 2006).

Settlement Programs

In comparison to the evolution of the legislative and constitutional framework for settlement, integration, and inclusion as well as immigra-tion policy (Triadafilopoulos 2012; Beach, Green, and Reitz 2003; Kelley and Trebilcock 1998; Knowles 1997; Hawkins 1991) or refugee policy changes (Dirks 1977), the evolution of settlement, integration, and inclu-sion programs has been far less explored (Vineberg 2010; Lanphier and Lukomskyj 1994).

Canada's approach to settlement has evolved considerably with the introduction of the so-called "modernized approach to settlement" introduced in 2008. In essence, this approach combines all of the former settlement streams into one macro settlement program (Smith 2010). The former approach, which included Language Instruction for Newcomers to Canada (LINC), the Immigrant Settlement Adaptation Program (ISAP), and the HOST program, are well covered elsewhere, so we will not de-scribe them here (Biles and Winnemore 2006).[4] In addition, the last decade has seen a significant increase in actors investing resources in facilitating the settlement and integration of newcomers, with provincial and muni-cipal governments in particular expressing greater interest in becoming involved (Andrew et al. 2011, Biles et al. 2011, Biles 2008, Mulholland and Biles 2004).[5]

For all this activity, the bulk of expenditures are geared towards meeting newcomers' more immediate settlement needs and are provided by CIC's settlement program. In the 2010–11 fiscal year this was expected to include expenditures of nearly $960 million. These were complemented by mod-est multiculturalism expenditures of $11 million in 2010–11 (CIC 2010c) used to address broader and longer-term integration needs. Inter-Action, the multiculturalism grants and contributions program, underwent re-structuring and renewal in 2010 and consists of two streams: Projects and Events, both in support of the goal of building an integrated and socially cohesive society. The Projects stream provides contributions for multi-year projects, usually selected through a call-for-proposals process, and Events provides grants to one-time community-based events.

Other recent activities of the Multiculturalism Program can be found in the annual report tabled in Parliament (CIC 2011). Analysis of the evolution of projects funded by the program over the last 30 years indicates a marked shift from cultural retention in the 1980s, to race relations in the late 1980s and early 1990s, and since the mid-1990s, towards inclusion and integration of minorities within "mainstream" society and institutions (McAndrew et al. 2008).The most recent iterations of the objectives of the program, updated in 2009, emphasize building an integrated society through, for example, ensuring equality of opportunity for individuals of all origins, promoting shared democratic values and civic knowledge, and providing opportunities for positive interaction among members of diverse communities to encourage inter-cultural and inter-faith dialogue.[6]

The settlement program is delivered directly by CIC in all provinces except British Columbia, Manitoba, and Quebec where various agreements have transferred responsibility for delivery of the settlement program to the provincial government. Nevertheless settlement in these jurisdictions largely mirrors that in the rest of the country, albeit with different governance and delivery arrangements. The post-2008 "modernized" settlement program focuses on four major outcomes: information and orientation, language training and skills development, labour market access, and welcoming communities. According to the Immigration-Contribution Accountability Measurement System (iCAMS), 171,291 individual clients (outside of Quebec, Manitoba, and British Columbia) were served in 2010.[7]

Information and orientation approaches encompass hard-copy publications, in-person orientation sessions, and web-based information products. On average, CIC's Going to Canada Immigration Portal receives 960,000 visits per year. In 2009, 150,000 copies of "Welcome to Canada" in English and 50,000 in French, along with 150,000 copies of the bilingual booklet "Key Information Sources," were printed and distributed.

In 2009–10, more than 18,000 immigrants received in-person orientation sessions prior to their departure for Canada. These include group orientation sessions, individual counselling, needs assessment, path finding, and referrals.

In Canada, through the network of service provider organizations funded by CIC, 68 percent of clients received a needs assessment, and 59 percent of those accessing settlement services received para-counselling and problem-solving and referral services.

Language training and skills development programming enhance the ability of clients to communicate in an official language and develop the skills required to succeed in Canadian society and workplaces. In 2008–09, 43,896 newcomers' language skills were assessed for placement in language training programs, and 55,031 clients received language training.

Regarding labour market access, 29,279 clients received employment-related services in 2008–09. Close to half of the participants in the Enhanced Language Training programs found employment. Employers and business councils have been key partners in 28 of the 34 Local Immigration Partnerships in Ontario. In addition, five regional newcomer employment networks have been established in Ontario.

Finally, welcoming communities, which include activities such as Settlement Workers in Schools (SWIS), Library Settlement Partnerships (LSP), Local Immigration Partnerships (LIPs), and the Small Centres Toolbox, have been a growing area of focus. In 2009–10, 1,310 schools and 56 libraries were served by SWIS and LSP. Also worth mentioning are the 14,822 volunteers who supported the delivery and administration of the full range of settlement programs.

Similarly important is the support for official language minority communities to attract and retain francophone newcomers. In 2009, among other activities, 9,918 francophone permanent residents not destined for Quebec were landed, four research projects were undertaken, and 51 information sessions were held. Over the course of 2009–10, CIC collaborated to create and strengthen 12 francophone immigration networks from coast to coast (CIC 2010d).

FORMAL AND SUBSTANTIVE EQUALITY: HOW ARE WE DOING?

Formal Equality

It has become commonplace in Canada to distinguish between formal and substantive equality. The former requires that a law apply equally to all the people to whom it was designed to apply, while the latter is more concerned with outcomes and accepts that there are circumstances where treating everyone the same does not result in treating everyone equally (OWJN 2008). Traditionally, international comparisons tend to focus on formal equality because it is far simpler to ascertain what legal frameworks are in place. For example, according to the Migrant Integration Policy Index (MIPEX), Canada has one of the strongest legal frameworks to promote the social integration of immigrants. MIPEX assesses the integration policies and legal frameworks of 31 immigrant-receiving countries across North America and Europe and has found Canada to have, behind Sweden and Portugal, the overall third-best integration policies.

Even though Canada's MIPEX score in a number of areas demonstrates that it has established strong policies and legal frameworks to support the formal equality of immigrants, Canada does not fare as well in other areas of social integration. For example, Canada's efforts at facilitating the political participation of newcomers rank eighteenth. According to MIPEX, immigrant consultative bodies are not involved in the development of

FIGURE 3
MIPEX 2011 Score Overview

Source: Huddleston et al. (2011). Reproduced with permission.

integration policy and, although permanent residents have political liberties in Canada, they have no electoral rights.

Canada's low score on political rights reflects an oft-cited criticism of MIPEX that it considers the factors in isolation and ignores the effect of their interplay. Canada's inclusive approach to citizenship, where naturalization is encouraged and the required residency period to become a citizen, three years, is the shortest among all of the evaluated countries (processing times can be around two years, so the majority of those eligible naturalize within five years). The relatively few permanent residents who do not opt to naturalize face minimal obstacles: they are prevented from voting and running for public office, and they receive less preferential treatment for federal government jobs. That said, as Siemiatycki (2007, 2006) argues, given the large-scale migration to Canada, substantial numbers of newcomers in some cities, particularly Toronto, Vancouver, and Montreal, are effectively "disenfranchised" for a period.

Canadians researchers and policy-makers are sceptical of the formal consultative measure as it seems to privilege a European hierarchical model of consultation. There are regular consultations with various actors including a deputy minister advisory committee and provincial/regional umbrella organizations of settlement service provider organizations that are regularly attended by a wide range of actors. There is significantly less quibbling by Canadian researchers with the formal electoral measures and the score meted out to Canada in this regard.

Substantial Equality

Except for the limited opportunities for permanent residents to participate in the formal electoral processes in their first few years in Canada, there is little question that, overall, Canada has a fairly comprehensive approach to formal equality. However, the proof is in the pudding. It is necessary to look beyond the policies and legislation in place, which is another limitation of MIPEX, and examine outcomes more closely. Given the consistency with which many of the same aspects are deployed in policy debates and public discourse, it seemed reasonable to us to assess how we are faring, after 40 years of multiculturalism and government involvement in the integration of newcomers, in striving towards creating an integrated society, all the while acknowledging that an integrated society is an aspiration, not an attainable end state.

No indicators project is ever comprehensive or agreed upon unanimously. However, we have selected a set of indicators that emerged out of more than a decade of work by Metropolis with the widest possible array of stakeholders drawn from all facets of society. The indicators have been workshopped at interdepartmental committee meetings within the federal government, and at academic conferences. Each set of indicators (social, cultural, civic, and economic) was developed and drafted by top scholars in their field and focuses on both sides of the two-way street of integration. Using these, we are able to gather a snapshot of how near, or far, we are from being an integrated society (Biles, Burstein, and Frideres 2008). Obviously these four domains are not mutually exclusive; the components cut across domains and interact. Nevertheless, we have sought to analyze them with the available evidence base to identify where policy and program attention needs to be focused (see Table 2).

Of interest is both how close the host society is to being an integrated society and how newcomers are faring in terms of integrating into this pre-existing society.

Civic/Political

There is little evidence that newcomers in the aggregate are any less likely to try to participate in the civic/political life of Canada than the Canadian born (although there is evidence that some minority communities like

TABLE 2
Indicators of Integration

Economic	Social	Cultural	Civic/Political
Annual income	Associational involvement	Intercultural competency	Citizenship
Occupation	Feeling of security and belonging	Cultural participation	Voting
Labour force participation	Intermarriage rate	Intercultural dialogue	Political engagement
Unemployment	Immigrant/host contacts	Language proficiency	Political representation
Educational achievement	Perceived discrimination	Immigrant content in mainstream media	Knowledge of rights and responsibilities
Expertise/job match	Residential concentration	Cultural labour force participation	Knowledge of Canadian politics
Use of social services	Resistance to integration	Level of volunteerism	
Poverty rates	Understanding of Canadian institutions	Literacy rate	
Duration of job	Outreach services to newcomers	Intercultural events	

Source: Biles, Burstein, and Frideres (2008).

Chinese[8] and Korean-origin Canadians are less likely to participate regardless of place of birth) (Derouin 2004; Tossutti 2005). Indeed, an extremely high level of naturalization denotes a conscious effort on the part of most newcomers to join the Canadian polity (Tran, Kustec, and Chui 2005). Findings suggest that, potentially related to the actual naturalization process itself, newcomers are more likely to demonstrate knowledge of Canadian politics and rights and responsibilities than the Canadian born (Henderson 2005). On other measures like voting and civic and political engagement, newcomers converge towards the Canadian norm over 15 to 20 years (Tossutti 2005). The most significant measure where there is a serious disparity is the representation of newcomers and minorities in elected and appointed political bodies. Research suggests that the gap is more structural than individual – in other words, newcomers and minorities seek to become involved but encounter obstacles (Andrew et al. 2008). As the MIPEX project suggests, one of these obstacles is the extension of the franchise at the municipal level prior to naturalization (Siemiatycki 2006). However, in terms of representation, Canada fares well in comparison to many other countries. Canada's elected bodies are not fully representative of immigrant population but are more so than other countries at least at the national level: 13 percent foreign born Canadian members of the federal Parliament versus 19.3 percent of population (2001 census); in the UK, 4.5 percent vs. 7.5 percent; France, 6.2 percent vs. 10.6 percent; US, 2 percent versus 14.7 percent, and Australia: 11 percent versus 23 percent (Adams 2007).

Social and Cultural

Overall, despite public discourse to the contrary, the evidence gathered so far suggests that in most social and cultural areas, Canada is not facing serious obstacles to fostering an integrated society. Canadians regardless of background or place of birth are generally likely to volunteer and be involved in associations and donate to charity. Initially there is a 9 percent gap between the Canadian and foreign born who volunteer, but this converges over time (Vallée and Caputo 2010). First, second, and further generations of Canadians feel attached to Canada and are proud to be Canadian. Indeed, the foreign born report higher levels of attachment than the Canadian born (Jedwab 2007). Connections among Canadians of diverse backgrounds is on the increase, even among newcomers (with length of time spent in Canada). Measures of bridging social capital suggest that the negative impact of ethnic and cultural diversity on social capital found in other countries is not the case in Canada; indeed, trust measures are positively correlated with diversity in Canada (Kazemipur 2009). Inter-marriage rates (the most extraordinary measure of minimized social distance) indicate that many Canadians form unions with partners of different language, faith, or racial background, and the number of these unions continues to climb (Statistics Canada 2010a). Finally, Canadians and newcomers are generally interested in, and participate in, cultural activities of both the "mainstream" and ethnic cultures. Some groups, like Italian-Canadians, however, are more likely to donate to only those cultural organizations that are focused on their own culture (Solutions Research Group 2006). And while newcomers are represented within Canada's arts labour force in rough proportion to their numbers in the labour force in general, visible minorities are 50 percent underrepresented (Hill Strategies 2005).

In spite of the generally positive outlook, concerns remain around both attachment/belonging and inclusion/exclusion that are central to fostering an integrated society. Looking first at attachment and belonging, high-profile media cases and hot issues that have provoked public debates indicate that the theme of interfaith and intercultural understanding deserves further attention, including representation in the media (Belkhodja 2008; Mahtani 2008; Potvin 2008). Such cases have included the controversy around wearing the niqab in Quebec and the related bill introduced by the provincial government; the banning of the wearing of kirpans in the Quebec National Assembly in spite of the Supreme Court's 2006 ruling that Sikhs have a constitutional right to carry kirpans in public contexts; earlier debates on introducing Sharia law in the legal system of Ontario; and recurrent instances of anti-Semitism and negative representations of Islam in public and media discourses. Relatedly, Canada has experienced instances of "imported conflicts" or interest in "homeland politics" like the Tamil Canadian protests in the spring of 2009; recently, discussions were rekindled around the involvement of Sikh Canadians in historic homeland tensions, and the suspicions of "citizenship of convenience" that arose at the time of the 2006 Lebanon war still resurface, usually in synch with international crises. These examples suggest the importance of the provisionally termed indicator "resistance to integration" (to denote purposeful non-participation in Canadian society and culture[9] and, instead, maintaining strong transnational ties and adherence to "home" culture, language and ethnic group). We need to better understand to what extent this indicator poses a challenge to an integrated society, in at least influencing perceptions, if not also in substance.

Secondly, on the inclusion and exclusion front, there is solid evidence to suggest that racism and discrimination affect Canadians in multiple facets of their lives. To mention just a few examples, incomes and employment rates of visible minority Canadians are consistently lower (independent of their other characteristics) (Hou and Coulombe 2010); perceptions or racism and discrimination emerge in multiple public opinion and statistical surveys (Leger Marketing 2007, Statistics Canada 2003); discrimination in employment occurs in many ways including discrimination triggered by different accents and foreign-sounding names; and race and ethnicity account for a large part of reported hate crimes (Statistics Canada 2010b; MacDougall 2009; Oreopoulos 2009). While we have enough evidence to determine that action is needed to address racism and discrimination, there is a pressing need for quantitative data on how it affects different groups, as well as need for evidence on the effectiveness of various anti-racism and discrimination approaches.

In a similar vein, while the Government of Canada spends nearly $1 billion annually on settlement services, most of these resources are focused on delivering services to newcomers, and little is devoted to facilitating the development of welcoming communities and the long-term integration of both immigrant and Canadian born members of ethno-cultural, visible minority, and religious groups. This imbalance is increasingly problematic as newcomers begin to settle outside the large metropolitan areas. Rural areas as well as small towns are experiencing difficulties attracting and retaining much-needed immigration, for reasons of lack of information, inadequate settlement services and infrastructure; racism and discrimination resulting from local communities being unaccustomed to ethnic, racial, and religious diversity; and social and cultural isolation (Burstein 2007). Francophone minority communities as well as communities with significant Aboriginal populations are experiencing unique issues in relation to welcoming diversity (Belkhodja 2008). In Western Canadian cities like Edmonton, Calgary, and Winnipeg, but also to some extent in Toronto and Ottawa, very rapidly growing urban Aboriginal and recent newcomer populations increasingly share physical, social, and economic ground, which poses new challenges and calls for developing more focused approaches to fostering an integrated society. Large metropolitan areas, where the majority of immigrants settle, are generally struggling: for example, the high volume of incoming immigrants presents a challenge to providing adequate services, housing, and transportation, especially considering the increasing suburbanization of immigrant settlement (Preston et al. 2009; Heisz and Schellenberg 2004). Most importantly, economic considerations and persistent urban poverty may hinder social integration (Kazemipur and Halli 2000; Galabuzzi 2006), and declining health outcomes are cause for concern (Gushulak 2007).

Finally, language and literacy remain key challenges for participation in all facets of Canadian society. Immigrants with low levels of official language proficiency have lower rates of voluntarism, participation in associations, and voting (Boyd 2009). Language proficiency is deemed essential in expanding social networks (Kazemipur 2009) and, of course, it is vital to participatation in the labour market (McDonald et al. 2010). The 2005 Longitudinal Survey of Immigrants to Canada (LSIC) found the two most-cited difficulties for newcomers to be finding an adequate job (46 percent) and learning an official language (26 percent). A study of newcomer labour market integration found that 66 percent of employers cited a lack of occupation-specific language proficiency as an obstacle to hiring immigrants (Lochhead and Mackenzie 2005). Further, three different analyses of census data conducted between 1992 and 2003 revealed that the average earnings of immigrant workers in Canada who were fluent in an official language were between 11 percent and 49 percent higher than those of immigrant workers who lacked this skill (Chiswick and Miller 1992, 1995, 2003). Aydemir and Skuterud estimated that roughly one-third of the deterioration in entry earnings of immigrants could be explained by a shift in source countries resulting in weakening English and French language abilities of new immigrants (2004).

The International Adult Literacy Skills Survey (IALSS), while ambiguous[10] as to the literacy skills of newcomers, indicates that immigrants (regardless of their length of stay in Canada) make use of written forms of English and French at levels below what is deemed essential for success in Canada's knowledge economy. Overall, about 60 percent of immigrants were below Level 3 in prose literacy compared to 37 percent of the Canadian born population. About 2 percent of university-educated Canadian born scored at the lowest level (Level 1) of prose literacy proficiency. In comparison, 14 percent of university-educated established immigrants and 18 percent of recent immigrants scored at this level, with a total of 47 percent of recent immigrants scoring below level 3 (Statistics Canada 2005b). There is a sense that literacy needs are poorly understood by newcomers and that employers should be playing a greater role. Teasing out the differences between language learning needs and literacy is vital to appropriately fashioning policy and program responses. Finally, there is a definite need for better evaluation of language and literacy programs to ascertain what works most effectively (Toronto Dominion 2009).

Economic

By international comparisons, Canada is at the top of OECD's lists of countries when considering immigrants' outcomes. As the minister of Citizenship and Immigration Canada recently noted, "When compared to immigrants in other OECD countries, immigrants in Canada continue to have the greatest equality in the labour market . . . the job quality of those who live here for more than a decade matches or exceeds that of workers born in Canada . . . With few exceptions, immigrant labour market outcomes improve with time spent in Canada" (Media Q 2010).

The economic outcomes of newcomers to this country have received a great deal more attention than the social, cultural, and civic outcomes already discussed, so we have the opposite problem of too much data, although there is more of a data gap related to the examination of outcomes for minorities.[11] Perhaps as a result of the extensive data on economic outcomes for newcomers, considerable policy activity has been undertaken in this sphere on the most commonly cited barriers – language, experience, and foreign credentials. We will reiterate here the need for policy work in this area, but take it as a given that this work is underway and while important, does not constitute the full range of economic challenges faced by newcomers and minorities in Canada.[12]

Turning first to the indicators of inclusion upon which Canada is already faring well, it is apparent that, in the aggregate, immigrants are eager to contribute to and become part of Canada's labour market, as demonstrated by their high (and increasing) level of participation.[13] Though below the rate of the Canadian born, the employment rates for all immigrants increased between 2001 and 2006. In fact, data from the Longitudinal Survey of Immigrants to Canada suggest that within four years the employment to population ratio among the foreign born surpassed that of the Canadian born (Xue 2010).

Immigrants are also highly educated. Of recent immigrants (those who immigrated between 2001 and 2006), 51 percent had a university degree – more than twice the proportion of degree holders among the Canadian born population (20 percent) and much higher than the proportion of 28 percent among immigrants who arrived in Canada before 2001. Interestingly, immigrants also account for a large proportion of doctorate (49 percent) and master's degree (40 percent) holders in Canada – populations often associated with innovation (Statistics Canada 2008a).

Another clear indicator of whether Canadian society is inclusive of immigrants is the extent to which Canadian born children of immigrants grow up to be fully engaged and self-reliant adults. The educational and economic outcomes of second generation Canadians (those who have at least one parent born in another country) are, on average, equal or better than those of their Canadian born counterparts (Statistics Canada 2007a). However, the economic outcomes of second generation visible minority men are worrying. By virtue of being born and educated in Canada, these children of immigrants do not face the same barriers to labour market integration as their parents, yet research indicates that barriers continue to exist. Studies show that second generation men whose parents come from West Africa, the Caribbean, and some Latin American countries have equal or greater levels of education but lower earnings than those with parents from traditional source countries (North America, Northern and Western Europe) (Corak 2008).

This concern dovetails with worrying signs that the latest cohorts of immigrants have experienced stagnating economic outcomes, and associated poverty and inequality indicators are increasing. In 2006, the unemployment rate for recent immigrants was 11.5 percent, more than double the rate of 4.9 percent for the Canadian born population (Statistics Canada 2007b). They also often find themselves in low-income, low-skilled jobs despite high levels of qualifications (Reitz 2007). This is particularly true for immigrant women. They have comparatively high levels of education, with 18 percent of immigrant women having university education, compared to 14 percent of Canadian born women, but are still more likely to be underemployed or unemployed or represented heavily in manufacturing rather than professional occupations such as education, social services, government, religion, recreation, and culture (Statistics Canada 2005a).

In spite of the increasing economic focus of immigrant selection during the 1990s, in 2005, according to the 2006 Census, immigrant men earned 63 cents for every dollar earned by a Canadian born male worker. Twenty-five years ago the ratio was 85 cents to a dollar. There was a more dramatic drop for immigrant women – from 85 cents to 56 cents (Picot and Sweetman 2005). Other research suggests that this pattern is also highly concentrated among black or Latin American origin men (Hum 2006).

These outcomes are not unresolvable. When immigrant outcomes are disaggregated based on the immigration category under which an immigrant was selected to come to Canada on a permanent basis, solid earning and employment results are seen for those newcomers selected under the Federal Skilled Worker Program (FSWP) (CIC 2010e). Clearly the new emphasis on human capital attributes under the Immigration and Refugee Protection Act (2002) appears to be leading to better outcomes.[14] Ongoing evaluations will show whether outcomes for newcomers arriving through other streams including the provincial nominee programs will prove equally positive.

Despite the glimmers of hope for future economic outcomes, it is clear that many visible minorities experience economic disadvantage. This is seen when looking at the low-income cut-off (LICO) rates of Toronto area residents. The overall LICO rate for Toronto in 2001 was 14 percent. Yet among the visible minority population, 32 percent of Toronto area Aboriginal persons lived below LICO and 45 percent of Arab and West Asian and Black individuals lived below the cut-off.

Economic disadvantage also disproportionately affects those individuals of minority religious status, with Muslim families being most acutely affected. Studies show that almost a fourth of all Muslim families earned less than $30,000 per year, compared to 15 percent of Protestant families (Ornstein 2008, cited in CIC 2010b). Less than half of Muslim women participated in the labour market in 2001; their unemployment was double the national rate for women in general. Muslim women earned 10 percent less than women in general, and were underrepresented in skilled professions (Hamdani 2004). Muslims also face discriminatory barriers. For example, in the manufacturing, sales, and service sector, 41 percent of those who wore the hijab were informed that they would need to remove it to be employed (Persad and Lukas 2002).

The lower initial earning upon arrival to Canada has contributed to an increase in poverty rates among new immigrant families (Picot and Sweetman 2005). According to HRSDC's Market Basket Measure (MBM), the incidence of low income for all working-age economic families was 9.0 percent, but for recent immigrant families it was 22.3 percent, which was marginally higher than for off-reserve Aboriginal families (22.1 percent) but significantly better than that for unattached 45–64 year olds (32.8 percent) (HRSDC 2009). Interestingly, while newcomers are more vulnerable to falling into poverty, and that enhanced vulnerability remains true for several years after arrival, newcomers are marginally more likely to exit poverty the following year than are their Canadian born counterparts (Fleury 2007).

Recent immigrants are also generally employed full-time, full-year, in smaller proportions than Canadian born workers. In fact, the gap between recent immigrants and the Canadian born in the proportion of workers employed full-year, mostly full-time, increased between 2000 and 2005 and might have contributed to the growing earnings disparities between recent immigrants and Canadian born workers (Statistics Canada 2008b).

Understandably, with long-term declines in their income, recent immigrants are receiving a larger proportion of their income from government transfers than in the past. However, per capita transfers are similar to or lower than those for comparable Canadian born individuals and families; indeed, a higher percentage of newcomer individual and family income is derived from employment than for the Canadian born (Statistics Canada 2008b).

The declining economic indicators are clearly cause for concern, and further analytic work needs to be undertaken to ascertain which sub-populations are at greatest risk and what solutions might most effectively mitigate this risk.

Finally, just as visible minority representation in decision-making bodies remains problematic, the federal public sector, in contrast to the federally regulated private sector, shows a significant lack of representation of visible minorities in comparison to labour force availability – much of this coming within the Canadian Forces and to a lesser extent the Royal Canadian Mounted Police but also true of the core public service (Labour Program 2009). Older research also suggested significantly lower odds of promotion within the public service for visible minorities (Pendakur et al. 2000). Interestingly, these data are omitted for the public service in the latest Employment Equity report, but included for federally regulated industries; an update would allow us to ascertain whether this problem persists. Beyond just the public service, discrimination in the workplace in general was often cited by respondents to the Ethnic Diversity Survey, with 35 percent of visible minorities reporting that they had experienced discrimination in general, and of those incidents, 56 percent took place in the workplace (Statistics Canada 2003). In summary, while we appear to have a handle on both the most operative challenges to economic integration for newcomers and those areas where policy levers can most directly impact upon them (language, credential recognition, and experience), many studies have documented various economic inequalities experienced by minorities (both newcomer and Canadian born), which, if they persist over time, raise concerns for social cohesion and will impair the fostering of an integrated society.

Conclusions and Looking to the Future

In general terms, Canada is doing reasonably well in developing an integrated society. In some areas like language, foreign credential recognition, and the need for Canadian experience, CIC already has significant policy work underway, and we need to remain vigilant and committed to tackling these stubborn issues. However, there appear to be an additional six areas needing to be further explored.

First, there is the fundamental question of whether or not the "mainstream" Canadian situation is compatible with an integrated society. Examining whether the Canadian born exhibit the characteristics of "integrated" citizens rather than just focusing on newcomers' outcomes challenges some assumptions. For example, when considering residential concentration, overall low rates of civic literacy and participation, and increasing economic inequality in Canada between the affluent and impoverished, it becomes apparent that the variances are not necessarily uniquely between the Canadian born and foreign born but there are significant variances in outcomes among the Canadian born. In short, we find that newcomers are not being asked to integrate into an already integrated society but into a work in progress. This suggests that we need to work on moving the Canadian yardsticks on these measures of integration (which will of necessity involve partnerships with those organizations that control the necessary levers) as well as facilitating newcomer integration into Canadian society and ensuring that Canadians of all backgrounds are participating fully and equitably in all aspects of Canadian life.

Second, there is ample evidence that insufficient attention has been paid to the reception side of the two-way street of the immigrant integration process. Representation on elected and appointed decision-making bodies (as well as within the public service) remains significantly below levels reflecting Canadian diversity. In addition, as newcomers settle in a wider range of Canadian communities, there is mounting evidence that these communities do not have all of the tools they need to be welcoming and to enhance the probability that these desperately needed residents will remain to contribute to these communities. Relatedly, more attention on intercultural and interfaith connections is required to ensure that Canadians of all backgrounds have opportunities for positive interaction, which should lead to strengthened shared democratic values and sense of Canadian citizenship

Third, we need to better understand the contours of the challenges we face, particularly in terms of racism and discrimination and "resistance to integration." We need up-to-date data to allow us to effectively target the specific manifestations of racism and discrimination as well as the particular challenges that different communities face, and we need to effectively evaluate what programming actually has an impact. In the case of "resistance to integration" on the part of immigrants, this inchoate fear has resulted in an eclectic list of potential indicators of problems, few of them backed by research evidence. Without being able to define the contours of these challenges, it is very difficult to construct effective policy responses. This area may well be the one that most requires intensive focus.

Overall we find the evidence base to guide effective policy development on integration and inclusion to be thin. Despite the very productive Metropolis network, there remains insufficient evidence across the gamut covered by the work on an "integrated society." The large-scale data sets we do have are now almost a decade old, and there is a need to refresh it to guide ongoing policy development. Consequently, we can establish general trends in most cases, but we remain unable to dig deeper and ascertain which sub-populations are the most affected, or adequately assess the extent to which Canadian society, community, and institutions help foster a sense of belonging, and therefore where scarce resources should be focused.

It would appear that aggregate categories like "newcomers" or "visible minorities" may be insufficient to gauge our progress in building an integrated society. These categories may hide as much as they illuminate. For example, Portuguese Canadians are not classified as visible minorities and yet have educational attainment challenges similar to black Canadians and Aboriginals (Nunes 2008, 1998). Similarly, the simple binaries of the twentieth century do not explain a more complex twenty-first century Canada. Racism and discrimination can flow in multiple directions; indicators of engagement or exclusion can suggest some communities are doing well in some areas and not in others, thus challenging the metrics we utilize to ascertain level of integration.

In addition, critics of Canada's approach to multiculturalism and integration often articulate positions with implicit definitions of successful integration that are internally contradictory, with few ethnocultural communities exhibiting either all or none of the characteristics of the well integrated. For example, Italian-Canadians (a community generally no longer considered to be poorly integrated) are one of two communities overrepresented in elected bodies, and yet large numbers of Italians read Italian media and vote in Italian elections and have a far greater tendency to donate to cultural organizations of their own cultural heritage in comparison to a wide range of visible minority communities of much more recent immigrant vintage in Canada. In short, we need to acknowledge that few Canadians demonstrate all elements of any implicit definition of integration, and thus we need more finely grained research to ascertain the scale of any "resistance to integration" and to devise tailored policy responses if necessary.

Lastly, and perhaps most troubling, is the overall economic situation of newcomers and minorities in Canada. True, some communities fare better than others, but in general the indicators are not positive and are trending downwards. A large and growing body of research addresses the question of the racialization of poverty and the range of ills its growth portends for an integrated society. Clearly, more policy focus needs to be brought to these challenges, and innovative solutions need to be explored. We know that the federal skilled workers are faring far better in the labour market; the forthcoming evaluation results on the Provincial Nominee Program outcomes will also be illustrative. Not everything can be handled via selection. For example, employers (at least those that are federally regulated) appear to lead in terms of hiring visible minorities and yet lag in terms of their engagement in training and hiring newcomers. This may be an area for fruitful exploration.

Hand in hand with these strategies to ensure the economic inclusion of those newcomers and minorities already in Canada, a tighter connection between selection policies and settlement outcomes also seems advisable. The kind of information this connection could yield would assist potential newcomers in deciding whether immigrating to Canada would lead to the desired results. In some cases, it would allow those who apply to better prepare, and, of course, it would deter others who were least likely to be successful. Support for mass immigration to Canada is dependent upon both the newcomers and the communities they join perceiving mutual benefit and gain. We must ensure that this perception continues to be the case.

NOTES

We would like to thank our colleagues from across the country who provided invaluable feedback to us.

1.   The division of labour between the settlement programming of the department tasked with immigration (Manpower and Immigration in the early 1970s) and the Multiculturalism Program at Secretary of State was settled at a Cabinet discussion on 6 June 1974 with the Cabinet decision that created the settlement program and established that the immigration department would maintain responsibility for "the reception of immigrants and their settling into the community, including employment, accommodation, and establishing an understanding of social services available to the individual immigrant and his family"; the Secretary of State would be "responsible for the longer-term aspects of integration concerning the development of a society which is receptive to and understanding of, the needs and desires of Canada's immigrant community and for stimulating initiatives in the immigrant community to assist in its own development within a Canadian context" (Vineberg 2010, 20).
     At the same meeting, a report on assistance to voluntary organizations led to a Cabinet directive that "whenever possible, departments and agencies avail themselves of the services of Canadian voluntary organizations as a means of fulfilling their respective mandates instead of increasing the numbers of departmental staff" (21).
2.   The *Employment Equity Act* defines a visible minority as "persons, other than Aboriginal peoples, who are non-Caucasian in race or non-white in colour."
3.   Crowley (2009) adroitly summarizes the available evidence that suggests that immigration numbers would have to increase substantially to have a significant impact, although present levels are sufficient to have some impact.
4.   While it would have been optimal to draw on evaluation reports to illustrate the efficacy of this new program, unfortunately none will be available until at least 2013–14. Readers interested in evaluations of the former settlement programs can consult evaluation reports found at http://www.cic.gc.ca/english/resources/evaluation/index.asp.

5. It is worth noting that while these volumes provide much-needed analysis of provincial and municipal actors and cast some light over the thicket of civil society actors involved in settlement, integration, and inclusion activities, this latter field remains poorly researched in Canada (Kobayashi 2000; Handy and Cnaan 2000).

6. The evolution of priorities established for the Multiculturalism Program can be found in note 14 of Biles (2008).

7. Data for settlement and integration outputs presented here are drawn from an article posted in *CIC Insider* no. 7, included on the CIC intranet 10 November 2010. It should be noted that data extracted from the iCAMs database are provided by service provider organizations (SPOs) as part of the accountability provisions that accompany contribution agreements with CIC. Thus, data only cover settlement outside of Quebec, Manitoba, and British Columbia, which have separate arrangements for data collection and service delivery. In addition, data may slightly vary depending upon date of extraction from the database, given ongoing data input from SPOs. Finally, prior to July 2010, some data for HOST and ISAP (roughly 20 percent) were entered in an aggregate format, so it is not possible to identify all individual clients who may have accessed information and orientation services for this period.

8. Interestingly, international research on Chinese origin voters has found this to be true in Malyasia, Indonesia, and the United States (Freedman 2000).

9. The issues span a spectrum from residential concentration, home language use, and similar issues at one end and conflict with the law and radicalization at the other.

10. Language experts are concerned that the IALSS Survey conflates two things: language proficiency and literacy. They believe that the astrophysicist with poor English or French skills is not illiterate: (s)he just has not yet acquired the language, although (s)he possesses an understanding of how language in general functions. How one provides second language training to this kind of individual is fundamentally different than for a poorly educated individual who is not literate in any language.

11. While the economic outcomes for newcomers have long been a major concern for CIC and it has invested significant resources into data collection, the arrival of the Multiculturalism Program in the department has widened the scope of concern and data collection has yet to catch up. For example, CIC has not yet added a visible minority question to the Labour Force Survey module that the department supports.

12. The department has committed in its strategic plan to "develop a policy framework for language assessment across the immigration, integration and citizenship continuum" and to "implement the Pan-Canadian Framework for the Assessment and Recognition of Foreign Qualifications" (CIC 2010a). In addition, changes to the points system are under development to adjust the grid to recognize the challenges with recognizing foreign experience. Bridge-to-work labour market settlement programming has also been developed, and the Canadian Experience Class has also been introduced to tackle this experience challenge amongst others.

13. The *labour force participation rate* refers to the proportion of the overall working age population (15+) who work or are available to work. It is expressed

as a percentage of the population 15 years of age and over in that group. The *employment rate* for a particular group is the number of employed in that group expressed as a percentage of the population 15 years of age and over in that group (those in the working age population who work).

14. With a structural shift towards a knowledge economy, the nature of the labour market has changed. Jobs requiring education, credentials, and strong communication skills have increasingly replaced those requiring lower level of skills. In 2002, responding to the evolving needs of the Canadian labour market, changes were made to the immigration program. The previous federal legislation that regulated immigration to Canada, the *Immigration Act* of 1978, was replaced by the *Immigration and Refugee Protection Act* (IRPA), and the basis of selection of immigrants admitted for their contribution to Canada's economy through the FSWP was updated. Points are no longer allocated for specific occupations but rather for broad skills and capabilities that make an immigrant labour market ready to contribute to positive economic returns in the long run, such as official language ability, educational attainment, and age. Recent evaluations of this human capital approach in the selection of skilled workers show that these immigrants are doing far better economically than their predecessors who came to Canada under the pre-IRPA selection system. They have been able to capitalize on their higher education and better knowledge of official languages and not only more quickly obtain employment but do so in occupations that pay considerably better than for those who arrived pre-IPRA.

References

Adams, M. 2007. *Unlikely Utopia: The Surprising Triumph of Canadian Pluralism.* Toronto: Viking Canada.

Andrew, C., J. Biles, M. Burstein, V. Esses, and E. Tolley, eds. 2011. *Immigration and Diversity in Ontario.* Montreal and Kingston: McGill-Queen's University Press.

Andrew, C., J. Biles, M. Siemiatycki, and E. Tolley. 2008. *Electing a Diverse Canada.* Vancouver: University of British Columbia Press.

Aydemir, A. and M. Skuterud. 2004. "Explaining the Deteriorating Entry Earnings of Canada's Immigrant Cohorts: 1966–2000." Analytical Studies Branch Research Paper Series 2004225e. Statistics Canada, Analytical Studies Branch.

Beach, C.M., A.G. Green, and J.G. Reitz, eds. 2003. *Canadian Immigration Policy for the Twenty-First Century.* Kingston and Montreal: McGill-Queen's University Press.

Beaujot, R. and D. Matthews. 2000. *Immigration and the Future of Canada's Population.* Discussion Paper no. 00-1. Population Studies Centre University of Western Ontario.

Belkhodja, C., ed. 2008. "Immigration and Diversity in Francophone Minority Communities." Special issue of *Canadian Issues* (Spring).

Biles, J. 2008. "Integration Policies in English-Speaking Canada." In *Immigration and Integration in Canada in the Twenty-First Century*, ed. J. Biles, M. Burstein, and J. Frideres, 139-86.

Biles, J., M. Burstein, and J. Frideres, eds. 2008. *Immigration and Integration in Canada.* Montreal and Kingston: McGill-Queen's University Press.

Biles, J., M. Burstein, J. Frideres, E. Tolley, and R. Vineberg, eds. 2011. *Immigration and Inclusion across Canada.* Montreal and McGill-Queen's University Press.

Biles, J., and E. Panousos. 1999. *The Snakes and Ladders of Canadian Diversity.* Ottawa: Department of Canadian Heritage.

Biles, J. and L. Winnemore. 2006. "Canada's Two-Way Street Integration Model: Not without Its Stains, Strains and Growing Pains." *Canadian Diversity/Diversité canadienne* 5(1):23-30.

Boyd, M. 2009. "Official Language Proficiency and the Civic Participation of Immigrants." Paper presented at Metropolis, 22 October.

Burstein, M. 2007. "Promoting the Presence of Visible Minority Groups across Canada." *Our Diverse Cities* 3 (Rural Issue): 42-6.

Chiswick, B.R. and P.W. Miller. 1992. "Language in the Immigrant Labor Market. In *Immigration, Language and Ethnic Issues: Canada and the United States,* ed B.R. Chiswick, 229-96. Washington, DC: American Enterprise Institute.

— 1995. "The Endogeneity between Language and Earnings: International Analyses." *Journal of Labor Economics* 13(2):246-88.

— 2003. "The Complementarity of Language and Other Human Capital: Immigrant Earnings in Canada." *Economics of Education Review* 22(5):469-80.

Citizenship and Immigration Canada (CIC). 2009. *Facts and Figures. Immigration Overview. Permanent and Temporary Residents.* At http://www.cic.gc.ca/english/resources/statistics/facts2009/index.asp (accessed 8 July 2010).

— 2010a. "Strategic Plan: Citizenship and Immigration Canada 2010–2015." Internal document, CIC Intranet website.

— 2010b. "Canada's Multiculturalism and Citizenship Policy." Presentation to Multiculturalism Grants and Contributions National Meeting, June.

— 2010c. "Report on Plans and Priorities." At http://www.tbs-sct.gc.ca/rpp/2010-2011/inst/imc/st-ts01-eng.asp (accessed 31 March 2011).

— 2010d. "Successful Integration of Newcomers to Canada." *CIC Insider* 7 (November).

— 2010e. "Evaluation of the Federal Skilled Worker Program." http://www.cic.gc.ca/english/resources/evaluation/fswp/index.asp (accessed 20 February 2012).

— 2011. *Annual Report on the Operation of the Canadian Multiculturalism Act 2009/2010.* At http://www.cic.gc.ca/english/resources/publications/multi-report2010/index.asp (accessed 31 March 2011).

Corak, M. 2008. "Immigration in the Long Run: The Educational and Earning Mobility of Second-Generation Canadians." *IRPP Choices* 14(13).

Crowley, B.L. 2009. *Fearful Symmetry: The Fall and Rise of Canada's Founding Values.* Toronto: Key Porter.

Day, R.J.F. 2000. *Multiculturalism and the History of Canadian Diversity.* Toronto: University of Toronto Press.

Derouin, J. 2004. "Asians and Multiculturalism in Canada's Three Major Cities: Some Evidence from the Ethnic Diversity Survey." *Our Diverse Cities* 1:58-62.

Dirks, G.E. 1977. *Canada's Refugee Policy: Indifference or Opportunism?* Montreal and Kingston: McGill-Queen's University Press.

Dreisziger, N.F. 1988. "The Rise of a Bureaucracy for Multiculturalism: The Origins of the Nationalities Branch, 1939–1941." In *On Guard for Thee: War, Ethnicity, and the Canadian State, 1939–1945.* Ottawa: Ministry of Supply and Services.

Ferguson, T. 1975. *A White Man's Country: An Exercise in Canadian Prejudice.* Toronto: Doubleday Canada.

Fleury, D. 2007 "A Study of Poverty and Working Poverty among Recent Immigrants to Canada." At http://www.hrsdc.gc.ca/eng/publications_resources/research/categories/inclusion/2007/sp_680_05_07_e/page01.shtml (accessed 13 April 2011).

Freedman, A.L. 2000. *Political Participation and Ethnic Minorities: Chinese Overseas in Malaysia, Indonesia, and the United States.* New York: Routledge.

Galabuzi, G.-E. 2006. *Canada's Economic Apartheid: The Social Exclusion of Racialized Groups in the New Century.* Toronto: Canadian Scholars Press.

Green, A. and D. Green. 1999. *The Economic Goals of Canada's Immigration Policy: Past and Present. Canadian Public Policy* 15(4).

Gushulak, B. 2007 "Healthier on Arrival? Further Insight into the 'Healthy Immigrant Effect.'" *CMAJ* 8(10):176.

Hamdani, D. 2004. "Muslim Women: Beyond the Perceptions: A Demographic Profile of Muslim Women in Canada." Report prepared for the Canadian Council of Muslim Women, November.

Handy, F. and R.A. Cnaan. 2000. "Religious Nonprofits: Social Service Provision by Congregations in Ontario." In *The Nonprofit Sector in Canada: Roles and Relationships*, ed. K.G. Banting, 69-106. Montreal and Kingston: McGill-Queen's University Press.

Hawkins, F. 1991. *Critical Years in Immigration: Canada and Australia Compared.* Kingston and Montreal: McGill-Queen's University Press.

Heisz, A., and G. Schellenberg. 2004. "Public Transit Use among Immigrants." *Canadian Journal of Urban Research* 13(1):170-92.

Henderson, A. 2005. "Ideal Citizens? Immigrant Voting Patterns in Canadian Elections." *Canadian Issues* (Summer):57-60.

Hill Strategies. 2005. "Diversity in Canada's Arts Labour Force: An Analysis of 2001 Census Data." At http://www.arts.on.ca/Page589.aspx (accessed 15 January 2012).

Hou, F. and S. Coulombe. 2010. "Earnings Gaps for Canadian-Born Visible Minorities in the Public and Private Sectors." *Canadian Public Policy* 36(1).

Huddleston, T. and J. Niessen, with E.N. Chaoimh and E. White. 2011. "The Migrant Integration Policy Index." Brussels: British Council and Migrant Policy Group.

Hum, D. 2006. "Revisiting Visible Minorities and Immigration Adjustment in Canada's Labour Markets." At http://www.umanitoba.ca/faculties/arts/economics/simpson/CERF%20Paper%20Montreal.pdf (accessed 16 July 2010).

Human Resources and Skills Development Canada (HRSDC). 2009. "Low Income in Canada, 2000–2007, Using the Market Basket Measure – August 2009." At http://www.hrsdc.gc.ca/eng/publications_resources/research/categories/inclusion/2009/sp-909-07-09/page08.shtml (accessed 17 June 2010).

Jedwab, J. 2007. "The Young and the Rootless: Measuring Ethnicity and Belonging in Canada." At http://www.acs-aec.ca/pdf/polls/11882297694378.pdf (accessed 31 March 2011).

Joshee, R. 1995. "Federal Policies on Cultural Diversity and Education, 1940–1971." PhD dissertation, University of British Columbia, Vancouver.

Kazemipur, A. 2009. *Social Capital and Diversity: Some Lessons from Canada.* Bern: Peter Lang.

Kazemipur, A. and S.S. Halli. 2000. *The New Poverty in Canada: Ethnic Groups and Ghetto Neighbourhoods.* Toronto: Thompson Educational Publishing.

Kelley, N. and M. Trebilcock. 1998. *The Making of the Mosaic: A History of Canadian Immigration Policy.* Toronto: University of Toronto Press.

Knowles, V. 1997. *Strangers at Our Gates: Canadian Immgration and Immigration Policy, 1540–1997.* Toronto: Dundurn Press.

Kobayashi, A. 2000. "Advocacy from the Margins: The Role of Minority Ethnocultural Associations in Affecting Public Policy in Canada." In *The Nonprofit Sector in Canada: Roles and Relationships*, ed. K.G. Banting, 229-66. Montreal and Kingston: McGill-Queen's University Press.

Labour Program. 2009. *Employment Equity Act: Annual Report 2008.* At http://www.hrsdc.gc.ca/eng/labour/publications/equality/annual_reports/2008/docs/2008report.pdf (accessed 17 June 2010).

Lanphier, M. and O. Lukomskyj. 1994. "Settlement Policy in Australia and Canada." In *Immigration and Refugee Policy: Australia and Canada Compared*, vol. 2, ed. H. Adelman, A. Borowski, M. Burstein, and L. Foster, 125-48. Toronto: University of Toronto Press.

Leger Marketing. 2007. "Racial Tolerance Report." At http://www.legermarketing.com/documents/spclm/070119ENG.pdf (accessed 16 June 2010).

Li, P. 1998. *The Chinese in Canada.* 2nd ed. Toronto: Oxford University Press.

Lochhead, C. and P. Mackenzie. 2005. "Integrating Newcomers into the Canadian Labour Market." *Canadian Issues/Thèmes canadiens* (Spring):103-6.

MacDougall, A. 2009. "Hearing Audible Minorities: Accent, Discrimination, and the Integration of Immigrants into the Canadian Labour Market." Presentation at Metropolis Presents on Language, October. At http://canada.metropolis.net/events/metropolis_presents/LanguageSeminar/Presentations/Macdougall%20-%20Presentation.pdf (accessed 17 June 2010).

Mahtani, M. 2008. "How Are Immigrants Seen – and What do They Want to See? Contemporary Research on the Representation of Immigrants in the Canadian English-Language Media." In *Immigration and Integration in Canada*, ed. J. Biles, M. Burstein, and J. Frideres, 231-52.

McAndrew, M., D. Helly, C. Tessier, and J. Young. 2008. "From Heritage Languages to Institutional Change: An Analysis of the Nature of Organizations and Projects Funded by the Canadian Multiculturalism Program (1983–2002)." *Canadian Ethnic Studies* 40(3):149-70.

McDonald, T., E. Ruddick, A. Sweetman, and C. Worswick, eds. 2010. *Canadian Immigration: Economic Evidence for a Dynamic Policy Environment.* Montreal and Kingston: McGill-Queen's University Press.

Media Q. 2010. "Minister of Citizenship, Immigration and Multiculturalism Jason Kenney Addresses the Economic Club of Canada on 'The Future of Immigration in Canada.'" Transcript prepared for Citizenship and Immigration Canada, 9 June.

Mulholland, M.-L. and J. Biles. 2004. "Newcomer Integration Policies in Canada." At www.welcomingcommunities.ca/docs/newcomer.doc (accessed 31 March 2011).

Nunes, F. 1998. "Portuguese-Canadians: From Sea to Sea." Report prepared for the Portuguese National Congress. At http://manuelcarvalho.8m.com/nunes1.html

—2008. "Striking a Balance in Canada's Diversity Dialogue." *Canadian Diversity* 6(2):121-5. At http://dc.msvu.ca:8080/bitstream/handle/10587/581/Nunes-

Striking%20a%20Balance%20in%20Canada's%20Diversity%20Dialogue.
pdf?sequence=1 (accessed 17 June 2010).

Ontario Women's Justice Network. 2008. "The Development of the Canadian
Equality Test: S. 15(1) of the Charter." At http://www.owjn.org/owjn_new/
index.php?option=com_content&view=article&id=109&Itemid=107 (accessed
31 March 2011).

Oreopoulos, P. 2009. "Why Do Skilled Immigrants Struggle in the Labor Market?
A Field Experiment with Six Thousand Résumés." Metropolis Working Paper.
At http://mbc.metropolis.net/assets/uploads/files/wp/2009/WP09-03.pdf
(accessed 16 June 2010).

Ornstein, M. 2008. "Ethno-Racial Inequality in Montreal." Presentation at the
Quebec Inter-University Centre for Social Statistics, 11 February.

Pendakur, R., F. Mata, S. Lee, and N. Dole. 2000. "Job Mobility and Promotion in
the Federal Public Service." At http://www.tbs-sct.gc.ca/res/dwnld/jmp-eng.
pdf (accessed 17 June 2010).

Persad, J.V. and S. Lukas. 2002. "No Hijab Is Permitted Here: A Study on the
Experience of Muslim Women Wearing Hijab Applying for Work in the Manufacturing, Sales and Service Sectors." Report prepared for Women Working
with Immigrant Women, December.

Picot, G. and A. Sweetman. 2005. "The Deteriorating Economic Welfare of Immigrants and Possible Causes: Update 2005." Statistics Canada Catalogue
No. 11F0019MIE2005262.

Potvin, M. 2008. *Crise des accommodements raisonnables: Une fiction mediatique?*
Montreal: Athena Editions.

Preston, V. et al. 2009. "Immigrants and Homelessness – At Risk in Canada's
Outer Suburbs." *Canadian Geographer* 53(3):288-304.

Reitz, J.G. 2007. "Immigrant Employment Success in Canada, Part 2: Understanding the Decline." *Journal of International Migration and Integration* 8(1):37-62.

Roy, P.E. 2003. *The Oriental Question: Consolidating a White Man's Province, 1914–41.*
Vancouver: UBC Press.

Siemiatycki, M. 2006. "Municipal Franchise and Social Inclusion in Toronto: Policy and Practice." At http://maytree.com/PDF_Files/MaytreePolicyInFocus
Issue1.pdf (accessed 31 March 2011).

—2007. "Extend the Right to Vote to Non-Citizen Residents in Canada's Diverse
Cities." At http://maytree.com/PDF_Files/MaytreePolicyInFocusIssue1.pdf
(accessed 18 April 2011).

Smith, A. 2010. "CIC's Modernized Approach to Settlement Programming: A
Brief Description." At http://integration-net.ca:81/infocentre/2010/001e.pdf
(accessed 31 March 2011).

Social Cohesion Network. 1998. "Rekindling Hope and Investing in the Future."
Report of the Social Cohesion Network to the Policy Research Committee.

Solutions Research Group. 2006. "Diversity in Canada." Powerpoint presentation
provided to Canadian Heritage, 24 March.

Statistics Canada. 2003. "Ethnic Diversity Survey: Portrait of a Multicultural
Society" Catalogue No. 89-593-XIE. At http://www.statcan.gc.ca/pub/89-
593-x/89-593-x2003001-eng.pdf (accessed 16 June).

—2005a. "Women in Canada: A Gender-Based Statistical Report." At http://www.
statcan.gc.ca/pub/89-503-x/89-503-x2005001-eng.pdf (accessed 16 June 2010).

—2005b. "International Adult Literacy and Skills Survey." *The Daily*. At http://www.statcan.gc.ca/daily-quotidien/051109/dq051109a-eng.htm

—2007a. "Economic Integration of Immigrants' Children." *Perspectives on Labour and Income* 8(10). At http://www.statcan.gc.ca/pub/75-001-x/2007110/article/10372-eng.htm (accessed 16 June 2010).

—2007b. "Canada's Immigrant Labour Market." *The Daily*. At http://www.statcan.gc.ca/daily-quotidien/070910/dq070910a-eng.htm (accessed 16 June 2010).

—2008a. "Educational Portrait of Canada – 2006 Census." At http://www12.statcan.ca/census-recensement/2006/as-sa/97-560/pdf/97-560-XIE2006001.pdf (accessed 17 June 2010).

—2008b. "Earning and Incomes of Canadians Over the Past Quarter Century, 2006 Census." At http://www12.statcan.ca/census-recensement/2006/as-sa/97-563/pdf/97-563-XIE2006001.pdf (accessed 11 April 2011).

—2009a. *2006 Census: Immigration in Canada : A Portrait of the Foreign-Born Population, 2006 Census: Findings*. Catalogue 97-557-XIE2006001. At http://www12.statcan.ca/census-recensement/2006/as-sa/97-557/index-eng.cfm (accessed 8 July 2010).

—2009b. *2006 Census: Educational Portrait of Canada, 2006 Census: Findings*. Catalogue 97-560-XIE2006001. At http://www12.statcan.ca/census-recensement/2006/as-sa/97-560/index-eng.cfm (accessed 8 July 2010).

—2010a. "A Portrait of Couples in Mixed Unions." At http://www.statcan.gc.ca/pub/11-008-x/2010001/article/11143-eng.htm (accessed 15 June 2010).

—2010b. "Police-Reported Hate Crimes." *The Daily*, 14 June. At http://www.statcan.gc.ca/daily-quotidien/100614/dq100614b-eng.htm (accessed 16 June 2010).

—2010c. *Projections of the Diversity of the Canadian Population 2006-2031*. Catalogue 91-551-X.

—2011. "Canada: Estimated Aging Index." At http://www.canadaimmigrants.com/qualityoflife/agingpopulation.asp (accessed 7 April 2011).

Toronto Dominion Financial Group. 2009. *Literacy Matters: Helping Newcomers Unlock Their Potential*. At http://www.td.com/document/PDF/economics/special/ca0909_literacy.pdf (accessed 15 January 2012).

Tossutti, a. 2005. "Electoral Turnout and Canada's Changing Cultural Make Up: Interviews with Three Municipal Leaders." *Canadian Issues* (Summer):53-6.

Tran, K., S. Kustec, and T. Chui. 2005. Becoming Canadian: Intent, Process and Outcome." *Canadian Social Trends*. At http://www.statcan.gc.ca/studies-etudes/11-008/feature-caracteristique/5018920-eng.pdf (accessed 17 June 2010).

Triadafilopoulos, T. 2012. *Becoming Multicultural: Immigration and the Politics of Membership in Canada and Germany*. Vancouver: University of British Columbia Press.

Trudeau, P. 1971. *House of Commons Debates*. 8 October, 8545-8.

University of Calgary. 2001. *The Peopling of Canada, 1891–1921*. Applied History Research Group. At http://www.ucalgary.ca/applied_history/tutor/canada1891/6frame.html (accessed 8 July 2010).

Vallée, M. and T. Caputo. 2010. "Synthesis Paper on Newcomers and Volunteering." Prepared for Human Resources and Skills Development Canada.

Vineberg, R. 2010. "A History of Immigration Settlement Services." Submitted to Integration Branch, Citizenship and Immigration Canada.

Ward, P.W. 1990. *White Canada Forever: Popular Attitudes and Public Policy Toward Orientals in British Columbia.* 2nd ed. Montreal: McGill-Queen's University Press.

Xue, L. 2010. "A Comprehensive Look at the Employment Experience of Recent Immigrants during Their First Four Years in Canada." In *Canadian Immigration: Economic Evidence for a Dynamic Policy Environment,* ed. T. McDonald, E. Ruddick, and A.Sweetman, 11-40. Montreal and Kingston: McGill-Queen's University Press.

CHAPTER 5

MIGRANT WORKERS IN CHINA

PETER S. LI AND EVA XIAOLING LI

Since China's reforms in 1979 adopting an open-door economic policy and expanding the market economy, the country has experienced spectacular growth. Between 1980 and 1994, the average annual increase in China's gross domestic product was 18.4 percent; between 1994 and 2008, the average annual increase was 14 percent (National Bureau of Statistics of China 2010a). Even when population increases are taken into account, the per capita GDP growth averaged 16.7 percent every year from 1980 to 1994, and 13 percent every year from 1994 and 2008 (ibid.). One factor contributing to this sustained prosperity is the large supply of migrant workers from rural areas moving into the cities to provide the labour supply necessary to fuel the country's rapid industrial and urban growth. Estimates vary as to how many migrant workers there are in China, but the latest official statistics suggest the number reached almost 230 million people in 2009 (National Bureau of Statistics of China 2010b). The sheer size of the migrant population, as well as the social and legal barriers to integrating them into the cities, has created a policy dilemma for China. On the one hand, migrant workers are essential to its continuous economic development; on the other hand, they are illicit migrants, moving to the city from the countryside without seeking prior official approval.

Although they are technically internal migrants, migrant workers in China have to overcome many legal and social barriers in trying to be accepted in the city. In this way, their experiences bear some similarities to the experience of illegal migrants in the West. The experiences of China's migrant workers reflect the country's urban and rural divide and the many institutional and social barriers that deter their integration in cities. This paper discusses the process that has produced the migrant workers' population in China, the size and features of this workforce, and

International Perspectives: Integration and Inclusion, ed. J. Frideres and J. Biles. Montreal and Kingston: Queen's Policy Studies Series, McGill-Queen's University Press. © 2012 The School of Policy Studies, Queen's University at Kingston. All rights reserved.

the resulting unequal opportunities facing migrant workers in the city. The paper also makes use of interview materials to show the plight and aspirations of recent migrant workers in the city of Xi'an in western China.

THE MAKING OF MIGRANT WORKERS

Several terms have been used to describe workers in urban China who are officially designated as belonging to agricultural households in the countryside but have moved to the city on their own to take advantage of job opportunities created by urban development and economic prosperity. These terms include "China's floating population" (Liang and Ma 2004), "rural migrant workers" (Han 2010), "rural migrants" (Zhang and Wang 2010), "migrant workers" (Windrow and Guha 2005) and "migrant labour" (Chan 2010). Officially, they are referred to as *nongmin gong* or "farmers-turned-workers" (National Bureau of Statistics of China 2010b), and academically, they are most commonly called "rural migrant workers" or "migrant workers" (Han 2010; Windrow and Guha 2005). The National Bureau of Statistics of China classifies migrant workers as made up of those who are officially registered as belonging to an agricultural household but have been working for six months or more in a year as non-agricultural workers either in their local area or in regions outside their region of registration (National Bureau of Statistics of China 2010b).

Two factors, one historical and one contemporary, explain why the number of migrant workers has been rising since 1980, and why prior to 1980, there was no sustained migration from rural areas to the city under communist rule, except for a few years prior to the introduction of the household registration system and in short periods when urban growth necessitated recruitment of labour from the countryside (Banister 1987; Howe 1971; Kirkby 1985). The historical factor has to do with the entrenchment of the *hukou* system, the system of household registration that since 1955[1] has linked household registration to entitlements to necessities of life, including the food coupons needed to purchase monthly staples, housing that has become state controlled, and access to transportation such as purchase of a train ticket (Cheng and Selden 1994). The contemporary factor is the outcome of economic reform that makes access to necessities of life increasingly unrelated to household registration and frees up surplus labour in the countryside as farming production becomes more efficient.

Under the *hukou* system of registration, urban residents and state employees were classified as belonging to urban and non-agricultural households, which were given entitlements to grain rations (Cheng and Selden 1994; Windrow and Guha 2005). In addition, urban householders received various types of benefits provided by the state, including retirement benefits, health care, education, and subsidized housing, but peasants were left to farm collectives to look after their livelihood under the dogmatic belief that the countryside had the sufficiency and flexibility to absorb excess labour (Cheng and Selden 1994). Thus, the type of household registration determined the range of benefits to which agricultural and non-agricultural householders were entitled. In essence, the *hukou* system tied farmers to the land without providing them with the benefits enjoyed by urban workers; at the same time, the agricultural sector had to bear the burden of feeding the urban work force and paying taxes to the state. The control of population movement was rationalized on the grounds that it would ensure an orderly development of an urban industrial workforce and a rural collective farm economy, and such a rationale was reinforced by the socialist conviction that urban workers and collective farmers would eventually converge in a classless society (Cheng and Selden 1994, 652). As it turned out, the *hukou* system limited the mobility of rural residents by preventing them access to urban employment and opportunities; it denied them the choice to move elsewhere even when their subsistence was threatened, as during massive farm failures in the aftermath of the Great Leap Forward in the late 1950s when tens of thousands in the countryside died of starvation (MacFarquhar 1983; Selden 1993).

The historical *hukou* system was effective in undermining the free mobility of citizens guaranteed under the 1954 constitution; the state used the system to grant or deny residents access to food and other essentials of life (Cheng and Selden 1994). Unless the transfer of household registration was officially approved, those who ventured to the city on their own received no entitlement, since their agricultural household registration card would not allow them access to employment, food rations, and housing in the city. The registration system, in combination with other controls, has hardened the divide between urban and rural life. From the start, China adopted a bifurcated approach towards workers in the city and peasants in the countryside. Since the 1950s, the state has assumed responsibilities in looking after unemployed workers in the city and turning them into productive industrial workers (ibid.). At the same time, it has viewed the peasants as food producers and as future farm workers who would be eventually incorporated into collectivized farm production.

Prior to the 1980s, the *hukou* system was successful in slowing urbanization in China. However, since the market reform of 1979, several factors have contributed to the weakening of the complex system of registration that controlled geographic mobility. First, the process of privatization in China has enabled the free market to expand in practically every aspect of life. As food supply becomes readily available in the open market and as people's earnings increase, the traditional mechanism of using food coupons to control access to basic staples has become obsolete. The housing market too has become increasingly privatized, as work units (establishments under which employees work) and the state no longer wish to assume responsibilities for providing housing, and many urban workers have had to raise private funds to purchase housing in the open market. Access to public transportation has improved, and there is little restriction to transportation such as control of access to train tickets. As rural residents no longer depend on household registration to access food coupons for basic staples, it becomes possible for them to move to the city. Second, the economic growth in urban centres has created rising demand for labour in manufacturing, construction, transportation, and other sectors. As the income level of urbanites rises, there is a corresponding demand for various types of services related to a higher consumption level and a more luxurious lifestyle. The economic prosperity in the city that has generated a higher demand for labour and the resulting higher earnings of urbanites have served as pulling forces drawing rural residents to the city, initially from surrounding areas of the coastal region where development first occurred and later in central and interior parts of China. Third, as China becomes more industrialized, the country's proportional reliance on agriculture production in building national wealth decreases; the rural area generates large quantities of labour no longer needed in more mechanized and innovative forms of agricultural production. This surplus agricultural workforce serves as a pushing force to propel migration to the city. Basic economic data confirm the shift in production. For example, in 1980 about 30 percent of China's GDP came from primary industry and 22 percent from the tertiary sector; in 2008, primary industry only contributed 11 percent to GDP while the tertiary industry contributed 40 percent (National Bureau of Statistics of China 2010a).

The above factors explain why large numbers of migrants from rural areas have been moving to the city, even though officially under the *hukou* system still in effect, they belong to agricultural households in the countryside. Since the *hukou* system remains an institutional barrier by which access to urban benefits are determined, migrant workers in the city are typically not entitled to subsidized medical care, housing, and other benefits or to quality education for their children, even though the state's control over staple rationing has become obsolete. Thus, changes in China have resulted in the *hukou* system producing two somewhat contradictory effects – freeing rural peasants from the historical constraints of migration while at the same time barring them from gaining what some researchers refer to as "urban citizenship" (Chan 2010; Chen 2005; Zhang and Wang 2010).

The persistence of the obsolete *hukou* system suggests that there are underlying structural reasons that sustain it. Chen (2005) argues that the central government of China has been benefiting from the system, using it as a means to economize on costs of financing educational and welfare benefits for migrant workers. The central government accepts as a fact the large population flow from rural to urban areas, but instead of taking responsibility for looking after the welfare of migrant workers and the education of their children, it downloads the responsibility and costs onto municipal and local governments. The bifurcation of rural and urban citizenship enables the central government to redefine its responsibility of looking after what would amount to universal rights of all citizens so that it becomes a responsibility of municipal and local governments to determine the entitlements of local citizens. In turn, municipal governments devise complex hierarchical systems to include or exclude different types of residents in the city for benefit considerations. In the case of Shanghai in the early 2000s, the municipal government used nine strata to classify residents of Shanghai, including those who moved to Shangahi from elsewhere; people in different strata had full, partial, or no access to the treatment and benefit enjoyed by full citizens of Shanghai depending on whether they had Shanghai household registration or permanent Shanghai resident permission, and on their educational level (Chen 2005). In short, the municipal government granted the urban *hukou* and its corresponding benefits to migrant workers based on individual workers' contribution to the city, not on their physical presence or duration of stay there (Zhang and Wang 2010).

Size and Features of Migrant Population in China

Population flow from the rural area to the urban area has been rising as China becomes more industrialized, greatly contributing to the expansion of the urban population. In 1980, the urban population made up about 20 percent of China's population; by 2008, officially it rose to slightly less than 35 percent of China's population, although the de facto urban population accounted for over 45 percent (Chan 2010). Thus, roughly 10 percent of China's population have become "illegal" migrants in the sense that they are supposed to be agricultural householders in the countryside but have moved to the city and remained there as migrant workers.

The issue of migrant workers has become so persistent and pervasive that on 31 March 2009 China's State Department set up a special branch to monitor and survey migrant workers (Finance and Economic Net 2009). Its report indicates that in 2009 the migrant population reached 229.8 million people (see Table 1). Of these, 84.5 million or 37 percent operated in their local region. In other words, these were officially designated agricultural householders who had worked for six months or more as non-agricultural workers in the region where they had their agricultural household registration. The remaining 145.3 million, or 63 percent of all migrant workers, worked in a region outside of their region of household registration.

TABLE 1
Number of Migrant Workers by Region, China, 2009

			China		
		Total	*Eastern*	*Central*	*Western*
Migrant workers in	N	84,450,000	53,794,650	18,494,550	12,160,800
local region[a]	%		54	26	21
Migrant workers in	N	145,330,000	46,360,270	53,045,450	45,924,280
outside region[b]	%		46	74	79
Total migrant workers	N	229,780,000	100,184,080	71,461,580	58,134,340
	%		100	100	100

[a] Includes those who hold agricultural household registration in a local region but have worked for six months or more as non-agricultural workers in the same region.
[b] Includes those who hold agricultural household registration in a local region but have worked for six months or more as non-agricultural workers in a region outside the region where they hold agricultural household registration.
Source: National Bureau of Statistics of China (2010b).

The economically more developed eastern part of China in 2009 attracted 100 million migrant workers, or 44 percent of all migrant workers, compared to 31 percent in central China and 25 percent in western China. In addition, 54 percent of migrant workers in eastern China came from the immediate local region, whereas in central and western China, 74 percent and 79 percent respectively came from outside regions (see Table 1). These differences reflect the ability of the more developed eastern China to attract migrant workers from surrounding areas as well as from further regions. There is no doubt that migrant workers are more inclined to move to areas of intense development, as, for example, the Pearl River Delta in Guangdong, which in 2009 attracted 30 percent of all migrant workers who worked in outside regions (National Bureau of Statistics of China 2010b).

Migrant workers in China tend to be young and not well educated. In 2009, about 42 percent of migrant workers who ventured to other regions outside their region of registration were between 16 and 25 years of age[2] (Table 2). About 62 percent were 30 years of age or younger. The vast majority did not complete senior secondary school. In 2009, about three-quarters of migrant workers had an education of no more than junior secondary school. Only about 10 percent had more than secondary school education. The young age of the migrant workers and their relatively low educational level meant that they would likely be in menial and low-paying jobs in the city.

Migrant workers tend to work in manufacturing, construction, and service industries. Official statistics indicate that 39 percent of migrant workers in cities worked in manufacturing, 17 percent in construction, and 12 percent in service industries. These three industries accounted for 68 percent of migrant workers who worked in regions outside of their region of registration (ibid.).

The income profile of migrant workers indicates that about 39 percent earned less than 1,200 yuan a month in 2009 and 34 percent earned between 1,200 to 1,600 yuan a month.[3] In 2009 the per capita disposable income in urban China was 17,175 yuan a year or 1,431 yuan a month, but the rural

TABLE 2
Selected Characteristics of Migrant Workers in Region outside Their Region of Household Registration, China, 2009

	Percent
Age	
16–25	41.6
26–30	20.0
31–40	22.3
41–50 .	11.9
Over 50	4.2
Total migrant workers	100.0
Educational level	
Illiterate	1.1
Primary	10.6
Junior secondary	64.8
Senior secodary	13.1
More than secondary	10.4
Total migrant workers	100.0
Income per month (yuan)	
Under 600	2.1
600–800	5.2
800–1200	31.5
1200–1600	33.9
1600–2400	19.7
More than 2400	7.6
Total migrant workers	100.0
Type of housing	
Dormitory provided by employer or work unit	33.9
In workplace or shop	10.3
In location of production	7.6
Co-renting	17.5
Renting on one's own	17.1
Commuting	9.3
Own housing unit	0.8
Other	3.5
Total migrant workers	100.0
Total number of migrant workers	*145,330,000*

Source: National Bureau of Statistics of China (2010b).

per capita disposable income was only 429 yuan a month (*China Daily* 2010). Thus, at least 39 percent of migrant workers earned less than the urban per capita disposable income in 2009. However, compared to the average disposable income in the rural area, the majority of migrant workers had a much higher earning level in the city. The housing condition of migrant workers also indicates their poor quality of life. In 2009, over half of migrant workers lived in employer-provided dormitories or in the workplace, and less than 1 percent lived in housing units that they owned.

There are strong indications that migrant workers are not well protected by existing labour regulations in China and are not properly covered by various types of benefits that urbanites enjoy. For example, about 90 percent of migrant workers worked in excess of the 44 hours a week limit set by the labour law (National Bureau of Statistics of China 2010b). In fact, in 2009 migrant workers in manufacturing, construction, accommodation and food sectors, services, and wholesaling and retailing worked between 58 to 61 hours a week (ibid.).

Statistics on insurance coverage (see Table 3) also suggest that only a small proportion of migrant workers in the city in 2009 were covered for work injury, medical care, and other benefits. Only 8 percent had access to old age insurance; 12 percent had medical care insurance; and 4 percent had unemployment insurance. In terms of work injury insurance, about 22 percent of migrant workers had such coverage, but the rate of coverage was higher in eastern China (25 percent) than in central (14 percent) or western China (16 percent). Childbirth insurance was available to only 2.3 percent of migrant workers. There were wide variations among industries in terms of the extent of insurance coverage for migrant workers. For example, the percentage of migrant workers covered by work injury insurance was 27.5 percent in manufacturing, 10.7 percent in transportation and mail delivery, 15.6 percent in construction, and 11.7 percent in accommodation and food services (ibid.). Medical care insurance was available to 14.7 percent of migrant workers in manufacturing, but only to 4.4 percent in construction (ibid.).

TABLE 3
Percent Covered by Type of Insurance in Eastern, Central, and Western China, Migrant Workers in Region outside Their Region of Household Registration, China, 2009

Type of Insurance	China			
	Total	Eastern	Central	Western
Old age	7.6	8.8	5.2	4.2
Work injury	21.8	24.6	14.3	15.7
Medical care	12.2	13.9	8.6	7.4
Unemployment	3.9	4.6	2.6	2.0
Childbirth	2.3	2.8	1.4	1.0

Source: National Bureau of Statistics of China (2010b).

To sum up, the statistical data on migrant workers indicate that migrant workers are typically young and not well educated; in the city they tend to live in low-quality housing such as dormitories or the workplace; they tend to be concentrated in labour intensive industries such as manufacturing, construction, and service, with little access to various types of insurance. Most do not have old age insurance and medical care coverage, and in 2009 only about 22 percent had access to work injury insurance.

EXPERIENCES OF MIGRANT WORKERS

Despite differences in background, migrant workers in China share a common goal: to find work in the city to improve their livelihood. This section, based on interviews with 36 migrant workers collected in 2009 in the city of Xi'an in western China, provides qualitative accounts of the experiences of migrant workers in the city.[4] The interview materials confirm many of the statistical findings reported earlier, especially regarding the low educational level of migrant workers and their tendency to be in manual and service jobs. The interview materials also provide fresh insights into the difficulties that migrant workers face in trying to integrate into the city, and about their quest for a better livelihood in the city and their hopes of receiving full recognition of urban citizenship rights and entitlements.

The migrant workers interviewed in Xi'an came from a wide variety of backgrounds, with some from the neighbouring countryside and others from other provinces and cities. Most of them went to the city in search of work to supplement their farm earnings, but at the same time many kept some farmland and maintained ties with family members at home. Many migrant workers left the farm because it was hard to make a living on the land or because of the low income from farming. Ms Zhang, a 47-year-old woman who went to the city in 1990, described her family background and why she took a city job:[5]

> My family is in Henan Province ... in a farming village. The conditions were not good. I have a husband at home. We have two sons. My husband is 49, but he has no job. In the village, he works on the land and grows crops. He is the only one left in the home village now ... I came to the city in 1990 at a time when my older child was ten and the younger was six or seven. There was no money at home; we needed money to look after the children. It happened a factory was recruiting workers in our home village. (Interview transcript, case 012)

Mr Li, a 31-year-old security guard, had been working in different jobs in many cities as a migrant worker. He described the hardship in his home village when the government encouraged some peasants not to farm in order to reclaim the land for forest preservation:

> The policy to compensate for peasants not to farm does not work at all. The compensation is not enough to live on – only 200 catties[6] of grain for every *mou*[7] of land and less than 100 yuan per year. My family for instance had 3 *mou* of land, and after returning 2 *mou*, we got 400 catties of grain and less than 200 yuan a year. What could we do? ... 90 percent of the young people in my home village now work outside ... They must work outside no matter how low wages are – that beats working on the farm ... People in my home village do not have much education; some went to Hebei Province to work in coal mines. But it is very dangerous ... I heard one could make 4,000 to 5,000 yuan a month, but the work is tiresome, hard, and dangerous. I dare not go there. (Interview transcript, case 017)

Migrant workers typically have a low level of education; those with secondary school education are among the better educated. There are many reasons as to why they are unable to complete even a secondary school education, including poor academic performance, changes in the family, and economic pressures, as well as some parents' belief that girls need not be educated the same as boys and that girls ought to contribute to the family's financial well-being as early as possible. The experiences of Ms Chen and her two sisters illustrate how some migrant workers had their education terminated when they were young. Ms Chen was 17 years old and worked as a waitress. She came from a farming family in Northern Shaanxi Province, but her father lost money as a construction contractor and had to come to Xi'an to make a living. At the time of the interview, the parents and three of their children were in Xi'an, leaving the grandparents behind to farm. Ms Chen described how she and her sisters had left school:

> No one in my family completed junior secondary school ... My elder sister did not do well in school, and my father told her not to go to school anymore ... I completed elementary school but only attended junior secondary school for a few days. My teacher asked to see my parents, and after my father heard the teacher's complaint against me, my father told me not to go to school anymore. I was hurt when I heard what my father said, but I had no choice but listen to him. He believes that if I cannot do well in school, I should just as well work and earn some money. (Interview transcript, case 005)

Due to the limited education of many migrant workers, they tend to work mainly in manual or service jobs. These jobs are typically low-paying and unstable, involving long hours and often harsh conditions. Migrant workers tend to move frequently from job to job to try to improve their earnings. Ms Zhang has been working for many years as a migrant worker. She described her working experiences:

> I worked in the factory to make cartons for about one year ... I started at 7 in the morning. When I finished my work for the day, I had to work on designing boxes, and when machines broke down, I had to try to repair them. I sometimes worked till 11 or 12 o'clock at night ... Later, I was repairing machines all day ... My family did not allow me to continue. Meals were not good there; the pay was not high. I got 150 yuan a month; other workers got 100 yuan ... I returned home for a year, but my children needed money to go to school. I came out again, this time washing dishes for a restaurant ... Later, others told me I could use a recruitment agency. I paid the agency... but I felt it was not good because the agency only knew of jobs in small restaurants and outfits. The employer did not look after meals or accommodation ... sometimes the owner did not pay you and kicked you out ... You worked from 8 in the morning till midnight ... you could only lean on the table to rest a bit over lunch ...
>
> In 1998 I saved a bit of money and started a small restaurant. I made some money at the beginning, but later, it failed, for many reasons – business was not good; I was inexperienced; officials from different departments came and refused to give me the licences needed. We migrant workers could not do this. The officials kept saying the place was unhygienic, violations here and violations there. I lost money after a few years. (Interview transcripts, case 012)

Among the many problems of integration in the city is the issue of education of migrant workers' children. The urban schools that migrant workers can afford to send their children to are likely to be poor-quality public schools. Their children also tend to come from rural schools with poor academic backgrounds that prevent them from entering good schools in the city. Mr Zhang, a 36-year-old factory worker, explained his difficulty in educating his children in the city:

> I came to Xi'an as soon as I graduated from secondary school. It is very hard for someone like me to try to stay in Xi'an. I brought my children to the city. We cannot afford private schools and can only send them to public schools. Public schools now provide nine years of compulsory education; the fees are not high. But the quality is not good. Other city kids can go to good schools, such as Jiaotong University Secondary School, Railroad Secondary School. Our kids can only go to ordinary schools ... These schools are free, but the environment is no good. We paid various fees to the government, but we are still not officially counted in Xi'an. Our children are still not counted, all because we do not have the Xi'an household registration. (Interview transcript, case 023)

Many migrant workers aspire to buying an apartment in the city, and some try desperately to save up in order to do so. But the high cost of purchasing an apartment relative to their low level of savings makes the dream of home ownership hard to realize. Mr Zhang, who had paid to buy the Xi'an household registration, talked about his aspiration to buy his own apartment and the difficulty of achieving that goal:

> If you imagine two people working in the city and saving 10,000 yuan a year, how hard it is to save enough to buy an apartment. One square metre costs at least 2,000 yuan. Without 200,000 yuan, it is not possible. Maybe it will take 20 years of saving to buy an apartment … banks won't give me a mortgage because my job has no security … I heard banks require mortgage payments to be about 30 percent of income. Like us both working and earning about 1,000 yuan – our 30 percent is only 300 to 400 yuan. In case we cannot make the payment, the bank would go after us. (Interview transcript, case 017)

The desire to buy their own apartment and the frustration for not being able to do so is evident in the story of many migrant workers. Mr Zhang echoed this frustration:

> I have land in the home village … but I cannot pull the land from there and put it here. I also spent a lot of money to build a house in the home village. Our accommodation unit in the city is exceptionally small, but the house in the home village is large with no one living there. Actually I do want to get rid of the land, and convert it to cash to prepare for buying an apartment here … But for us migrant workers, buying an apartment is beyond us … Our country now allows people like us to work and earn enough to maintain a living, but buying an apartment is really hard. We can't even afford to buy the low-cost housing units in the city. Many houses are being built here, but people like us are being excluded. When rich people buy, they can afford to buy several units, but we wage-earning people cannot afford even one. (Interview transcript, case 023)

Some migrant workers have been in the city for many years but remain concerned for their future, especially when they get old. Mr Zhang explained his dilemma in wanting to stay in the city and at the same time worrying about not having old age support:

> My household registration is still agricultural; I am still called a migrant worker …When I look back, 20 years have lapsed … How many more years can I live? If you let me go back to farm, I think it is impossible … Many co-workers like me do not wish to return to the village. If it is really true that we cannot work here anymore, then it is fine to find me another place. But I am worried about old age insurance. If I work till 65, will the government give me a pension? A pension is given to officially recognized workers in

the city. Do we get it? If you send us to our home village then, we would be too old to be able to work on anything. (Interview transcript, case 023)

CONCLUSION

The case of migrant workers in China reflects the dilemma of the country's economic development and the difficulty in integrating rural workers into the cities. On the one hand, the continuation of economic development in China depends on having large numbers of migrant workers from the rural areas working in the city; on the other hand, migrant workers who have left the countryside without official permission are officially designated as belonging to agricultural households. It remains a policy challenge to integrate into cities a migrant population of about 230 million people who are not supposed to be there but are needed for urban and industrial development.

The household registration system or *hukou* system launched in China in 1955 has produced a bifurcated rural and urban system. Under this system, all citizens are classified as belonging to agricultural or non-agricultural households depending on where the family was originally designated, and not on whether the person lives in the city or not. Urban citizens have access to better jobs, better housing, and better education. In addition, they have entitlements to various types of state-supported insurance to cover old age security, hospitalization, medical care, work injury, and unemployment. In contrast, migrant workers do not have access to many of the urban citizenship rights due to their agricultural household registration and their "illegal" status in the city.

Ironically, the rapid economic development of China since the late 1970s has dislodged the surplus labour tied to the land but at the same time institutionalized a two-tiered system of citizenship. Prior to China's adoption of an economic open-door policy in 1979, the *hukou* system was effective in controlling population movements in China since the system was linked to food rationing, employment, and housing entitlement. Since the reform and the proliferation of the free market, food rationing and government job assignment have become obsolete; rural peasants can now move to the city because they have access to the essentials of life. However, they are not officially accepted by municipal and local governments as bona fide urban citizens and are excluded from many benefits that urban citizens enjoy. There are some indications that the central government condones the system of bifurcation as a means to pass on the responsibility and costs of providing universal citizenship benefits by allowing local and municipal governments to devise bureaucratic categories of urban citizenship as a basis of social inclusion or exclusion.

Migrant workers are typically drawn to the more developed regions of China. Eastern China, for example, attracted about 44 percent of the 230 migrant workers in 2009. The highly developed Pearl River Delta region in Guangdong Province absorbed about 30 percent of migrant workers who worked outside their region of registration in 2009.

Official statistics indicate that migrant workers are typically young and not well educated. As a result they tend to take up manual and service jobs in the city. In all, the manufacturing, construction, and service sectors accounted for 68 percent of all migrant workers working outside their region of registration in 2009. At least 39 percent of them had earnings below the 2009 per capita urban disposable income. Ninety percent of migrant workers worked in excess of the 44 hour limit set by the government; most had no access to various types of work-related benefits or insurance protection.

Interview data from the city of Xi'an confirm many of the statistical findings. In addition, the personal stories of migrant workers give a vivid picture of why they came to the city and how they change jobs frequently. Migrant workers express frustration at not being able to send their children to good schools in the city. They show a strong desire to buy an apartment in the city but find it difficult to do so due to their low levels of saving. While many maintain small farm lands in their home village and leave behind some relatives to tend the land, they see themselves as staying permanently in the city. At the same time they worry about not being able to look after themselves when they become old.

Despite the *hukou* household registration system losing the effectiveness of many of its original purposes, it remains an institutional arrangement by which a bifurcated citizenship is produced and sustained. In the long run, such a system is inconsistent with the open-market economic development of China. The continuous arrival of migrant workers in the city and the lack of an attainable process by which such workers can become true urban citizens are creating a substantial social problem for the future.

NOTES

The authors would like to thank Hongming Cheng, Shibao Guo, and Yan Guo for their helpful comments.

1. In 1955, the State Council passed the "Directive Concerning Establishment of a Permanent System of Household Registration" that initiated a countrywide *hukou* system. Prior to 1955, the state established the regulations requiring all residents to notify the local public security organ on change of residence and to apply for a permit to do so. Shortly after the 1955 registration law, the state set up the staple rationing system that included rationing grain, cooking oil, cotton, cloth, and other items by issuing grain-supply cards to registered householders (Cheng and Selden 1994).

2. Unless otherwise stated, statistics regarding characteristics of migrant workers in this section apply to those migrant workers who operated in regions outside their region of household registration.

3. One yuan was about US$0.146 towards the end of 2009.
4. The study was designed by Peter Li and conducted in May 2009 by faculty members and graduate students in the Department of Sociology, Xi'an Jiaotong University. Graduate students in a graduate research method class conducted all the 36 interviews under the guidance of faculty members. Each interview lasted from about one hour to several hours; they were tape recorded and later transcribed.
5. Pseudonyms are used in interview materials cited in this section.
6. One *catty* is equivalent to 500 grams.
7. One *mou* is approximately 0.165 acre.

REFERENCES

Banister, J. 1987. *China's Changing Population*. Stanford: Stanford University Press.
Chan, K.W. 2010. "The Household Registration System and Migrant Labor in China: Notes on a Debate." *Population and Development Review* 36(2):357-64.
Chen, Y. 2005. "Peasant Labor: System and Identity." *Sociological Studies* 3:119-32.
Cheng, T. and M. Selden. 1994. "The Origins and Social Consequences of China's *Hukou* System." *China Quarterly* 139 (September):644-68.
China Daily. 2010. January 22. "China's Urban, Rural Income Gap Widens." At www.chinadaily.com.cn/bizchina/2010-01/22/content_9361049.htm
Finance and Economic Net. 2009. April 1. "State Department Commences System of Monitoring and Surveying Migrant Workers." At www.caijing.com.cn/2009-04-01/110131529.html
Han, D. 2010. "Policing and Racialization of Rural Migrant Workers in Chinese Cities." *Ethnic and Racial Studies* 33(4):593-610.
Howe, C. 1971. *Employment and Economic Growth in Urban China, 1949–1957*. Cambridge: Cambridge University Press.
Kirkby, R.J.R. 1985. *Urbanization in China: Town and Country in a Developing Economy, 1949–2000 A.D.* London: Croom Helm.
Liang, Z. and Z. Ma. 2004. "China's Floating Population: New Evidence from the 2000 Census." *Population and Development Review* 30(3):467-88.
MacFarquhar, R. 1983. *The Origins of the Cultural Revolution*. Vol. 2, *The Great Leap Forward 1958–1960*. New York: Oxford University Press.
National Bureau of Statistics of China. 2010a. *2009 China Statistical Yearbook*. Beijing: China Statistics Press.
—2010b. *2009 Report of Monitoring and Surveying Migrant Workers*. At www.stats. gov.cn/tjfx/fxbg/t20100319 402628281.htm
Selden, M. 1993. *The Political Economy of Chinese Development*. Armonk: M.E. Sharpe.
Windrow, H. and A. Guha. 2005. "The *Hukou* System, Migrant Workers, and State Power in the People's Republic of China." *Northwestern University Journal of International Human Rights* 3 (Spring):1-18.
Zang, L. and G. Wang. 2010. "Urban Citizenship of Rural Migrants in Reform-Era China." *Citizenship Studies* 14(2):145-66.

CHAPTER 6

THE SOCIAL INTEGRATION OF IMMIGRANTS IN FINLAND

TUOMAS MARTIKAINEN, KATHLEEN VALTONEN, AND ÖSTEN WAHLBECK

We begin this overview of immigrant social integration in Finland with a presentation of the national context and the composition of the country's immigrant population, and proceed to discuss and evaluate ideologies, policies, and programs on social integration. Next we highlight certain obstacles to integration, discuss unique aspects of Finnish society, and address future challenges. Our focus is on labour markets and social security, but we also touch on matters related to educational and cultural policy.

Finland, a North European country located by the Baltic Sea, has been an independent nation-state since 1917. From 1809 to 1917 the region was part of Russia and previously had been part of Sweden. Over the course of the twentieth century, Finland changed from a poor, peripheral North European society to a successful welfare state and is today one of the most prosperous Western societies, with a high GNP and low income differences, similar to neighbouring Scandinavian countries. Finnish society is characterized by the Nordic welfare state model, which strives to actively encourage equality among the population of the country. Finland joined the European Union in 1995.

Finland's population was 5.4 million in 2009 (Statistics Finland 2010). Constitutionally it is a bilingual country, with a majority of Finnish speakers, and a Swedish-speaking population of approximately 300,000, mainly living in the coastal regions of the country (McRae 1997). Other well-established, smaller cultural minorities with a long minority history in Finland include (in order of estimated size) Roma, Sami, Jews, and Muslim Tatars. The social rights of Swedish speakers, Sami, and Roma

International Perspectives: Integration and Inclusion, ed. J. Frideres and J. Biles. Montreal and Kingston: Queen's Policy Studies Series, McGill-Queen's University Press. © 2012 The School of Policy Studies, Queen's University at Kingston. All rights reserved.

are stated on the constitutional level, and the constitution also includes a general clause regarding the protection of the linguistic and cultural rights of all minorities (Constitution of Finland 1999, Section 17).

Historically, Finland has been a relatively multicultural meeting place between East and West, but it did not experience major immigration in the post–World War II reconstruction period (Joronen, Pajarinen, and Ylä-Anttila 2002). It became a country of immigration after the end of the Cold War and in the era of globalization. Political changes in the neighbouring Soviet Union in the early 1990s made immigration from the East possible, and increased economic prosperity made Finland more attractive for immigrants. The country has developed an integration policy within the framework of its traditional Nordic welfare state policies. The resettlement of so-called quota refugees, selected in cooperation with the UNHCR, started in 1979 and grew in the late 1980s. Thus, integration policies were initially focused on the resettlement of refugees.

The Nordic welfare state ideology includes a strong emphasis on the role of work for the integration of all citizens. Employment for all citizens retains high priority, and different measures to battle unemployment constitute a central part of the postwar welfare state policies. The principle that everyone of working age should be active in the labour market has been regarded as a primary way to prevent social exclusion (Svallfors, Halvorsen, and Andersen 2001; Blomberg-Kroll 2004). The strong emphasis on employment has consequences for immigrant integration policies, which are primarily focused on integrating immigrants into the labour market (cf. Valtonen 1998; Wahlbeck 2007).

The Finnish welfare state has, however, undergone considerable change since the 1990s. This restructuring has been described as a move from a "planning economy" to a "competition economy" (Alasuutari 2006), which is captured in the notions of "competitiveness society" (Heiskala 2006) and "project society" (Sulkunen 2006). The restructuring is part of a broader global trend of neoliberal policies whereby the state to an extent retreats from some of its previous societal core functions or at least redefines its role in service provision and opens new spaces for market forces to operate (cf. Arestis and Sawyer 2005; MacGregor 2005).

While the net effects of these changes are complex and layered in changing forms of governance,[1] they have led to, among other outcomes, outsourcing and privatization of welfare services, and the growth of projects. Previous structures have to some extent been replaced, eroded, or complemented by more temporary and market-based solutions. While the implementation of these policies has proceeded unevenly in different societal sectors, they are noteworthy in immigrant integration services, as integration policy has developed simultaneously with state restructuration, and hence there has been less institutionalized friction and opposition to change.

A Brief History of Immigration

International migration in Finland has ebbed and flowed significantly during the last 150 years with varying patterns of emigration and immigration. The country has experienced two main periods of emigration. The first was from the 1860s until the 1930s, when up to 350,000 people crossed the Atlantic to the United States and Canada (Kero 1997, 13). In the second period, over 560,000 Finns moved to Sweden since World War II, especially in the 1960s and 1970s, where they still form the largest minority of postwar immigrants (Korkiasaari 2000, 156; Statistics Finland 2010). Both of these migration waves were economically motivated and coincided with structural changes in Finnish society. An estimated 1.2 million Finns and their descendants are living abroad today (Koivukangas 2002, 25).

· Immigration to Finland has been minor in comparison and has to a large extent consisted of return migration from North America and Sweden (Kero 1996, 255; Korkiasaari 2000, 160-1). The major exceptions are related to both forced and voluntary population movements during the two world wars. It is also worth noting that Finland needed to resettle 425,000 people – 10 percent of the total population at the time – due to loss of territory to the Soviet Union after World War II (Korkiasaari 2000, 137). Overall, from a Western European perspective, Finland was until the 1980s a country of emigration like Ireland and Portugal.

Net migration turned positive during the 1980s and rose rapidly after the collapse of the Soviet Union in 1991 and again in the 2000s. This period coincided with the Finnish economy's opening to global market, membership in the European Union, and heightened globalization (Forsander 2002a, 25-6). The growth can be characterized by increasing diversity in both countries of origin and reasons for migration, even though most of it is from areas nearby. Of a total population of 5.4 million by the end of 2009, the number of foreign born people was 233,000, 4.4 percent of the total population. However, as late as 1980, the number was less than 40,000 (Statistics Finland 2010).

The new immigration to Finland has been very heterogeneous, consisting of marriage-related immigration and immigration of low-skilled and high-skilled employees, entrepreneurs, international students, and refugees and asylum seekers. Alongside other return migrants, some 20,000 to 30,000 ethnic Finns – so-called Ingrians – have moved from the former Soviet Union to Finland since the early 1990s. Even the numbers of the foreign temporary workforce have increased. The most common reason to move to Finland, though barely noticed in public and political discourse (Forsander 2002a, 17-22; Martikainen 2007), has been family related. It has been estimated that between 1990 and 2010 about 60–65 percent of all immigration was family related, while the rest was composed mainly of refugees (15 percent), returnees (10 percent), work migrants (5–10 percent), and others (5–10 percent, e.g., students) (Ministry of Labour 2006a, 15).

The largest groups of immigrants originate from neighbouring countries, especially from the areas of the former Soviet Union and Western Europe, but significant numbers of immigrants also come from developing countries. Figure 1 illustrates foreign born population by area of birth from 1990 to 2009. It shows that the vast majority of immigrants are from Europe, but also that the share of African and Asian migrants has risen somewhat. The four largest foreign nationality groups as of 31 December 2009 were citizens of Russia (28,210), Estonia (25,510), Sweden (8,506), and Somalia (5,570) (Statistics Finland 2010). Many immigrants, however, have already been naturalized. Refugees have arrived both as asylum seekers and within the framework of organized resettlement programs administered by the UNHCR (cf. Wahlbeck 1999). Between 1973 and 2008, Finland accepted altogether 31,769 quota refugees, asylum seekers, and their family members, about 15 percent of all immigrants in that period (Statistics Finland 2009, 7).

FIGURE 1
Foreign Born Population by Area of Birth in Finland, 1990–2009

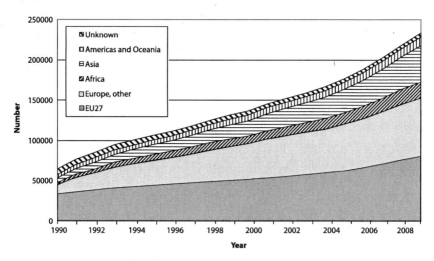

Source: Statistics Finland (2010).

Almost half of all immigrants live in the vicinity of the Helsinki metropolitan area. More immigrants live in the larger cities than rural areas, where the number of immigrants is small. However, some small municipalities have refugee reception centres, and in certain areas, a temporary foreign workforce is periodically used in agriculture. Also, many Russians live in southeast Finland, often due to (female-dominated) marriage migration. The age and gender structures of migrant groups from different countries of origin vary greatly. For instance, groups of refugee origin are on average younger and have a balanced gender structure because of the family reunification policy. Migrants from countries dominated by other reasons for migration tend to be older, with either a male or female bias, reflecting Finnish men and women's international spousal preferences.[2] Fertility rates between various groups also differ (Martikainen 2007; Statistics Finland 2010).

An issue of emerging focus is children of immigrants born in Finland, i.e., the second generation (Martikainen 2009). Martikainen and Haikkola (2010, 30) have estimated that approximately 8 percent of all children born in Finland after 1988 have at least one immigrant parent. As migration has grown since the 1990s, this implies that the majority of the second generation is rather young. The age structure of the first generation (born abroad), second generation (born in Finland to two immigrant parents) and 2.5 generation (born in Finland to one immigrant and one native parent) in 2007 is presented in Figure 2.[3] It shows that the first generation is mainly people of working age and that the second and 2.5 generations are predominantly under the age of twenty. It should be noted, though, that at the time of arrival approximately one-fifth of the migrants have been under the age of fifteen (Martikainen 2007, 48-9). While statistical information on the second generation is still scarce, it is known that the total size of second and 2.5 generations was 120,000 in December 2007 (Väänänen et al. 2009, 15). Altogether the first, second, and 2.5 generations constituted about 6 percent of the total population in 2007.

FIGURE 2
Age Structure of First, Second, and 2.5 Generations in Finland, 2007

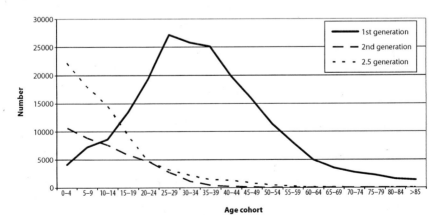

Source: Statistics Finland (2009); Väänänen et al. (2009, 15).

How Does Finland Define "Social Integration"?

The definition of social integration of immigrants in Finland is outlined in several official publications and legal documents. Finnish laws and regulations concerning immigration have been the object of many debates and have gone through constant changes (cf. Lepola 2000). However, the general understanding of the process of social integration has stayed more or less the same since the arrival of the first major refugee and immigrant groups in the late 1980s.

In this context, the most central legal document is the *Act on the Integration of Immigrants and Reception of Asylum Seekers* (*Integration Act 1999*), which came into force on 1 May 1999. According to the first section of this law, the purpose of the act is to promote the integration, equality, and freedom of choice of immigrants through measures that help them acquire the essential knowledge and skills required to function in society. Furthermore in section 2 of the act, "integration" is explicitly defined as follows:

1) *Integration* means the personal development of immigrants, aimed at participation in working life and society while preserving their own language and culture; and
2) integration also means the measures taken and resources and service provided by the authorities to promote and support such integration, and consideration for the needs of immigrants in planning and providing other public services and measures. (*Integration Act 1999*, Section 2)

Two central features of the way social integration is understood in Finland are evident already in first sections of the act mentioned above. Firstly, the major focus is on the individual's integration in the labour market, and secondly, on the active involvement of the welfare state institutions in this process. The later sections of the act outline the division of labour between different state institutions and local government institutions in this process. Thus, refugees and immigrants in Finland are easily perceived as clients of the welfare state institutions.

The Ministry of the Interior, since 1 January 2008, has been responsible for the general development and coordination of immigration and integration policies, including the reception of asylum seekers. However, as outlined in the *Integration Act* (1999), the implementation of integration policies is the responsibility of regional and local authorities. The regional Employment and Economic Development Centres[4] are responsible for the regional coordination of the integration of immigrants. These centres, jointly with the Employment Offices, are responsible for providing labour market services that promote and support the integration of immigrants. These regional government institutions are also responsible for the possible instruction in reading and writing and for basic education for adult immigrants registered as job-seekers.

The Employment Offices and respective municipalities cooperate in the organization of measures and services to promote and support integration, and in the provision of information about them. In the end, the local municipalities have the general and coordinative responsibility for developing, planning, and monitoring the integration of immigrants residing in the municipality. As outlined in the *Integration Act* (1999), the municipalities organize measures and services promoting and supporting the integration of immigrants. In practice, this is largely an economic issue decided within the framework of the municipal budget. As described below, immigrants belonging to certain groups should receive a personalized integration plan drawn up jointly by the individual, the employment office, and the municipality. In the municipality this plan is often the task of social workers.

The main focus of the official integration measures in Finland are refugees and immigrants who live permanently in the country. In practice, most integration measures have targeted only a limited selection of immigrants, mainly refugees, for whose needs most of the services were initially created. In general, rights and services in Finland tend to be connected to whether one is a permanent resident of the country or not. Most public services are provided by the municipalities, who provide services to everyone, regardless of nationality, who is a permanent resident of the municipality. The National Health Insurance System also equally covers everybody who lives permanently in the country. Thus, the immigrant integration policies are in Finland implemented at the local level. It can be argued that, in general, all permanently settled immigrants have relatively strong social rights (cf. Wahlbeck 2008). However, the question is to what extent these social rights can be realized and whether the structures of Finnish society really permit true social integration of immigrants. All foreign citizens who have lived in the country permanently for two years have the right to vote in the local elections. To vote in the state elections, however, Finnish citizenship is required.

The *Integration Act* (1999) also names the preservation of immigrants' "own language and culture" as an explicit goal. This is an explicit statement for multiculturalism or collectivism (cf. Constitution of Finland 1999, Section 17) and has led to the development of educational and cultural policy supporting linguistic and cultural diversity. For example, funding is available to immigrant associations, at both municipal and state levels, to conduct cultural activities. Furthermore, elementary and high schools are obliged to provide education in the pupil's own language and religion, once there is sufficient demand. The teaching of minority religions and certain minority languages at schools predates contemporary integration legislation but has expanded due to immigration since the 1990s (Ministry of Education 2009; Saukkonen 2010).

POLICIES AND PROGRAMS TO PROMOTE SOCIAL INTEGRATION

The range of policies and programs with potential for promoting social integration of immigrants is broad, since the comprehensive social security system with its social insurance, social services, and welfare arrangements is available to all immigrants settling on a permanent basis. Individuals are considered to be settling permanently when they move as returning migrants, refugees, or asylum seekers who have been granted a residence permit valid for at least 12 months. Permanent residence status is granted also to persons coming to Finland for family reasons or to those having a regular job in Finland for a period of at least two years (Ministry of Labour 2003). While immigrant and refugee settlement takes place in the context of the state welfare system, the policies are implemented and shaped to a critical extent at local municipal level. Every individual establishing permanent residence becomes a resident of some municipality. There were 342 municipalities in Finland in 2010.

Integration services were fashioned as an outgrowth of the welfare system in response to the initiation of the UNHCR quota refugee reception program in the latter 1980s. Over the next two decades this bundle of services and benefits was honed in various ways to cater primarily to the integration related needs of "forced" migrants and their relatives arriving under the family reunification program. However, the need for integration services for other settling groups is now seen as an important area for attention. With increasing ethnocultural and socioeconomic diversity among refugee cohorts and gradual numerical growth of immigrants in general, issues of entitlement and degrees of entitlement to integration services have come to the fore. One outstanding question is how the Finnish welfare state will adapt, respond to, and also affect future immigration.

Social policy in Finland has been developed within the frame of "social citizenship," and is seen as the operationalization of social rights that focus in a substantive way on programs and services in the areas of health, education, housing, the labour market, and social and welfare services. Social security benefits include, for example, family allowance, sickness allowance, unemployment allowance, and national pensions. Parental leaves related to the birth of a child, child-care, and early childhood education, cash benefits for parents, child-care subsidies, and child home care allowances are central components of family policy.

Subject to certain basic conditions (such as being unemployed and / or a recipient of income support, having been given a Social Security number), immigrants settling permanently in the country have the right to a personal integration plan as a means of utilizing existing vocational guidance resources and effectively consolidating their integration activities. The integration plan might include, for example, language training, work experience, general education, vocational training, or professional development. Individuals with integration plans can receive a labour market subsidy for a maximum of three years, as a form of integration assistance (Ministry of Labour 2003, 2006a, 2006b).

Effective language instruction and labour market training programs are hallmarks of the Finnish settlement program. Labour market training can be viewed as the state's investment in ethnic equality and its thrust to expand the skill base in the immigrant labour force. Special orientation services that target resettling refugees automatically include Finnish language education, which generally extends over a period of three years. Similar to mainstream basic and higher education activity in Finland, this period is underwritten by income support mechanisms that facilitate participation. In families with children, child-care services enable both parents to take part in language courses in the early years of residence. State child-care programs, as gender equity promoting services, have in principle improved female immigrants' formal position in the labour market and facilitated their participation in paid employment (Valtonen 1997). Women have been included as important participants in the labour market and guaranteed the right to choose between paid work and full-time care work in the family (Satka 1993). The fact that immigrants often face a situation in which their qualifications are not recognized in practice (see, for example, Forsander 2002a) weakens the effectiveness of programs that should promote labour market participation.

Asylum seekers who are minors and who arrive without a guardian are accommodated in group homes or family group homes. Children are always placed in a group home while the situation is assessed. Unaccompanied minors who have relatives can be placed with them once the assessment has been made. In the initial period, children of school age attend a preparatory training class intended for immigrants (*Integration Act* 1999).

Projects have become the key platform for developing immigrant services. A survey by Ruhanen and Martikainen (2006) of 139 immigrant projects from the late 1990s to ca. 2005 found that about three out of four projects were related to improving immigrants' labour market skills, providing educational opportunities, and improving general integration practices; the remainder focused on special target groups, mainly women. Most of the projects dealt with people of refugee background, but efforts have been made to reach other targeted groups as well. Many projects are run by local and state authorities, but private companies and NGOs also have a strong presence. Major sources of funding are a few national and European funds, notably Finland's Slot Machine Association and the European Social Fund. The extent of the project environment is difficult to estimate as, beyond external funding, projects have become vital instruments in developing activities in general. Often they have a number of partners, including steering group representation and other forms of networking, and a diversity of funding. We could even argue that much of the national integration discourse in the public and third sectors is on the shifting emphasis of funding opportunities.

EVALUATION OF POLICIES AND PROGRAMS

The welfare system has been argued to be one of the most important inclusion mechanisms, as the basic accessibility of benefits and services is seen as a fundamental "enabling" mechanism that reinforces wide participation in other areas of Finnish society. It is becoming increasingly recognized, however, that membership in the welfare state has not of itself opened the doors to full participation, especially in the areas of employment and higher education (Valtonen 2008). The scope of social security programs cannot compensate for needed structural modifications that would promote participation in the labour market.

A smaller percentage of immigrants are part of the labour force compared to the general population, which can be explained by the higher than average number among immigrants of people receiving education and women staying at home taking care of children. Among the immigrant population of working age in 2009, about 60 percent were part of the labour force, while the percentage was about 75 percent among the total population (Ministry of the Interior 2009). The unemployment level is higher among immigrants in the labour force than among Finnish citizens – in general, three times higher. In December 2007, during a relatively good economic period, the unemployment rate was 21.5 percent among immigrants and 6.8 among the total population. However, there are significant differences in the unemployment rate between different nationality groups and genders. In 2007, the unemployment among female immigrants was 25.2 percent and among male immigrants 15.8 percent. As described in Figure 3, there is also a large difference in the unemployment rate among different nationality groups.

The unemployment rate seems to be particularly high among nationality groups characterized by a refugee background. For example, in 2007, the highest unemployment rate (65 percent) was among Iraqi nationals, who also have constituted one the largest refugee groups in 2000–10 (ibid.).

The high level of immigrant unemployment, coupled with inclusive labour market programs to build the language and other human capital of immigrants, indicates structural obstacles to immigrant hiring and employment. While considerable progress has been made in equivalency procedures in the fields of medicine and information and communications technology (ICT), generally immigrants with higher educational or professional background meet a decisive career path impasse, since their qualifications and experience are rarely recognized (Forsander 2002b; Ministry of the Interior 2009). This non-commodification of immigrants' human capital calls for formal intervention to overcome this barrier. This issue

FIGURE 3
Unemployment Rate among Finnish and Foreign Citizens in Finland, December 2007

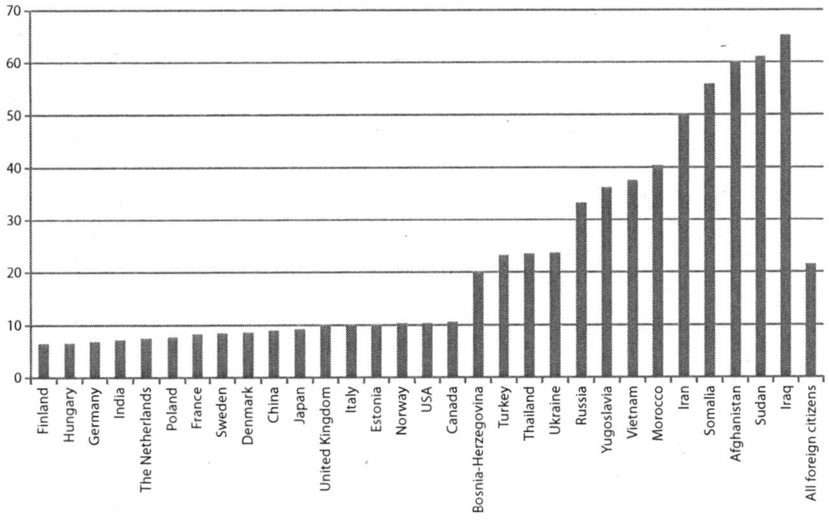

Source: Ministry of the Interior (2009).

has been raised in recent times in the public debate. With regard to social security, individuals with large gaps in their employment record are in a weak position since the main components of social insurance (sickness/disability; unemployment; pensions) are earnings related. The universal flat-rate benefits are low and can be supplemented by the last resort of means-tested, discretionary payments of income support. In this situation, however, individuals in chronic unemployment eventually become relegated to peripheral areas of the social welfare system.

In the educational sector, some immigrant groups are underachieving in comparison to the majority population (Kuusela et al. 2008), even though they are gaining higher education than their parents (Kilpi 2010). Again, the groups that seem to be hardest hit are those of a refugee background, despite the fact that socio-economic background explains part of the differences. Some of the differences appear to be related to a lack of social support networks at crucial stages of transition, but also parental under- or over-expectations, as well as discrimination. However, signs of over-achievement are also present, as elsewhere in Europe (cf. Heath, Rothon, and Kilpi 2008).

Findings in cultural policy show inconsistent results as well; Saukkonen (2010) notes a lack of support for immigrant specific needs as the majority has a tendency to view immigrant issues as separate from normalized activities. Hence, there seems to be a large degree of institutional inertia that does not recognize the special needs of minority groups in general.

At least part of institutional difficulties in responding to new needs can be related to the emergence of the "project society." While all public institutions have to a degree undergone structural changes, some are more affected than others. Activities in immigrant affairs have been developed by and through projects and thus have often remained in the periphery of institutional power.

The concentration of integration measures under state and local municipal responsibility has advantages in that funding is relatively secure, and standards can be monitored. However, this model clusters the linking activity of immigrants with authorities and officials, making for relations of "clienthood" (Valtonen 2008). As mentioned above, the service delivery of the institutional welfare system, including integration services, is being partially devolved to the third sector although subsidized by the state, European Union, and national lottery funds. There is also rather high-profile multicultural project activity sector that has integration aims. In this sector, as in the mainstream social and human service delivery arena, immigrants' productive participation as actors and service providers needs to be placed strategically on the policy agenda (cf. Valtonen 2008; Tuori 2009).

WHAT ARE THE MAIN ISSUES IN ACHIEVING THE SOCIAL INTEGRATION OF IMMIGRANTS?

The international regime is directing attention to ways in which the benefits of global migration can be harnessed (UNDP 2009). One of the main areas of focus is on the utilization, exchange, transfer, and building of human capital. In the main, these processes must take place on the local level, with attention paid to structural barriers in national labour markets. Moreover, participation in the labour market proper is the only sustainable path to integration for the majority of immigrants. Thus a prime indicator of integration is representation of persons of immigrant background across the different sectors of employment and at all levels in workplaces.

Despite the measures taken by Finnish authorities to support integration in the labour market, many immigrants are in a disadvantaged position. They are overrepresented among the segments of people who are the last to be hired and the first to let go, depending on the economic situation (Forsander 2002a, 283). Furthermore, because of the difficulties in getting into the general labour market, some immigrants end up as self-employed. Self-employed immigrants often work under difficult economic and social conditions in the restaurant sector, which does not support a true social integration (Wahlbeck 2007). Annika Forsander (2002a), who has done the most extensive study of immigrants' position in the Finnish labour market, argues that access to that market seems to be hampered by many different factors. According to Forsander, the Nordic welfare state is based on the ideal of national homogeneity, and social structures do not adapt easily to respond to the growing diversity of present-day society. Furthermore, the immigrants who manage to get a job often remain in a vulnerable position. The various obstacles they face in getting access to the labour market have obvious negative consequences for their social integration into Finnish society.

The Finnish labour market largely seems to be closed to many immigrants, but those who do manage to enter are well protected by the law. General legal practices in the labour market as well as the legal access of immigrants to the labour market were rated as very good in Finland in a recent evaluation of EU countries by the Migrant Integration Policy Index (MIPEX). Finland represented the best practice on the security of employment and rights associated with work, including anti-discrimination legislation (MIPEX 2010). This good legal position of immigrants is in sharp contrast to the above-mentioned serious problems immigrants face in getting into the labour market. Although a good legal framework is in place, the social and economic reality in the Finnish labour market does not support the social integration of all immigrants.

Responsibility for the implementation of settlement and integration policies lies with regional and local authorities. Progressive policy interpretation at the municipal level as well as the effective operation of integration-oriented programs places a singular demand on municipalities. In many cases, there is a need to draw in new ideas and vision as well as appropriate expertise in areas of diversity. Institutional capacity-building to manage diversity is critical if the benefits of human mobility are to be recognized and reaped. The difficulties of knowledge transfer can in part be attributed to the vast differences in local immigrant populations and their histories. Whereas policy and services have responded fairly extensively in larger urban settlements, smaller municipalities have remained outside these information flows. Further, actors in the field have identified a chronic lack of resources (e.g., Saukkonen 2010).

UNIQUE ASPECTS OF SOCIAL INTEGRATION IN FINLAND

Finland is a developed welfare state with strong social rights and integration measures, yet the integration of immigrants in the general labour market has been slow and difficult. This specific feature of Finnish society has been outlined by Kathleen Valtonen (2001, 2004), who argues that "citizenship has been compromised by lack of specific anti-discrimination mechanisms that would strengthen immigrants' exercise of civil rights to equal treatment in the labour market" (2004, 92). According to Valtonen,

Finnish society features a specific form of "differential exclusion" where strong social rights of immigrants can occur alongside weak labour market status.

The official integration policy of Finland shows characteristics of multiculturalism or collectivism and is composed of three main blocs: (1) integration of individual immigrants to Finnish society, and especially to working life; (2) the right of ethnic and cultural communities to preserve their distinct identity; and (3) accommodation of Finnish society and population to changed circumstances (Valtioneuvosto 2008, 17). According to Pasi Saukkonen (2010), Finnish integration policies in practice, however, are more pragmatic than ideological and more assimilative than often presumed. The focus has mostly been on the integration of individuals, while support for communities has remained at a low level. Despite many accommodations in society, it remains open as to how deeply existing practices and attitudes have changed. In general, integration programs have been constantly under-resourced in relation to official policy goals.

Another peculiarity of Finnish integration policy is that it was originally designed to cater to the needs of forced migrants and, to a lesser extent, Ingrian returnees. This focus has left other migrant groups at the outskirts of integration measures, despite recognition of their needs. Labour migration has received more attention in policy debates in the past decade, but a coherent and holistic integration policy is yet to emerge. In this sense the situation is in marked contrast to many West European countries where labour migration has played a more dominant role in public policy and debates.

FUTURE CHALLENGES

Immigrant integration has gradually climbed on the national political agenda, although many politicians have been reluctant to take strong stances on what has been regarded as a contentious issue. However, about 2005 the Finnish government started proposing an active immigration policy to combat a feared future labour shortage created by a rapidly aging population. This initiative implies a shift from reactive to proactive migration policy and from refugee to labour migrant issues. Since the municipal elections of October 2008, immigration and integration policies have become increasingly controversial, and anti-immigration sentiments played a role in the parliamentary elections of March 2011. The political consequences still remain open, but as the new parliament now has a vocal anti-immigration lobby, further politicization of immigration and integration policies can be expected.

A current focus of national policy-making is on broadening the scope of immigration discourses and policy beyond labour migrants and refugees, in order to achieve more holistic policies as diversity increases in the immigrant population. Contemporary forms of immigration and transnational mobility present novel challenges for a system that is based on the notion of permanent settlement. Circular migration, international student mobility, and increasing contract work inside the EU are examples of migratory flows that are expected to grow. The importance of new transnational communities and diasporas will become more evident in politics, culture, and the economy. A nation-state centred view of migration management is not likely to succeed, and the contemporary politicization of social cohesion, immigration policy, and immigrant integration poses new challenges that may tempt some to political opportunism to gain short-term victories.

In the same vein, after two decades of the "new migration," we can better assess limits in the capacity of the mature welfare state structure to function as the prime vehicle for immigrant incorporation. It would be timely to consider the potential of immigrant incorporation strategies outside the frame and constraints of the welfare state. Energies, synergies, and initiatives in the broader and "informal" domains of human activity and interaction can be more strongly supported and valued as quality components to integration measures. Community organization activity and collaborative programs that involve immigrant partners in joint decision-making as well as resource-sharing are invaluable bridging mechanisms with the potential of lowering existing institutional thresholds. Much needed proactive on-the-ground integration efforts can only be done on collaborative and power-sharing bases. Growing diversity in the immigrant population opens opportunities for developing new forms of two-way solidarities that underpin integration.

Although the scope of future labour shortages remains open, labour migration will likely continue to grow in importance due to further family migration, increasing international marriages, and diversification of the population in the long run. The apparent difficulty of Finland's labour markets to accommodate already existing immigrants casts doubt on how economically effective future labour migration can be. If the labour markets do not open more effectively, there is a major risk of ethnification and the social exclusion as at least part of both current and future migrants are consigned to the less desirable segments of working life (Wrede and Nordberg 2010). Existing ethnic hierarchies have hit visible minorities and other stigmatized groups the hardest (Jaakkola 2009, 52-60), as is already evident in the immigrant unemployment figures discussed above.

Another long-term challenge is to what extent the Finnish welfare state will be able to compensate for the disadvantage to those of the second generation whose parents have suffered from unemployment and lack of human and social capital and other skills needed in Finnish society. This issue cannot be solved by integration or educational policy alone but rather is related to general structural features of society, as income differences and variations in life opportunities in different social groups have increased over the past two decades (Riihelä, Sullström, and Tuomala 2004). In this sense, the children of immigrants may be good indicators of future social change in Finland.

The humanitarian overtones of the initial resettlement program for UNHCR quota refugees were instrumental in facilitating what we see today as the first phase of the "new" migration to Finland. Resettling refugees of Vietnamese, Kurdish, Iranian, Iraqi, and Somalian descent has paved the way for the ethnocultural diversity that is more evident in the current population. Much of the achieved accommodation on the part of the majority and minority groups is not visible and inevitably is not measured or acknowledged. Successful acculturation is unlikely to take place unless the newer citizens can get to assume more socially visible and valued roles of responsibility in economic and social life. In the case of immigrant integration, the pivotal issue of equality becomes one of role sharing in the mainstream of public life.

To some extent, Finland has benefited from experiencing immigration slightly later than many other Western European countries. At least in principle, this has made it possible to learn from possible mistakes elsewhere and adopt recognized good practices in other countries. However, despite good intentions, Finnish immigration policies often seem to be too much guided by various short-term domestic political and economic goals rather than a coherent long-term integration policy.

CONCLUSION

Finland, a Nordic welfare society, has become an immigration society mainly since the 1990s. Its official policy of social integration is a version of multiculturalism that is focused on labour market integration but gives space to linguistic and ethno-cultural diversity. In practice, however, more resources are dedicated to labour market integration than to other types of integration activities. The results are mixed, and a large portion of immigrants have remained outside of the labour force or unemployed. People of refugee background have had the greatest difficulties. Nevertheless, the differences between individuals and groups are large, and there is not one single trajectory for social integration.

Paradoxically, despite the labour shortage that is predicted for the future, many of the immigrants already in the country find it difficult to get access to the labour market. In Finland the supply and the demand for labour clearly do not meet, but there are also indications that immigrants are discriminated against and that the marginalization and exclusion they often experience in the general labour market are reflected in a relatively high rate of unemployment. Furthermore, the jobs available to them tend to be unskilled and insecure.

The future of Finnish welfare society is open, and it is premature to evaluate the broader significance of post-1990 changes in welfare state structures. We may, however, estimate that immigrants are especially vulnerable to a thinning of state support, if inclusionary mechanisms do not improve. Immigrants initially lack many of the skills and networks needed for social mobility, but if their children too cannot achieve those, then the welfare project has failed them.

NOTES

The article has been written in association with Transnational and Local: The Social Integration of Immigrant Communities Project, funded by the Academy of Finland (project no. 131720). The authors would also like to thank Dr Pasi Saukkonen for his comments on the manuscript, many of which were taken into account.

1. Brenner, Peck, and Theodore (2010, 189) argue that "market-oriented regulatory reform ... [is] associated with unpredictable 'layering' effects in relation to inherited institutional landscapes," which also makes the evaluation of these changes a demanding task of case-by-case analysis, because the changes take different forms in different social structures and are embedded as well in "transnational fields of policy transfer" (ibid.).
2. An example of an almost single-gender dominated immigration stream in Finland is Thais, of whom 78 percent were women, predominantly women in their twenties, thirties, and forties, whereas most Thai male immigrants were under the age of twenty and likely the children of Thai women immigrants. Immigration of Thai women began growing in the 1990s and was based on increased tourism to Thailand, where many Finnish men found spouses.
3. For the definitions of immigrant generations, see Rumbaut 2007.
4. On 1 January 2010, the regional Employment and Economic Centres were merged with the former Road Districts, Regional Environmental Centres and State Provincial Offices. These regional state authorities formed 15 new centres called "Centres for Economic Development, Transport and the Environment."

REFERENCES

Alasuutari, P. 2006. "Suunnittelutaloudesta kilpailutalouteen: miten muutos oli ideologisesti mahdollinen?" (From planning economy to competition economy: How was the change ideologically possible?). In *Uusi jako: Miten Suomesta tuli kilpailukyky-yhteiskunta?* (New deal: How did Finland become a competitiveness society?), ed. R. Heiskala and E. Luhtakallio, 43-64. Helsinki: Gaudeamus.
Arestis, P. and M. Sawyer. 2005. "Neoliberalism and the Third Way." In *Neoliberalism: A Critical Reader*, ed. A. Saad-Filho and D. Johnston, 177-83. London: Pluto Press.
Blomberg-Kroll, H. 2004. "Integration through Work in a Multicultural Society?" In *New Challenges for the Welfare Society*, ed. Vesa Puuronen et al., 237-54. Joensuu: University of Joensuu.

Brenner, N., J. Peck, and N. Theodore. 2010. "Variegated Neoliberalization: Geographies, Modalities, Pathways." *Global Networks* 10(2):182-222.

Constitution of Finland (731/1999). 1999. At http://www.finlex.fi/fi/laki/kaannokset/1999/en19990731.pdf.

Forsander, A. 2002a. *Luottamuksen ehdot: Maahanmuuttajat 1990-luvun suomalaisilla työmarkkinoilla* (Conditions of trust: Immigrants in the 1990s Finnish labour market). Helsinki: Väestöliitto.

—ed. 2002b. *Immigration and Economy in the Globalization Process: The Case of Finland*. Helsinki: Sitra.

Heath, A., C. Rothon, and E. Kilpi. 2008. "The Second Generation in Western Europe: Education, Unemployment, and Occupational Attainment." *Annual Review of Sociology* 34:211-35.

Heiskala, R. 2006. "Kansainvälisen toimintaympäristön muutos ja Suomen yhteiskunnallinen murros" (Changes in international environment and the societal change in Finland). In *Uusi jako: Miten Suomesta tuli kilpailukyky-yhteiskunta?* (New deal: How did Finland become a competitiveness society?), ed. R. Heiskala and E. Luhtakallio, 14-43. Helsinki: Gaudeamus.

Integration Act (Act on the Integration of Immigrants and Reception of Asylum Seekers [493/1999]). 1999. At www.finlex.fi/en/laki/kaannokset/1999/en19990493.pdf

Jaakkola, M. 2009. *Maahanmuuttajat suomalaisten näkökulmasta: Asennemuutokset 1987–2007* (Immigrants from a Finnish point of view: Attitude changes over 1987–2007). Helsinki: Helsingin kaupungin tietokeskus.

Joronen, T., M. Pajarinen, and P. Ylä-Anttila. 2002. "From Hanseatic Trade to Hamburger Chains – A Historical Survey." In *Immigration and Economy in the Globalization Process: The Case of Finland*, ed. A. Forsander, 48-65. Helsinki: Sitra.

Kero, R. 1996. *Suureen länteen: Siirtolaisuus Suomesta Pohjois-Amerikkaan* (To the Great West: Immigration from Finland to North America). Turku: Siirtolaisuusinstituutti.

—1997. *Suomalaisina Pohjois-Amerikassa: Siirtolaiselämää Yhdysvalloissa ja Kanadassa* (As Finns in North America: Immigrant life in the United States and Canada). Turku: Siirtolaisuusinstituutti.

Kilpi. E. 2010. "Toinen sukupolvi peruskoulun päättyessä ja toisen asteen koulutuksessa" (The second generation after high school and in secondary education). In *Maahanmuutto ja sukupolvet* (Immigration and generations), ed. T. Martikainen and L. Haikkola, 110-132. Helsinki: Suomalaisen Kirjallisuuden Seura.

Koivukangas, O. 2002. "The Need for Multicultural Approach in Finland." In *Entering Multiculturalism: Finnish Experience Abroad*, ed. O. Koivukangas, 24-35. Turku: Institute of Migration.

Korkiasaari, J. 2000. "Suomalaiset Ruotsissa 1940-luvulta 2000-luvulle (Finns in Sweden from the 1940s to 2000s)." In *Suomalaiset Ruotsissa* (Finns in Sweden), 135-496. Turku: Siirtolaisuusinstituutti,

Kuusela, J., A. Etelälahti, Å. Hagman, R. Hievanen, K. Karppinen, L. Nissilä, U. Rönnberg, and M. Siniharju. 2008. *Maahanmuuttajaoppilaat ja koulutus – Tutkimus oppimistuloksista, koulutusvalinnoista ja työllistämisestä* (Immigrant students and education – A study of educational results, educational choices and employment). Helsinki: Opetushallitus.

Lepola, O. 2000. *Ulkomaalaisesta suomenmaalaiseksi* (From foreigner to Finlander). Helsinki: Suomalaisen Kirjallisuuden Seura.

MacGregor, S. 2005. "The Welfare State and Neoliberalism." In *Neoliberalism: A Critical Reader*, ed. A. Saad-Filho and D. Johnston, 142-8. London: Pluto Press.

Martikainen, T. 2007. "Maahanmuuttajaväestön sukupuolittuneisuus, perheellistyminen ja sukupolvisuus" (The gender, family, and generational structure of the immigrant population). In *Maahanmuuttajanaiset: Kotoutuminen, perhe ja työ* (Immigrant women: Integration, family, and work), ed. T. Martikainen and M. Tiilikainen, 38-67. Helsinki: Väestöliitto.

—2009. "The Study of Immigrant Youth in Finland." *Forum 21: European Journal on Child and Youth Research* 4 (December):23-7.

Martikainen, T. and L. Haikkola. 2010. "Johdanto: Sukupolvet maahanmuuttajatutkimuksessa" (Introduction: Generations in immigrant research). In *Maahanmuutto ja sukupolvet* (Immigration and generations), ed. T. Martikainen and L. Haikkola, 9-43. Helsinki: Suomalaisen Kirjallisuuden Seura.

McRae, K.D. 1997. *Conflict and Compromise in Multilingual Societies: Finland*. Waterloo: Wilfrid Laurier University Press.

Ministry of Education. 2009. *Opetusministeriön maahanmuuttopoliittiset linjaukset* (Ministry of Education's policies of immigration). Helsinki: Opetusministeriö.

Ministry of Labour. 2003. *A Home in Finland: Information for Immigrants about Living, Studying and Social Security*. Helsinki: Ministry of Labour.

—2006a. *Työministeriön selvitys eduskunnan hallintovaliokunnalle maahanmuuttajista aiheutuvista kustannuksista* (A report of the Ministry of Labour of the expenses of immigrants to the Administration Committee of Parliament). Helsinki: Työministeriö.

—2006b. *Finland: Your New Home. Information on Integration for Immigrants*. Helsinki: Ministry of Labour.

Ministry of the Interior. 2009. *Maahanmuuttajien työllistyminen ja kannustinloukut* (Employment of immigrants and inactivity traps). Helsinki: Ministry of the Interior At http://www.intermin.fi/intermin/biblio.nsf/D5A6B24123947AC EC225754C004B836E/$file/22009.pdf

Migrant Integration Policy Index (MIPEX). 2010. "Country Profiles: Finland." At www.integrationindex.eu/topics/2355.html

Riihelä, M., R. Sullström, and M. Tuomala. 2004. "On Recent Trends in Economic Poverty in Finland." In *New Challenges for a Welfare Society*, ed. V. Puuronen et al., 40-60. Joensuu: University of Joensuu.

Ruhanen, M. and T. Martikainen. 2006. *Maahanmuuttajaprojektit: Hankkeet ja hyvät käytännöt* (Immigrant projects: Projects and best practices). Helsinki: Väestöliitto.

Rumbaut, R. 2007. "Ages, Life Stages, and Generational Cohorts: Decomposing the Immigrant First and Second Generation in the United States." In *Rethinking Migration: New Theoretical and Empirical Perspectives*, ed. A. Portes and J. DeWind, 342-87. Oxford: Berghahn Books.

Satka, M. 1993. "Social Service Professionals in Finland under the Pressures of a Depressed Economy and European Integration." *Scandinavian Journal of Social Welfare* 2(4):397-444

Saukkonen, P. 2010. *Kotouttaminen ja kulttuuripolitiikka: Tutkimus maahanmuutosta ja monikulttuurisuudesta suomalaisella taiteen ja kulttuurin kentällä* (Integration and cultural policy: A study on immigration and multiculturalism in the fields of art and culture in Finland). Helsinki: Cupore.

Statistics Finland. 2009. *Suomi lukuina* (Finland in numbers). Helsinki: Statistics Finland.

—2010. *StatFin Service, Population, Population Structure.* At www.stat.fi/

Sulkunen, P. 2006. "Projektiyhteiskunta ja uusi yhteiskuntasopimus" (Project society and a new social contract). In *Projektiyhteiskunnan kääntöpuolia* (The flip sides of the project society), ed. K. Rantala and P. Sulkunen, 17-38. Helsinki: Gaudeamus.

Svallfors, S., K. Halvorsen, and J.G. Andersen. 2001. "Work Orientations in Scandinavia: Employment Commitment and Organizational Commitment in Denmark, Norway and Sweden." *Acta Sociologica* 44(2):139-56.

Tuori, S. 2009. *The Politics of Multicultural Encounters: Feminist Postcolonial Perspectives.* Åbo: Åbo Akademi University Press.

United Nations Development Program (UNDP). 2009. *Human Development Report 2009 – Overcoming Barriers: Human Mobility and Development.* New York: United Nations Development Program.

Väänänen, A., et al. 2009. *Maahanmuuttajien integroituminen suomalaiseen yhteiskuntaan elämän eri osa-alueilla* (Immigrant integration into Finnish society in different areas of life). Helsinki: Työterveyslaitos, Kuntoutussäätiö ja Terveyden ja hyvinvoinninlaitos.

Valtioneuvosto. 2008. *Valtioneuvoston selonteko kotouttamislain toimeenpanosta* (The government's report on the implementation of the Integration Act). Valtioneuvosto: Helsinki.

Valtonen, K. 1997. *The Societal Participation of Refugees and Immigrants: Case Studies in Finland, Canada and Trinidad.* Turku: Institute of Migration.

—1998. "Resettlement of Middle Eastern Refugees in Finland: The Elusiveness of Integration." *Journal of Refugee Studies* 11(1):38-59.

—2001. "Cracking Monopoly: Immigrants and Employment in Finland." *Journal of Ethnic and Migration Studies* 27(3):421-38.

—2004. "From the Margin to the Mainstream: Conceptualizing Refugee Settlement Processes." *Journal of Refugee Studies* 17(1):70-96.

—2008. *Social Work and Migration.* Farnham, Surrey: Ashgate.

Wahlbeck, Ö. 1999. *Kurdish Diasporas: A Comparative Study of Kurdish Refugee Communities.* Basingstoke: Macmillan.

—2007. "Work in the Kebab Economy: A Study of the Ethnic Economy of Turkish Immigrants in Finland." *Ethnicities* 7(4):543-63.

—2008. "Citizenship and Immigration in Finland: The Nationality Act 2003 in Context." *Canadian Diversity/Diversité Canadienne* 6(4):47-50.

Wrede, S. and C. Nordberg, eds. 2010. *Vieraita työssä: Työelämän etnistyvä eriarvoisuus* (Strangers at work: The ethnification of inequality in work-life). Helsinki: Gaudeamus.

Chapter 7

Israel: An Immigrant Society

Moshe Semyonov and Anastasia Gorodzeisky

Introduction

Israel has long been viewed as the prototype of an immigrant society, a society inhabited mostly by Jewish immigrants and by sons and daughters of these immigrants. The Jewish immigrants arrived in Israel throughout the last century from a wide variety of countries and compose the overwhelming majority of the state's population. In addition to the majority group population, Israel is inhabited by two sizable non-Jewish minority groups: Israeli Arabs and global labour migrants. Israeli Arabs have been living in the region for generations and can thus be viewed as indigenous to the region. They are citizens of the state. Labour migrants have been arriving in Israel only in recent decades. They are neither citizens of Israel, nor can they become citizens or permanent residents. Their arrival in Israel can be understood within the context of the recent and ever increasing trend of global labour migration

Arabs constituted a numerical majority of the region's population at the time that Jews began immigrating to the country to re-establish their homeland in Palestine. (Jews had begun immigrating to Palestine in sizable numbers toward the end of the nineteenth century and the turn of the twentieth.) Arab populations living in Palestine were mostly traditional-rural, with little exposure to modern culture. After establishment of the State of Israel and following the War of Independence, Arabs became a subordinate minority group, in terms not only of numbers but also of their social, economic, and political status in the state. Currently, Arabs, the overwhelming majority of whom are of the Muslim faith, comprise roughly 20 percent of the citizens of Israel. Although they are citizens and as such can fully participate in the country's political system, they

International Perspectives: Integration and Inclusion, ed. J. Frideres and J. Biles. Montreal and Kingston: Queen's Policy Studies Series, McGill-Queen's University Press. © 2012 The School of Policy Studies, Queen's University at Kingston. All rights reserved.

are highly segregated from the Jewish majority population and, when compared to Jews, are disadvantaged in terms of attainment of social and occupational positions and economic rewards (e.g., Lewin-Epstien and Semyonov 1993). Since Arabs are not an immigrant population, they and their relative status in Israel are not discussed in detail in this chapter.

The second major non-Jewish group residing in Israel is composed of labour migrants, often referred to in Israeli society as "foreign workers." Labour migrants began arriving in the country, for all practical purposes, only in recent decades, mostly to replace Palestinian workers from the West Bank and Gaza who used to participate in the Israeli economy before the Intifada. According to estimates provided by various official sources, this group accounts for about 8 percent of the Israeli labour force. It is further estimated that half of the "foreign workers" population are living and working in Israel without legal work permits and are therefore considered to be undocumented migrants (often referred to as "illegal workers"). Their presence in Israel should be understood within the framework of the growing trend of global labour migration with globalization. Indeed, contemporary Israel should be viewed and understood as not only a society of Jewish immigrants but also as a multi-ethnic society inhabited by multiple groups of immigrants alongside an indigenous Arab population. That is, Israel should be understood as a society inhabited by Jewish immigrants who arrived from practically every corner on the globe, as well as by Arabs who have lived in the region for generations, and by labour migrants who recently arrived in the country.

In what follows we first explain the unique meaning of immigration in the context of Israeli society; second, we provide a descriptive overview of the immigration flows to Israel throughout the last hundred years; third, we discuss the emergence of a new group of global migrants, their presence in the country, and the implications of their presence for Israeli society; fourth, we describe the impact that immigration has had on patterns of social and economic inequality in Israeli society; and fifth, we evaluate the role of the state in incorporating immigrants in its social and economic systems.

THE MEANING OF IMMIGRATION IN ISRAEL

By 2009, the population of Israel accounted for almost 7.5 million residents. Three-quarters of these are Jews; 20 percent are Arabs (the overwhelming majority Muslims, the rest Christians and Druze); the remainder are non-Jewish immigrants, including labour migrants. By way of comparison, in 1948, when the state was established, the Jewish population residing in Israel amounted to only 600,000 persons and the Arab population amounted to 156,000 persons. When these numbers are put in historical perspective, it becomes apparent that within six decades the Jewish population of Israel increased dramatically. That is, within sixty years, the Jewish population increased almost tenfold, and more than half of the growth of the Jewish population can be attributed to immigration inflows (Della Pergola 1998). Currently, one-third of the Jewish population of Israel is first generation immigrants and one-third is second generation. The proportion of immigrants in Israeli society is considerably higher than in other traditional immigrant societies such as the United States, Canada, or Australia, and dramatically higher than the new immigrant receiving countries of Western Europe such as Germany, France or the United Kingdom (ibid.). In fact, the proportion of the immigrant populations in Israel is the highest in the world.

Immigration not only accounted for the dramatic increase in the size of the Jewish population but has also changed the ethnic composition of Israeli society, making its population much more heterogeneous. That is, immigration has brought to Israel Jews from practically every corner of the world. Over the years Israel became home to Jews from Eastern and Western European countries such as Germany, Poland, the United Kingdom, Hungary, France, Romania, and the Former Soviet Union; from the United States and Canada, Argentina, Mexico and Chile in the Americas; from Iraq, Iran, Yemen, and India in Asia; from Egypt, Morocco, Libya, and Tunis in North Africa and Ethiopia in East Africa; and from Australia, South Africa, and New Zealand in Oceania. Immigration has shaped the population composition of Israeli society as well as its collective identity and its patterns of social and economic inequality.

Jewish immigration to Israel is different from most other immigrant societies. It is not viewed as an economic migration but as a "returning diaspora" (e.g., Semyonov and Lewin-Epstein 2003). Since Israel is considered the homeland of the Jewish people, every Jew has the right to immigrate there. Therefore, immigrants are referred to not as immigrants but as *olim*, a term with a positive connotation, meaning ascending or going up. Likewise, immigration is referred to as *aliya*. Following this logic, Israel applies a system *of jus sanguineous* for inclusion of Jewish immigrants in society, while excluding non-Jewish immigrants. This system is clearly evident in the Law of Return (1950) and the Law of Nationality (1952). According to these laws, every Jew and family members of Jewish immigrants have the right to settle in Israel and to be awarded Israeli citizenship upon arrival. The state not only enables Jewish immigrants and family members to make Israel their home but also provides generous financial and institutional support to ease their transition from their country of origin and to facilitate their integration into society during their first years in the new country.

Indeed, the State of Israel and the Israeli public have established a social contract with the immigrants; they are fully committed to the successful integration of immigrants into society; they grant immigrants immediate and unconditional acceptance to their new society. The state not only provides support to immigrants to smooth their integration into society but in many cases actively encourages immigration of Jews from widespread diasporas. In many cases, Israel has not only admitted Jewish immigrants but actually sponsored rescue operations around the world to bring Jews under threats to survival to safety in the "homeland." Immigration has played a major role in the development of Israeli society and as such has become a major component of its collective identity.

THE FLOW OF IMMIGRANTS TO ISRAEL: HISTORICAL PERSPECTIVE

Jewish immigration to Israel can be best understood within a series of major flows or currents of immigrants that have taken place from the turn of the twentieth century to the present. Here we adopt the five periods typology identified and offered by Amit and Semyonov (2008):

1. Immigration in the pre-statehood era (ca.1900–48)
2. Mass immigration after the establishment of the State of Israel (1948–52)
3. Sporadic immigration during the following three decades (1952–89)
4. Mass immigration (mostly) from the former Soviet Union following its downfall (1989–95)
5. Sporadic immigration from various (mostly Western) countries (1995–present)

As noted, immigration flows have shaped the size and composition of the population of Israel. Two major geo-cultural (or ethnic) groups are commonly distinguished within the Jewish population: Jews of European or American origin (mostly Ashkenazim) and Jews of Asian or North-African descent (mostly Sephardim). The two groups are of roughly equal size but the former group is, on average, characterized by higher social and economic characteristics (including education, occupational positions, earnings, and wealth and place of residence) than the latter. Much of those disparities were formed and shaped by immigration and can be attributed, at least in part, to circumstances associated with immigration to Israel.

Figure 1 displays the size of immigrants flows to Israel from 1948 (when official statistics had become available for the first time) to the present. Two major peaks can be observed. The first took place immediately after statehood when the newly established state received a mass of immigrants that arrived both from Europe and from Asian and North African countries within a very short time interval. The second peak occurred after the downfall of the Former Soviet Union (1989) when a mass of nearly one million immigrants left the Soviet Republics in order to make Israel their new home.

FIGURE 1
Number of Jewish Immigrants to Israel per Year by Continent of Origin (in Thousands)

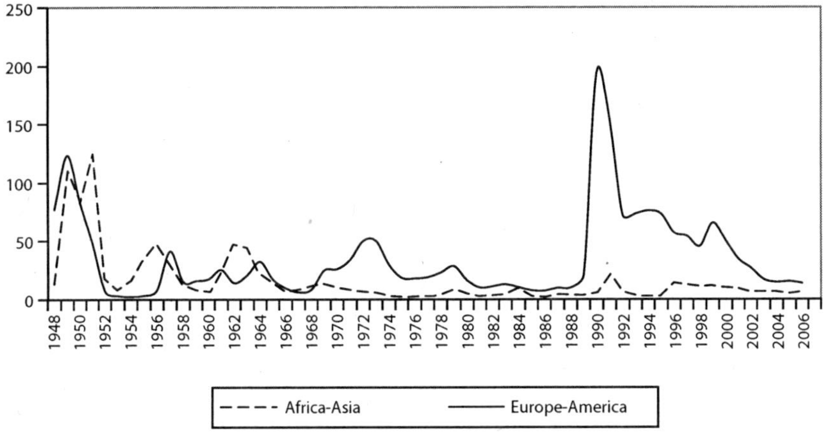

Source: Central Bureau of Statistics in Israel (1996, 2007).

The first Jewish immigrants arrived in Israel (then Palestine) toward the end of the nineteenth century, mostly from Central and Eastern Europe, with the primary goal of establishing a Zionist state as a homeland for the Jewish people. Indeed, this was an ideological immigration joined by almost half a million Jews throughout the five decades preceding the establishment of the state. The pre-state immigrants established new Jewish communities and economic, social, civic, and political institutions. By 1948, early immigrants of European origin were in control of the newly established state's institutions and occupied positions of status, power, and prestige.

Immediately after its establishment, Israel was faced with almost a million Jewish immigrants, most of them, for all practical purposes, refugees. These immigrants can be divided into two major geo-cultural groups of roughly equal size. The first group was composed of survivors of the Holocaust in Europe, the second group of refugees from the Muslim countries in Central Asia, the Middle East, and North Africa. To appreciate the scope and problematic nature of this wave, one must consider that within a period of five years, following a bloody war of independence, 600,000 Jewish residents of the newly established state had to absorb 900,000 new immigrants. The combination of limited and scarce resources (of both the state and the immigrants) coupled with the heterogeneous nature of this influx made the absorption process very difficult. The state had to control, direct, and navigate the process by finding housing and jobs for the new immigrants, establishing new localities in the periphery of the state, and training and retraining many immigrants for life in their new country.

The three decades that followed were characterized by much more scattered and sporadic immigration and smaller numbers of immigrants. During this third period, immigration was influenced more by "push" than "pull" factors. That is, immigrants were influenced more by social, political, or economic events or crises in their country of origin than by the social and economic situation in Israel. For example, when the Former Soviet Union changed its immigration policies in the 1970s and became less restrictive, a stream of immigrants from the former Soviet republics began arriving in Israel. The uprising in Hungary brought a stream of Hungarian Jews; likewise, during the Iranian revolution, an increased number of Iranian Jews made Israel their country of destination. Political unrest in South Africa, Argentina, and Romania brought greater numbers of immigrants from those countries. However, when compared to the previous periods, the stream of immigration during this third immigration period was relatively low. Hence, the integration process could be carried out under less pressure than in earlier periods and with many more resources.

A turning point for immigration to Israel came in 1989. Following the economic and political crisis in the Soviet Union leading to its eventual downfall, a massive number of immigrants from all Soviet Republics had begun leaving their old homes searching for new ones. Although Israel was not the only country of destination, it undoubtedly became the primary viable destination for most Soviet Jews and their family members (an estimated one-quarter of Soviet immigrants were not Jewish). If we take into consideration that Israel, a country of 4.5 million residents, was faced with almost a million Soviet immigrants within less than a decade, we can understand the massive scope of this immigration wave. Some 400,000 Soviet immigrants arrived in Israel between 1989 and 1991, and 300,000 additional immigrants arrived over the next four years. Currently, Soviet immigrants comprise approximately 20 percent of Israel's Jewish population. They are characterized by high levels of education (two-thirds came with some academic education) and by professional and scientific training. Yet, and despite considerable government support, many experienced considerable hardships in finding employment suiting their human capital resources and occupational skills. Consequently, many experienced considerable downward mobility upon arrival in Israel (e.g., Raijman and Semyonov 1995). Although recent studies reveal that with the passage of time these immigrants have experienced some upward occupational and economic mobility, many still lag far behind the Israeli born in the attainment of occupational positions and earnings (Gorodzeisky and Semyonov, 2011).

During the influx of immigrants from the former Soviet Union, a relatively large number of Ethiopian Jews (approximately 100,000 persons) immigrated to the country. In fact, many were airlifted to Israel by state authorities in two major rescue operations. The Ethiopians, unlike the immigrants from the Former Soviet Union (FSU) were characterized by low levels of formal education and were unequipped with occupational skills needed for success in a modern economic system. Consequently, many Ethiopian immigrants continue to face serious difficulties and disadvantages in attaining jobs and economic rewards in the Israeli labour market (Raijman 2009; Offer 2004; Bank of Israel 2007).

By 1995 the stream of immigrants from the FSU had, for all practical purposes, come to its end, with only 50,000 immigrants arriving in the decade between 1995 and 2006. Most recent immigrants have arrived from economically prosperous places such as United States, Canada, and France as well as Argentina, and most are academically educated and hold professional occupations. That is, unlike many of the previous immigrants (many of whom can be viewed as refugees with Israel their one and only viable destination), these immigrants can choose among several destination countries along with the option of staying in their country of origin. They choose Israel mostly on the basis of Zionist ideological grounds and for religious reasons – mainly to live among Jews in the homeland of the Jewish people. If they are economically and socially unsuccessful in Israel, they have the option of returning to their country of origin. However, they appear to integrate and see success and are likely to make Israel their homeland (Raiman 2009; Amit and Chachashvili 2007).

GLOBAL LABOUR MIGRANTS

Labour migrants in Israel should be viewed as part of the growing phenomenon of global labour migration. In recent decades, labour migrants from relatively poor countries have begun leaving their homes in search of economic opportunities in more developed countries in order to improve the quality of life and standard of living of family members in the homeland (Massey et al. 1998; Semyonov and Gorodzeisky 2008). Israel has become a destination and home to many labour migrants. Similar to "guest workers" in many other societies, labour migrants in Israel (often referred to as "foreign workers") are used as cheap labour to fill low-status, low-paying jobs that the native population is reluctant to take and perform. Currently the number of foreign workers in Israel is estimated around 200,000. Half are believed to be undocumented, and most reside in the run-down neighbourhoods of Tel Aviv. They arrive in Israel from a variety of countries including several African countries, Latin America, Thailand, the Philippines, China, Turkey, and Romania.

Israel began relying on migrant non-citizen labour following the 1967 Six-Day War. Immediately after the war, Palestinian workers from the West Bank and Gaza Strip began finding employment in the Israeli labour market. Daily workers who commuted from their place of residence in the morning and returned home at night, they were recruited mostly for employment in construction, agriculture, and service sectors, mostly in blue-collar menial jobs. Their earnings were considerably lower than those of Jewish workers in the same jobs, yet considerably higher than the earnings they could possibly attain in the labour market in the West Bank or Gaza. The number of the Palestinian workers in Israel grew rapidly, by 1987 reaching over 150,000 persons and composing approximately 10 percent of the Israeli labour force (Semyonov and Lewin-Epstein 1987).

Following the first Intifada (the Palestinian uprising in 1987), Palestinians became an unreliable source of labour. Frequent border closings, curfews, and violent events made commuting between Israel and the West Bank or Gaza very difficult. Employers exerted pressure on the Israeli government to replace Palestinians workers with other foreign workers. The government responded (Bartram 1998) by issuing permits for the recruitment of temporary guest workers from other countries. Romanians and Turks were recruited for the construction industry (currently Chinese workers are taking their place), and Thais were hired on agricultural sites. Filipinos came in as caretakers, and many Africans and Latin Americans (mostly undocumented) found jobs as domestic help. The number of work permits and subsequently the number of foreign workers in Israel grew steadily. In 1987 the Ministry of Labour issued only 2,500 permits; by 1993 the number increased to 9,950; in 1996 it exceeded 100,000. Along with the documented workers (those having a work permit), an increasing number of labour migrants without permits began arriving, coming mostly from Africa, Latin America, and Eastern Europe.

Figure 2 clearly shows that the decrease in Palestinian workers commuting to Israel on a daily basis coincides with the rise in the number of global migrants. In the early 1990s the proportion of Palestinian workers in the Israeli labour force was considerably larger than that of the foreign workers; by 1994 the two groups of non-citizen workers reached parity. By the mid-1990s the relative proportion of the foreign workers had systematically increased; in 2000 the proportion of foreign workers reached 10 percent while the proportion of Palestinian workers declined to approximately 2 percent. The data presented suggest that Palestinian workers had been replaced by global labour migrants in the Israeli labour market.

The data displayed in Table 1 pertain to the distribution of foreign workers in Israel according to country of origin and sector of employment (Raijman 2009). Labour migrants from Thailand and China worked mostly in agriculture; labour migrants from the Philippines (but recently also from India, Sri Lanka and Bulgaria) worked as domestic help; labour migrants from Romania, the former Soviet Union, Turkey, and China were invited to work in the construction industry.

FIGURE 2
Percentage of Global Labour Migrants and Palestinian Workers in the Israeli Labour Force, 1990–2006

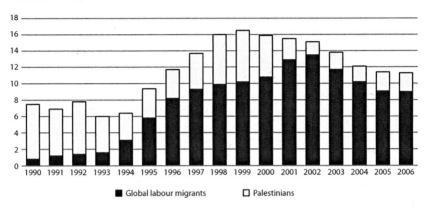

■ Global labour migrants   ☐ Palestinians

Source: Israel Ministry of Labor and Welfare (2001); Bank of Israel (2007).

TABLE 1
Distribution of Foreign Workers with a Permit in Israel by Sector of Employment and Country of Origin, 2002

Sector of Employment	Number of Migrants	Percent	Country of Origin
Agriculture	30,000	27.0	Thailand, China
Construction	32,000	28.9	Romania, FSU, China, Turkey
Industry	5,000	4.5	Romania, FSU, Latin America
Domestic help/caretaking	40,000	36.0	Philippines, India, Sri Lanka, Bulgaria
Restaurants	3,000	2.7	Philippines, China, Thailand
Hotels	1,000	0.9	Africa, FSU

Source: Raijman (2009).

IMMIGRATION AND SOCIO-ECONOMIC INEQUALITY

The immigration flows to Israel affected not only the ethnic composition of Israeli population but also patterns of socio-economic inequalities among the sub-populations. For the purpose of the present discussion, we identify three main axes (or dimensions) of inequality in Israeli society. We contend here that these axes have been shaped mostly by immigration flows: the three-axes have been formed on basis of citizenship (citizens versus non-citizens), the Jewish-Arab split, and ethnic or geo-cultural cleavage within the Jewish population (i.e., between Jews of European or American origin and Jews of Asian or African origin).

The sharpest and most pronounced cleavage in Israeli society lies between citizens (whether Jews or Arabs) and non-citizens (foreign workers). The cleavage is evident in terms of social and economic status in society but mostly in terms of access to rights and privileges that the Israeli welfare system provides. In other words, labour migrants who have arrived in Israel (especially in recent years) have almost no chance of becoming citizens of the state and having equal access to social, political, and economic rights and privileges to which other citizens (whether Jews or Arabs) are entitled. They are highly segregated in terms of occupational positions. Placed at the bottom of the Israeli labour market, they take menial low-status, low-paying jobs that Israeli citizens are reluctant to take. Nowadays labour migrants are highly concentrated in three major industries: construction, agriculture, and domestic services, including care taking. Specifically, about 28 percent of labour migrants holding work permits are employed in construction, about 27 percent in agriculture, and around 40 percent employed in domestic service.

The occupational distribution of the labour migrants in Israel does not reflect their educational credentials nor the occupations they held in their country of origin prior to arrival in Israel. For example, although the educational level of labour migrants from Latin-America and Africa is relatively high (average number of schooling years is about 12), and although 34 percent of labour migrants from Africa and about 15 percent of those from Latin America held professional or technician occupations in their country of origin, the overwhelming majority of these immigrants (82 percent among Africans and 75 percent among Latin Americans) work in domestic help (i.e., house-cleaning). The gap between occupational status in a country of origin and in Israel reflects the high occupational cost associated with migration (Raijman 2009). However, labour migrants are willing to accept this occupational cost because the wages they receive in Israel are considerably higher that those they could at home. Sizable portions of the earnings that labour migrants make in the destination countries are remitted to combat poverty and improve standard of living of family members left behind at home (see, for example, Semyonov and Gorodzeisky 2008 for Filipino overseas workers).

Similar to the situation in many other societies, labour migrants in Israel suffer from the worst working conditions in the country; their wages are considerably lower than those of Israeli citizens, in many cases below minimum wage; they seldom receive employment benefits or have access to the Israeli welfare system. Most live in the poorest neighbourhoods (primarily in South Tel Aviv); the undocumented workers are under a constant threat of deportation. In sum, foreign labour migrants in Israel can be viewed as the most vulnerable and disadvantaged sub-population in every aspect of social stratification.

The second axis of socio-economic inequality in Israel is based on the distinction between Jews and non-Jews (mostly between Jews and Arabs). According to this distinction, Jews form the superordinate group and Arabs are the subordinate disadvantaged group. In general, the disadvantages of the Arab population in Israel are largely understood within the context of the Jewish-Arab conflict and the definition of Israel as the homeland for the Jewish people (Al-Haj and Rosenfeld 1988; Lewin-Epstein and Semyonov 1993). Since Jewish immigrants are considered "returning diasporas," they benefit (as compared to Arabs) from priority in access to employment opportunities, housing, and a variety of state services.

The last axis of inequality formed by immigration flows to Israel is based on the distinction between two major ethnic or geo-cultural groups within the Jewish population (i.e., between Jews that arrived from Europe or America – mostly Ashkenazim – and Jews that arrived from Central Asia and North Africa – mostly Sephardim). Socio-economic disparities between these two major ethnic groups have long been attributed to geo-cultural differences and particularly to patterns of immigration flows to the country (e.g., Ben Rafael 1982). Four distinct ethnic sub-populations of immigrants are now recognized in Israeli society: Jews of European and American origin (Ashkenazim); Jews of Asian and African origin (Sephardim) who arrived prior to 1989; immigrants from the former republics of the Soviet Union who arrived after the downfall of the Soviet Union in 1989 (most of European origin), and Ethiopian immigrants who arrived in the late 1980s and early '90s. The socio-economic status of these four sub-groups is often linked to the circumstances associated with their arrival in the country.

Most of the immigrants in pre-statehood era came to Israel from Eastern and Central European countries; thus they were in a better position than any other group to occupy the most desirable positions in the social, economic, and political system of the new state. Shortly after statehood (1948), Israel began absorbing a large influx of immigrants (mostly refugees) from Muslim countries in Central Asia and North Africa along with European survivors of the Holocaust. Within a five-year period, Israel's population almost tripled. At the same time the state, with very little resources, had to supply housing, jobs, food, and services to many of the new immigrants and help absorb them into society. Many were housed in temporary tent communities and many, especially immigrants of Asian or North African origin, were directed to newly established communities and rural villages in the periphery of the country where occupational, economic, and educational opportunities were more limited and scarce than in the centre. These immigrants were characterized by large families, traditional orientation, and few connections to those who controlled resources. Consequently they experienced greater difficulties and greater hardships in integrating and adjusting to the Israeli social and economic system than immigrants of European origin. In fact, whereas Jews of

European or American origins were able to close socio-economic gaps with native born Jews, immigrants of Asian or African origins were less successful in doing so (e.g., Semyonov 1996).

Even today, more than 60 years after the establishment of the state, immigrants of Asian and North African origins are still disadvantaged in terms of attainment of socio-economic rewards (e.g., Cohen, Haberfeld, and Kristal 2007; Haberfeld and Cohen 2007). First and second generation immigrants from European and American countries have been placed at the top of the Israeli stratification ladder; they have achieved the highest occupational status and earn the highest salaries. First and second generation immigrants from Asian and African countries have achieved lower occupational status and earned lower salaries than either first or second generation immigrants from European and American countries (Gorodzeisky and Semyonov, 2011). For example, in 2004–06 the average occupational status (on a 100 point scale) of European-American origin men was 56 and 60 points (for first and second generation immigrants, respectively), while the occupation status of Asian-African origin men was 40 and 43 points (for first and second generation immigrants, respectively).

New immigrants who arrived in Israel after 1989 from the Former Soviet Union faced considerable hardships in finding high-paying and high-status positions matching their educational credentials and occupational skills and hence experienced downward occupational mobility (Raijman and Semyonov 1998). However, FSU immigrants did not enter the Israeli labour market at the bottom of occupation hierarchy. Even shortly after arrival, their occupational positions were of higher status than that of first and second generation Asian-African Jews (Gorodzeisky and Semyonov, 2011). Yet taking into consideration the very high level of education among FSU immigrants (14.7 and 14.8 years of schooling in average for men and women, respectively), they are still disadvantaged in attainment of both occupational status and earnings as compared to other Jewish groups. That is, FSU immigrants have been less successful than comparable Jews who arrived to Israel before 1989 in converting education to occupational positions. Moreover, the earnings disadvantage of FSU immigrants is substantial as compared to earlier immigrants even after controlling for occupational distribution, especially when compared to European-Americans. For example, around 2005, the earnings of FSU immigrants who arrived in Israel in 1990–91 was 30 percent lower than earning of comparable groups who arrived in Israel in previous immigration waves (Gorodzeisky and Semyonov, 2011). Although intermediate assessments indicate that FSU immigrants are improving their relative occupational status and earnings, they are still lagging behind other groups of Jewish immigrants; according to an estimation provided by Haberfeld and Cohen (2007) it will take more than 30 years for them to close the socio-economic gap with previous immigrants.

Ethiopian immigrants arrived in Israel in the late 1980s and early '90s (most were rescued from a developing–poor country under difficult and severe conditions). They are placed at the bottom of the social stratification ladder and face considerable hardships in integrating into the Israeli society. Their educational level is the lowest in Israel. For example, in 1995 the average years of formal schooling among Ethiopian immigrants was only 3.3 years; by 2005 their average level of formal years of education had increased, but only up to an average of seven years; it is still considerably lower than average level of years of formal education in the population (13.7 years). The increase in years of formal education reflects, to a great extent, exposure of young Ethiopian immigrants (and second-generation immigrants) to the Israeli educational system. The odds for participating in labour market activity among Ethiopians are also considerably lower than that for all other Jewish sub-populations (Raijman 2009). These odds remain low even after controlling for differences in levels of education. It has been suggested that Ethiopian immigrants are not only disadvantaged by their low level of human-capital resources and skills that are inadequate for the Israeli economy but also by the discrimination they face in the Israeli labour market (e.g., Offer 2004). Currently, only 16 percent of Ethiopian men and 18 percent of Ethiopian women hold professional, technicial, and managerial occupations as compared to 44 percent of the Israeli population. Moreover, average monthly earnings among Ethiopian immigrants amount to only about 50 percent of the average monthly earnings of the Israeli population (Raijman 2009). Indeed, Ethiopian immigrants are the most vulnerable population among the Jewish population in Israel in terms of socio-economic inequality.

THE ROLE OF THE STATE

Israel views itself as the homeland of the Jewish people and thus is committed ideologically and institutionally to the successful integration of Jewish immigrants into society. The state has established a ministry and a series of organizations, agencies, and institutions to support immigrant integration. Although the scope, amount, and type of state support have changed over the years, in financial terms it is quite substantial. This support frequently includes travel and relocation funds, Hebrew courses, housing loans and allowances, tax exemptions, training and retraining programs, and assistance in finding a job.

Throughout most of its history, the state has also been intensively involved in shaping the opportunity structure and immigration policies to facilitate a smooth incorporation of immigrants into society. Although state involvement is aimed at supporting and helping immigrants, it can also lead to a dependency of immigrants on the state system and institutions. In many cases, state actions directed at supporting immigrants' incorporation have had long-term detrimental consequences for their social and economic status. Perhaps the most apparent consequences are associated with immigrants from North Africa who arrived in the 1950s (i.e., during the period of mass immigration after the establishment of the State of Israel). This period was characterized by scarce societal resources and by high levels of state control on the ways that these resources were allocated (e.g., Semyonov and Lewin-Epstein 2003). During this period the state had to furnish housing and create jobs for the new immigrants. At the same time it launched a policy of population dispersion and established new development towns with labour intensive industries in the peripheral regions of the country to provide housing and jobs to the new immigrants. New immigrants, especially those from North African countries, were directed and channelled in disproportional numbers to these newly created peripheral towns. Consequently, the new immigrants from North Africa were not only introduced to an inferior opportunity structure in the social and geographical periphery of the country but also became extremely dependent on state agencies. Even today North African immigrants and their sons and daughters are overrepresented in the peripheral areas of the state where economic and educational opportunities are limited and housing values are low. This seems to be one of the reasons why second and third generation immigrants from North Africa are still lagging far behind Jews of European and American origin in every aspect of socio-economic stratification.

Absorption and support policies implemented by the state have changed over the years to fit changes in composition and scope of immigrant populations. In the fourth period of immigration – the second mass migration, mostly from the Former Soviet Union between 1989 and 1995 – the state launched a new policy of absorption: direct absorption. According to this policy, resources were given directly to immigrants with a low level of state control. Immigrants from the FSU received a "basket of absorption" – cash and services – and could choose among various strategies and modes of incorporation with state support. The "basket of absorption" included a lump sum of money of approximately $10,000 (depending on the size of family), housing subsidies, language instructions, job retraining programs, tax exemption, and free academic education for qualified students (Doron and Kargar 1993). Immigrants could choose where to live, whether to buy apartment or to rent one, and when and where to enter the labour market. Although Soviet immigrants experienced downward occupational mobility upon arrival in Israel, intermediate assessments indicate improvement in their socio-economic status and achievements, especially among younger immigrants. This policy has continued for all practical purposes into the fifth period of immigration (1995–present) in which immigrants from Western and economically developed countries arrive in Israel. Nevertheless, at the same time that the policy of "direct absorption" was implemented, immigrants from Ethiopia also arrived in Israel. Since Ethiopian immigrants were viewed as a "weak" population, state involvement in every aspect of their incorporation process was much more intensive, and the support was more generous. Despite these state strategies, this group of immigrants continues to experience severe difficulties in their socio-economic incorporation into Israeli society (e.g., Offer 2004, 2007; Kaplan and Salamon 2004).

Whereas the state of Israel provides considerable support to Jewish immigrants, it does not welcome non-Jewish labour migrants. More specifically, contrary to the immediate and unconditional acceptance and support granted to Jewish immigrants, the state makes it very difficult, almost impossible, for non-Jewish immigrants to become permanent residents, let alone Israeli citizens. Immigration policy towards foreign labour migrants has been implemented mainly through decisions regarding the number of work permits (quotas) to be allocated to employers, coupled with a policy of deportation of undocumented migrants. Since in Israel work permits are granted to employers and not to the migrants, labour migrants with permits become a "captured" labour force (Rozenhak 2000). In fact, labour agencies and employers are those that receive permits for recruiting and hiring foreign workers while the state itself does not participate in the process, apparently so that the state can avoid assuming responsibility for the welfare and the working conditions of foreign workers (Raijman 2009; Kemp and Raijman 2008). Indeed, although the community of labour migrants in Israel has become a sizable and integral part of social reality, the state has not yet established a clear policy on the status of foreign workers in Israel (Raijman 2009).

CONCLUSIONS

Israel is an immigrant society with a high proportion of foreign born population. Data show that flows of Jewish immigrants from practically every corner of the world have contributed more than any other social factor to the dramatic increase in the size of the Israeli population. Migration flows have also shaped the diverse ethnic composition of the population and influenced patterns of ethnic-linked socio-economic inequality. Since Israel is considered the homeland of the Jewish people, every Jew has the right to immigrate to Israel and to receive citizenship upon arrival. As the state is fully committed to successful social and economic integration of its Jewish immigrants, it is actively involved in helping Jewish immigrants to settle. Jewish immigrants are viewed as a "returning diaspora," and the state grants them generous financial and institutional support to facilitate their smooth incorporation into society. Indeed, the successful integration of most immigrants into Israel society, despite the scope of immigration flows and the diverse nature of the immigrant populations, can be attributed in part to state policies and state support.

However, whereas Jews are fully welcomed and accepted by state authorities and by the public, non-Jewish labour migrants are faced with social and legal exclusion. Contrary to its policy that embraces and facilitates full inclusion of Jewish immigrants, Israel has implemented a policy of total exclusion toward non-Jewish global labour migrants. Viewed by the state and the public as temporary workers, not permanent immigrants, they cannot become citizens, nor can they become permanent residents. Thus, Israel should be viewed as a pluralist society inhabited by diverse groups of immigrants with differential access to privileges, rights, and opportunities for success. In this immigrant society, differential state policies toward different subgroups may affect immigrant opportunities for success.

REFERENCES

Al-Haj, M. and H. Rosenfeld. 1988. *Arab Local Government in Israel*. International Center for Peace in the Middle East, Tel Aviv.
Amit, K. and S. Chachashvili. 2007. *The Ruppin Index: An Index of Immigrant Integration in Israel, Report 2*. (In Hebrew.) Submitted to Ministry of Absorption.
Amit, K. and M. Semyonov. 2006. Israel as Returning Disapora. *Metropolis World Bulletin* 6:11-14.
Bank of Israel. 2007. "The Labor Market." In *Accounting 2006*, 165-99. (In Hebrew.) Jerusalem: Bank of Israel.
Bartram, D. 1998 "Foreign Workers in Israel: History and Theory." *International Migration Review* 32(2):303-25.
Ben Rafael, E. 1982. *The Emergence of Ethnicity: Cultural Gaps and Social Conflict in Israel*. Westport, CT: Greenwood Press.
Central Bureau of Statistics. 1996. *Statistical Abstracts of Israel*, Jerusalem: Hemed Press.
—2007. *Statistical Abstracts of Israel*, Jerusalem: Hemed Press.
Cohen, Y., Y. Haberfeld, and T. Kristal. 2007. "Ethnicity and Mixed Ethnicity: Educational Gaps among Israeli-Born Jews." *Ethnic and Racial Studies* 30(5):896-917.
Della Pergola, S. 1998. "The Global Context of Migration to Israel." In *Immigration to Israel: Sociological Perspectives*, ed. E. Leshem and J. Shuval, 51-92. New Brunswick: Transaction.
Doron, A. and H.J. Kargar. 1993. "The Politics of Immigration Policies in Israel." *International Migration* 31(4):497-512.
Gorodzeisky, A. and M. Semyonov. 2011 "Two Dimensions to Immigrants' Economic Incorporation: Soviet Immigrants in the Israeli Labour Market." *Journal of Ethnic and Migration Studies*, 37 (7): 1059-1077
Haberfeld, Y. and Y. Cohen. 2007. "Gender, Ethnic and National Earnings Gaps in Israel: The Role of Rising Inequality." *Social Science Research* 36(2):654-72.

Israel. Ministry of Labor and Welfare 2001. *Report by the Committee on Employment of Foreigners in Israel*. Jerusalem: Ministry of Labor and Welfare.

Kaplan, S. and H. Salamon. 2004. "Ethiopian Jews in Israel: A Part of the People or Apart from the People?" In *Jews in Israel: Contemporary Social and Cultural Patterns*, ed. U. Rebhun and C. Waxman, 118-48. Hanover and London: Brandeis University Press.

Kemp, A. and R. Raijman. *Migrants and Workers: The Political Economy of Labor Migration in Israel*. (In Hebrew.) Hakibbutz Hameuchad Publishing House.

Lewin-Epstein, N. and M. Semyonov. 1993. *Arabs in Israel's Economy: Patterns of Ethnic Inequality*. Boulder, CO: Westview Press.

Massey, D.S., J. Arango, G. Hugo, A. Kouaouci, A. Pellegrino, and J.E. Taylor. 1998. *Worlds in Motion: Understanding International Migration at the End of Millennium*. New York: Oxford University Press.

Offer, S. 2004. "The Socio-Economic Integration of the Ethiopian Community in Israel." *International Migration* 42(3):29-55.

——2007. "The Ethiopian Community in Israel: Segregation and the Creation of a Racial Cleavage." *Ethnic and Racial Studies* 30(3):461-80.

Raijman, R. 2009. "Immigration to Israel: Review of Patterns and Empirical Research, 1990-2006." (In Hebrew.) *Israeli Sociology* 12(2):340-79.

Raijman, R. and M. Semyonov. 1995. "Modes of Labor Market Incorporation and Occupational Cost among New Immigrants to Israel." *International Migration Review* 29(2):375-93.

——1998. "Best of Times, Worst of Times, and Occupational Mobility: The Case of Soviet Immigrants in Israel." *International Migration* 36(3):291-310.

Rozenhak, Z. 2000. "Migration Regimes, Intra-State Conflicts and the Politics of Inclusion and Exclusion: Migrant Workers and the Israeli Welfare State." *Social Problems* 47:49-67.

Semyonov M. 1996. "On the Cost of Being an Immigrant in Israel: The Effects of Tenure, Ethnicity and Gender." *Research in Social Stratification and Mobility* 15:115-31.

Semyonov, M. and A. Gorodzeisky. 2008. "Labor Migration, Remittances and Economic Well-Being of Households in the Philippines." *Population Research and Policy Review*, 27: 619-637.

Semyonov, M. and N. Lewin-Epstein. 1987. *Hewers of Wood and Drawers of Water: Non-Citizen Arabs in the Israeli Labor Market*. Ithaca, NY: ILR Press.

——2003. "Immigration and Ethnicity in Israel: Returning Diasporas and Nation Building." In *Diasporas and Ethnic Migrants in 20th Century Europe*, ed. R. Muenz. London: Frank Cass.

CHAPTER 8

IMMIGRATION AND SOCIAL INTEGRATION IN JAPAN

NANA OISHI

Although Japan is often referred to as a homogeneous nation, it has long been a multicultural and multi-ethnic society.[1] In the first half of the twentieth century, Japan's invasions of neighbouring countries resulted in both voluntary and involuntary migration of people. These migrants, mostly Koreans and Chinese, were "integrated" as Japanese nationals with limited socio-economic and political rights under the colonial rule. Yet those who remained in the country after World War II were "disintegrated" again after their countries of origin became independent from Japan, and they lost Japanese citizenship and its associated rights. These populations have constituted Japan's major ethnic communities. Given these situations, together with the presence of other ethnic minorities such as the Ainu and Okinawans, some scholars have stated that Japan's claim to ethnic homogeneity is an "illusion" (Weiner 1997).

In the postwar period the country's economic growth led to the new immigration patterns, further accelerating ethnic diversity. In 2010, approximately 2.1 million migrants from 191 countries were living in Japan (MOJ 2011). While this proportion comprises only 1.7 percent of the national population, the actual level of ethnic diversity is more significant than what the number indicates, because the data only refer to foreign citizens and do not include those who became naturalized.[2] The large majority of migrants are from neighbouring Asian countries, but a considerable proportion has also come from South America, particularly from Brazil. Despite the growing size and diversity of its migrant population, however, the Japanese government has had no formal policy or vision on social integration at the national level, and has provided only limited support for migrants and ethnic minorities. Official support was

International Perspectives: Integration and Inclusion, ed. J. Frideres and J. Biles. Montreal and Kingston: Queen's Policy Studies Series, McGill-Queen's University Press. © 2012 The School of Policy Studies, Queen's University at Kingston. All rights reserved.

only available at the level of municipalities in which migrants were concentrated. However, the government gradually recognized the need for integration and announced its Plan for the Promotion of Multicultural Coexistence in 2006. What is "multicultural coexistence,"[3] and how does it differ from multiculturalism? Are the current policies and programs effective in integrating migrants and ethnic minorities? Starting with a brief historical overview of immigration and social integration in Japan since the nineteenth century, this chapter analyzes the recent policy changes and remaining challenges for social integration in Japan.

THE HISTORY OF IMMIGRATION AND INTEGRATION IN JAPAN

Pre-World War II Period: Assimilation under Colonialism

After a 215-year policy of national isolation during the Edo period, Japan reopened itself to the world in 1854. Initially the high poverty rate resulted in significant emigration to North America. However, there was also some immigration from the United States and Europe of highly skilled professionals invited by the Meiji government to work as engineers and professors for the country's industrial development. In the late 1880s, 2,936 people from the United States, United Kingdom, Germany, and France entered Japan under this category, while others were missionaries or merchants (Uemura 2008). Given that Japan's total population at that time was 3.5 million (Cabinet Office 2004), this figure was extremely small – less than 0.1 percent. The majority lived in Japan on a temporary basis, although a few married and stayed in the country.

The major immigration to Japan began in 1910 when Japan colonized Korea. Although several hundred Koreans were already working in coal mines in the western part of Japan, after the colonization the number of Koreans in the country increased nearly tenfold, from 30,189 in 1920 to 298,091 in 1930 (Yamawaki 2003). Taiwan also became Japan's colony in 1895, when China ceded it after its defeat in the Sino-Japan War. Immigration from Taiwan to Japan, however, was much more limited than that from Korea.

Under the Japanese colonial rule, Koreans and Taiwanese legally became Japanese nationals with some rights. Koreans and Taiwanese men (of the age 25 or above) living in Japan enjoyed full political rights, both the right to vote and the right to stand for office.[4] One Korean even became a national legislator; Choon-Geum Park was elected to the House of Representatives (Oguma 1998). Other Koreans worked as civil servants in the Japanese government, municipal governments, and military forces, though they were still a small minority among all Koreans in Japan.

After the Japanese military took power in the 1930s, the forced cultural assimilation of Koreans and Taiwanese intensified. Under the slogan of establishing the Greater East Asian Co-Prosperity Sphere, the Japanese military government promoted the policy of *Kominka*, forcing Koreans and Taiwanese to identify themselves as subjects of the Japanese emperor. In Korea and Taiwan, the colonial government denied local cultures and imposed Japanese-language education, religious rituals, clothing, cuisine, and even Japanese names.

Postwar Transitions: 1945 to Mid-1970s

When World War II ended, there were 2.3 million Koreans and 34,000 Chinese (including Taiwanese and Mainland Chinese) in Japan, most of whom returned home. According to the estimates, some 600,000 Koreans and 14,000 Taiwanese chose to remain in Japan and for a while retained their legal status as "Japanese nationals" (Ryang 2000; Komai 2001). However, in 1952 when the San Francisco Peace Treaty entered into force, all Koreans and Taiwanese in Japan lost their Japanese citizenship. They became "foreigners" and lost all the socio-economic and political rights that they had enjoyed in Japan during the colonial period. They were removed from the national pension and health insurance schemes.

The Japanese government did not take substantial measures to alleviate their socio-economic hardships. The only exception was Notification 382, issued by the Ministry of Welfare in 1954, enabling municipal governments to apply the welfare system, *mutatis mutandis*, to foreign residents living in extreme poverty (AMDA 2001). In 1965, when diplomatic relations were re-established between Japan and South Korea, South Korean residents were reintegrated into Japan's national health insurance system, while North Koreans and other foreign citizens remained excluded until 1979 (Minegishi 2004).

Municipalities with large migrant populations tackled integration issues much more seriously than the national government during this period. In Kawasaki City, which was home to a large number of Koreans, the city government had been adopting various social integration policies on its own. In 1972, it provided health care coverage for all foreign citizens, although the national government officially denied their membership. The Kawasaki City government argued that North Koreans and South Koreans should be treated equally because of their common historical background. Subsequently, the city government struck the citizenship requirement from the welfare provision, public housing, and childcare subsidies (ibid.).[5]

New Postwar Immigration and the Policy Shift toward Equality: Late 1970s–1989

As Japan recovered from the war damages and began to experience strong economic growth, migrants from various countries started arriving in the late 1970s. The first to arrive were North American and European businessmen working for multinational corporations. Most stayed in Japan only on a temporary basis to expand their businesses in Asia. The second category of migrants was "entertainers," although more than 90 percent of them worked as hostesses in bars, according to the survey by the Immigration Bureau (*Asahi Shimbun* 1996). Most were women from Asian countries such as the Philippines and Thailand. A significant number of them married Japanese men and settled in the country. However, the "entertainers" visa has also been criticized for disguising trafficking of sex workers. By 2004, approximately 60,000 entertainers arrived in Japan annually, though numbers declined to 11,000 in 2009 due to the anti-trafficking campaigns (MOJ 2010).

The third category of migrants consisted of Japanese returnees from China. Most had been young children when World War II ended, and had been entrusted by their destitute parents to Chinese families. Since 1981, 6,396 people have returned to Japan, the total number, including spouses, children, and grandchildren, reaching over 20,000 (MHLW 2010). The vast majority were unable to speak, read, write, or understand Japanese and thus have had difficulty in establishing themselves in Japan. There has been insufficient public assistance for language education, and these migrants were relatively old to learn a new language. Thus many have experienced economic difficulties and have had to rely on public assistance (MHLW 2005).

Foreign students have also emerged as a major component of Japan's migrant population. Since Prime Minister Nakasone launched a plan to accept 100,000 foreign students in 1983, the number of students grew fivefold, from 10,428 to 52,405 within ten years. While being officially allowed to take up employment for up to only 28 hours a week, many foreign students have reportedly been working longer hours to cover their tuition and high living expenses. Although many are serious students, some are more inclined to work, filling the demand for unskilled labour (Asano 2004). After a slight decrease in 1996–97, the number of students has continued to rise, reaching 201,511 in 2010 (MOJ 2011). A further increase is expected as the government has announced a goal of accepting 300,000 foreign students by 2020 (MEXT 2008).

Immigration flows into Japan significantly expanded in the late 1980s because of the growing "bubble economy." Although the government refused for a long time to accept unskilled migrants, the acute labour shortage in urban areas in the late 1980s could no longer be met by workers from rural areas. Many Japanese employers gradually turned to migrants from abroad, including irregular migrants.

Two important shifts in Japan's integration policies in the late 1970s and early 1980s should be noted. One was the government's ratifications of two international laws – the International Covenant on Economic, Social and Cultural Rights and the International Covenant on Civil and

Political Rights in 1979, which obliged the state to treat citizens and non-citizens equally. After these ratifications, the citizenship requirement for the national health insurance system and public housing for low-income population were officially abolished.

The second shift came about when the Japanese government ratified the Convention Relating to the Status of Refugees in 1982, responding to international pressures to accept Indochinese refugees after the Vietnam War. Though the actual number of acceptances was only about 200, the result of the ratification of this important refugee law eventually led to the abolishment of the citizenship requirement for the national pension scheme and childcare subsidies. The eligibilities were not only applicable to refugees but extended to all migrants including Koreans, Taiwanese, and other foreign citizens living in Japan.[6]

Progress was also made in the area of economic integration in the 1970s as local governments gradually lifted the citizenship requirement for employment eligibility. In 1973, six cities and one town in the Hanshin area abolished the citizenship requirement for employment eligibility in the local civil service. Such initiatives have been gradually followed by other local governments. At present, 11 prefectures and 12 major cities have abolished the citizenship requirement for the local civil service, and more than 1,000 foreign citizens are working as local civil servants; about 200 foreign citizens hold teaching positions in public schools (SNMJ 2009, 117). However, foreign citizens do not necessarily have equal access to public sector employment. Local governments still maintain a certain range of jobs that are inaccessible to foreign citizens, and set the upper limit of the promotions of foreign public officials as well. The rationale is not legally founded but is based on the views issued by the Cabinet Legislation Bureau (CLB) in 1953. According to the CLB, it is "natural" to require Japanese citizenship for civil servants who could exercise public power and participate in the state decision-making (Nishikawa 1997, 221).

New Immigration Law, Settlement, and Local Integration, 1990–2004

In 1990, the *Immigration Control and Refugee Recognition Act* was revised partly in response to the growing demand for unskilled labour. While it kept the stance of not accepting unskilled foreign labour, it established a special provision allowing people of Japanese descent (*Nikkeijin*) to live and work in Japan. Since there was no limit in the type of occupations that they would take, many South American *Nikkeijin* – mostly from Brazil and Peru – engaged in unskilled work. The number of Brazilians in Japan swelled from 4,000 in 1986 to 313,000 in 2008. Even though their number declined for the first time to 267,000 in 2009, they still comprise the third major migrant group in Japan (MOJ 2010).

Another significant change under this immigration law was the establishment of two new schemes for "trainees" from developing countries.
The Industrial Trainee Program (ITP) was meant to allow migrants to
learn Japanese language and culture for the first four months and receive
"on-the-job training" at small or medium sized corporations for the following eight months.[7] Then, most of the trainees would proceed to the
Technical Intern Program (TIP) and officially work as "technical interns"
for two more years. In 2009, there were 65,000 trainees and 122,000 technical interns, about 80 percent from China and the rest from other Asian
countries such as Vietnam, the Philippines, and Indonesia (MOJ 2010).
Although both programs were officially designed to provide training for
workers from developing countries, they have been actually functioning
as a "side door" for bringing in migrants to fill the demand for cheap
unskilled labour. Many employers do not pay the wages specified in the
contract and often pay very little for overtime. Most trainees keep silent
out of fear of losing their job, especially since they must recover the high
migration fees paid to the agent prior to their arrival in Japan (Oishi 1995;
Tabuchi 2010).

When the bubble economy burst in 1991, the Japanese economy entered
the longest recession of the postwar period. Nevertheless, the number of
migrants continued to increase, reaching 2.2 million in 2008 (MOJ 2010).[8]
Contrary to expectations among the Japanese public that migrant workers
would eventually leave, they remained and settled down in the country,
bringing in family members. Although the global financial crisis resulted
in serious job losses among migrant workers, the majority of them have
stayed in Japan because of the meagre employment opportunities in their
home countries and also out of concern for their children's education.
Only 26 percent of Japanese Brazilians, for instance, left Japan between
2008 and 2010 (MOJ 2011).

Family formation and settlement have been the major trend among
other migrants as well. The number of foreign spouses has been rising
steadily to 241,000 in 2009 (MOJ 2010). This rise is attributable to growing incidences of international marriage as well as family reunification.
In 2007, 5.6 percent of all marriages registered in Japan were between
Japanese and foreign citizens, a significant increase from 0.9 percent in
1980 (MHLW 2007). Furthermore, as more short-term migrants obtained
permanent residency, their spouses and relatives began to join them.
Migrants who hold a spouse visa comprise 12 percent of the total migrants
in Japan. Many of these spouses eventually apply for permanent resident
status or become naturalized after several years, disappearing from the
data on foreign spouses. The actual number of foreign born migrant
spouses is thus estimated to be much higher than is often perceived.

Given such a rapid increase of migrants, some municipalities slowly
began to search for a way of integrating them politically. In 1992, Osaka
Prefecture established its Advisory Panel on Foreign Residents Issues

in Osaka, with over half of its members foreign residents. In 1996, the Kawasaki City government established a forum called the Kawasaki City Representative Assembly for Foreign Residents, made up of foreign residents only, so that they could contribute their opinions and policy recommendations to the mayor. Comprised of 26 elected members, the assembly has been enabling foreign residents to take part in policy-making processes on local issues and to have their voices heard (Kawasaki City 2010). Similar attempts at political integration have been made in other municipalities, though most of them prefer the structure of having both Japanese and foreign residents on their advisory panels.

Early in the previous decade, many municipalities adopted an inclusive approach to the political integration of migrants and ethnic minorities. One of the factors behind this direction was the structural reorganization of municipalities. When small cities, towns, and villages were to be merged, many municipalities held a local referendum on the merger decision and included foreign residents. Over 200 local governments passed a decree allowing the participation of foreign residents in referenda (SNMJ 2009). While referenda are only held when extraordinary local matters arise, and foreign residents remain excluded from regular local elections, these gradual changes indicate that local communities in Japan were gradually accepting foreign residents as fellow community members. Even at the prefectural level, by 2009 the majority of councils had passed resolutions supporting the official provision of local suffrage to foreign permanent residents (*Sankei Shimbun* 2010). This was a significant step forward in the political integration of migrants.

Some local governments with large numbers of migrants also began to engage in political lobbying. In 2001, 13 cities jointly established the Council for Municipalities with Large Migrant Populations (CMLMP)[9] to exchange information on local policy practices and to submit their own policy proposals jointly to the national government. In situations where the national government provided no long-term vision or national policy on social integration, municipalities with large migrant populations had to respond to growing needs and concerns, despite their limited resources. Recognizing that many of the issues concerning migrants were related to the restrictive nature of national legislations and systems beyond the purview of municipal governments, these cities formed an alliance to pressure the national government to take actions on integration issues (CMLMP 2001).

The social integration of migrants and ethnic minorities in Japan has thus been initiated and driven by municipal governments. While government has adopted exclusivist citizenship policies at the national level, local governments have been supplementing these policies by conferring on migrants some degree of "local citizenship" (Tsuda 2006) and trying to integrate them as community members.

Multicultural Coexistence Policies, 2005–Present

It is noteworthy that the term "social integration" has rarely appeared in media and policy discourses about the incorporation of migrants and ethnic minorities in Japan. In the 1970s, municipalities grounded their social integration policies on the human rights principle; the more recently adopted principle is "multicultural coexistence" (*tabunka kyosei*). This concept has been defined in various manners. The Ministry of Internal Affairs and Communications (MIC) defines it as the situation in which "people of different nationalities and races live together as members of local societies while recognizing cultural differences and trying to establish equal relationships" (MIC 2006a, 5)

The idea of "multicultural coexistence" gradually garnered wide social support both at the local and national levels in the late 1990s and to the middle of the next decade. At the national level, the term gained official recognition in 2005 when the MIC designated "the efforts to establish a society based on multicultural coexistence" as a major policy focus (Yamawaki 2005). The MIC also issued its "Promotion Plan for Multicultural Coexistence" in 2006. This policy document requested all municipal governments across the country to take specific measures to promote multicultural coexistence with foreign citizens (MIC 2006b). These measures were in four arenas:

1. Communication support (e.g., assistance in Japanese language acquisition, provision of multilingual information, etc.);
2. Life support (e.g., provision of orientation programs, assistance with children's education, information provision for employment, health care, and emergency situations such as earthquakes);
3. Development of multicultural communities (e.g., launching awareness raising campaigns, promoting the social participation of migrants and minorities); and
4. Policy coordination for promoting multicultural coexistence policies (e.g., establishing a specially designated office for multicultural coexistence).

Furthermore, the document advocated for integrating migrants into communities through neighbourhood associations, cultural events, and policy-related hearing processes (MIC 2006b). This was the very first time any arm of the Japanese government had set a clear policy guideline for incorporating migrants in the society.

Among the most recent and significant measures taken by the national government was the creation of a new office for social integration policies within the Cabinet Office on 9 January 2009. The Office for the Promotion of Measures for Foreign Residents, which consists of four staff members and two supervisory positions under the director general, became responsible for drafting policy plans for foreign citizens. By the end of January 2009, the office announced the "immediate support measures for foreign residents" such as housing assistance,[10] educational assistance for foreign children in transition,[11] and employment assistance for unemployed foreigners in the form of subsidies and skill-upgrading training, among others (Cabinet Office 2009).

The other milestone was the establishment of the Council for the Promotion of Measure for Foreign Residents in March 2009. Chaired by the minister of State, the council is composed of 22 top officials from all ministries except Defense and Environment to plan and coordinate policies for foreign residents in Japan. This is the national government's first policy coordination body dealing with issues including social integration. The objective of the council is to "promote the policy efforts for foreign residents as a whole government" (ibid.). Such an initiative can be understood as the national government's belated response to the needs of social integration.

MULTICULTURAL COEXISTENCE AND SOCIAL INTEGRATION

Following the MIC's Plan for the Promotion of Multicultural Coexistence, various social integration programs have been adopted and implemented at the local level. Under the first category of "communication support," most municipalities with a substantial number of migrants have made available multilingual information services and low-cost Japanese language lessons. Reflecting the experiences of Kobe and Osaka, the major concern for municipalities has been the ways in which they could reach out to migrants and provide them with information in cases of natural disasters such as the earthquakes and typhoons that frequently hit Japan. Many municipalities have prepared information booklets on emergency evacuation procedures in several languages.

Integration of migrants into the information network has become a challenge for local governments as well. For instance, in 2009, many municipalities struggled with informing foreign residents of H1N1 (swine flu) when it spread across the country. To protect migrants as well as Japanese citizens by containing the infection zone, establishing an effective outreaching system became indispensable. The Tokyo Metropolitan Government is currently examining the possibility of introducing a new multilingual information system for foreign residents by using mobile networks. Having been proposed by the Committee on the Promotion of Local Internationalization, this measure, once adopted, will integrate migrants into the mobile-based information system at the time of their residency registration (Tokyo Metropolitan Government 2010).

Under the MIC's category of "life support," some municipalities have provided local schools with additional Japanese language teaching staff for migrant children. The extent to which municipalities support local schools, however, varies greatly. For instance, Toyota City in Aichi prefecture offers special education programs for migrants' children whose mother tongue is not Japanese.[12] Children with limited understanding of the Japanese language can receive their math and Japanese education in separate classrooms. The programs, which are tailored to the different levels and needs of children, can be offered until their graduation. However, most cities do not offer such programs. Mitaka Cty in Tokyo, for instance, provides migrant children with a special education program only up to 40 hours per child. A one-time-only program, its duration cannot be extended except in special circumstances. Such a measure is far from being sufficient. Education programs for migrant children have varied enormously among municipalities in terms of quality and quantity due to factors such as available financial resources and institutional will.[13]

Other social integration programs under the category of life support include measures such as providing migrants with medical interpreters to hospitals, offering assistance with housing applications, and supporting employment searches.

The Assessment of Policies and Programs for Multicultural Coexistence

The concept of multicultural coexistence has gradually been accepted in Japanese society, especially after the MIC adopted it as a major policy focus in 2005. Nevertheless, even apart from the repercussions of the economic crisis, the concept has faced criticism. First, "multicultural coexistence" lacks clarity and precision in the values that it attempts to project. In fact, it is a confusing term and has given rise to much misunderstanding and criticism on both conservative and progressive grounds. Some conservatives claim that it will lead to more resource allocations to foreigners and are thus opposed to it. They believe that Japanese taxpayers' money should be spent on helping low-income Japanese citizens instead of low-income foreigners. Anti-migrant groups such as Zaitokukai claim that foreign residents (particularly Koreans) already have too many privileges, including welfare benefits, that are very difficult to obtain even for Japanese. They argue that the social protection of Japanese citizens should take priority over that of foreign residents (Zaitokukai 2011).

Other conservatives criticize the concept of multicultural coexistence from a different standpoint, equating "multicultural coexistence" with "multiculturalism" or the effort to devalue Japanese culture. For example, Hasegawa (2009) has interpreted the concept: "In other words, if the number of foreign residents increases in Japan, the Japanese culture will be eventually simply one of other many cultures existing in Japan. And the idea of 'multicultural coexistence' accepts it *as a good thing*. It is indeed scary" (Hasegawa 2009, author's translation). From the perspective of these conservative polemicists, multicultural coexistence will spoil the purity of Japanese culture and threaten its hegemony in the country.

Some progressives have also argued against the concept of multicultural coexistence, mainly on the grounds that such a policy slogan conceals inequalities and oppressions in Japanese society. Fujioka (2008) points out that no official policies and programs concerning multicultural coexistence have mentioned the forced migration and settlement of Koreans and Chinese in Japan as a result of Japanese colonialism during World War II. The naïve celebration of cultural diversities, she argues, tends to hide this historical past and the discrimination against ethnic minorities, which still remains strong. According to Fujioka, the current "state-led multicultural coexistence" does not recognize or attempt to rectify ongoing discrimination and inequality.

Higuchi (2008) echoes Fujioka by stating that the current policy of multicultural coexistence lacks a structural perspective. He emphasizes the importance of addressing the inequality in opportunities, resources, and outcomes. He insists that for the success of multicultural coexistence it is necessary to provide migrants and ethnic minorities with recognition and redistribution. These two elements can be made possible, he suggests, through affirmative action policy and heritage language acquisition.

Some minorities themselves take a critical stance toward multicultural coexistence policies. Seungkoo Choi views such policies and programs as paternalistic, maintaining that both national and local governments decide what they consider appropriate for foreign residents without fully including them in the decision-making process (Choi 2008). Indeed, with limited political rights, migrants and ethnic minorities have very little influence over policy-making that could directly affect them. Even many foreign residents councils are organized and governed by municipal governments – including the process of selecting the members. According to Choi, these councils do not always allow foreigners and minorities to express their needs and demands freely, much less translate them into policy; rather, local governments often use these committees to back up the policy that they have already prepared (ibid.).

The policies and programs for multicultural coexistence also lack the perspective of equal rights. As seen in the phrase "*trying to* establish equal relationship" in its official definition, multicultural coexistence presumes an "unequal" relationship between Japanese citizens and foreign citizens. This is quite different from multiculturalism policies in other Western countries which are founded upon the principle of equality for all.[14] For instance, Article 9 of the Canadian Multiculturalism Act stipulates, "It is hereby declared to be the policy of the Government of Canada to ensure that *all individuals receive equal treatment and equal protection under the law*, while respecting and valuing their diversity" (Canada 1985, italics added).

Such a discrepancy might arise partly because the Japanese concept of "multicultural coexistence" is intended for foreign citizens who do not have the same socio-economic and political rights enjoyed by Japanese citizens.[15] Therefore, the majority of Japanese might simply assume an "unequal relationship." However, Japan has ratified the International Covenant of Economic, Social, and Cultural Rights and the International Covenant on Civil and Political Rights, both of which endorse equality between citizens and non-citizens in terms of basic human rights. Therefore, the rights perspective should be more substantially incorporated into the actual policies and programs concerning multicultural coexistence. Foreign citizens and minorities are still discriminated against in employment, have limited access to social services, and have extremely limited political rights.

Ito (2009) argues that the lack of rights perspective derives from the fact that the Japanese government perceives multicultural coexistence as only one of the solutions to population aging and economic globalization. By comparing and contrasting the state policies on multicultural coexistence and gender equality, she concludes that in both cases political ideals such as human rights and equality simply became the tools for achieving economic goals rather than realizing principles and values. Like gender-related policies, multicultural coexistence policies have been promoted for utilitarian purposes: the Japanese government wants to use them to facilitate more immigration to maintain Japanese economic competitiveness.

One argument has it that "multicultural coexistence" in Japan has more in common with "integration" in European countries than with "multiculturalism" (e.g., Kondo 2008). However, when examined closely, the Japanese policies and programs for multicultural coexistence can be seen to differ from European policies on integration as well. In Europe, integration policies are often founded upon the rights principle, under which legislation has been passed to ensure the equality and rights of migrants and ethnic minorities, and various measures have been adopted and implemented to protect these groups from racial and ethnic discrimination. However, multicultural coexistence policies in Japan are not backed by anti-discrimination legislation or measures, as seen in the Racial Equality Directive of 2000/43/EC in Europe (European Union 2000).

Moreover, the principle of multicultural coexistence in Japan lacks the perspective of mutuality. The vast majority of programs have been assisting migrants' adaptation with multilingual social services and language acquisition programs. These programs are certainly a welcome move, but very few of them are offered to address concrete efforts on the part of the mainstream Japanese population to better accommodate migrants and minorities. For instance, very few awareness-raising programs on anti-discrimination and protection of migrants' rights have been implemented for the local population so far.

This situation presents a stark contrast to the concept of social integration, understood in recent years as a mutual process between the mainstream population and migrants (and ethnic minorities). The European Union, for instance, defines social integration as follows:

> Social integration is a dynamic, long-term, and continuous *two-way process* of mutual accommodation, not a static outcome. *It demands the participation not only of immigrants and their descendants but of every resident.* The integration process involves adaptation by immigrants, both men and women, who all have rights and responsibilities in relation to their new country of residence. *It also involves the receiving society, which should create the opportunities for the immigrants' full economic, social, cultural, and political participation.* Accordingly, Member States are encouraged *to consider and involve both immigrants and national citizens in integration policy, and to communicate clearly their mutual rights and responsibilities.* (European Union 2004, emphasis added by author)

Clearly, there are tremendous differences in the vision and orientations between the EU concept of social integration and the Japanese policies for multicultural coexistence. While the Japanese policies for multicultural coexistence certainly opened a new policy horizon for integration, their scope is still much more limited than those in Europe. It would be more appropriate to call the Japanese policies and programs "assimilative social integration" in that they stress foreign residents learning the Japanese language, culture, and social norms. While language programs and socio-cultural classes certainly help foreign residents and ethnic minorities, more attention should be paid to how their cultures will be valued and their rights can be protected. According to the director of a migrant NGO in Tokyo, all foreign students, including Koreans and Chinese children, are compelled to bow to the Japanese flag and sing the Japanese national anthem at public school ceremonies; all children must conform to Japanese cultural practices. The education at Japanese public schools encourages students with diverse cultural backgrounds to behave like Japanese without allowing them to claim their own cultural heritage. Heritage language programs are offered in a few municipalities but not even considered as a policy agenda at the national level.

Furthermore, it is difficult for migrants' children to attend ethnic schools not only because of the high tuition but also because of institutional marginality. The Japanese government does not recognize the high school diploma of most ethnic schools as a sufficient requirement to apply for Japanese universities since their curricula do not follow the Japanese academic guidelines. Graduates of ethnic high schools cannot attend Japanese universities unless they pass the government exam based on the Japanese high schools curriculum. If they decide to work instead, they cannot even be recognized as high school graduates, so their employment prospects are extremely limited.

FUTURE CHALLENGES FOR SOCIAL INTEGRATION IN JAPAN

Social integration of migrants and ethnic minorities in Japan continues to face numerous challenges. Foremost among these is the national government's dearth of commitment to integration issues. Policy-makers still believe that integration should be dealt with at the local level. While many proposals have been submitted to the government to establish an independent state agency in charge of immigration and integration, no action has been taken except for the establishment of a small office within the Cabinet Office in early 2009.

The second challenge is the backlash against multicultural coexistence. Since the financial crisis hit the country in 2008 and unemployment among Japanese workers has risen, anti-immigrant sentiments have begun to grow. Partly reflecting such sentiments, the initial enthusiasm for multicultural coexistence has waned. The backlash also seems to be associated with the attempt by the Democratic Party of Japan (DPJ) to pass a law on local suffrage[16] for permanent foreign residents in 2009 and 2010. Various anti-migrant groups launched extensive political campaigns against this attempt and received wide public support. For instance, the membership of an anti-migrant group, Zaitokukai, almost doubled from 5,000 in 2009 to over 10,000 in 2011 (Zaitokukai 2011). Although it was the top DPJ leaders who initiated and pushed this proposal, the DPJ finally gave up submitting it to the national legislature in the face of fierce objections from inside and outside the party.

The third challenge in relation to such backlash lies in establishing more substantial legal measures against growing racial/ethnic discrimination, xenophobia, and hate crimes. Although the Japanese government ratified the International Convention on the Elimination of All Forms of Racial Discrimination in 1995, it has suspended the provisions of Article 4 (a) and (b) outlawing the dissemination of ideas based on racial superiority or hatred, out of concern for restricting freedom of expression and speech. Because of these reservations, the Japanese government has not yet enacted any anti-discrimination laws (SNMJ 2009). Particularly since the issue of local suffrage for foreign residents became a topic of heated national debate, harassment of foreign residents, ethnic restaurants, and ethnic schools has been growing (*Migrants Network* 2010; *Yomiuri Shimbun*, 22 May 2010). To ensure multicultural coexistence, however, such acts must be officially condemned and outlawed by establishing the new legislation against racial/ethnic discrimination and hate crimes.

CONCLUSION: BEYOND THE MONOCULTURAL MYTH

In recent years, there has been a consensus among scholars on the policy convergence of immigration and integration policies in industrialized countries (Entzinger and Biezeveld 2003; Joppke 2007; Surak 2008). The case of Japan can to a certain extent be contextualized in this converging trend. After having adopted exclusivist policies on immigration and ignored the need of migrant incorporation for many years, the Japanese government finally recognized its de facto cultural diversities and in 2006 shifted its policy focus to multicultural coexistence. The actual programs are becoming more similar to those in Europe and North America than in the past, though there remain many significant discrepancies. The financial crisis and the local suffrage issue, however, triggered anti-migrant sentiments and a backlash against multicultural coexistence among municipal governments and the local population, only three years after the declaration of the policies that promoted it. While other industrialized countries have been facing a multiculturalism backlash after many years of trials and errors, Japan had not even fully implemented the policies and programs for multicultural coexistence before the backlash started.

A further xenophobic approach, however, will eventually undermine Japan's position in the global economy. In demographic terms, Japan has no option but to become more open to migrants, given its rapidly increasing aging population and declining birthrates. The Japanese labour force will decline by 50 percent by 2055, resulting in a serious labour shortage. By that time, one retiree will be supported financially by 1.3 working persons, a situation that is literally unfeasible (Japan Business Federation 2008). The United Nations estimated that Japan would need to accept 10 million migrants between 2005 and 2050 in order to maintain the dependency ratio[17] at the 1995 level, which would be desirable for the Japanese social security system (United Nations 2000).

Of course, increasing immigration alone will not solve all of the demographic problems; other measures for increasing the population and reforming the social security system will be required. Nevertheless, accepting a substantial number of migrants is at least one of the measures that Japan will have to take. Even a former secretary general of the conservative Liberal Democratic Party and other politicians issued a policy proposal that Japan should officially become an open immigration country, and accept 10 million migrants by 2050 (LDP 2008). Policy-makers, government officials, and business leaders have finally recognized the seriousness of the country's demographic crisis. They have also realized that Japan is losing the global competition for the highly skilled migrants it needs to survive in the knowledge economy.

As Ito (2009) has pointed out, such utilitarian motivations should not be the only foundation of integration policies. This is particularly so for Japan, which invaded neighbouring countries during World War II, resulting in the formation of major ethnic communities in the country. To establish a solid foundation for multicultural coexistence at the local level, such efforts must start with acknowledging historical legacies and incorporating the historical background of cultural diversities in school education programs. At the same time, multicultural education programs should also respond to the current realities of growing cultural diversities and inequalities as well as future immigration needs of the country.

At present, the Japanese government has not fully committed itself to social integration in terms of allocating sufficient resources to local programs for multicultural coexistence. Nor has it formulated comprehensive policies for social integration at the national level. Financial and human resource responsibility for integration has still fallen upon local governments. While it is perfectly suitable for local governments to make efforts to integrate migrants, the national government should also provide a long-term vision on immigration and integration, and establish the national policy framework based on such a vision. No matter how much the backlash grows, migrants will still remain our fellow neighbours. Accommodating their cultural diversities and building a community with them will not be an option but an inevitable reality that the mainstream Japanese population must tackle.

Many Japanese still have difficulties in abandoning the myth of homogeneity. However, the Japanese population has always been diverse, and with more immigration and international / interethnic marriages, its diversity will continue to increase. Educational opportunities and awareness campaigns for the majority Japanese population to recognize this reality would be a starting point for the successful integration of migrants and ethnic minorities. Only by recognizing the reality of diversity as well as the importance of rights and equality for all will the efforts for multicultural coexistence begin to bear fruit in Japan.

NOTES

Due to the unavailability of the data at the time of preparing this draft, the author could not include the impact of the Great East Japan Earthquake in March 2011 in this chapter. The author's separate analysis on the impact of the disaster on migration in Japan will become available later in 2012.

1.   While this chapter focuses on the integration of migrants and their descendants, the author would like to mention that Japan long had ethnic minorities who were not necessarily migrants. In the northern part of Japan, indigenous people called the Ainu had been maintaining their distinct culture for centuries until the Meiji government began to impose its strong assimilation policy in the late nineteenth century. In southern Japan, the Okinawans, who used to have their own Ryukyu Kingdom, had been controlled by a Japanese feudal lord since 1609 and were eventually coerced into becoming Japanese citizens by the Meiji government in 1879.

2.   In Japan the terms "migrants" and "immigrants" are not used in official documents or statistics. The government only uses "foreign residents" or

"foreign citizens." Data on the "foreign born" population are not available. Though "migrants" and "foreign residents" are not synonymous in a strict sense, I use these terms interchangeably whenever appropriate. I will also use the term "ethnic minorities" to refer to those who became naturalized as Japanese citizens and the second and third generation Korean residents who were born in Japan but do not have Japanese citizenship.

3. The Japanese term *Tabunka Kyosei* is also translated as "multicultural community building."

4. Koreans and Taiwanese men living in overseas territories (their traditional residence) did not enjoy such political rights. Women did not have political rights at all regardless of their residence or origin. Even Japanese women were denied suffrage until 1945.

5. Osaka Prefecture also abolished the citizenship requirement for the public housing application in 1975.

6. However, given that the national pension scheme officially requires 25 years of financial contribution and the typical retirement age was 60 in Japan in 1982, the government did not allow in the national pension scheme those who were already above 35 years old. Therefore, many foreigners remained excluded. However, some local governments provide the supplementary allowance for these people (Tsujimoto 2007, 127).

7. During the "on-the-job training" period, most trainees were actually serving as low-wage labourers while receiving only a "training allowance" far below the official minimum wage. This problem was finally rectified in July 2010 when the ITP and TIP were reformed. Trainees are now recognized as workers as soon as they start on-the-job training and are covered by labour laws. The monitoring system was also introduced to protect trainees from abuse and exploitation (MOJ 2010).

8. Migrants who arrived in the latter part of the past decade include care workers. Under the Economic Partnership Agreement with Indonesia (2008) and the Philippines (2009), 455 nurses and 732 caregivers entered Japan between 2008 and 2010. This scheme has been heavily criticized, however, as these migrants can work only as "assistants" until they pass the Japanese national exams, and in reality, only 4 percent have passed the exams so far due to the language difficulty. Those who fail must eventually return home.

9. The membership expanded to 28 cities by 2009.

10. When many foreign residents, particularly Japanese Brazilians, lost their jobs, they also lost their accommodation, because most of them lived in dormitories or apartments provided by the companies. This has also been a problem for Japanese employees, but foreign residents have had a particularly hard time finding accommodation for financial reasons and also because of discrimination.

11. Because of the financial crisis, many migrants lost their jobs and could not afford to send their children to ethnic schools. Nevertheless, few of these children enrolled in Japanese public schools due to the language barrier. This new state measure helped foreign children with their transition to Japanese public schools.

12. The author's field trip to Toyota City, 27 February 2009.

13. In 2009 the national government finally started allocating some resources for language assistance programs for migrant children in cities with a large

number of migrants – an emergency measure in response to the growing number of migrant children dropping out of ethnic schools after the global financial crisis. However, even under this program, a migrant child can get language assistance for only six months.

14. Tessa Morris-Suzuki (2002) criticizes the Japanese case as "cosmetic multiculturalism."

15. For instance, as discussed earlier, Notification 382 of the Ministry of Welfare in 1954 enabled municipal governments to apply the welfare system to foreign residents in extreme poverty. However, foreign citizens have again been excluded from the welfare system since 1990 unless they are permanent residents, long-term residents, or their spouses. This change was communicated orally by the Ministry of Welfare to each local government (Tsujimoto 2007).

16. This proposal referred only to the right to vote in local elections, not the right to run for office.

17. The ratio of retirees and working-age population. The dependency ratio in Japan right now is 3.3, meaning that 3.3 working-age persons are supporting one retiree.

REFERENCES

AMDA International Medical Information Center. 2001. "Obasutei no Gaikokujin to Seikatsuhogo." Newsletter no. 38. At http://amda-imic.com/modules/NewsLetter/index.php?content_id=192 (accessed 11 July 2010).

Asahi Shimbun (newspaper). 1996. "Houmusho, Nyukokukijun wo Minaoshi." 18 April.

Asano, S. 2004. "The Situation of Chinese Students and the Shifts in the Acceptance Policy." *Rodo Horitsu Junpo* (25 May).

Cabinet Office. 2004. *Shoshika Shakai Hakusho.* Tokyo: Gyosei.

—2009. *Teijugaikokujin Shiennikansuru Taisakuno Suishinnitsuite.* At http://www8.cao.go.jp/teiju/suisin/taisaku_z.html (accessed 29 January 2012).

Canada. Department of Justice. 1985. *Canadian Multiculturalism Act.* c.24, 4th Supp. At http://laws.justice.gc.ca/en/C-18.7/ (accessed 31 January 2010).

Choi, S. 2008. "Kyosei no Machi Kawasaki wo Tou." *Nihon ni Okeru Tabunka Kyosei toha Nanika – Zainichi no Shitenkara*, ed. P. J. Seok and C. Ueno, 151-90. Shinyosha.

Council for Municipalities with Large Migrant Populations (CMLMP, Gaikokujin Shuju Toshi Kaigi). 2001. Hamamatsu Declaration and Proposals. At http://homepage2.nifty.com/shujutoshi/siryo/pdf/20011019hamamatsu.pdf (accessed 10 March 2010).

Entzinger, H. and R. Biezeveld. 2003. *Benchmarking in Immigrant Integration.* European Research Centre on Migration and Ethnic Relations (ERCOMER), Erasmus University. Rotterdam.

European Union. 2000. "Council Directive 2000/43/EC of 29 June 2000 Implementing the Principle of Equal Treatment between Persons Irrespective of Racial or Ethnic Origin." *Official Journal L 180*, 19/07/2000:22-6.

—2004. *Common Basic Principles for Immigrant Integration Policy in the European Union*. 14776/04.

Fujioka, M. 2008. "Kansei Tabunka Kyosei wo Tou." *NGO to Shakai* 3. 15 April.

Hasegawa, M. 2009. "Hontoha Kowai Tabunka Kyosei." *Sankei Shimbun*. 19 January.

Higuchi, N. 2008. *Kyosei de Haijo to Kakusa ha Nakunaruka – Ijusha no Genjo kara*. At http://www.tv.janjan.jp/movie/shiminkisha/0806169792/ngo_higuchi. pdf. (accessed 14 March 2010).

Ito, R. 2009. "Tabunka Kyosei to Jinken – Nihon no Bunmyaku kara." *Gakujutsu no Doko*. Japan Science Support Foundation (January):47-51.

Japan Business Federation. 2008. *Jinko Gensho ni Taioshita Keizai Shakai no Arikata*.

Joppke, C. 2007. "Transformation of Immigrant Integration in Western Europe: Civic Integration and Antidiscrimination Policies in the Netherlands, France, and Germany." *World Politics* 59(2):243-73.

Kawasaki City. 2010. *Gaikokujin Shimin Daihyousha Kaigi no Shikumi*.

Komai, H. 2001. *Foreign Migrants in Contemporary Japan*. Trans Pacific Press.

Kondo, A. 2008. *Migration and Globalization: Comparing Immigration Policy in Developed Countries*. Akashi Shoten.

Liberal Democratic Party of Japan (LDP). 2008. *Jinzai Kaikoku! Nihongata Iminseisaku no Teigen – Sekaino Wakamonoga Ijushitai to Akogareru Kuni no Kochikuni Mukete*. 12 June.

Migrants Network (magazine). 2010. "Zainichi Chugokujin no Jinken." No. 130 (June):15.

Minegishi, K. 2004. "Kawasaki-shi no Gaikokujin Shimin Seisaku to NPO." In *Imin wo Meguru Jichitai no Seisaku to Shakaiundo*, ed. H. Komai. Akashi Shoten.

Ministry of Education, Science and Technology (MEXT). 2008. "Ryugakusei 30 Mannin Keikaku Kosshino Sakuteini Tsuite." 27 July. At http://www.mext. go.jp/b_menu/houdou/20/07/08080109.htm (accessed 12 July 2010).

Ministry of Internal Affairs and Communication (MIC). 2006a. *Tabunka Kyosei no Suishin ni Kansuru Kenkyukai Hokokusho* (March).

—2006b. *Chiikiniokeru Tabunka Kyosei Suishin Puran*.

—2009. *Tabunka Kyosei no Suishin ni Kakawaru Suishin Keikaku no Sakutei Jokyo*.

Ministry of Justice (MOJ). Various years. *Immigration Statistics*. At http://www. immi-moj.go.jp/toukei/index.html (accessed 27 September 2011).

—2010. The Summary of Revisions and Stipulations of the Ministerial Ordinance concerning the Reassessment of the International Training System and the Technical Internship Program. At http://www.moj.go.jp/content/000033310. pdf (accessed 27 July 2010).

Ministry of Health, Labour, and Welfare (MHLW). 2005. *Chugoku Kikokusha Seikatsu Jittaichousa no Gaiyo*. At http://www.mhlw.go.jp/toukei/saikin/hw/ kikokusya/03/index.html (accessed 10 March 2010).

—2007. *Jinkou Doutai Toukei Nenpo*.

—2010. "Nikkeijin Rishokushani Taisuru Kikokushien-Jigyou no Shuryo ni Tsuite." Press release, 18 January.

—2010. *Chugoku Zanryu Kojit to heno Engo*. At http://www.mhlw.go.jp/bunya/ engo/seido02/ (accessed 18 March 2010).

Morris-Suzuki, T. 2002. "Immigration and Citizenship in Contemporary Japan." In *Japan – Change and Continuity*, ed. J. Maswood, G. Jeffrey, and H. Miyajima. London: RoutledgeCurzon.

Nishikawa, S. 1997. "Naikaku Houseikyoku – Sono Seidoteki Kenryokueno Sekkin." *Seikeironnso*:185-251.

Oguma, E. 1998. *Nihonjin no Kyoukai. Shinyosha*. Tokyo.

Oishi, N. 1995. *Training Abroad: German and Japanese Schemes for Workers from Transition Economies and Developing Countries*. With C. Kuptsch. ILO International Migration Paper No. 3, International Labour Office. Geneva.

Ryang, S. 2000. "Introduction: Resident Koreans in Japan." In *Koreans in Japan: Critical Voices from the Margin*, ed. S. Ryang. London: RoutledgeCurzon.

Sankei Shimbun (newspaper). 2010. "Gaikokujin Sanseiken Hantai 28 Ken, Sansei wo Gyakuten Todofukengikai." 21 March.

SNMJ (Solidarity Network with Migrants Japan). 2009. *Taminzoku Tabunka Kyosei no Korekara: NGO kara no Seisaku Teigen*. Gendai Jinbunsha.

Surak, K. 2008. "Convergence in Foreigners' Rights and Citizenship Policies? A Look at Japan." *International Migration Review* 42 (3):550-75.

Tabuchi, H. 2010. "Japan Training Program Is Said to Exploit Workers." *New York Times*. 20 July.

Tokyo Metropolitan Government. 2010. *Chiiki ni Micchakushita Kokatekina Joho Teikyo no Shikumi Zukuri*. Local Internationalization Promotion Committee. 22 January.

Tsuda, G. T., ed. 2006. *Local Citizenship in Recent Countries of Immigration: Japan in Comparative Perspective*. Lanham, MD: Lexington.

Tsujimoto, H. 2007. "Jinkentoshiteno Tabunka Kyosei – Gaikokujin Mondai." In *Kenkyu Kiyo* 13 (March):103-47. Buraku Liberation Research Institute Hyogo.

Uemura, S. 2008. "Salaries of Oyatoi [Japan's Foreign Employees] in Early Meiji. (In Japanese.) *Ryutsukagaku Daigaku Ronshu* 21, no.1:1-24.

United Nations. 2000. *Replacement Migration: Is It a Solution to Declining and Ageing Populations?* Population Division. Department of Social and Economic Affairs. United Nations Secretariat. New York.

Weiner, M., ed. 2009. *Japan's Minorities: The Illusion of Homogeneity*. 2nd ed. Routledge.

Yamawaki, K. 2003. "Foreign Workers in Japan: A Historical Perspective." In *Japan and Global Migration: Foreign Workers and the Advent of a Multicultural Society*, ed. M. Douglass and G.S. Roberts, 38-51. University of Hawaii Press.

—2005. "2005 nen wa Tabunka Kyosei Gannen?" *Jichitai Kokusaika Forum* (May):34-7.

Yomiuri Shimbun (newspaper). 2010. "Chosen Gakkou Chushou no Gaisen Ihan de 100 Manen." 22 May.

Zaitokukai. 2011. "Zaitokukai Gaiyo." At www.zaitokukai.info (accessed 21 July 2011).

CHAPTER 9

INTEGRATION IMMIGRATION GOVERNANCE POLICIES IN SPAIN: A PRACTICAL PHILOSOPHY

RICARD ZAPATA-BARRERO

DOES A SPECIFIC APPROACH TO THE INTEGRATION OF IMMIGRATION EXIST IN SPAIN?

Spain established immigration legislation for the first time after almost a decade of democracy in 1985 and as a compulsory condition for its admission to the European Union a year later. Two decades have since passed, with structural and legal changes and a clearer definition of the management strategies that help to orient Spain's integration policies. However, the country has yet to reach the critical point of going back to discuss the terms of its political and social contract, founded on a constitution and a system of regulations based on national and local autonomy. This operative stage is still to come. For the moment, paradoxically, the Spanish constitution is part of the problem that needs resolving. Likewise, certain dimensions of the country's institutional structure are unhelpful in managing these new issues. The structure of the labour market discriminates against immigrants in different areas of their daily lives. This new context of diversity resulting from the arrival and permanency of immigrants is now exposing weaknesses of the Spanish liberal democratic system. The issues arising from the management of immigration provide us with an opportunity to diagnose not only Spain's capacity to govern immigration but also to look at the policies being proposed for addressing the challenges of governance: the so-called Immigration Governance Policies (IGPs). A critical revision of the main issues that trouble Spain is also an opportunity for constituting an agenda.

International Perspectives: Integration and Inclusion, ed. J. Frideres and J. Biles. Montreal and Kingston: Queen's Policy Studies Series, McGill-Queen's University Press. © 2012 The School of Policy Studies, Queen's University at Kingston. All rights reserved.

If we define "philosophy of integration" as a set of explicit and co-herently developed policies for managing integration policies, Spain's philosophy of immigration is undoubtedly a practical one. It is based not on a preconceived idea but rather on the questions and answers that the day-to-day governance of immigration generates. It provides the strategic guidelines for approaching political action. In addition, this practical philosophy has the advantage for Spain of being able to observe the experience of other European states, and on this basis, build its own philosophy. Knowing the outcomes of policies in other states, it is able to reflect on and evaluate them in devising its own IGPs.

Given this framework, we pose two questions: What are the charac-teristics of IGP in Spain? What are the future challenges for ensuring governance? To answer these questions, we will consider nine policy areas related to the management of integration of immigration in Spain: 1) The distribution of powers with the decentralized structure of the Spanish state; 2) welfare policies; 3) immigrant associations; 4) the approach to citizenship; 5) the right to vote; 6) anti-discrimination policies in the labour market; 7) Muslim immigrant communities; 8) gender policies related to immigration; and 9) the management of identity in Spain. However, first a brief overview of the short history of Spanish immigration followed by the theoretical framework will help us to our focus critical analysis.

IMMIGRATION IN SPAIN: A SHORT HISTORY

Immigration has been an important political issue in Spain only since 2000, when political parties started to include the issue in their electoral campaigns and immigration became institutionalized after several legisla-tive changes. The year 2000 also saw the first debates on the social integra-tion of immigrants, after riots against Moroccan immigrant workers took place in El Ejido, a market-gardening town (*ciudad-cortijo*) in southeastern Spain. Other incidents of social unrest (such as immigrant strikes to obtain papers or civil, cultural, social, and economic rights), racism, and ethnic prejudice have triggered further public and political debate. More recently, the accommodation of cultural and religious claims raised by the Muslim community has entered the debate (Zapata-Barrero 2006).

Spain has a diverse immigrant population. The economic and historical connections with Northern Africa (source of 23 percent of foreign resi-dents) and South America (35 percent) have triggered the main immigra-tion flows into the country, but Europeans also represent a large group of foreign residents (22 percent). Conflicts of migration related to diversity have largely been provoked by the cultural and religious demands of those immigrants who are most "visible" within Spanish society: Muslims. However, it is important to recognize that these conflicts appear because the Muslim demands collide with historical and identitarian elements of Spain that hinder the management of diversity (such as the support to the Christian religion and the Spanish language).

The social and political debate has been focused more on the management of immigration flows than on integration. In the aftermath of 9/11, immigration became increasingly linked to security, resulting in the enhancement of border control, combating irregular immigration flows, and restricting immigration law. The fluctuations in Spanish immigration law over the past six years demonstrate that a political discourse on immigration is still under construction. Overall, the development of immigration policy is to a large extent still a matter of controlling immigration flows (prevention), while effective policies for the social integration of immigrants are lacking.

The change in government in March 2004 had an impact on policy orientations. Before 2004, when the right-wing Partido Popular was in government, migration policy was focused on security, trying to control migration flows by toughening the Foreigner's Law; policies were concentrated on building barriers. This restrictive approach encouraged the black-market economy and had negative results in terms of irregular immigration. However, the arrival in government of the Partido Socialista has seen some changes, the most important being that the focus has moved from security towards one linking immigration to the labour market. Policies are now concentrated on the capacities of the Spanish labour market to absorb immigration. This focus has driven the most recent regularization process, called the "normalization process," with the purpose of "normalizing" the lives of irregular immigrants already working in Spain in the informal economy.

Even though the number of immigrants has increased in the last decade, immigration is still mainly perceived as a matter of economic necessity, and the priority for politicians is border control. In a way, this explains why currently in Spain the immigrant is considered as *homo economicus,* a conceptualization that makes it difficult to move to more in-depth debate or further vision, in which immigrants are integrated not only in the labour market area but also in other spheres such as the political.

Having undergone many structural and legal changes since 1985, defining step by step the strategy of management of immigration, immigration policy in Spain is still under construction. Moreover, some elements of the institutional structure, like the Spanish Constitution, discriminate against immigrants in different ways. These elements exacerbate the management of challenges posed by new contexts and dynamics, as in the case of the arrival and permanence of immigrants, reinforcing the necessity of reviewing the bases for a new social and political contract.

With this context in mind, we next introduce a theoretical framework for analysis, the Immigration Governance Policies (IGPs).

THEORETICAL FRAMEWORK: IMMIGRATION GOVERNANCE POLICIES

This chapter is interested not only in the governance of immigration but also in analyzing the policies being proposed and implemented for guaranteeing it and the main challenges facing it in future. Hence, we establish the link between policy and governance. Our theoretical framework proposes the critical analysis of specific issues related to IPGs.

We take "governance" in its conventional sense and apply it to the management of immigration, not just as a set of government actions but rather as the capacity to politically face and respond to the challenges of society and to coordinate government actions for maintaining stability and social cohesion. From World Bank definitions and governance indicators, we can assemble the following definition: "The use of institutional resources to manage society's problems and affairs" and "the capacity of government to formulate and implement sound policies, and also the use of institutions and their capacity to create a context of collaboration for allocating resources and coordinating the government's activity" (World Bank 1991).

Governance here is related to the capacity to manage the realities of diversity and to cope with the contradictory and extreme conditions of the liberal democratic system. In addition, the term involves "the consequences of the excessive demands" that these situations provoke (ibid.).

In terms of function as opposed to measures such as capacity to manage, the governance of immigration is related to the results achieved – that is, stability and cohesion. Here we are also referring to the capacity to foresee the effects of the arrival of immigrants.

According to the diagnosis made in 1975 by the Trilateral Commission in response to the welfare state crisis (Crozier, Huntington, and Watanuki 1975),[1] a widely accepted cause of ungovernability is that it is a result of an overload of demands on government and the difference between the volume of demands and the capacity to respond. This is an issue that is considered strictly within the liberal democratic context and its capacity to provide a response to the questions that arise from the new dynamics of diversity of society (Zapata-Barrero 2010a). As a political category, a redefinition that includes immigrants within the semantic field is required; otherwise, we might end up with a reactive discourse that assumes that immigrants give rise to problems in democratic governance because they challenge the needs of ordinary citizens, including national citizens in a precarious social situation who are dependent on the welfare state.[2] Therefore, the concept of the governance of diversity should be considered as one affecting the system and not the needs of national citizens. This vision of governance is fundamental in understanding the orientation of the issues that follow.

We would also like to add to this theoretical framework an important dimension of the meaning of governance: the capacity of government to introduce adjustments and innovations to respond to the challenges of diversity arising from immigration. Therefore, this framework links governance and processes of social change in which the different economic, social, political, public, and private actors play specific roles.

In this theoretical framework, the issues selected form part of the most immediate agenda of IPGs in Spain. Our main intention is to describe the current situation and the normative questions it poses for the future.[3]

However, we do not wish to review governance policies in Spain without a central argument. In this regard, we propose that the approach to the policies for the governance of immigration in Spain is based on a practical philosophy – not on a preconceived idea but rather on the questions and answers that the practice of governance of immigration itself generates.

NINE BASIC AREAS OF IMMIGRANT INTEGRATION

Management of the Distribution of Powers

Distribution of powers is a deep-rooted issue in Spain, one that is always present in political and social debates. It is linked to the way the process of political and administrative decentralization was agreed upon during the transition to democracy, with no time limit and no minimum and maximum powers established for any of the parties involved. It has therefore always been an ongoing process since the Spanish Constitution of 1978.

The subject of immigration falls within this framework as an area that has not been defined in terms of powers, and which therefore has not been defined in terms of the administrative distribution of tasks and functions (the "who does what" in terms of immigration involving different government bodies). The powers in immigration were not discussed during the transition to democracy and are not included in the Constitution of 1978. However, this lack of an administrative reference on how powers on immigration are distributed in administrative and territorial terms is no hindrance to the orientation of practices that are increasingly well defined and recognized. It is in this area that the argument that Spain is pursuing a practical philosophy is most apparent.

Indeed, government action and institutional practice itself means that while the management of frontiers and everything related to flows is the exclusive responsibility of the central government, issues related to integration have fallen to the autonomous regional governments and especially to local governments, which are responsible for practically all reception and integration issues. In this respect, the government has sought to support immigrant integration initiatives by distributing the budget for the integration and reception of immigrants between town councils and autonomous community governments. This financial distribution has been undertaken through the bodies managing immigration policies in each autonomous region, and with accredited demographic and objective criteria. In turn, the government has started to divert responsibilities for the internal management of immigration to the autonomous communities, as required and recognized in the statutes of these communities. For example, the responsibility for reception and integration of immigrants is recognized in Catalonia, as is management of work permits.[4]

The biggest problem is that the present distribution of powers prevents the autonomous communities from developing comprehensive public policies on immigration, although it is also true that conflicts of powers in this area have to date been scarce (Miret 2009).

The current regime of autonomous regions, which enables towns to register their inhabitants without taking into account the criteria of the state, is also an unusual feature of Spain. It enables immigrants in an irregular situation to register. Here again, this practical philosophy, which is the basis for the governance of immigration in Spain, is apparent. Considering strategic objectives – basically, cohesion and stability – the preference is to make the problem visible (by registering individuals in an irregular situation) rather than keeping it invisible and unprotected. In these circumstances, the practical philosophy of the state is also interesting, as it is aware of the situation but does not seek conflict with the councils. There is a tacit understanding of and indirect consent for the councils' action. This practical philosophy ensures the governance of immigration in Spain.

This situation leads to a number of challenges for the improvement of governance, such as establishing right from the beginning well-known mechanisms for coordination among the state, autonomous communities, and local government bodies in terms of public policies on immigration, and between the autonomous communities. Considering the division of powers being established in practice, the participation of the autonomous communities and local government should be increased by establishing state policies for immigration, including controlling flows and setting quotas. However, there is also lack of a more explicit recognition of what is a fact on the ground: that leadership in the management of migratory policies falls to town councils. The most appropriate measure would be a national agreement on aliens and immigration, in which (among other issues) areas of competence would be precisely defined, the mechanisms for coordination between various government bodies would be specified, and the financing mechanisms would be determined for facing the challenge that immigration presents for Spanish society today (ibid.). This agreement would need to be be based on political consensus, institutional coordination, and social harmony. Perhaps we should also include here the creation of an immigration agency whose main role would be to ensure compliance and to guarantee the implementation of the contents of the agreement.

Management of Welfare Policies

The Spanish welfare state is young compared to that in other European countries. Historically, it has two important distinguishing characteristics. It was set up after the crisis of the welfare states during the 1970s without the presence of immigrants, whereas in France and Germany immigrants contributed to the rebuilding of society after the Second World War. This may help to explain some of the Spanish welfare state's weaknesses. Another issue, already intrinsic to the other European welfare states, is how welfare, identity, diversity, and opportunity have become gradually linked. This link is central to understanding the logic behind Spanish governance of immigration. The biggest problem is the social exclusion of immigrants and second-generation immigrants who will become incorporated in the labour market during the next decade. Yet again, the debate on this issue will contribute to constituting the practical philosophy that guides policy for governing diversity in the area of welfare.

According to Moreno (2009), the arrival of immigrants presents us with the opportunity to identify the weaknesses of our welfare system with the aim of guaranteeing its future sustainability. In Spain there is a very characteristic link between welfare and integration. On one hand, social security programs protect against determined risks such as invalidity, unemployment, or retirement for immigrants who have worked in the formal economy. On the other hand, universal programs of education, health, and, to some extent, social services provide a basic network of protection that guarantees a series of elementary social rights and acts as a redistribution mechanism – which in turn guarantees life opportunities and the development of immigrants' potential. It is also worth mentioning the transformation that the traditional Spanish family has undergone due to changes in society, such as the increasing participation of women in the workforce, the evolution of family structures, and a reduction in the expectations of intergenerational care. These changes represent opportunities for immigrant workers to develop niches in the labour market in the area of social reproduction (ibid.).

With this framework, Spain could pave the way forward in the issue of social mobility. An important part of the effort made to design viable models of incorporation will come from the need to guarantee the possibility of vertical social mobility for immigrants' descendants, as well the application of effective anti-discrimination policies so that equal opportunities are guaranteed (ibid.). Welfare should thus be linked to the promotion of equal treatment and non-discrimination in terms of racial or ethnic origin, in a way that no other European country has highlighted so willingly. The achievement of these objectives will be of great importance to paving the way for the children of the immigrants, who have grown up and been educated in a bicultural context in Spanish society.

The practical philosophy that guides policy for the governance of diversity in Spain develops tools for foreseeing events such as those that occurred in November 2005 in France, where citizens of immigrant origin rebelled against the state that excluded them despite their having been educated in the republican values of equal opportunities. The French experience is a clear warning to the weak Spanish welfare state. These "Spanish of immigrant origin" will have the same personal and labour expectations as their native born colleagues and will not be as willing to accept the jobs or the working conditions their parents once did – jobs that once represented a significant qualitative improvement over life in countries of origin. Likewise, the fight against the social exclusion of immigrants, who have fewer resources for combating social inequalities, is related to the precarious immigrant labour market. Therefore, the area of social protection policies is the one most in need of development (ibid.). The lines of action for diversity originating from immigration should be adjusted in two basic ways: guaranteeing equality (access to benefits and services) and advancing towards equity (the achievement of equal results even if this means differential treatment). One of the practical dimensions embodying this debate is deciding how to respond to the specific demands of ethnic diversity: through general services or through the establishment of a specialized parallel system. The debate on the advantages and disadvantages of both models remains open, although the Spanish practical philosophy tends to defend the logic that generalizes and standardizes.

Management of Immigrant Associations

Immigrant associations are one of the most deep-rooted indicators of our recent democratic history. In Spain, there are very close links between immigrant associations and social movements, in that it is assumed that one of the functions of immigrant associations is social criticism and pressure with a view to effecting social change. This is no coincidence and is part of the history of Spain, where the right of association was semi-criminalized and, as such, associations and mobilization against Franco's dictatorial regime were implicitly linked. This deep-rooted phenomenon in Spanish tradition is being reproduced among immigrant associations, as they find themselves in a political situation that denies them certain rights and makes it difficult for them to express their religious and cultural practices. This situation partially explains why immigrant associations are a tool for social and political demands, a means of channelling immigrants' demands and passing them on to the public political system. With their links to government bodies, immigrant associations are nonetheless assuming another role, not so much in terms of making demands but at the level of implementation of policies aimed at immigrants. In this area, immigrant associations are making the transition from being a movement to becoming NGOs. In Spain, this dual role of immigrant associations, as an altruistic social movement providing welfare, is a fact. Most welfare services are partly fostered by the associations' relationship with governments in general, and local governments in particular, and where the associations become "allies" of local politics in the design and especially the implementation of policies.

This situation leads to a dilemma that each town council resolves in a different way: there is no state-wide response or any political guidelines for local government to design a specific way of relating to immigrant associations. The dilemma is between promotion and generalization. To include immigrant associations within the network of citizens' associations as a whole, with no distinction or specific treatment, is one of the central focuses for debate regarding the governance policy of associationism among immigrants in Spain (Zapata-Barrero 2004, 147-59). Once again, the focus of this debate highlights a practical philosophy.

On this point, local integration policies that promote the development and consolidation of associations among immigrants contribute to ensuring that they are included in the city's effective and active *demos* (Morales, Gonzalez, and Jorba 2009). However, the issue involves determining which policies promoting immigrant associations are the most effective. In this case, the dilemma arises between policies that identify immigrant associations as a separate group and therefore promote the formation and consolidation of associations by and among immigrants, and the more general policies for promoting associations that do not provide more facilities for immigrants in particular to form associations. The former policies tend to facilitate the creation of a separate network of associations among immigrants; they can in some cases become segregated from the associations of the population as a whole. The aim of the latter policies is for immigrants not to form their own associations based around their own cultural identities but to join existing citizen associations.

Immigrant associations are means of transfer, and agents for the reception and implementation of public policies aiming to enable immigrants and their descendants to integrate, as they fulfil certain essential tasks for recognition and redistribution among the groups present in the city (ibid.). Associations enable demands to be aggregated and to be defended from platforms with greater symbolic power; they allow the participation of their members to be channelled and promoted. Furthermore, associations are institutions of first contact and provide psychological-emotional support in the migratory process, clearly complementing the work of the institutions of the host society. Finally, they enable collective self-expression, and the maintenance of identity is something that is valuable to the individuals who sustain it.

Management of the Citizenship Approach

While most European countries make use of the "citizen" rhetoric to assign a restrictive policy forcing immigrants to pass a civic test in order to access rights to residency and/or citizenship (e.g., the Netherlands, Denmark, and Germany; see Zapata-Barrero 2009b), the use made in Spain of the category of citizenship is precisely contrary to any regime establishing obligations or examinations, which even Spanish citizens do not have to pass. The category of citizenship has a conservative connotation and a reactive sense in practically all European countries, but in Spain it has a progressive connotation and a proactive sense. Here Spain is radically distancing itself from the general European tendency. This attitude might be explained by the fact that Spain, as a relatively new country in terms of the immigration tradition, is at the beginning of the process of managing the effects of immigration on society, or is aware of these other policies, and wants to intentionally disassociate itself from this conservative logic. The first case would be possible if it coincided with the situation in other countries that have recently become incorporated in the immigration tradition, as is the case of Italy and Greece. However, reality shows that these two southern countries are choosing to adopt a reactive approach to the category of citizenship. Undoubtedly, there is a third element: the secondary effects that the introduction of citizen tests would have in highlighting the plurality of identities that exists in Spain. In this case, perhaps the progressive option is better than the conservative one. While the debate on immigration is hardly ever contextualized in Spain in terms of identity, the language of identity is intrinsic to the political debate in its different non-state nations, and impregnates their political philosophies (Gil 2009). In this last case, the use made of citizenship is a mixture of both conservative and proactive logics. Perhaps it is the management of this balance that shapes the distinctive Catalan philosophy in these issues.

In this contextual framework, citizenship in Spain has become a category with an assigned political focus and a way of formulating immigration plans and programs at all levels of the administration, from the Spanish government's Strategic Plan for Citizenship and Integration, 2007–10 to the Catalan autonomous government's Citizenship and Immigration Plan, 2004–08, as well as the citizenship plans that exist in many local administrations. This approach to citizenship is unique to Spain; it incorporates the principles of equality and inclusion and explicitly includes the aim of treating immigrants as citizens in its integration policies. The approach provides a framework for making demands for legislative change, especially constitutional change that enhances effective equal rights for all citizens (de Lucas 2009). There is also a republican component to this approach insofar as it defends the practice of citizenship by immigrants and the criteria for residence through registration mechanisms, also unique to Spain.

In this regard, the use made of citizenship in Spain is very much linked to the urban concept of citizenship, citizens as inhabitants of the city. Therefore, all inhabitants are worthy of all the rights bestowed by the municipality without any legal differentiation between citizen and immigrant. One of de Lucas's (2009) conclusive arguments is that the census should be treated in a positive sense as a list of residents and not in a negative sense as an instrument of police control.

This approach is also used as a guide for proactive discourses, both for establishing policies that manage immigrants as full citizens (the inclusion rhetoric) and for contextualizing policies that are centred on managing the interaction between immigrants and citizens (the accommodation rhetoric) (Zapata-Barrero 2009a, 102-14). If we adopt the citizenship rhetoric discourse, all mention of immigrants as "new citizens" should be criticized, as this concept conceals all the inequalities that immigrants suffer compared with citizens.

Management of the Right to Vote

Currently, the right to vote is one of the main debates linked to the governance of immigration in Spain. Initially social, the debate has already begun to enter the parliamentary sphere. Claims for the promotion of this right become more apparent before any type of election, not only by immigrant associations but also by other social actors and some left-wing political parties. The Spanish United Left Party (Izquierda Unida) has spoken out in favour of this democratic right.

In this respect, the Spanish practical philosophy is two-dimensional. The "dimension of territory" questions the territorial level at which immigrants should be allowed to vote: local, autonomous, or state. The "legal dimension" includes at least three arguments: first, the criteria of nationality (all immigrants must obtain Spanish nationality before accessing the right to vote), and second, the principle of reciprocity in the Spanish constitution, a polemic element in the management of the right to vote in Spain.[5] The third argument deals with length of residence in Spain before gaining the right to vote (Zapata-Barrero and Zaragoza 2009).

There are two legal elements that hinder the promotion of the right to vote. Efforts made to promote immigrant voting rights clash with issues such as the technical difficulty of changing the constitution, political party fears around changing it, and the fact that it is an issue that can negatively affect the electoral interests of the governing party. In addition, there is an evident "ethnicization" of the Civil Code, which discriminates against immigrants by origin when it comes to granting Spanish nationality, the only way of achieving the right to vote. It is evident that this "ethnicization" is structural rather than social or political. A reform of the Civil Code would be an important step in reconciling access to Spanish nationality without discriminating by nationality, culture, or origin, therefore promoting immigrant voting rights without discriminating on the grounds of origin.

Currently, it appears that the government is taking the first steps to promote immigrant voting rights, with the appointment of a special ambassador to improve reciprocity agreements and the decision to create a sub-commission in the Congress of Deputies to study possible constitutional and legal reforms. However, these first steps may come to nothing if there are no constitutional changes in the meantime. Without this reform, the promotion of reciprocity agreements will mean conceding the fundamental right to vote through bilateral agreements with direct implications for the different legal status of immigrants, depending on whether or not "their" states have negotiated in favour or against. Definitively, all the arguments indicate a practical philosophy, although in this case not as straightforwardly expressed as in others: the need for constitutional change in the medium term in order to avoid the perpetuation of inequalities between groups of different origin. Here constitutional change is essential to promote immigrant voting rights on the basis of length of residence and without any other type of exclusion.

Management of Anti-Discrimination in the Labour Market

Discrimination against immigrant workers in Spain is directly linked to the informal sector. In this situation, immigrants are faced with hard working conditions without rights or protection. EU legislation was introduced in Spain before the social and political debate on equal treatment and opportunities for immigrant workers began. Its transposition occurred without a political debate and with the marginal use of tools for making it effective, especially in terms of the legal framework of the Commission for Equal Treatment. From the beginning, these directives have stimulated the evolution of anti-discrimination policies and considerations relevant to the fight against discrimination in collective negotiations. However, the fight against discrimination against immigrant workers continues to be limited to the fight against the exploitation of irregular workers and largely depends on local initiatives and non-governmental agencies.

Likewise, the reception and application in Spain of EU directives should be evaluated in the specific context of the diversity process. Although immigration has become a consolidated reality of Spanish society, the policies that deal with ensuring governance are in the first stage (Zapata-Barrero 2004). This first stage is focused mainly on equal access to rights, while it is only in the second stage, when equal rights are guaranteed or no longer a priority of the debate, that the issue of discrimination appears.

In fact, while there is a growing concern about how to manage diversity in the workplace (for example, the demands of Muslim workers in relation to their daily religious practices), demands are not tackled from the perspective of non-discrimination or equal opportunities but are perceived as a practical problem to be dealt with in a pragmatic fashion by companies, often outside the negotiations of collective agreements. The lack of debate on discrimination is not the only problem; its application is a concern as well (Cachón 2009). Therefore, we propose two practical routes: on one hand, local administrations need to apply anti-discrimination policies in order to stop "institutional discrimination"; on the other, we must optimize the development of redistribution policies, recognition, and representation in the field of immigration and in all groups that may be victims of discrimination.

Bearing in mind the constitutional framework, especially Article 14 of the Constitution, which states, "Spanish people are equal under law, without discrimination on the grounds of birth, race, sex, religion, opinion or any other personal or social condition or circumstance," the fight against discrimination must constitute a key element for judging the policies and practices of public and private actors in Spain (ibid.). This has been the case in the fight for gender equality, but the fight against discrimination must be incorporated at all levels in all its shapes and forms: race, ethnicity, age, disability, religious convictions, sexual orientation, and other aspects worthy of special protection.

According to Cachón (2009), in the normative field we need to advance towards a general law for equal treatment and equal opportunities. This law should include and be in keeping with regulations already in force in Spain, clarifying and uniting the normative texts; legislation should be revised in light of community directives and international instruments that propose more advanced tactics in the fight against discrimination. In the discussion framework on the policies that can be established for ensuring the governance of immigration, we include the importance of having a law that includes equal treatment and opportunities – a law that can be implemented in conjunction with the relevant actors and can take advantage of knock-on social and pedagogical effects in terms of the stereotypes and prejudices at the heart of discriminatory practices.

Management of Muslim Communities

Policies for governing issues related to Muslims are directly linked to the way that Spain manages religious pluralism. The Muslim presence forms part of the Spanish tradition, considering the historical background of eight centuries of Muslim presence in Spain. However, later, as we know, there were constructions of Spanish identity based on *Hispanidad* or "Spanishness" to wipe out this Muslim legacy (Zapata-Barrero 2006). The main issues concerning Muslim communities are related to religious infrastructures and education. The greatest problem has been the limited implementation of the 1992 Agreement, a very open and liberal regulation of the relation between the Muslim community and other religions in Spain and the state, along with the difficulty the state has had in finding representatives to negotiate with.

In this respect, the process of the incorporation of Islam in the system of cooperation between state and church makes us question the capacity of the Islamic Commission and the federations of associations to represent the growing Muslim community and to fulfil the relative functions for implementing the 1992 Agreement, as well as the capacity and willingness of local administrations to develop it (Alvarez-Miranda 2009). The stumbling blocks met in the implementation of the agreement, such as conflicts around the construction of mosques, complaints about the lack of teachers of Islam, or cases of Muslim girls being expelled from schools for wearing traditional clothes, bring public debates to Spain that have long existed in other European countries. Alvarez-Miranda (ibid.) points out that comparisons with Britain, Germany, and France show that, although all those states guarantee freedom of worship and permit plural religious teaching, the institutional adjustments and the levels of support given to the collective practice and teaching of Islam vary. The Spanish design appears to resemble more the German one, which is more liberal than other two.

In addition, Spain cannot escape from the governance problems posed by the links between security, Islam, and terrorism at a global level, nor the need to reposition its relation with the Catholic Church in order to ensure a secular state, which is considered to be one of the likely responses to Muslim demands.

The issue of the space and support that should be given to Islamic worship and teaching thus poses wider questions in relation to the effects that religious recognition may have on the integration of immigrants. Spain has yet to resolve the dilemmas generated by the demands of people of the Islamic faith. In this regard, Spanish policies of governance need to take steps in the practical field rather than in the theoretical field of the 1992 Agreement, which has hardly been implemented.

Many questions must still be resolved around the accommodation of the Muslim community. If wide recognition of religious difference is achieved, will there be a tendency towards multicultural coexistence, isolating communities and prolonging inequalities? If recognition is denied, will there be a reaction of dissatisfaction and badly channelled demands around the issues of Muslim identity? Which of these two cases promotes coexistence between religious communities and the numerous Europeans and immigrants from Muslim countries who do not practice any religion?

Management of Immigrant Gender

An academic tradition exists about how Spain reacts in the face of structural inequalities related to gender. The greatest challenge is how Spain incorporates women immigrants as subjects of gender and equality policies. As Parella so well theorizes, what is new is the way in which two dynamics of inequality – of being a woman and an immigrant – are united. This link generates multiple discrimination situations unresolved by Spanish policy. Perhaps we are in the stage of identifying the problem; however, there are few measures for ensuring equality for women in irregular situations and/or who work in the informal domestic service sector, care work, and other work sectors occupied by immigrants.

Another issue that contributes to the problem of the governance of immigrant gender is the fact that we are dealing with an interpretative framework that tends to follow a "family based" welfare system, which guarantees "the management of care work" on the basis of processes of subordination of immigrant women (Parella 2009). At the same time, the legislative measures aimed at promoting gender equality or facilitating the management of care work understand women as a theoretical homogenous category. However, this homogeneity does not exist, and measures for governing gender only address the needs and interests of certain groups of women (ibid.). The situation guarantees the availability of cheap female workers for families to manage care work, a responsibility that is no longer entirely assumed by women in an unpaid capacity and not attributed to the social system as a whole.

What are the main normative challenges for overcoming gender inequalities, considering the multiple connections and intersections with different types of discrimination, on a structural scale and in the processes of elaborating policies? Parella (ibid.) proposes a series of arguments that could orient IGPs in this area. First, current immigration regulation hinders the integration of immigrant women in the labour market outside the "domestic service" sector. Procedures for validating and accrediting academic and professional qualifications should be revised, as well as the criteria for obtaining permission to work for people reunited with their families. Second, and continuing on from the changes necessary for ensuring governance, legal changes are needed to ensure dignified and non-discriminatory working conditions for domestic work relative to other sectors of the labour market. To this end, the withdrawal of the Special Regime for Domestic Employees (REEH) and its subsequent upgrading to the General Regime should be a priority.

Management of Identity

Perhaps the manner in which Spain manages different forms of belonging and different ways of answering the question "Who am I?" in terms of national identity forms part of its history. That history has been unable to resolve the issue of multiple national identities and to encourage mutual recognition. In the face of this complexity, we must add the issue of the identities that immigrants bring with them. Each territorially delimited national identity (e.g., Catalonia, Galicia, and the Basque Country) can be affected by the way the Spanish state manages the issues related to the identities of immigrants. Hence, situations arise that have not yet been diagnosed in depth. Zapata-Barrero (2008, 2009c) has opened this analysis, taking into account the Catalan perspective and the multinational Spanish state. However, at state level an ethnicization of the nationality code exists. As we have pointed out, some nationalities have special privileges when it comes to the right to vote; for example, Latin Americans, Filipinos, and members of the old Spanish colonies in general require fewer years of residence in Spain before applying, while other nationalities are excluded – for example, immigrants in the Moroccan community, one of the largest groups in Spain.

As we have pointed out in our assessment of the approach to citizenship, debate on identity does not exist in Spain, despite this structural reality. Perhaps this is one of the most visible differences from debates that exist in other European countries. If we examine parliamentary discourses as direct sources of argument, hardly any references to identity are found (Zapata-Barrero 2009b, 119). Gil (2009) states that the lack of debate makes it difficult to talk about a Spanish philosophy of integration of immigrants. What it means to be a Spanish (state) citizen has more than one interpretation. The question of national belonging in Spain is an unresolved issue.

We can take as a premise that the Spanish approach to the management of identity and the focus on ethnic affinities that permeates Spanish migration and nationality policies are still very much linked to the colonial past. Gil (2009) interprets the situation in terms of power relations, explicit in the superiority that the term *Hispanidad* evokes in its peninsular setting. For example, the inclusion of children and grandchildren of Spaniards in Spanish nationality and the privilege given to those considered most similar (and most readily assimilated), as well as the exclusion of many who inhabit Spanish territory, reinforce this idea of ethnic superiority and clearly show the links between citizenship policies and the myths about the foundation of the country.

Nonetheless, if we move from the state framework to the national non-state framework, in Catalonia, for example, the identity debate that already forms part of the national tradition is shaping issues related to immigrants. We can identify different questions in Catalonia to those posed by the state, especially in terms of competencies in the management of immigration but also in terms of identity (Zapata-Barrero 2009). In addition, responses in Catalonia to questions shared with the state may differ – for example, the rejection by Catalonia of Spanish as the only valid language for permitting the entry of Latin American immigrants. Immigration policy is slowly becoming a language policy, especially with regard to the issue of the Catalan language, and a policy that reconceptualizes the actual notion of national community (Zapata-Barrero 2009b).

In the face of this national non-state scenario, Gil (2009) offers a critical analysis, insofar as these issues may also conceal differences in the socioeconomic realities of immigrants. Consequently, she argues that current dominant assumptions understand the main differences permeating Catalan society as linguistic issues and issues related to origin, leaving references to the transversal categories of social class and cultural capital in the background. The 1980s slogan "Become integrated and therefore become Catalan" appears to have given way to the reverse: "Become Catalan and therefore become integrated." An immigrant in Catalonia can perfectly say, "Parlo català pero encara no em sento integrat" – that is, "I speak Catalan but I do not feel integrated yet" (Zapata-Barrero 2009b). This concept, of cultural linguistics as the principal differentiating facet under which other inequalities are silenced or subsumed, explains why Spanish-speaking Latin American immigrants have been identified as a possible threat to the extension of the nationalist project. A practical philosophy is still being constructed on these issues, a philosophy that will undoubtedly bring Catalonia face to face with the Spanish state to debate how they coincide and diverge in their ways of questioning and responding to the issue of identity that the arrival of immigrants inevitably provokes.

CONCLUSION

This chapter has critically analyzed nine areas where the focus of integration policies in Spain is apparent. The argument we have advocated is that the Spanish approach is the result of a very practical integration philosophy, based on a question/answer logic in terms of dealing with immediate considerations. We have also seen that institutional structure is the main restriction in terms of answering the immediate questions arising from this practical philosophy of integration. This institutional structure dates back to Spain's transition to democracy, when immigration was not part of either its political or social agendas.

We have also argued that, because of this practical approach, integration policies in Spain are policies that thereby achieve the governance of immigration. If these policies were not so closely linked with practice, perhaps we would now be talking about Spain at least in terms of the international debate on integration, and in the context of this volume, as an example of ungovernance. The fact that Spain is managing the integration of first-generation immigrants continues to play an important role, and we will have to wait to confirm this approach and perhaps make the practical focus into a model that is also able to provide responses for the second and third generations. Most young immigrants have yet to reach Spain's universities and the Spanish labour market, and the majority of those who are working have not been trained in this country. In the near future we will be considering the same questions for a different generation. We will see whether the practical approach becomes a model.

NOTES

This chapter is an adaptation of the introduction and conclusion of *Políticas y gobernabilidad de la Inmigración en España*, ed. R. Zapata-Barrero (2009). The material was first presented as a paper at the Seventeenth International Conference of the Council for European Studies in Montreal on 15 April 2010 in the panel A Changing European Multiculturalism: Comparative Perspectives on the Crises and Reconfigurations of "National Models," thanks to a travel grant from the Centro de Investigaciones Sociológicas (CIS) of the Spanish Ministry of the Presidency.

1. See other authors such as J. Habermas, J. O'Connors, G. Peters, D. Bell, and K. Offe, who shaped the 1970s debate.
2. See Zapata-Barrero (2009a), which justifies the revision process of the policy categories that the phenomenon of immigration provokes and introduces the foundations of the reactive discourse.
3. Although we shall keep them in mind, we shall not deal with the issues related to the diversity linked to multinational structure in Spain, nor the link between this dynamic of diversity with the dynamics posed by immigrants. For this approach, see Zapata-Barrero (2009b, 2010a).
4. See the powers for Immigration of the *Statute of Autonomy of Catalonia*, Art. 138, and the *Statute of Autonomy for Andalucia*, Art.62
5. This principle is determining the voting rights of immigrants in Spain, by relating them to the rights received by Spanish emigrants in their receiving countries.

REFERENCES

Alvarez-Miranda, B. 2009. "La acomodación del culto islámico en España. Comparación con Gran Bretaña, Alemania y Francia." In *Políticas y gobernabilidad de la Inmigración en España*, ed. R. Zapata-Barrero, 185-206. Barcelona: Ariel.

Cachón, L. 2009. "Políticas antidiscriminatorias para la población inmigrante y gestión del mercado de trabajo." In *Políticas y gobernabilidad de la Inmigración en España*, ed. R. Zapata-Barrero, 165-84.

Crozier, M., S. Huntington, and J. Watanuki. 1975. *The Crisis of Democracy: Report on the Governability of Democracies to the Trilateral Comission*. New York University Press.

Gil, S. 2009. "La gestión de la cuestión nacional: España y Cataluña en perspectiva." In *Políticas y gobernabilidad de la Inmigración en España*, ed. R. Zapata-Barrero, 227-46.

Lucas, J. de. 2009. "El enfoque de la ciudadanía: cuestiones normativas." In *Políticas y gobernabilidad de la Inmigración en España*, ed. R. Zapata-Barrero, 93-112.

Miret, A. 2009. "La gestión de la división de competencias en materia de inmigración." In *Políticas y gobernabilidad de la Inmigración en España*, ed. R. Zapata-Barrero, 51-72.

Morales, L., A. Gonzalez, and L. Jorba. 2009. "Políticas de incorporación y la gestión del asociacionismo de la población de origen inmigrante a nivel local." In *Políticas y gobernabilidad de la Inmigración en España*, ed. R. Zapata-Barrero, 113-38.

Moreno, F. J. 2009. "La gestión del bienestar y la inmigración en España." In *Políticas y gobernabilidad de la Inmigración en España*, ed. R. Zapata-Barrero, 73-91.

Parella, S. 2009. "La gestión política del género y la mujer inmigrante." In *Políticas y gobernabilidad de la Inmigración en España*, ed. R. Zapata-Barrero, 207-26.

World Bank, Managing Development. 1991. *The Governance Dimension*. Washington, DC.

Zapata-Barrero, R. 2004. *Multiculturalidad e Inmigración*. Madrid: Editorial Síntesis.

— 2006. "The Muslim Community and Spanish Tradition: Maurophobia as a Fact and Impartiality as a Desideratum." In *Multiculturalism, Muslims and Citizenship: A European Approach.*, ed. T. Modood, A. Triandafyllidou, and R. Zapata, 143-61. London: Routledge.

— 2008. "Policies and Public Opinion towards Immigrants: The Spanish Case." *Journal of Ethnic and Racial Studies* 32 (7):1101-20.

— 2009a. *Fundamentos de los discursos políticos en torno a la inmigración*. Madrid: Trotta.

— 2009b. "Building a Public Philosophy of Immigration in Catalonia: The Terms of Debate." In *Immigration and Self-Government: Normative Questions and Institutional Prospects*, ed. R. Zapata-Barrero, 125-61. Witney, OX: Peter Lang / Col. Diversitas.

— 2010a. "Dynamics of Diversity in Spain: Old Questions, New Challenges." In *The Multiculturalism Backlash: European Discourses, Policies and Practices*, ed. S. Vertovec and S. Wessendorf, 181-200. London: Routledge.

— 2010b. "Managing Diversity in Spanish Society: A Practical Approach." *Journal of Intercultural Studies* 31(4):383-402

— ed. 2009c. *Immigration and Self-Government: Normative Questions and Institutional Prospects*. Witney, OX: Peter Lang / Col. Diversitas.

Zapata-Barrero, R. and J. Zaragoza, J. 2009. "La gestión del derecho al voto de los inmigrantes." In *Políticas y gobernabilidad de la Inmigración en España*, ed. R. Zapata-Barrero, 139-64.

CHAPTER 10

IMMIGRANT INTEGRATION AND POLICY IN THE UNITED STATES: A LOOSELY STITCHED PATCHWORK

IRENE BLOEMRAAD AND ELS DE GRAAUW

The United States is known, in the collective imagination of its citizens and by many around the world, as the quintessential immigrant nation, one that has successfully integrated millions of newcomers over its history. Today, the descendants of the massive waves of nineteenth and early twentieth century European migrants are part of the American mainstream. Their incorporation was symbolized in the 1960s by the election of President John F. Kennedy, a Catholic Irish-American, over a hundred years after the Know Nothing movement advanced political candidates opposing Irish Catholic immigration. Some might read the 2008 victory of President Barack Obama, the son of a Kenyan born father and Kansas born mother, as a new chapter in the integration story, extended to non-white immigrants and their descendants. Given that the United States is often held up as a model, how does integration work?

We argue that the dominant view of the American public and the prevailing policy stance of the US government is one of laissez-faire integration: immigrants are largely expected to use their own resources, family, friendship networks, and perhaps the assistance of local community organizations to survive and thrive in the United States.[1] Since there is no coordinated national integration policy, there is no official definition of "social integration" in the United States. We can, however, identify a widespread view of integration, or assimilation, from public and academic debates. According to this common view, social integration is achieved when we see an absence of significant difference between immigrants and the native born in, for example, their language use, their labour market participation, or their political viewpoints.[2]

International Perspectives: Integration and Inclusion, ed. J. Frideres and J. Biles. Montreal and Kingston: Queen's Policy Studies Series, McGill-Queen's University Press. © 2012 The School of Policy Studies, Queen's University at Kingston. All rights reserved.

Beneath the dominant laissez-faire outlook, we do find examples of federal, state, and municipal policies aimed at immigrants' integration. Indeed, the Migrant Integration Policy Index – an international survey of policies that affect immigrants' labour access, family reunification rights, education, political participation, and access to nationality – scored the United States as ninth out of 31 highly developed countries on integration policy in 2010.[3] In this chapter, we examine some of the most salient national policies as part of the patchwork of government initiatives that affect immigrants' ability to fully access the opportunities, rights, and services available to the native born population.

Because of limited action by the national government, local communities – including non-traditional and new immigrant destinations such as suburbs, rural areas, and new gateway cities in the South – have found themselves, de facto, confronted with the challenges of integration, often without the resources or know-how to address them. We argue that the patchwork of policies that exist do not, together, form a coherent response to the issue of immigrant inclusion. Immigrants can be treated very differently across political jurisdictions and regions of the United States. Furthermore, not all policies seek inclusion. Some aim to exclude the foreign born from social services, education, and jobs, all key pieces of social integration. It appears that variation in local integration approaches is increasing, and the move toward exclusion is intensifying.

Remarkably, despite public reservations about immigration and the national government's laissez-faire attitude, social scientists report that many immigrants and their children are integrating successfully into the labour market, education system, popular culture, and, to a lesser extent, politics. One comparative assessment concluded that, on the whole, immigrants integrate more successfully in the United States than in most European countries, but less successfully than in Canada (Vigdor 2011). However, patterns of inclusion are heavily stratified by migrants' educational and economic resources, racial inequalities, and legal status, which prevent a significant proportion of immigrants from being fully included. Given evidence that official refugees in the United States – the only migrants who receive some concerted government assistance with integration – tend to have better outcomes than similarly situated non-refugees, we suggest that patterns of successful integration in the United States occur despite rather than because of the laissez-faire attitude. If more concerted policy action were taken, across all levels of government, we speculate that integration would be even more successful.

IMMIGRATION TO THE UNITED STATES: LAW AND PEOPLE

The popular image of the United States is one of enduring immigration. In reality, immigrants and issues of integration faded into relative insignificance for a large stretch of the twentieth century. As Figure 1 shows, the ebbs and flows of migration to the United States have been dramatic. In 1890, the foreign born made up 15 percent of the population, but by 1970, this figure dropped to under 5 percent. In 2010, the United States was again an immigrant nation: almost 40 million foreign born people constituted 12.9 percent of the country's 309 million residents, a proportion four times the global average.[4] Behind the numbers lies a complex history of immigration laws and US military and foreign policy decisions, as well as the relative attraction of the American labour market, an attraction at times encouraged by US employers seeking out immigrants.[5] While the history of US immigration law is well-covered elsewhere (Daniels 2004; Reimers 1992; Tichenor 2002; Zolberg 2006), its broad contours can be told as a story in four periods.

FIGURE 1
Foreign Born Population in the United States, 1850–2010

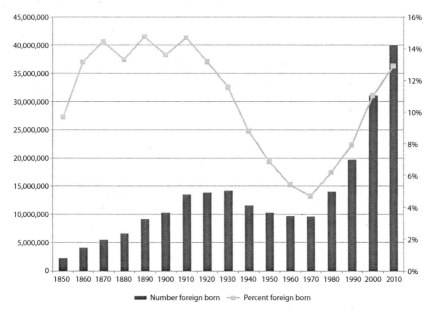

Source: Campbell and Lennon (1999); 2000 US Census of Population and Housing and 2010 American Community Survey.

The History of Migration to the United States

From its founding to the 1880s, the United States had an open-door policy with virtually no federal regulation of migration. Individual states sometimes regulated passenger ships, and cities enforced residence requirements in poor laws. Both affected migrants' ability to enter or reside in particular places, but in general people were able to migrate with relative ease, and millions did.

Starting in the 1880s, the door gradually closed through a series of laws demonstrating the racial hierarchy informing American policy-making (Ngai 2004). Starting with the *Chinese Exclusion Act* of 1882, Congress first suspended, then effectively ended, Chinese migration to the United States. Legislators also denied Chinese immigrants access to US citizenship through naturalization. Racial exclusion was extended to Japanese migrants under the "Gentlemen's Agreement" of 1907–08, and then to the entire Asian continent with the imposition of an "Asiatic Barred Zone" in the *Immigration Act* of 1917. In 1921 and 1924, national origin quotas effectively ended mass migration from Eastern and Southern Europe, targeting Italians, Greeks, Russians, Poles, and other groups viewed as racially inferior by many Americans of the time.[6]

The national origin quota laws of the 1920s and the 1965 *Immigration and Nationality Act*, also known as the *Hart-Celler Act*, bookend the third period of "non-migration." Few migrants were able to enter the United States during this time, so the proportion of immigrants in the country declined dramatically. However, two types of migration served, in hindsight, as harbingers of the current period. After World War II, refugees – first from war-torn Europe and then from countries in which the United States had a foreign policy interest – were given entry outside the quotas. The US government also entered into agreements, known as the Bracero program, starting in World War II and continuing to 1964 with Mexico and Caribbean countries to bring in temporary migrants to fill labour shortages. By the 1970s, special refugee admissions would explode, and with the end of bilateral labour agreements, temporary migration would transform into clandestine migration.

Today, the fourth chapter of the story is a dramatic rise in the number of new migrants. In 2010, over a third of all immigrants, 35 percent, had entered the United States in 2000 or later; less than two-fifths had lived in the country for more than two decades. The 1965 *Hart-Celler Act* ended national-origin quotas, ushered in a new era of mass migration, and changed the sources of immigration, as seen in Table 1. Today, Europeans constitute a small minority of the total, while over half of all immigrants were born in Mexico, Central or South America, or the Caribbean, with Mexicans the largest group. Most of these migrants speak Spanish, so debates over linguistic inclusion and bilingual education focus heavily on the Spanish language, and perceptions of immigrants as a "cultural threat" often centre on the feared displacement of English by Spanish (Zolberg and Woon 1999; Huntington 2004).

The 1965 act still structures immigration today through a series of preference categories that determine admission. Only individuals sponsored by an immediate family member who is a US citizen can avoid the quotas imposed by Congress, set between 416,000 and 675,000 per year

TABLE 1
Top 25 Countries of Birth of the US Foreign Born Population, 2007–09

Country of Birth	Number	Percent of All Foreign Born
Mexico	11,498,849	30.2
Philippines	1,693,963	4.4
India	1,603,933	4.2
China*	1,586,442	4.2
Vietnam	1,128,775	3.0
El Salvador	1,112,340	2.9
Korea	1,023,297	2.7
Cuba	980,156	2.6
Canada	823,360	2.2
Dominican Republic	768,535	2.0
Guatemala	751,541	2.0
United Kingdom	688,445	1.8
Germany	633,879	1.7
Jamaica	627,011	1.6
Colombia	600,460	1.6
Haiti	534,610	1.4
Poland	467,821	1.2
Honduras	457,872	1.2
Russia	406,147	1.1
Ecuador	404,889	1.1
Italy	394,490	1.0
Peru	392,150	1.0
Brazil	348,754	0.9
Taiwan	347,248	0.9
Iran	340,120	0.9

*China includes Hong Kong, not Taiwan.
Source: US Census Bureau, 2007–09 American Community Survey.

by the 1990 *Immigration Act*. The preference categories emphasize family reunification as well, so two-thirds to three-quarters of those who migrate in any given year do so because they have family already in the country. The remainder of legal immigrants enter as economic migrants, usually as high-skilled workers sponsored by US employers, or as refugees or asylees.[7]

The United States is also home to a significant undocumented population, migrants who enter the country clandestinely or overstay legal visas for tourism, study, or temporary work. It is estimated that, as of 2008, between 11.5 and 12 million people lacked legal residency papers – about 31 percent of all foreign born individuals in the United States (Hoefer, Rytina, and Baker 2009; Passel and Cohn 2009). Undocumented, or "illegal," migration has become a defining feature of American immigration debates. Indeed, a majority of US residents think most immigrants in the country are illegal.[8] The prevailing belief, among the public and many policy-makers, is that more border control is the best way to deal with undocumented migration, which encompasses calls for more border patrol officers, more fencing, and more high technology surveillance. Border enforcement was already a priority of the Immigration and Naturalization Service (INS) before the terrorist attacks of 11 September 2001, but since 2003, when immigration and enforcement were transferred to the new Department of Homeland Security, policing borders has become deeply intertwined with national security.

Contemporary Integration Issues: How Are Immigrants Doing?

How well are these migrants fitting into American society? Statistical comparisons of foreign born and US born residents provide some evidence of successful integration; labour market participation among immigrants is particularly high. But statistics also show that language access, policies related to children, income inequality, and poverty are particularly salient issues for the foreign born.

In terms of language, Table 2 shows that the overwhelming majority of foreign born residents, 84 percent, speaks a language other than English at home, compared to only 10 percent of the native born. Of those who do not speak English at home, 52 percent report not speaking English "very well," and probably a higher percentage have difficulty with written English. As we outline below, many policies targeted at immigrants deal with language issues, from integrative policies providing non-English speakers with access to public services to exclusionary policies imposing English as the only language of government.

Child welfare and education policies also heavily affect immigrant families. Forty-four percent of immigrant families have at least one child under the age of 18 in the household, compared to only 29 percent of native born families. Indeed, 23 percent of all children under the age of 18, 16.3 million children, live in a household with at least one immigrant parent. The overwhelming majority of these children are US born and thus US citizens. Scholars and policy-makers often judge the success of this "second generation," from their educational attainment to their living conditions, as an important indicator of integration and social inclusion, even if children born in the United States are citizens and not technically immigrants.

The mixed legal status of many immigrant families, with children who are citizens but parents who are non-citizen legal residents or un-documented, generates fierce debates over whether such families should receive public benefits, which in the United States are sometimes tied to citizenship or legal status. Such debates are consequential since 15 percent of immigrant families fall below the federal poverty line, compared to 9 percent of native born families. At least one study claims that the

TABLE 2
Selected Characteristics of the Foreign Born and Native Born US Population, 2007–09

	Foreign Born	Native Born
Total population	38,090,166	266,230,299
Families with children under 18 yrs	43.6%	29.1%
Language ability (5 yrs+)		
Speaks only English at home	15.6%	90.2%
Speaks English less than "very well"	52.1%	1.9%
Educational attainment (25 yrs+)		
Less than high school diploma	32.2%	11.8%
Bachelor's degree or higher	27.0%	27.9%
Employment status (16 yrs+)		
In labour force	68.2%	64.8%
Unemployed	4.7%	4.9%
Income and earnings (2009 US dollars)		
Median annual household income	47,671	51,919
Male median earnings, full-time, year-round workers	34,558	47,750
Female median earnings, full-time, year-round workers	30,264	36,009
Poverty – families under poverty threshold	15.2%	9.0%
Housing		
Owns home	53.5%	68.4%
1.01 or more occupants per room	11.7%	1.7%
US citizenship	42.6%	100.0%

Source: US Census Bureau, 2007–09 American Community Survey.

problem is much worse; an alternative measure of economic deprivation reveals that nearly half of children in immigrant families live in poverty (Hernandez, Denton, and Macartney 2009). Poverty measures are frequently used to determine eligibility for means-tested public benefits, from food aid to health insurance coverage.

Even when they do not fall below the poverty line, immigrant households – with or without children – have lower incomes than the native born. Median household income was US$4,200 less for immigrant families (US$47,700) than for native born families (US$51,900). This income difference is not because immigrants are not working. To the contrary, 68 percent of all immigrants are in the labour force, with only 4.7 percent reporting they are unemployed, compared to 65 percent and 4.9 percent among the native born, respectively.[9] Rather, the difference stems from a substantial earnings gap: for example, a full-time male immigrant worker earned US$34,600 compared to US$47,800 for a native born worker. The low level of schooling among a large proportion of immigrants explains part of the gap – 32 percent of immigrants do not hold a high school diploma – but education does not account for the entire difference, raising questions about employment equity and discrimination. Evaluating immigrants' economic incorporation is thus a mixed bag: the foreign born work more, but they earn less and are more likely to live in poverty than those born in the United States.

The portrait of social inclusion sketched out in these statistics finds some response in the policies we discuss below. On the whole, however, we find these policies inadequate; there is room for additional policy intervention. To the extent that policy often flows from political pressure and voter preferences, the low level of citizenship among US migrants – only 43 percent have naturalized – makes it hard to promote policies for the nearly 22 million foreign born shut out of the voting booth.[10] Without a direct political voice, non-citizen immigrants must rely on intermediaries such as community-based organizations and advocacy groups to promote their interests, or they can demonstrate and take their concerns to the street. These strategies have produced integration policies in certain localities (de Graauw 2008), but they are less likely to inspire comprehensive integration policies at the national level.

PHILOSOPHIES OF INTEGRATION: FROM AMERICANIZATION TO LAISSEZ-FAIRE

The editors of this volume ask how different countries define and understand the "social integration" of immigrants. In the United States, the quick answer is that the federal government has no such definition because immigrants' social integration is not their purview. The word "integration" does not appear in the mission statement of the US Citizenship and Immigration Services (USCIS), which is to "secure America's promise as a nation of immigrants by providing accurate and useful information to our customers, granting immigration and citizenship benefits, promoting an awareness and understanding of citizenship, and ensuring the integrity of our immigration system."[11] At most, the main federal agency dedicated to immigration touches on civic integration: USCIS adjudicates citizenship applications and does some limited work to facilitate US citizenship.[12] Starting in 2009, for example, USCIS administered a competitive Citizenship and Integration Grant Program to fund local citizenship preparation efforts. With just US$1.2 million in its first year, US$8.1 million in its second, and US$9 million in its third, the program can only serve a fraction of the nearly 22 million non-citizen immigrants (USCIS 2011a). The White House puts slightly more emphasis on immigrants' economic contributions – "President Obama recognizes that an orderly, controlled border and an immigration system designed to meet our economic needs are important pillars of a healthy and robust economy" – but despite a

Democratic president with a foreign born father, immigrant integration is not on the executive agenda.[13]

We can read an implicit definition of integration in the formal documents used by government authorities to grant legal residence or US citizenship. These documents assess whether applicants contribute economically (by working or going to school, paying taxes, and not using welfare); they evaluate immigrants' "good moral character" by making sure they have committed no crimes (including hate crimes, terrorism, and bigamy); and they verify that men between the ages of 18 and 25 have signed up for the selective service (to be used in the event of a military draft). The implicit message from the official documents builds on that of the White House: integration means obeying the law and making an economic contribution to society. For those who want to become a citizen, naturalization also requires a basic knowledge of the English language, US government, and American history. To the extent that the national "glue" holding the United States together rests on attachment to the US Constitution, political values such as liberalism and democracy, and free-market capitalism, immigration officials reiterate these values in their forms and the naturalization exam.

The government response both reflects and influences public perceptions over appropriate policy. Many Americans are ambivalent about immigration – 54 percent see immigration more as a problem than an opportunity – but concern centres largely on illegal migration.[14] Asked about *legal* immigrants, two-thirds to three-quarters of Americans disagree with suggestions that newcomers are a burden on social services, increase crime, or increase the likelihood of a terrorist attack. When the question is framed as about *illegal* migrants, however, a majority associates illegal migrants with increases in terrorism and crime, and almost three-quarters see the undocumented as a drain on social services. Unlike in many European countries, immigrants' cultural and religious diversity does not raise as much concern. Two-thirds of Americans feel that immigration enriches the culture of the United States. When asked whether it is better for a country if almost everyone shares the same customs and traditions, 71 percent of Americans disagreed, a higher proportion than in eight other countries surveyed.[15] The legal status of migrants – not their culture or work ethic – is the central public policy issue in the United States.[16]

Despite the lack of a coordinated or overarching federal integration policy, immigrants can benefit from programs seeking the social integration of all US residents, and naturalized immigrants can access the same programs as citizens. With its history of slavery and second-class African-American citizenship, the United States also has a range of policies and programs directed to ethnic and racial minorities, such as preferential hiring and contracting policies (affirmative action) and anti-discrimination protections in housing and the workplace. Many of these initiatives are extended to and used by immigrants if they are deemed an ethnic or racial minority. Indeed, in the MIPEX international comparison of integration policies, the United States stood out, with Canada, as having the strong-est anti-discrimination infrastructure.[17] Finally, as we outline below, some federal agencies oversee initiatives or implement laws directed to linguistically isolated individuals who do not speak English, a population overwhelmingly composed of immigrants.

Sub-national governments – sometimes states, but often municipal-ities – are also increasingly the site of integration debates, especially as a result of immigrants' increased dispersion to new metropolitan and rural locales and after federal efforts at comprehensive immigration reform failed in 2007. This pattern can be seen in the growing number of state bills and local ordinances proposed, and sometimes enacted, by policy-makers (Laglagaron et al. 2008). Some bills aim to facilitate im-migrant integration; others seek exclusion. Media have also constructed immigrant integration as a problem for local government; one analysis of newspaper coverage finds that journalists' accounts view integration as a policy "non-problem" for federal officials (Abu-Laban and Garber 2005).

American society and government have not always been so "hands-off" regarding immigrants' social integration. In the early twentieth century, private groups of citizens, settlement houses, social workers, employ-ers, schools, and some government agencies worked to "Americanize" newcomers. By encouraging immigrants to shed their Old World ways – from language to culture, political attitudes to ways of dress – these groups hoped to hasten immigrants' transition into an industrial economy and a democratic political system (Gosnell 1928; Higham 1988; Ziegler-McPherson 2009). The US Department of Education, for example, worked with local school boards to provide textbooks to teach children and adults about US citizenship, and businesses such as the Ford Motor Company provided English-language classes to their workers (Smith 1926). While in some cases helpful, many of these initiatives also denigrated immi-grants' cultures of origin, promoting a unilateral and one-way process of assimilation.

The cauldron of the first and second world wars served as a further melting pot as wartime service brought soldiers from various ethnic backgrounds together to fight in common cause against a foreign enemy. Following World War II, these adult children and grandchildren of European migrants benefited from programs for war veterans, such as the GI Bill, which helped to send a generation of young men to college, and mortgage programs that facilitated homeownership in the suburbs. While not frequently acknowledged in public discussions, such postwar social policies played a critical role in the social integration of twenti-eth century European migrants and their descendants (Brodkin 1998; Katznelson 2005).[18]

Today, academics in the United States debate whether the experiences of European immigrants and their children serve as a guide to contemporary migrants' integration. Due to educational and language barriers, many first generation migrants will not achieve full integration in their lifetime, but the American belief in equality and economic mobility implies that the experiences and outcomes of the second generation should be like those of other native born peers. According to some, there are grounds for optimism: young adults with immigrant parents living in New York City do better than their parents (as measured by educational attainment and occupation), and better than US born peers of similar minority status (Kasinitz et al. 2008). According to Richard Alba and Victor Nee (2003), US anti-discrimination policy and Americans' social acceptance of diversity ensure that the children and grandchildren of today's immigrants will become part of a mainstream where their background has little effect on their lives.

Such a view is disputed by other scholars who conclude that the prospects of today's second generation are mixed at best and dim for many. Previously, a strong industrial sector with well-paying jobs offered an economic ladder to successive generations; it is argued that the post-industrial economy rewards those with high education but traps migrants with less human capital in a low-wage service economy (Gans 1992; Portes and Zhou 1993). Economic obstacles are also aggravated by racism, which is still prevalent despite anti-discrimination legislation (Telles and Ortiz 2008). Some second generation Americans will succeed by integrating into the white mainstream or using their human, cultural, and social capital to get ahead, but a significant proportion faces limited educational success and bleak job prospects (Zhou 1999; Portes and Rumbaut 2001).

Both viewpoints, whether optimistic or pessimistic, envision a minimal role for government policy. The "new" assimilation model of Alba and Nee underscores the role of anti-discrimination legislation and, implicitly, the public school system, but it is a model primarily driven by individual immigrants' decisions to get ahead, rather than government policies promoting social integration. The less optimistic highlight the importance of government in structuring different paths of legal entry – as refugees, economic, family, or undocumented migrants – but they place much of the blame for integration failures on global capitalism, racism, and a new hourglass economy. As with public opinion and federal policy inaction, academics in the United States envisage no major role for government in immigrants' social inclusion.

Contemporary Social Inclusion Policies: A Loosely Stitched Patchwork

The United States has a federal system of government, with power divided between a national (federal) government, 50 states, and close to 20,000 municipalities. The laws that the national government creates are, as stated in the US Constitution, "the supreme law of the land." Lower levels of government nevertheless have jurisdiction to set policy in certain areas such as education and social programs, and to impose taxes. In the absence of a uniform national integration policy, this tiered political system has produced a patchwork of social policies that affect newcomers. Certain policies are targeted directly at immigrants; some of these aim for inclusion, but others at exclusion. Other policies are not necessarily framed with immigrants specifically in mind but can facilitate immigrants' integration. These policies often flow from the legacies of the 1960s civil rights movement, when native born minorities led by African-Americans mobilized for equality in law and practice.

It is thus impossible to identify a coherent government response to the issue of immigrant inclusion. Rather, we provide an overview of the most salient policies that affect immigrants in language, education, health care, and social benefits. We focus on national policies current as of 2011, but occasionally we refer to notable developments at the state and local levels to reflect the increasing activity of sub-national governments around immigration. It is critical to underscore that our review does not cover all policies affecting or targeting immigrants, and that formal policy can be a poor guide to practice on the ground.[19] We nevertheless provide a sense of how governments in the United States have tried to increase opportunities and access for immigrants and, increasingly, where they exclude the foreign born.

Language

The great majority of recent immigrants to the United States do not speak English as their native language. Because language ability affects integration into, or exclusion from, other aspects of US society, language access and programs to learn English as a second language (ESL) are key policy arenas. There is a growing policy framework addressing linguistic access but much more limited action on adult ESL instruction.

Immigrants with limited English proficiency enjoy some language access guarantees to government information and public services. These policies have their roots in the civil rights movement of the 1960s. A crowning achievement of the movement, the 1964 *Civil Rights Act*, includes Title VI, which prohibits discrimination based on race, colour, or national origin in programs and activities receiving federal funds. Although the courts have consistently rejected attempts to equate language with national origin, Congress and the president have used Title VI as a statutory basis to intervene in language issues, most notably requiring administrative agencies at various levels of government to hire bilingual personnel and translate forms, notices, and applications for limited-English proficient (LEP) individuals. Following complaints about spotty implementation, President Clinton issued Executive Order 13166, "Improving Access for

Persons with Limited English Proficiency," in 2000. This order, which President Bush reaffirmed in 2002, aims to improve the enforcement and implementation of Title VI of the *Civil Rights Act* by requiring any agency or program that receives federal funding to provide meaningful access for LEP individuals. On the heels of this order, immigrant gateway cities such as San Francisco, Washington, DC, and New York have adopted their own, more expansive, language access policies. Mayor Bloomberg of New York, for example, signed Executive Order 120 in 2008, directing all city agencies to provide language assistance in the city's six most commonly spoken foreign languages: Spanish, Chinese, Russian, Korean, Italian, and French Creole.

Language access also surfaces in discussions over immigrants' access to the ballot box. Section 203 of the 1975 amendments to the *Voting Rights Act* of 1965 requires officials to provide bilingual voting assistance in communities where a single language minority group makes up 5 percent of the voting age population or has more than 10,000 voting age citizens and is limited-English proficient. Section 203 applies to persons of American Indian, Asian, Alaskan Native, or Spanish heritage, the groups that Congress found to face barriers in the political process. Despite intermittent public concern over the cost of Section 203 – which was originally intended as a temporary measure – Congress has reauthorized these provisions five times, most recently in 2006 for 25 years. As of 2002, a total of 466 local jurisdictions in 31 states were legally required to provide voting information and ballots in non-English languages (US Commission on Civil Rights 2006).

In contrast to relatively robust language access efforts, the federal government has done little to create and fund programs that teach English to adult immigrants. The *Adult Education and Family Literacy Act* (AEFLA), enacted as Title II of the *Workforce Investment Act* of 1998, is the main national program for adult English as a Second Language (ESL) instruction. In fiscal year 2003–04, the federal government allocated US$561 million for AEFLA, including nearly US$70 million benefiting 1.2 million individuals who had enrolled in English literacy and civics classes (US Department of Education 2006). Due to inadequate funding, however, AEFLA has not lived up to its potential. The federal government allocates funds to states and localities based on the number of LEP adults without a high school degree. In 2005–07, the United States counted 21.6 million LEP adults, of which 10.4 million had not completed high school (Capps et al. 2009). Consequently, 11.2 million LEP adults who hold a high school diploma are excluded from the federal funding formula, even though they are eligible for AEFLA-funded programs and often enrol in ESL classes. The underfunding has resulted in a nation-wide logjam: providers of ESL classes report long waiting lists, sometimes up to three years, and overcrowded, understaffed classrooms (Tucker 2006).

The case of adult ESL language instruction illustrates well the American public's laissez-faire philosophy to immigrant integration. In an opinion survey conducted in 2009 by the German Marshall Fund, 91 percent of Americans polled felt it very or somewhat important that immigrants speak English. However, only 30 percent felt that the government should pay for English language classes for immigrants, a level of support lower than the 48 percent of Canadians and 39 percent of Europeans who supported publicly funded language classes.[20]

Education

In the United States, education is primarily the purview of individual states, but during the civil rights movement the federal government stepped in to enforce civil rights laws in education. To this end, Congress enacted the 1968 *Bilingual Education Act* (BEA), the first piece of federal legislation for minority language speakers. BEA, which expired in 2002, served as a remedy for discrimination against students who did not speak English and provided federal funding for programs taught in languages other than English. Controversy over the form and effectiveness of BEA-funded programs was ongoing during the 34 years the act was in force, especially over whether it should provide only remedial or transitional English instruction, or whether it should also support the maintenance of minority languages and cultures, as favoured by supporters of multi-lingualism and cultural pluralism (Schmid 2001; Spolsky 2004).

The controversy over bilingual education has been especially heated in some states with large immigrant populations. California voters, for example, passed by a sweeping 61–39 percent margin Proposition 227, the "English for the Children" initiative, amid charges that bilingual school programs were ineffective and concerns that language diversity causes political disunity and the fragmentation of American culture. The 1998 initiative, which survived a federal court challenge, prohibits bilingual education programs for limited-English proficient students in the state's public school system and instead establishes one year of sheltered English instruction. Following California's example, voters in Arizona and Massachusetts adopted similar initiatives in 2000 and 2002, respectively, but voters in Colorado voted down a state ballot measure in 2002 attacking bilingual education.

When federal policy-makers allowed BEA to expire, they replaced it with the *English Language Acquisition Act* (ELAA). Congress enacted ELAA in 2001 as Title III of the *No Child Left Behind Act*, a landmark educational reform that aims to reduce the achievement gap among US primary and secondary schools through strict testing requirements and penalties for states and schools that fail to meet performance requirements in reading, math, and science. ELAA signals a clear departure in federal support for native-language instruction. The act contains no reference to "bilingual education" and prioritizes English-only instruction by measuring the success of school programs in English language proficiency alone. The change in teaching pedagogy that ELAA forces on states, some claim, will hurt the overall academic achievement of immigrant children and make it more difficult for them to adapt to life in the United States (England 2009).

Debate over school programs assumes that immigrant children have the right to attend public educational institutions. However, in 1975, the state of Texas challenged this assumption by enacting a law that denied funding to educate undocumented immigrant children and allowed local school districts to prevent these children from enrolling. The law was challenged in court and was ultimately argued before the US Supreme Court. In its 1982 *Plyler v. Doe* decision, the court struck down the law, ruling that undocumented children, like children who are US citizens and legal permanent residents, have a right to a free, public education.

As undocumented children have progressed through the school system, some immigrant advocates and policy-makers have shifted their attention to the plight of undocumented young people after they finish high school. In higher education, debate has zeroed in on whether undocumented students should be allowed to pay in-state tuition, a lower rate of tuition that public colleges and universities charge residents of their state, or whether they may attend college at all. Currently, an estimated 50,000 undocumented immigrants are enrolled in US colleges, but in 2011 only 12 states allowed these students to pay in-state tuition (NCSL 2011). Many worry about the career prospects of young people largely raised and educated in the United States but living without proper legal status. Such concerns have fuelled, since 2001, a series of legislative proposals for a "DREAM Act," which would provide undocumented immigrants who have five years of continuous US residency and a US high school diploma with the ability to legalize their status by attending college or joining the US military.[21] The act would also allow states to provide, without penalty, in-state tuition and other higher education benefits to students regardless of documentation status. As recently as 2010, the DREAM Act failed to pass Congress yet again.

Health Care

Congressional debates over health care reform in 2009–10 made clear that lack of health care coverage is an issue of national concern and one that affects substantial numbers of native born and foreign born individuals. The foreign born are, however, much more likely to lack health insurance. In 2007, 12.7 percent of the native born population was uninsured, compared to 17.6 percent of immigrants who had naturalized, 43.8 percent of non-citizen immigrants, and 57.1 percent of undocumented immigrants (DeNavas-Walt, Proctor, and Smith 2008; Passel and Cohn 2009). These percentages are perhaps surprising, since employment-based health insurance is the mainstay of the US health insurance system and immigrants are more likely to work than their native born counterparts. However, a series of private and public sector barriers hit immigrants particularly hard.

The majority of those with health insurance in the United States get coverage through their employers. As of 2011, however, no state or federal law requires private sector employers to provide health insurance benefits to their employees.[22] As health insurance plans become increasingly expensive, many small businesses and firms employing low-wage immigrant workers opt not to offer health insurance. The prohibitive cost of private health insurance also means that immigrants without employer-provided coverage cannot afford to buy insurance on their own.

These obstacles are aggravated by barriers to accessing public, government-funded health care programs, notably Medicaid, a federal/state funded health insurance program for the poor, and Medicare, the federal health insurance program that covers most people aged 65 and older. With some exceptions, undocumented immigrants have not been eligible for these programs, but legal immigrants previously had eligibility on par with US citizens. In 1996, this equality ended with the *Personal Responsibility and Work Opportunity Reconciliation Act* (PRWORA), commonly known as the *Welfare Reform Act*.[23] PRWORA made legal immigrants who entered the country after 22 August 1996 ineligible for Medicaid and Medicare during their first five years in the United States, a restriction also applied to the Children's Health Insurance Program (CHIP), which Congress created in 1997 to provide health insurance for low-income children who have no health insurance and are ineligible for Medicaid. Several states have stepped in to fill the health insurance void by providing state-funded health care to some non-citizens, especially children and pregnant women, but a significant gap in insurance coverage and access to health care remains between immigrants and native born Americans.[24]

Current health care policy, despite passage of new legislation seeking to extend health insurance to millions of residents lacking coverage, does not make us hopeful about the future course of immigrant integration in the United States. Undocumented immigrants remain explicitly excluded. Legal immigrants eligible for public health programs tend to be confused about the complex eligibility requirements. Many avoid using Medicaid due to the mistaken impression that doing so would make them a "public charge," possibly rendering them ineligible for US citizenship (Feld and Power 2002). Uninsured immigrants lack access to preventative services and often seek help only when they become critically ill, relying on costly emergency room visits to get medical care. Lack of linguistic and culturally competent medical services also affects the quality of care. All in all, health care barriers can have disastrous consequences for immigrants and result in an overextended emergency medical system.

Public Benefits

The poor, elderly, and disabled are eligible for a number of federally funded benefits that provide them with an important, though only minimal, government safety net. The major federal programs include food stamps, Supplemental Security Income (SSI, a monthly income supplement to the aged, blind, and disabled), welfare assistance to indigent families (known as Temporary Aid to Needy Families, or TANF), Medicaid, and Section 8 subsidized housing. Because many of today's newcomers are poorer than the native born population, federal benefits can provide much needed assistance with integration.

Undocumented immigrants are not eligible to receive federally funded public benefits other than emergency Medicaid. Legal immigrants used to be eligible for these benefits on the same basis as US citizens, but PRWORA instituted a citizenship criterion in 1996, limiting non-citizens' eligibility. In its original form, the act barred all legal immigrants from receiving food stamps and SSI, with the exception of refugees and legal immigrants with long work histories or military connections. The act also devolved some policy decisions to states, including whether or not to use state funds to offer TANF and Medicaid benefits to legal immigrants who arrived in the United States on or before 22 August 1996, the date PRWORA was enacted.[25] PRWORA rendered immigrants arriving after enactment ineligible for TANF and Medicaid for their first five years in the country.[26] As of 2011, many of the exclusionary provisions of PRWORA still stand, but some benefits have been restored. Congress restored SSI payments to pre-enactment immigrants, and it restored food stamps to immigrant children and disabled immigrants, regardless of date of entry into the country, as well as to pre- and post-enactment immigrants who have been in the country for at least five years.

The developments in welfare reform have two important consequences for immigrant integration. First, PRWORA shifted the burden of determining and financing social policy for immigrants from the federal government to state and local governments. These lower levels of government have not acted uniformly, thereby widening policy divisions between states and localities. In some jurisdictions, states stepped in to provide benefits for immigrants not covered in PRWORA, but in other places resentment over the new burden imposed by the federal government has combined with anti-immigrant sentiment and fiscal crisis to exclude non-citizens from social benefits. Second, current public benefit restrictions, at all levels of government, place the onus for help squarely on immigrants' families, friends, and a limited number of non-profit social service agencies. Since new immigrants – especially those with low human capital – often need some assistance to get on their feet and adjust to life in the United States, the burden falls on these networks of support and carries a significant psychological, social, and economic cost to immigrants and those around them. These developments do not bode well for the advancement of immigrants' social inclusion.

Social Exclusion

Our policy overview suggests that the trend in the United States is toward social exclusion rather than inclusion. Exclusion can be found at all three levels of government and across policy domains. In the area of labour market access, for example, the federal government started the E-Verify program in 1997, requiring employers with federal contracts to check a government database to verify employees' legal authorization to work.[27] Undocumented workers also lost some protections they previously had under labour law – generally applied to all workers, regardless of legal status – in 2002. In deciding the case of *Hoffman Plastic Compounds Inc. v. NLRB*, the US Supreme Court denied undocumented workers the right to sue for back wages, even when the employer was judged to use unfair labour practices.

Exclusionary policies are often a reaction to perceived problems associated with undocumented immigration, but not uniformly so, as our discussion of welfare reform at the federal level shows. The terrorist attacks of 2001 also spawned a series of laws undermining non-citizens' legal rights and their ability to carry out daily activities. For example, the *USA PATRIOT Act* of 2001 restricts immigrants' civil liberties by creating new grounds for deportation and making it easier for federal officials to detain foreign born individuals suspected of terrorist activities.[28] The *REAL ID Act* of 2005 requires proof of lawful immigration status to get valid state-issued photo identification.[29] This makes it impossible for undocumented immigrants to obtain a driver's licence, which in the United States is commonly used as identification for everything from using the public library to opening a bank account.

At the sub-national level, we also find a growing number of exclusionary laws and policies. These range from the 28 US states that have adopted – often by direct popular vote or referenda – policies that declare English the official language of government (English First 2011), to bills passed since 2007 by Alabama, Arizona, Georgia, Oklahoma, Tennessee, and West Virginia making it illegal for employers to hire undocumented workers. Such laws replicate existing federal legislation, passed in 1986, making it unlawful to employ undocumented migrants, but while the federal law has been largely unenforced (Brownell 2005), these states appear to be taking a more aggressive stance. Cities such as Hazleton, PA, Escondido,

CA, and Farmers Branch, TX, gained national attention in 2006 when they adopted tough ordinances that bar undocumented migrants from working and renting homes in their cities and make landlords responsible for verifying tenants' residence status. Other cities, such as Manassas, VA, have experimented with zoning laws that appear neutral but in reality are tools to drive away undocumented migrants (Jonsson 2006; Romero 2008). Finally, a total of 69 law enforcement agencies in 24 states had, by September 2011, entered into agreements with the Department of Homeland Security, pursuant to Section 287(g) of the 1995 *Immigration and Nationality Act*, to help federal officials enforce immigration laws by apprehending undocumented immigrants in their jurisdictions (USCIS 2011b). While many of these laws and policies are being challenged in court, exclusionary federal, state, and local policies contribute to a climate of fear and, we contend, hinder the social integration of immigrants, including those not directly targeted by legislation.

The Future of Immigrant Integration Policy in the United States

Some localities and states in the United States are formulating and implementing policies to promote the social integration of newcomers in their jurisdictions (de Graauw 2008). Large cities such as New York and San Francisco and smaller cities like Dayton, OH, and Littleton, CO, have developed programs to help immigrants access city services, benefit from social programs, and become active citizens of their communities. Yet while there are some bright spots, the overall picture is of gathering storm clouds threatening immigrants' successful integration. Governments at the federal, state, and local levels seem increasingly inclined to draw sharp distinctions between US citizens (native and foreign born) and non-citizens. Undocumented migrants, in particular, are painted as categorically unequal, not only ineligible for public benefits and services but also increasingly denied housing and other basic necessities as well as targeted by local police. Overall, we are pessimistic that this trend will reverse in the short term, especially as the United States grapples with high unemployment and large government deficits.[30]

We nonetheless end this chapter in search of a silver lining for medium- and long-term policy-making. It is important to emphasize that for many immigrants, and especially their children, the United States continues to be a land of opportunity, providing stable government under a rule of law, economic mobility for many, and a relatively open society that is generally tolerant of religious, cultural, and racial diversity. The general tolerance of diversity in the United States is not promoted by a national multicultural policy but is woven into American history and educational curricula that celebrate minority groups. It means that, unlike in a growing number of European countries, US policy-makers have made no serious proposals for cultural integration or Americanization programs. Many migrants move to the United States because, while no paradise, it offers a better way of life than many other places in the world.

This does not mean that exclusionary, or even laissez-faire, policy-making should continue. We believe that immigrants' integration would be faster, easier, and more successful for both newcomers and the host society if the United States instituted a comprehensive set of settlement policies; we think these should focus on language training and socio-economic security, not cultural instruction. Some question whether American political culture, and US voters, would support government intervention, especially given Americans' individualist ethos, suspicion of government, and "pull yourself up by the bootstraps" mentality to economic mobility (e.g., Pickus 2005). While there is clearly some truth to this portrait, such depictions ignore important examples of government action around immigrant incorporation, most notably, federal policy towards refugees.

Indeed, it is possible to identify a coherent US refugee resettlement policy, one accompanied by widespread agreement that the government should have a role in integrating refugees. Initially, federal involvement with refugee resettlement was ad hoc and fragmented in the years following World War II. Intervention grew modestly through aid to Cuban refugees in the 1960s, and then expanded further with the arrival of Southeast Asians in the 1970s and through programs for East Bloc refugees. In 1980, the *Refugee Act* transformed this patchwork of domestic resettlement programs into a single program for post-arrival assistance to all refugee groups. It also institutionalized the public-private partnerships that had long existed between government, religious institutions, and voluntary resettlement agencies. Today, the federal government provides most of the funding, but civil society organizations engage in most of the service work that assists refugees with short-term settlement and longer-term integration.

Unlike other immigrants, refugees have also been protected in welfare reform. Refugees remained eligible for SSI and food stamps, and they were exempt from the five-year bars on TANF and Medicaid. As of 2011, refugees are eligible for federally funded public benefits immediately upon arrival in the United States, and they retain eligibility over their first five to nine years in the country. Refugees also benefit from federal resettlement programs funded by the Office of Refugee Resettlement.[31]

Refugees' integration consequently takes place in a context of public-private partnerships that is more welcoming than the one faced by other immigrants. These policies and programs, which take money from the public purse, were initially justified as in the national interest of the United States, since many refugees came from communist countries. These policies are also defended, and increasingly so, on humanitarian grounds, a moral obligation to help people fleeing persecution in their homelands. Perhaps more consequential to tax-adverse Americans, we have evidence that refugee programs have improved integration outcomes for those who receive help, from better outcomes in education and the labour market (Portes and Rumbaut 2006) to greater civic and political integration (Bloemraad 2006).

If immigrant, and not just refugee, integration were seen as in the national interest and an important humanitarian endeavour, it might be possible for the United States to develop a comprehensive national policy.[32] This would, however, require vigorous advocacy by civil society groups and vocal support by a significant group of voters. Thus far, immigrants' political incorporation has lagged. Levels of citizenship, in particular, are low among the immigrant generation, and few foreign born people have succeeded in winning elected office (Bloemraad 2006; de Graauw forthcoming). Importantly, however, the United States has a longstanding tradition of *jus soli* citizenship, which ensures that all children born on US territory – even the children of undocumented migrants – acquire US citizenship at birth.[33] If this growing second generation is mobilized into political activity, and they take to heart the challenges faced by their parents, it is possible that the coming decades may witness change to US policies and thereby ameliorate the process of immigrants' social inclusion into the country.

NOTES

Our thanks to Tomás Jiménez, Helen Marrow, and the volume editors for their helpful feedback on an earlier draft of this chapter.

1. Schmidt (2007) also characterizes the US approach to immigrant integration as "laissez-faire."
2. Such views can be normative – immigrants *should* become like native born Americans – or an empirical statement of inter-generational outcomes (e.g., Alba and Nee 2003). Usually, the former view also values immigrants' cultural assimilation, whereas the latter envisions greater room for cultural and religious pluralism within a general pattern of economic, social, and political convergence.
3. See http://www.mipex.eu/usa.
4. The United Nations estimates that in 2005, 191 million people lived outside their country of birth, 3 percent of the world population (UNPD 2006). As with the global statistics, the US percentage counts the proportion of all foreign born individuals, regardless of legal status. Unless otherwise indicated, all US statistics are from the American Community Survey's 2010 data or 2007–09 three-year average. The American Community Survey is administered by the US Census; see http://www.census.gov/acs/www/ for more information.
5. The legacies of American foreign policy and military actions loom large in explaining US migration patterns. The United States has, at various times, controlled territories from the Philippines to the Caribbean, spurring

migration from these countries, and it has given preferential entry to refugees fleeing communism (such as Cubans, Vietnamese, Nicaraguans, and those from the former Soviet Union) while refusing asylum to those fleeing regimes supported by the United States (such as Salvadorians, Guatemalans, and Haitians) (Stanton Russell 1995; Zucker and Zucker 1992).

6. Restrictions did not apply to the "Western Hemisphere," which meant that Mexican and Canadian migration, in particular, could continue. The 1965 *Hart-Celler Act* instituted, for the first time, a cap on visas for the Western Hemisphere.

7. US immigration law distinguishes between refugees selected for resettlement outside the United States and aslyees who make an asylum claim on US territory.

8. According to a 2009 survey, 51 percent of Americans think most immigrants are illegal, a slight increase from the 48 percent with a similar view in 2008 (German Marshall Fund 2009).

9. These data were in part collected before the recession of 2008–09 hit the United States; there is evidence that immigrants were especially hurt by job losses, rendering their economic situation even more precarious (Orrenius and Zavodny 2009).

10. With the exception of a very few municipalities, non-citizens cannot vote in the United States. Non-citizens include immigrants who are eligible for US citizenship but have not applied, and almost 12 million individuals without legal residency who cannot access citizenship under their current status. Among those eligible for citizenship, there is some evidence of a slight increase in naturalization rate (Baker 2009).

11. Available at http://www.uscis.gov/aboutus. Like integration policy, many different federal agencies have jurisdiction over entry and deportation policy. See Davy, Meyers, and Batalova (2005) for a brief overview of this administrative maze.

12. To acquire citizenship, most applicants must demonstrate a basic command of English and knowledge of US government and history. USCIS, and INS before it, have historically provided little support for citizenship training or other integration efforts. There are small signs of change in recent years. For example, in addition to the grants program, USCIS now publishes a short guide that gives newcomers basic information on topics like getting a social security number and finding childcare, available on the web at http://www.uscis.gov/newimmigrants.

13. While this is in large part due to the belief that integration is not the purview of government, debates over legalizing the undocumented population and, more recently, concerns over terrorism also crowd out integration related issues. For the White House position, see http://www.whitehouse.gov/issues/immigration.

14. All opinion survey statistics, unless otherwise noted, are from the German Marshall Fund report, *Transatlantic Trends: Immigration, 2009.*

15. The data on sharing customs and traditions comes from the Globus International Affairs Poll, conducted by AP-Ipsos Public Affairs in 2004, surveying residents in the United States, Canada, Mexico, Japan, France, Germany, Italy, Spain, and the United Kingdom. The second highest level of

opposition to the statement came from Canadians, with 58 percent disagreeing that it is better for a country if almost everyone shares the same customs and traditions. See http://www.ipsos-na.com/news-polls/searchresults.aspx?search=GLOBUS.

Concern over how immigration-induced diversity might undermine social capital or social cohesion, widespread in countries such as the United Kingdom, has not gained much traction in the United States, either among academics or policy-makers. This is perhaps surprising, given that some of the most cited research linking diversity with reduced social capital focuses on the United States (e.g., Alesina and La Ferrara 2000, 2002; Putnam 2007). The muted reaction reflects both disagreement about how robust the findings are and the perception that any negative correlation in the United States occurs more due to the dynamics of race relations than immigration.

16. On the issue of working hard, Americans hold similar views on legal and illegal immigrants, with about nine out of ten judging that migrants are hard workers.

17. See http://www.mipex.eu/anti-discrimination. The United States was noticeably weaker in other integration policy areas.

18. Non-European veterans, including those of Asian and Mexican origin, faced barriers in accessing these benefits, as did native born African-American soldiers.

19. For example, we do not address the full range of anti-discrimination legislation, labour law (which in many cases protects undocumented workers), or policies related to the media and culture. US governments provide little public funding for "ethnic" culture; there is no national multiculturalism policy for the preservation of immigrants' cultural heritages. Here again we see a laissez-faire attitude, which allows immigrants to establish their own grassroots cultural groups as non-profit organizations and allows companies to seek profit by serving cultural communities. Especially noteworthy is the vibrant Spanish-language media sector and entertainment industry that count more than 700 Spanish-language newspapers in print, close to 900 Spanish-language radio stations, and approximately 200 television stations that broadcast in Spanish and that provide a rich range of products to Spanish speakers (Arbitron 2008; Latino Print Network 2008). On the disjuncture between law and practice, some recent scholarship examines "bureaucratic incorporation," the actions taken by public employees to accommodate immigrants (de Graauw 2008; Lewis and Ramakrishnan 2007; Jones-Correa 2008). It is worth noting, however, that although some officials accommodate immigrants by stretching, bending, or even breaking the rules, such bureaucratic inclusion is delimited by existing legislation and policies, our focus here (Marrow 2009).

20. Six European countries were polled: France, the United Kingdom, Germany, Italy, the Netherlands, and Spain. A virtually identical proportion of residents in the other countries, 89 percent, felt it important that immigrants know the national language, but only respondents in the United Kingdom were less likely to support government language classes, at 25 percent, while Canadians, at 48 percent, were most likely to support publicly funded language instruction for immigrants (German Marshall Fund 2009).

21. DREAM stands for "Development, Relief and Education for Alien Minors."
22. The state of Massachusetts adopted a law in 2006 requiring nearly all of its residents to obtain health insurance, but it does not require employers to provide insurance. In 2007, the city of San Francisco started a program, enacted the year before, to provide universal access to health care for residents, including undocumented immigrants. The program only requires employer contributions from large and medium-sized businesses.
23. This landmark federal law affected US citizens as well, by eliminating welfare as an entitlement, imposing time limits on public assistance, mandating that welfare recipients work, and increasing the power of states to administer welfare programs.
24. Federal law does mandate, however, that immigrants – regardless of citizenship, legal status, or ability to pay – cannot be denied medical services that protect their life and the health and safety of the public, including emergency services, immunizations, and diagnosis and treatment of communicable diseases.
25. Only Alabama decided to exclude pre-enactment immigrants from TANF, and only Wyoming decided to do so with regard to Medicaid (Fix, Capps, and Kaushal 2009).
26. PRWORA did not change eligibility for housing assistance, and all low-income legal immigrants, regardless of when they entered the country, remain eligible for public housing and Section 8 rental subsidies from the US Department of Housing and Urban Development.
27. Various states have subsequently enacted similar laws.
28. USA PATRIOT stands for "Uniting and Strengthening America by Providing Appropriate Tools Required to Intercept and Obstruct Terrorism."
29. REAL ID stands for "Rearing and Empowering America for Longevity against Acts of International Destruction."
30. Since the federal system facilitates policy "borrowing" between governments, we might see the diffusion of inclusive as well as exclusionary policies. Such borrowing, inclusive or exclusionary, will surely increase as immigrants increasingly settle in non-traditional destinations, including suburbs, rural areas, and new gateway cities in the South.
31. For example, the Refugee Cash Assistance and Refugee Medical Assistance programs are available for a period of eight months after arrival to refugees who do not meet the eligibility requirements of TANF or Medicaid.
32. See Jiménez (2007) for one attempt to make this case.
33. In another example of intensifying anti-immigrant sentiment, some federal and state politicians, as well as advocacy groups, have proposed legislation that would strip birthright citizenship from the children of undocumented parents, and perhaps even from legal temporary residents (e.g., http://www.cis.org/birthright-citizenship-for-visitors). Since, however, birthright citizenship is enshrined in the 14th Amendment of the US Constitution, and constitutional change is very difficult, the probability of ending birthright citizenship is remote. It is, nevertheless, an indication of the general animosity in some quarters against migrants in the United States.

REFERENCES

Abu-Laban, Y. and J.A. Garber. 2005. "The Construction of the Geography of Immigration as a Policy Problem: The United States and Canada Compared." *Urban Affairs Review* 40(4):520-61.

Alba, R. and V. Nee. 2003. *Remaking the American Mainstream: Assimilation and Contemporary Immigration.* Cambridge: Harvard University Press.

Alesina, A. and E. La Ferrara. 2000. "Participation in Heterogeneous Communities." *Quarterly Journal of Economics* 115:847-904.

—2002. "Who Trusts Others?" *Journal of Public Economics* 85:207-34.

Arbitron. 2008. "Hispanic Radio Today." At http://www.arbitron.com/television/hispanic.htm

Baker, B.C. 2009. "Trends in Naturalization Rates: 2008 Update." Fact sheet, Office of Immigration Statistics, US Department of Homeland Security. At http://www.dhs.gov/xlibrary/assets/statistics/publications/ois_natztrends_fs_2008.pdf

Bloemraad, I. 2006. *Becoming a Citizen: Incorporating Immigrants and Refugees in the United States and Canada.* Berkeley: University of California Press.

Brodkin, K. 1998. *How Jews Became White Folks and What That Says about Race in America.* New Brunswick, NJ/London: Rutgers University Press.

Brownell, P. 2005. "The Declining Enforcement of Employer Sanctions." Washington, DC: Migration Policy Institute. At http://www.migrationinformation.org/Feature/display.cfm?id=332

Campbell, G.J. and E. Lennon. 1999. "Historical Census Statistics on the Foreign-Born Population of the United States: 1850–1990." US Census Bureau Working Paper (29). Washington, DC: US Government Printing Office.

Capps, R., M. Fix, M. McHugh, and S. Yi-Ying Lin. 2009. *Taking Limited English Proficient Adults into Account in the Federal Adult Education Funding Formula.* Washington, DC: Migration Policy Institute.

Daniels, R. 2004. *Guarding the Golden Door: American Immigration Policy and Immigrants since 1882.* New York: Hill and Wang.

Davy, M., D.W. Meyers, and J. Batalova. 2005. "Who Does What in US Immigration." *US in Focus, Migration Information Source.* Washington, DC: Migration Policy Institute. At http://www.migrationinformation.org/USFocus/display.cfm?ID=362

de Graauw, E. Forthcoming (2012). "Thematic Essay: Immigrant Political Incorporation in the United States." In *An Encyclopedia of U.S. Immigration History,* ed. E. Barkan. Santa Barbara: ABC-CLIO Books.

—2008. "Nonprofit Organizations and the Contemporary Politics of Immigrant Incorporation in San Francisco." PhD dissertation, University of California, Berkeley.

DeNavas-Walt, C., B.D. Proctor, and J.C. Smith. 2008. "Income, Poverty, and Health Insurance Coverage in the United States." *Consumer Population Reports.* Washington, DC: US Department of the Census.

England, T.W. 2009. "Bilingual Education: Lessons from Abroad for America's Pending Crisis." *Washington University Law Review* 86(5):1211-39.

English First. 2011. At http://englishfirst.org/states

Feld, P. and B. Power. 2002. *Immigrants' Access to Healthcare after Welfare Reform: Findings from Focus Groups in Four Cities*. Washington, DC: Henry J. Kaiser Family Foundation.

Fix, M.E., R. Capps, and N. Kaushal. 2009. "Immigrants and Welfare: An Overview." In *Immigrants and Welfare: The Impact of Welfare Reform on America's Newcomers*, ed. M.E. Fix, 1-36. New York: Russell Sage Foundation Press.

Gans, H. 1992. "Second-Generation Decline: Scenarios for the Economic and Ethnic Futures of the Post-1965 American Immigrants." *Ethnic and Racial Studies* 15(2):173-90.

German Marshall Fund. 2009. *Transatlantic Trends: Immigration, 2009*. Washington, DC: German Marshall Fund. At http://www.gmfus.org/trends/immigration/

Gosnell, H.F. 1928. "Non-Naturalization: A Study in Political Assimilation." *American Journal of Sociology* 33:930-39.

Hernandez, D.J., N.A. Denton, and S. Macartney. 2009. *Children in Immigrant Families – The U.S. and 50 States: Economic Need beyond the Official Poverty Measure*. Child Trends and the Center for Social and Demographic Analysis, Research Brief Series. Albany: University at Albany, SUNY.

Higham, John. 1988. *Strangers in the Land: Patterns of American Nativism, 1860–1925*, 2nd ed. New Brunswick, NJ: Rutgers University Press.

Hoefer, M., N. Rytina, and B.C. Baker. 2009. "Estimates of the Unauthorized Immigrant Population Residing in the United States: January 2008." *Population Estimates*. Office of Immigration Statistics, Department of Homeland Security. At http://www.dhs.gov/xlibrary/assets/statistics/publications/ois_ill_pe_2008.pdf

Huntington, S.P. 2004. *Who Are We? The Challenges to America's National Identity*. New York: Simon & Schuster.

Jiménez, T.R. 2007. "From Newcomers to Americans: An Integration Policy for a Nation of Immigrants." *Immigration Policy in Focus* 5(11). Washington, DC: Immigration Policy Center (American Immigration Law Foundation).

Jones-Correa, M. 2008. "Immigrant Incorporation in Suburbia: The Role of Bureaucratic Norms in Education." In *New Faces in New Places*, ed. D. Massey, 308-40. New York: Russell Sage Foundation Press.

Jonsson, P. 2006. "To Curb Illegal Immigration, South Cracks Down on Housing Codes." *Christian Science Monitor* 98(36):3.

Kasinitz, P., J.H. Mollenkopf, M.C. Waters, and J. Holdaway. 2008. *Inheriting the City: The Children of Immigrants Come of Age*. Cambridge: Harvard University Press.

Katznelson, I. 2005. *When Affirmative Action Was White: An Untold History of Racial Inequality in Twentieth-Century America*. New York: W.W. Norton.

Laglagaron, L., C. Rodríguez, A. Silver, and S. Thanasombat. 2008. *Regulating Immigration at the State Level: Highlights from the Database of 2007 State Immigration Legislation and the Methodology*. Washington, DC: Migration Policy Institute.

Latino Print Network. 2008. At http://www.latinoprintnetwork.com

Lewis, P. and S.K. Ramakrishnan. 2007. "Police Practices in Immigrant-Destination Cities: Political Control or Bureaucratic Professionalism?" *Urban Affairs Review* 42(6):874-900.

Marrow, H.B. 2009. "Immigrant Bureaucratic Incorporation: The Dual Roles of Professional Missions and Government Policies." *American Sociological Review* 74(5):756-76.

National Conference of State Legislatures (NCSL). 2011. "Undocumented Student Tuition: State Action." At http://www.ncsl.org/default.aspx?tabid=12846

Ngai, M.M. 2004. *Impossible Subjects: Illegal Aliens and the Making of America.* Princeton: Princeton University Press.

Orrenius, P.M. and M. Zavodny. 2009. *Tied to the Business Cycle: How Immigrants Fare in Good and Bad Economic Times.* Washington, DC: Migration Policy Institute.

Passel, J.S. and D. Cohn. 2009. "A Portrait of Unauthorized Immigrants in the United States." Washington, DC: Pew Hispanic Center.

Pickus, N. 2005. *True Faith and Allegiance: Immigration and American Civic Nationalism.* Princeton: Princeton University Press.

Portes, A. and R.G. Rumbaut. 2001. *Legacies: The Story of the Immigrant Second Generation.* Berkeley/New York: University of California Press and Russell Sage Foundation.

Portes, A. and M. Zhou. 1993. "The New Second Generation: Segmented Assimilation and Its Variants." *Annals of the American Academy of Political and Social Science* 530:74-96.

Putnam, R.D. 2007. "E Pluribus Unum: Diversity and Community in the Twenty-First Century, The 2006 Johan Skytte Prize Lecture." *Scandinavian Political Studies* 30:137-74.

Reimers, D.M. 1992. *Still the Golden Door: The Third World Comes to America.* New York: Columbia University Press.

Romero, T.I. 2008. "No Brown Towns: Anti-Immigrant Ordinances and Equal Educational Opportunities for Latinos/as." *Journal of Gender, Race, and Justice* 12(1):13-56.

Schmid, C.L. 2001. *The Politics of Language: Conflict, Identity, and Cultural Pluralism in Comparative Perspective.* New York: Oxford University Press.

Schmidt, R. 2007. "Comparing Federal Government Immigrant Settlement Policies in Canada and the United States." *American Review of Canadian Studies* 37(1):103-22.

Smith, D.H. 1926. *The Bureau of Naturalization: Its History, Activities and Organization.* Baltimore: Johns Hopkins Press.

Spolsky, B. 2004. *Language Policy.* New York: Cambridge University Press.

Stanton Russell, S. 1995. "Migration Patterns of U.S. Foreign Policy Interest." In *Threatened Peoples, Threatened Borders: World Migration and U.S. Policy,* ed. M.S. Teitelbaum and M. Weiner, 39-87. New York: W.W. Norton.

Telles, E.E. and V. Ortiz. 2008. *Generations of Exclusion: Mexican Americans, Assimilation, and Race.* New York: Russell Sage Foundation.

Tichenor, D.J. 2002. *Dividing Lines: The Politics of Immigration Control in America.* Princeton: Princeton University Press.

Tucker, J.T. 2006. *The ESL Logjam: Waiting Times for Adult ESL Classes and the Impact on English Learners.* Los Angeles: NALEO Educational Fund.

United Nations Population Division (UNPD). 2006. *International Migration and Development Report 2006: A Global Assessment.* At http://www.un.org/esa/population/publications/2006_MigrationRep/report.htm

US Citizenship and Immigration Services (USCIS). 2011a. "USCIS Announces FY 2011 Citizenship and Integration Grant Program Recipients." At http://www.uscis.gov/portal/site/uscis/menuitem.5af9bb95919f35e66f614176543f6d1a/?vgnextoid=61e8a0920dc82310VgnVCM100000082ca60aRCRD&vgnextchannel=68439c7755cb9010VgnVCM10000045f3d6a1RCRD

—2011b. "Fact Sheet: Delegation of Immigration Authority Section 287(g) Immigration and Nationality Act." At http://www.ice.gov/news/library/factsheets/287g.htm

US Commission on Civil Rights. 2006. "Reauthorization of the Temporary Provisions of the Voting Rights Act." At http://www.law.umaryland.edu/marshall/usccr/documents/vrabriefingpaper_2-22-06.pdf

US Department of Education. 2006. *Adult Education and Family Literacy Act: Program Year 2003-2004*. At http://www2.ed.gov/about/reports/annual/ovae/2004aefla.pdf

Vigdor, J.L. 2011. *Comparing Immigrant Assimilation in North America and Europe*. New York: Manhattan Institute. At http://www.manhattan-institute.org/pdf/cr_64.pdf

Zhou, M. 1999. "Segmented Assimilation: Issues, Controversies, and Recent Research on the New Second Generation." In *The Handbook of International Migration: The American Experience*, ed. C. Hirschman, P. Kasinitz, and J. DeWind, 196-211. New York: Russell Sage Foundation Press.

Ziegler-McPherson, C.A. 2009. *Americanization in the States: Immigrant Social Welfare Policy, Citizenship, and National Identity in the United States, 1908–1929*. Gainesville, FL: University of Florida Press.

Zolberg, A.R. 2006. *A Nation by Design: Immigration Policy in the Fashioning of America*. Cambridge: Harvard University Press and Russell Sage Foundation.

Zolberg, A.R. and L.L. Woon. 1999. "Why Islam Is Like Spanish: Cultural Incorporation in Europe and the United States." *Politics and Society* 27(1):5-38.

Zucker, N.L. and N.F. Zucker. 1992. "From Immigration to Refugee Redefinition: A History of Refugee and Asylum Policy in the United States." *Journal of Policy History* 4(1):54-70.

PART 2

BEYOND POLITICS: INFRASTRUCTURE AND POLICY

CHAPTER 11

INTEGRATION POLICIES ACROSS THE ATLANTIC: HOW FAR BEHIND CANADA IS EUROPE, HOW FAR AHEAD?

THOMAS HUDDLESTON

The first systematic comparison of Canadian and European integration policies, the 2007 Migrant Integration Policy Index (MIPEX), elicited a mix of reassurance and surprise in Canadian public debate. Speaking to national press, Jack Jedwab, Canada's MIPEX national partner at the time, emphasized that Canada, the only traditional country of immigration in the study, came out at the top: "We [Canada] are a nation that's open to diversity, and set a high standard in a world where it is increasingly important to be sensitive to immigrants" (Canwest 2007). This interpretation (though Jedwab cautioned Canadians against being "too self-congratulatory") fits with how the country sees itself and is seen in intergovernmental and policy exchanges as a – if not *the* – global leader on migration and diversity.[1] Nearly all European practitioners, be they "selective immigration" supporters or die-hard multiculturalists, find the "best practice" they want in Canada.

Yet this selection of best practices is only part of the story, since Canada was at the top of the MIPEX but not *on* top. In fact, it fell behind Sweden, Portugal, Belgium, and the Netherlands and had to share fifth place with Finland. However, whether Canada's perceived integration success compared to Europe's is viewed with hubris or humility, the act of interpreting the MIPEX results reveals the areas of integration where both sides of the Atlantic still have to learn from each other. Indeed, many countries have faced – and are going to face – the same policy choices on integration.

International Perspectives: Integration and Inclusion, ed. J. Frideres and J. Biles. Montreal and Kingston: Queen's Policy Studies Series, McGill-Queen's University Press. © 2012 The School of Policy Studies, Queen's University at Kingston. All rights reserved.

The high-scoring MIPEX countries were working out their historically multiculturalist models at the same time as Canada, the United States, Australia, and New Zealand. Common fears of terrorism and radicalization, perceptions of "failed integration," and a growing politicization of immigration have tested traditional countries of immigration as well. All of them will be in competition not only for global talent but also for new successful integration practices for their increasingly diverse democracies. This chapter compares Canadian integration policies to those of the 27 European countries included in the 2007 MIPEX. Area by area, the chapter analyses what the MIPEX results add to our understanding of Canada's relative strengths and weaknesses in integration, the degree of convergence across EU member states, and the complementary and competing philosophies behind these policies.

MIPEX METHODOLOGY

The MIPEX policy indicators produce a country-coded comparative dataset for comparison as well as retrospective and prospective impact assessments on national laws and policies. All data are publicly available at www.integrationindex.eu. The 2007 edition used in this chapter included 142 indicators that were completed and peer reviewed by experts on the policies in place as of 1 March 2007 in 25 EU member states before the accession of Bulgaria and Romania, Norway, Switzerland, and Canada to MIPEX. The scoring operationalizes the equal treatment approach found within the integration literature and EU policy documents. Groenendijk, Guild, and Dogan (1998) argue that the importance of legal integration, especially residence rights, can hardly be overestimated as both "a firm base" for societal integration and also a "clear signal" committing public authorities to invest in integration as a two-way process. The equal treatment framework underlying the study's scores has a significant impact on immigrants' well-being, planning, and investments. Even so, equality of opportunity is neither the sole nor sufficient means for negotiating full participation of immigrants and nationals in an increasingly diverse society. On each indicator, a country can receive one of three possible scores. Three points (translating into 100 percent) are awarded to policies meeting the most inclusive international and European legal standards of equal treatment for non-nationals (or, in the EU context, non-EU nationals). For instance, the top position on the family reunion strand corresponds to what EU citizens enjoy when they live abroad in another EU country. A country gets one or two points (zero or 50 percent) on each indicator if policy-makers opt for more restrictive policies and minimum standards. A country receives a score on each indicator. Each score is then averaged into one dimension score and into the overall strand score. These benchmarks enable policy actors to assess whether the rights and responsibilities of non-EU citizens are levelling up or down in each member state and across the European Union as the result of domestic and international policy trends.

Published biennially, the MIPEX's ambition is to assess and compare the changes in national integration policy. Users can check for policy coherence by comparing areas of strength and weakness within a policy and between policies. The index has an additional longitudinal component to track policy changes over time. At the international level, a country's successful performance can be compared to those of its neighbours and its region as well as to the average across countries. It is important to highlight that policy indicators do not replace in-depth research. Rather, MIPEX's quantitative and comparable results make integration policies in Europe more accessible to a wider range of researchers and stakeholders as a framework for more comprehensive investigations.

OVERVIEW

TABLE 1
Difference on Overall Score for Canada and for Selected EU Member States for Six Integration Policy Areas

	CA	DK	FR	DE	GR	NL	PT	SE	UK
Overall	67	−23	−12	−14	−27	+1	+12	+21	−4

Source: MIPEX (2007).

Ten countries on the MIPEX rubric were found to set legal conditions that were at least slightly favourable for integration. Canada's, ranked fifth (with Finland), has one of the most inclusive legal frameworks, alongside new countries of immigration in the Western Mediterranean and the historically multiculturalist countries like Sweden, Finland, Belgium, the Netherlands, and the UK. The countries furthest from the Canadian approach are those slowly moving from historically assimilationist or exclusionary models, like Austria or Denmark, the Eastern Mediterranean, the Baltics, and Central Eastern Europe. Somewhere in the middle of these are France, Germany, Ireland, and Luxembourg, whose policy changes often move them both backwards and forwards on the MIPEX scales. Secondary analysis of the database identifies the highest degree of policy coherence in the countries with the most inclusive frameworks (Huddleston and Borang 2009). Canada's policies would rank among the most coherent, if one of the MIPEX areas (political participation) formed part of their local and provincial integration strategies (to be addressed later). Besides this Canadian outlier, most countries suffering the greatest policy incoherence are the new countries of immigration in Europe's South and East. The links between their various policies are generally weak and often non-existent. Only in areas of EU law like long-term residence and family reunion do their policies tend to be coherent, similar across countries, and close to the European average. The most challenging area for new countries of immigration is reforming nationality law and political rights.

THE STARTING POINT FOR LONG-TERM INTEGRATION

The integration of newcomers should be analyzed as a long-term and multi-dimensional process (Niessen and Huddleston 2007). On the face of it, EU member states' MIPEX scores suggest that their long-term residence policies are as good as Canada's for promoting integration in the many areas of public life. (See Table 2.) Across all countries, newcomers who can fulfill the criteria for long-term residence are granted a partially secure legal status and equal socio-economic rights as nationals. Specifically, their right to reside is covered by permanent – or otherwise long and renewable – permits and protected by judicial oversight. These legal protections may not extend to long periods abroad or full protection from expulsion. This degree of harmonization on security and rights has been a goal of the EU member states since the 1999 Tampere European Council Conclusions called for a common status for all long-term resident non-EU nationals and comparable rights and responsibilities as for EU nationals. Where member state governments were able to agree to ambitious minimum standards in the 2003/109/EC long-term residence directive, EU law has improved the security and rights of migrant families and long-term residence across Europe. The greatest impact has been observed by official evaluations in the Mediterranean, the Baltics, and Central Europe, where the integration infrastructure is still under construction.

TABLE 2
Difference between Canada and Selected EU Member States on Long-Term Residence

Long-Term Residence	CA	EU 25	AT	FR	ES	SE	UK
Overall	60	−1	−5	−12	+10	+16	+7
Eligibility	80	−22	−20	−40	−20	−10	−30
Conditions	33	+22	−11	−14	+57	+37	+47
Security of status	50	+4	+7	+21	+21	+29	+14
Rights associated	88	−17	−13	−38	−29	−4	−13

Source: MIPEX (2007).

The major difference between the Canadian and European approach to residence is when foreign residents are given a permanent perspective for integration. In Canada, potential migrants who meet more selective conditions are granted permanent residence and equal rights at the very start of their settlement in the country. By contrast, most EU member states keep long-term residence out of immediate reach. Several categories of non-EU temporary migrants are excluded from being eligible. These restrictions have greater impact in Europe, which receives more temporary work migration and asylum seekers than Canada, which allows for greater refugee resettlement and permanent work migration. Those who are eligible will not have to pass as many conditions as in Canada, but they must reside for approximately five years before they can apply. The consequence is that newcomers to the EU are denied an equal starting position in society during the key early years that will impact on their choices and investment in integration. That comparative disadvantage may become entrenched and compounded in the years leading up to eligibility for long-term residence.

Keeping newcomers in a temporary status is a dynamic influenced by choices and limits determined through European harmonization. The EC long-term residence directive is more binding on the security and rights attached to the long-term residence permit than on the eligibility criteria and conditions for acquisition. The EC concept of "civic citizenship" (European Commission 2000) tried to meet the Tampere ambition of comparable rights and responsibilities by detaching many rights from nationality and reattaching them instead to long-term residence. Partly to win over member states, this concept was introduced with a time lag. The state should grant a comparable position to non-EU nationals but only gradually over their years of residence. EU legislation set the maximum waiting period at five years, which most EU member states have adopted. The eligibility of students and various categories of workers is also left to the discretion of member states. Moreover, refugees and beneficiaries of subsidiary protection are not covered by the current scope of the EC long-term residence status.

A secure family life as a starting point for integration is also central to the policies of traditional countries of immigration, but only for a few EU member states. Only Sweden and Portugal have comparable family reunion scores to Canada. Western and Eastern European countries tend to ask sponsors to fulfill similar conditions as Canada does and grants them a similar degree of residence security. For example, like Canada, most do not impose language or integration assessments on sponsors or their spouses abroad (van Oers, Erboll, and Kostakopoulou 2010).

TABLE 3
Difference between Canada and Selected EU Member States on Family Reunion for Non-Nationals

Family Reunion	CA	EU 25	AT	DK	FR	PT	SE
Overall	76	−18	−41	−40	−31	+8	+16
Eligibility	100	−49	−60	−100	−70	0	0
Conditions	38	+12	−28	+9	−28	+13	+43
Security of status	63	0	−13	−13	0	+25	+25

Source: MIPEX (2007).

Again, the major gap is eligibility. In Canada, permanent adult residents, no matter how long they have lived in the country, can sponsor their spouse, common-law or conjugal partner, dependent children, parents, or grandparents, as well as other dependent relatives like orphaned minors. The European countries that modelled their demanding family reunion conditions on Canada's "selective immigration" approach did not copy its inclusive definition of the family. For instance, Austria, Denmark, France, and the Netherlands impose as many conditions on sponsors as Canada does while also imposing waiting periods and restricted definitions of the family.

The limits of European harmonization play a part in this dynamic.[2] The negotiations of the 2003/86/EC family reunion directive moved from a comparable definition of the family for non-EU and EU nationals to a wide range of possible restrictions. Member states can choose to limit sponsors to those who, according to authorities, have "reasonable prospects of obtaining the right of permanent residence," exclude unmarried or registered partners, dependent adult children or direct relatives in the ascending line, and impose minimum age limits on sponsors and spouses and maximum age limits and integration conditions on minor children. These restrictions are also found in the countries outside the bounds of this directive, where severe restrictions hamper the family reunion policies in Denmark[3] and Ireland.[4] Governments may wish to preserve this wide room for manoeuvring at the European level to fiddle with these definitions of the family and waiting periods to meet their divergent integration goals.

ECONOMIC INTEGRATION: INSIDERS AND OUTSIDERS

In most EU member states, once a legally resident third-country national finds a job, he or she generally has rights and security equal to those of their national co-workers. The differences between legally resident foreigners on the Canadian and EU member states' labour markets do not emerge from an analysis of their rights in employment; labour law often grants all legally employed workers equal footing after at least a few years' residence, if not immediately. MIPEX measured these rights in terms of unemployment benefits, trade union membership, and opportunities to change employers and sectors. Foreign born workers enjoy enough flexibility to adjust to the ups and downs of the labour market and their own careers.

Third-country nationals outside the labour market are those who suffer from unequal access and less favourable treatment than nationals and EU citizens. The legislation of EU member states to protect the employment security and rights of non-EU workers scored much better on the MIPEX rubric than legislation to get them into employment. In half the MIPEX countries, third-country nationals with the right to reside have a

TABLE 4
Difference between Canada and 25 EU Member States on Labour Market Access

Labour Market Access	CA	EU 25
Overall	80	−24
Eligibility	83	−40
Integration measures	67	−23
Security of status	75	−5
Rights associated	100	−21

Source: MIPEX (2007).

restricted eligibility to self-employment and certain private and public sector jobs. Moreover, non-EU nationals in most countries do not benefit from the same facilitated procedures for the recognition of qualifications obtained outside the EU. (See Table 5.)

TABLE 5
Difference between Canada and Selected EU Member States on Eligibility to Access the Labour Market

Labour Market Access	CA	AT	FR	DE	IE	IT	ES	SE	UK
Eligibility	83	−67	−83	−50	−67	0	0	+17	−33

Source: MIPEX (2007).

These protectionist countries include many Western European countries with significant non-national populations, including Austria, France, and Germany. For instance, France excludes non-EU nationals from the public sector, 50 occupations in the private sector, and several liberal, commercial, and craft professions.[5] Even countries with liberalized labour markets like Ireland and the United Kingdom impose these additional restrictions. Ireland's integration policies, at their infant stage, have made little progress with the National Qualifications Authority and entrepreneurship programs that actually restrict migrant self-employment in the first five years. Lonely at the top, only Canada, the Nordics, and a few new countries of immigration like Spain and Italy grant equal access to their labour markets as part of their integration strategy. The fact that both European states and immigrants often put economic participation as their top integration priority does not resolve these legal as well as the broader structural barriers imposed on labour market outsiders.

From Fighting Discrimination to Promoting Equality

Anti-discrimination is the area of integration where the European Union has seen the greatest and most recent progress. Because of the 2000/43/

EC Racial Equality and 2000/78/EC Employment Equality directives, most of the EU member states now have laws prohibiting discrimination on various grounds and the legal mechanisms to enforce them.[6] Nationals and non-nationals can bring forward a case of racial or ethnic discrimination in areas like employment, education, vocational training, housing, health, social protection, and social advantages. They have access to several types of procedures, where they benefit from protections against victimization and shifts in the burden of proof. Between 2004 and 2007 alone, MIPEX observed significant improvements to the legal framework in countries like France, Germany, Greece, and Luxembourg. The most robust legal frameworks are still found in the traditional settler countries as well as the historically multiculturalist countries that had elaborate anti-racism laws predating the directives: Belgium, Sweden, the Netherlands, and the United Kingdom (Niessen and Chopin 2004). Outside these pioneering countries, the implementation of the directives has produced some strong legislation in other EU member states, but not as yet strong results.[7] A large gap persists between the legal protections in Eastern and Western Europe. One characteristic of the countries with weaker anti-discrimination legislation is a lack of protection against nationality discrimination. A significant number of these countries of immigration, including Austria, Denmark, Greece, and Spain, permit forms of unequal treatment that severely undermine the ability of immigrants to exercise – and service-providers to deliver – comparable rights and responsibilities in many areas of life.

TABLE 6
Difference between Canada and Selected EU Member States on Anti-Discrimination

	CA	EU 15	EU 10	FR	DE	NL	ES	SE	UK
Overall	85	−19	−36	−4	−35	−4	−35	+9	−4
Definitions	88	−12	−26	−13	−25	−13	−25	+13	+13
Fields of application	100	−27	−55	0	−25	−33	−50	0	0
Enforcement	61	+10	−12	+17	−6	+39	+6	22	+6
Equality policies	100	−53	−58	−29	−86	−29	−79	0	−29

Note: EU 15 are member states before 2004 (e.g., Western Europe and Greece). EU 10 are new member states after 2004 (e.g., Baltics, Central Europe, Cyprus, and Malta).
Source: MIPEX (2007).

The major weakness in the non-discrimination laws of most EU member states is that most do not see a role for government in promoting equality (Bell 2009). States like Canada, France, the UK, and the Nordic countries have committed themselves to undertake public awareness-raising as well as social and civil society dialogue but tend to delegate this role to fledging equality bodies and NGOs. The Canadian government, as an employer, uses "employment equity" measures in recruitment and hiring to address the underrepresentation of visible ethnic minorities. The Swedish government, as a buyer of goods and services, obliges all winners of public contracts to respect non-discrimination legislation and has recently reinforced its own obligations in this area.[8] Despite some action at local level and noises by national politicians, few national administrations are role models in the mainstreaming of equality and adoption of positive actions and targets.

IMPORTANCE OF NATURALIZATION

Slightly favourable paths to citizenship are open in the traditional *ius soli*[9] countries (Canada, Ireland, the United Kingdom, and, not far behind, France) as well as the recently liberalized countries: Belgium (2000), Sweden (2001), and Portugal (2006). All these countries tend to require around five years' total residence for the first generation, grant conditional *ius soli* to at least the third generation, impose no income requirement for citizenship, protect against statelessness, and embrace dual nationality. This list is far from settled; liberalizing reforms can be done and undone (Howard 2009). The increasing politicization of naturalization (Bauböck 2005) can frustrate the development of a positive citizenship discourse and long-term integration goals, as most recently has happened in the UK.[10]

Paradoxically, European policy debates on integration often look to Canada for best practice, while missing the main goal of the policy: shared citizenship. Most EU member states do, like Canada, have inclusive policies for migrants to acquire long-term residence, but that fact has little to do with whether they encourage settled residents to become citizens (Huddleston and Borang 2009). That long-term residence has in many cases been facilitated in lieu of naturalization speaks to the continued identification of nationality with ethnicity in many parts of Europe: from Norway and Finland in the North to Spain and Italy in the South, from Ireland in the West to Hungary, Poland, and Romania to the East. Applicants in most EU member states must reside a range of five to twelve years and often have acquired long-term residence, which is increasingly one of the spillover effects of EU law (Huddleston 2009b). On average, they have to pass similar but more demanding conditions for naturalization than they did for long-term residence – and than they would for Canadian citizenship. (See Table 7.) The language fluency levels are higher, the integration / citizenship assessments more contested and sometimes subjective, the criminal record requirements less forgiving, and requirements about income or employment more onerous. The procedures for naturalization are more discretionary, allowing for more grounds for refusal and less room for judicial review. As such, the European Commission in its 2008 report to the ministers responsible for integration took note of the MIPEX finding that access to nationality was one of the greatest areas of weakness in most countries' thinking on integration.

TABLE 7
Difference between Canada and Selected EU Member States on Access to Nationality

	CA	EU 15	EU 10	BE	FR	DE	IT	PT	UK
Overall	67	−19	−30	+4	−13	−29	−34	+2	−5
Eligibility	75	−32	−60	0	−8	−25	−58	−8	−17
Dual nationality	100	−42	−68	0	0	−50	−75	0	0

Note: EU 15 are member states before 2004 (e.g., Western Europe and Greece). EU 10 are new member states after 2004 (e.g., Baltics, Central Europe, Cyprus, and Malta).
Source: MIPEX (2007).

Recent trends across Europe provide cause for greater optimism.[11] The steps that these countries have been most missing from the Canadian pathway to citizenship are also the most dynamic trend in Europe. These steps are the eligibility requirements and dual nationality regimes, which are the least coherent in the "new" member states (EU10), new countries of immigration, and countries with strong extreme right parties like Austria, Denmark, and Switzerland. Firstly, eligibility requirements for citizenship tend to be facilitated in democratic societies as the immigrant population becomes larger and longer settled. MIPEX has observed shortened residence periods for the first generation and double *ius soli* for the third generation in Portugal (2006), Luxembourg (2008), and Greece (2010). Secondly, the obligation to renounce one's previous nationality – often cited as one of the main disincentives for naturalization – is being removed either in part or in full in most policies in Europe: Germany (2000), Sweden (2001), Finland (2003), Luxembourg (2008), and Greece (2010). In fact, MIPEX secondary analysis indicates that the two elements are linked. Countries that facilitate residence and *ius soli* requirements are also more likely to accept dual nationality. In both cases, the reform legislation often changes the perception of naturalization into a sign of the willingness of foreigners to integrate.

The introduction of language and citizenship assessments is the other significant, if contradictory, trend in European naturalization policies. That a country asks its new citizens for a basic knowledge of one of its languages is rarely controversial (Jacobs 2008; Bernitz and Bernitz 2006). What remains unsettled (Bauböck and Joppke 2010) is whether increasingly demanding language and citizenship tests act as integration incentives or obstacles. The debate is essentially around their content and format: that is, what can be asked of new citizens that is not asked of the old (Michalowski 2009) and whether the policy enables them to succeed (European Commission 2010). It is still rather early to evaluate the efficiency and effectiveness of these recently adopted measures. Instead, the implementation of these tests in Europe is an opportunity for learning from the traditional settler countries. In Canada, Australia, and the United States, citizenship actors both inside and outside government are adopting discourses and good governance standards in order to promote both high naturalization rates and high public support for promoting naturalization. North American practices have already inspired new citizenship ceremonies in such diverse countries as Denmark, Estonia, France, the Netherlands, Norway, and the United Kingdom. This recent interest in ceremonies across Europe can be seen as an opening for greater transatlantic discussion about the role of state and local actors in shared citizenship.

THE MISSING LINK IN CANADA'S PATHWAY TO CITIZENSHIP

The political participation of immigrants is the one incoherent area in Canada's integration strategy and the second major area of weakness for half of the EU member states. (See Table 8.) Democratic inclusion in Canada comes through naturalization after three or four years. Before naturalization, the country only grants immigrants basic civil rights and funds political activities on a project basis. Only the newest countries of immigration have less developed political participation policies. Secondary analysis finds no trade-off between encouraging foreigners to become political actors and encouraging them to also become national citizens (Jacobs, Delmotte, and Herman 2009). Rather, there is a slight positive correlation, even if it is not very significant. The countries that open both political opportunities to foreigners and pathways to citizenship include the anglophone countries (Ireland and the UK), the Nordic countries (Sweden and Finland), and the Benelux countries (Belgium, the Netherlands, and recently Luxembourg). Local projects in democracy that engage newcomers in the political system can start off the path to national citizenship (Huddleston 2009a).

TABLE 8
Difference between Canada and Selected EU Member States on Political Participation Policies for Foreigners

	CA	EU 15	EU 10	DE	IE	NL	PT	ES	UK
Overall	32	+28	−12	+34	+27	+48	+47	+18	+14
Electoral rights	0	+43	+22	0	+100	+67	+33	+33	+50
Political liberties	100	0	−45	0	0	0	0	0	0
Consultative bodies	0	+51	+6	+69	+50	+69	+75	+50	0
Implementation policies	50	+12	−34	+40	−25	+40	+50	−10	+10

Source: MIPEX (2007).

Many countries have shown a renewed and spontaneous interest in political participation, as it has been incorporated into European "best practice."[12] The highest-scoring countries in this area have well-established policies of voting rights and consultative bodies dating back decades. Consultative bodies facilitate contact between immigrant representatives and policy-makers in cities in at least 15 EU member states and at the regional and national level in ten. For instance, over 400 local foreigners' councils have been organized in Germany alone (Gsir and Martiniello 2004). In Denmark, local councils are linked together into a national Council for Ethnic Minorities. The Dutch have a similar National Dialogue Structure for Ethnic Minority Groups, which provides a legal and financial basis for consultation with the government and the parliament. In the past ten years, voting rights have been extended to non-EU nationals (Czech Republic, Estonia, Lithuania, Slovenia, Luxembourg, Slovakia, and Belgium) and new consultative bodies established (e.g., Spain, Portugal, France, and Ireland). As of 2007, non-EU nationals could vote in local elections in 15 EU member states, stand as candidates in ten states, and vote in regional elections in five. The local enfranchisement of immigrants is regularly debated in all corners of Europe and even in North America.

Canada can learn from other federal or decentralized countries that have opened up their political opportunity structure at local and regional levels. Local actors in Toronto have already proposed the concept of local citizenship.[13] US states taking the lead on integration efforts have established New American committees including immigrant leaders, while several cities are discussing various forms of voting rights.[14] Ireland, where any legal resident can vote and stand in local election, has a major local information campaign[15] and is now exploring the idea of regional consultative bodies.[16] As a note of caution, consultative bodies can easily languish and disappear from a lack of political will or good governance rules. Constitutions and courts have often blocked the extension of voting rights (e.g., Austria, Germany, Italy, and Spain), in which case local and regional authorities need to invest in constitutional action. Despite what can be a long and complicated process, voting rights, once granted, are not revoked or seriously challenged. Few implementation costs are incurred. Moreover, in practice few of the feared negative effects play out, such as a decrease in naturalization or an increase in ethnic parties or foreign influence (Groenendijk 2008). Opening political opportunities to foreigners will be a dynamic construction site in the new integration governance, meriting further study at local, regional, and national levels as well as further international exchange.

Conclusions

In Canada and EU member states, migrants with the same legal status – be they legal workers, long-term residents, or reunited family members – enjoy largely the same residence security and access to rights. These immigrants share the same rights and responsibilities as nationals in most areas of public life. Moreover, the conditions to acquire these statuses, including family reunion and long-term residence, are increasingly similar on both sides of Atlantic. States tend to ask the same types of requirements for the acquisition of family reunion, long-term residence, and nationality. Canada's permanent-based migration is certainly more selective but much larger in scale, while European countries, on average, impose a greater number and level of conditions on naturalization. On these criteria, the policy of the average EU member state seems to have become as selective and as rights based as Canadian policies for newcomers.

Where EU member states fall short of the high standards set by traditional immigration countries is in granting immigrants a permanent perspective and a clear path to citizenship. Immigrants in the EU have a very different starting point for integration than in Canada. Few upon arrival are welcomed into an environment of equal rights and responsibilities. Barriers in the labour market, a limited definition of the family, and a long time in temporary status make integration take longer, while leaving many out of the process. While a traditional country of immigration like Canada can learn from new initiatives in EU member states to politically engage all residents, these countries have yet to appreciate their role to encourage these residents to become national citizens too. The same is true for anti-discrimination, where the complaints mechanisms in the courts are not reinforced in society by positive actions to encourage mainstream organizations to diversify. State support for citizenship and equality may set the conditions so that European societies may recognize their new-found diversity.

NOTES

1. For example, see the International Metropolis Project at http://international. metropolis.net/network_e.html.
2. See Odysseus Network (2007); Huddleston (2008); Groenendijk et al. (2008).
3. Denmark was the only MIPEX country in 2007 to have critically restrictive eligibility criteria for family reunion. For instance, the policy includes an attachment requirement whereby a sponsor and his or her spouse must prove more combined aggregated ties to Denmark than they have to any other country in the world. For more, see www.nyidanmark.dk/en-us/coming_to_dk/familyreunification/spouses/attachment_requirement.htm.
4. Ireland has no family reunion policy for non-EU nationals and may not have one in the future, according to the new Immigration, Residence and Protection Bill 2010. See Comments of Immigrant Council of Ireland, www.immigrantcouncil.ie/press_detail.php?id=143.
5. See the deliberation on this matter of the French national equality body, the High Authority for the Struggle against Discrimination and for Equality, at www.halde.fr/Emplois-fermes-aux-etrangers-15,12851.html.

6. For the results of the transposition of the anti-discrimination directives in EU member states, see the reports of the European Commission's network of independent legal experts in the non-discrimination field at www.non-discrimination.net.
7. For case law, see the national reports at www.non-discrimination.net as well as the monitoring of the EU's Fundamental Rights Agency at http://fra.europa.eu/fraWebsite/home/home_en.htm.
8. See the New Anti-Discrimination Act 2008: 567, at www.sweden.gov.se/content/1/c6/11/80/10/4bb17aff.pdf.
9. *Ius soli* is birthright citizenship or entitlement to a country's nationality through birth on its national territory. For a full overview of this area, see http://eudo-citizenship.eu/docs/Iseult_Honohan.pdf and http://eudo-citizenship.eu/modes-of-acquisition/190/?search=1&idmode=A02.
10. See the Runnymede Trust's consultation response to "Earning the Right to Stay – A New Points-Based Test for Citizenship," 26 October 2009, at www.runnymedetrust.org/uploads/policyResponses/EarningTheRightToStay.pdf.
11. For more on ongoing trends on the acquisition of nationality, see http://eudo-citizenship.eu/, which has followed up the well-known NATAC research project.
12. Number 9 of the 19 November 2004 Common Basic Principles for Immigrant Integration Policy in the European Union states, "The participation of immigrants in the democratic process and in the formulation of integration policies and measures, especially at the local level, supports their integration."
13. See the work of the Maytree Foundation (www.maytree.com) and the "I Vote Toronto" Campaign.
14. For an overview, see www.immigrantvoting.org.
15. See Dublin's Migrant Voters project, which is profiled on Cities of Migration at http://citiesofmigration.ca/did-you-know-you-can-vote-cities-and-democracy-at-work/.
16. See www.greenparty.ie/en/news/latest_news/white_seeks_expression_of_interest_for_council_on_integration.

References

Bauböck, R. and C. Joppke. 2010. "How Liberal Are Citizenship Tests?" EUI Working Paper RSCAS 2010/41.

Bauböck, R. E. Ersbøll, K. Groenendijk, and H. Waldrauch, eds. 2005. *Acquisition and Loss of Nationality: Policies and Trends in 15 European Countries*. Amsterdam: University Press.

Bell, M. 2009. "Benchmarking Standards in Anti-Discrimination Law and Policy." In *Legal Frameworks for the Integration of Third-Country Nationals*, ed. J. Niessen and T. Huddleston. Nijmegen: Brill.

Bernitz, H. and H. Bernitz. 2006. "Sweden." In *Acquisition and Loss of Nationality: Policies and Trends in 15 European Countries*, ed. R. Bauböck et al.

Canwest News Service, 2007. "Canada among Top Nations in Europe-Wide Immigration Study." At http://www.canada.com/cityguides/fortstjohn/story.html?id=3720ad5e-81aa-4f9e-9ad9-a3794ef086be&k=48765

European Commission. 2000. *Communication from the Commission to the Council and the European Parliament on a Community Immigration Policy.* COM (2000) 757. European Commission, Brussels, Belgium.

—2008. *Strengthening Actions and Tools to Meet Integration Challenges – Report to the 2008 Ministerial Conference on Integration.* European Commission, Brussels, Belgium.

—2010. *Handbook on Integration for Policy-Makers and Practitioners.* 3rd ed. European Commission, Brussels.

Groenendijk, K., E. Guild, and R. Barzilay 1998. *Security of Residence of Long-Term Residents.* Nijmegen: University of Nijmegen.

Groenendijk, K., R. Fernhout, D. van Dam, R. Oers, and T. Strik. 2007. *The Family Reunification Directive in EU Member States: The First Year of Implementation.* Centre for Migration Law, Radboud University, Nijmegen.

Gsir, S. and M. Martiniello. 2004. *Local Consultative Bodies for Foreign Residents: A Handbook.* Council of Europe, Strasbourg.

Howard, M. 2009. *Varieties of Citizenship in Europe.* New York: Cambridge University Press.

Huddleston, T. 2008. *What Future for Immigrant Families in Europe?* MIPEX Policy Impact Assessment.

—2009a. "Migration and Democracy: Migrant Participation in Public Affairs." Warsaw: Organisation for Security and Cooperation in Europe.

—2009b. "Promoting Citizenship: The Choices for Immigrants, Advocates, and European Cooperation." In *Citizenship Policies in the Age of Diversity: Europe at the Crossroads*, ed. R. Zapata-Barrero. Barcelona: CIDOB.

Huddleston, T. and F. Borang. 2009. "Correlations within Integration Policies in Europe: Internal Dynamics across National Contexts." In *Legal Frameworks for the Integration of Third-Country Nationals*, ed. J. Niessen and T. Huddleston. Nijmegen: Brill.

Jacobs, D. 2008. "Belgium and Its Struggle with Citizenship." *Canadian Diversity* 6(4):28-31.

Jacobs, D., F. Delmotte, and B. Herman. 2009. "Political Participation for Migrants: The MIPEX Result." In *Legal Frameworks for the Integration of Third-Country Nationals*, ed. J. Niessen and T. Huddleston. Nijmegen: Brill.

Michalowski, I. 2009. *Citizenship Tests in Five Countries – An Expression of Political Liberalism?* Wissenschaftszentrum Berlin für Sozialforschung.

MIPEX. 2007. *Migrant Integration Policy Index.* Ed. J. Niessen, T. Huddleston, and L. Citron. Brussels: British Council and Migration Policy Group. At www.integrationindex.eu

Niessen, J. and I. Chopin. 2004. *The Development of Legal Instruments to Combat Racism in a Diverse Europe.* Immigration and Asylum Law and Policy in Europe Book Series. Leiden: Martinus Nijhoff.

Niessen, J. and T. Huddleston. 2007. *Setting up a System of Benchmarking to Measure the Success of Integration Policies in Europe.* European Parliament, Brussels, Belgium.

Niessen, J., A. Balch, C. Bullen. and M.J. Peiro. 2005. *Civic Citizenship and Immigrant Inclusion Index.* British Council and Migration Policy Group, Brussels, Belgium.

Odysseus Network. 2007. *Report on the Implementation of Directive 2003/86/EC.* At www.ulb.ac.be/assoc/odysseus/CEAS/CEASstatus.ht

van Oers, R., E. Erboll, and D. Kostakopoulou. 2010. *A Re-Definition of Belonging?* Nijmegen: Brill.

CHAPTER 12

CITIZENSHIP AND EMPLOYMENT IN TWO COLD COUNTRIES: CANADA AND SWEDEN COMPARED

PIETER BEVELANDER AND RAVI PENDAKUR

Over the past three decades, both Canada and Sweden have liberalized citizenship acquisition regulations by reducing the required number of years of residency and recognizing dual citizenship. During the same period, both countries have witnessed changes in immigration patterns by country of birth, with greater numbers of immigrants arriving from non-Western countries.

In an era of increasing immigration and increasing diversity, and concomitantly a policy era in which countries both within and outside Europe are seeking to tighten citizenship acquisition rules, it is important to understand the socio-economic outcomes associated with naturalization.

This chapter explores the link between citizenship and employment probabilities for immigrants in Canada and Sweden, controlling for a range of demographic, human capital, and municipal characteristics such as city and co-ethnic population size. Specifically, we examine the degree to which citizenship acquisition affects employment outcomes, controlling for place of birth, personal characteristics, and the characteristics of the city within which immigrants reside. We pay particular attention to the size of the co-immigrant population within a municipality and ask if the size of the community impacts employment opportunities.

Using instrumental variable regressions to control for the impact of citizenship acquisition, we find that age, marital status, and educational level are important determinants of obtaining employment by foreign born men and women. For immigrants from outside the European Union and North America, we find that the size of the co-immigrant population

International Perspectives: Integration and Inclusion, ed. J. Frideres and J. Biles. Montreal and Kingston: Queen's Policy Studies Series, McGill-Queen's University Press. © 2012 The School of Policy Studies, Queen's University at Kingston. All rights reserved.

in a city often has a significant positive effect on the probability of being employed. In the same way, we find that the acquisition of citizenship makes a real difference to the probability of finding work and obtaining employment. Foreign born men and women who have acquired citizenship are far more likely to be employed than those who have not. The size of the co-ethnic population has a positive impact for many immigrant groups – as the co-ethnic population increases, the probability of being employed also increases.

IMMIGRATION AND EMPLOYMENT INTEGRATION

Both Canada and Sweden have witnessed substantial change in patterns of immigrant intake and citizenship acquisition rules. Postwar immigration to Sweden came about in two waves. Prior to the early 1970s the dominant sources for intake were from Europe, and Nordic countries in particular. Labour market regulations allowed Nordic immigrants to enter the Swedish labour market freely without applying for permanent residency. In 1995 these rights were granted to citizens from all EU member states. Immigration from outside Europe also increased, but through refugee intake and family reunification. Thus, prior to 1970, intake was primarily Nordic, while in the last three decades intake has become increasingly non-European. Most of the European intake arrives under a labour-market bound policy, while the bulk of non-European intake arrives under humanitarian policies.

As was the case for Sweden, Canada's immigration policy in the 1960s marked a profound change in immigration intake philosophy. Where previously policy had emphasized family reunification almost exclusively, new regulations introduced in 1962 also stressed skills and schooling (Pendakur 2000). The changes allowed immigration intake to rise rapidly, but in two distinct directions – skilled and sponsored. As well, regulations concerning regionally based (and hence discriminatory) intake were slowly removed, creating an arguably "colour free" immigration strategy. As a result, for the first time, the dominant source countries slowly shifted away from Europe toward Asia.

The new Canadian regulations encouraged intake from countries where potential migrants would have access to high levels of schooling and where extended families were the norm. The first wave of these immigrants would thus be highly skilled, and there was almost guaranteed to be a second wave of sponsored relatives who were not selected on the basis of skill requirements.

There is evidence to suggest that in both Canada and Sweden immigrants face barriers to labour market entry as well as career progression. Examples of such barriers include non-recognition of foreign credentials and experience, loss of networks, accent penalties, and more general discrimination. An examination of Sweden's employment integration suggests that almost all foreign born groups, and in particular newly arrived groups of refugees, have lower employment rates compared to the native born. The general pattern is that natives have the highest employment rate, followed by Europeans and thereafter non-Europeans (Bevelander 2009). Work at Human Resources and Skills Development Canada concludes that immigrants who have been in Canada for less than ten years are at higher risk of experiencing persistent poverty and have lower probabilities of employment than those born in Canada (HRSDC 2010). In 2005 Asian immigrants aged 25 to 54 had an employment rate of 63.8 percent, compared to 83.1 percent for their counterparts born in Canada. Latin American immigrants had an unemployment rate 2.1 times higher than their Canadian born counterparts. African born recent immigrants had an unemployment rate more than four times higher than that of their Canadian born counterparts. They also had lower employment rates (Galabuzi 2009).

CITIZENSHIP IN CANADA AND SWEDEN

Sweden has perhaps the most liberal naturalization rules in Europe; however, these are based on the *jus sanguinis* principle. Even if born in Sweden, the children of non-Swedish citizens are not automatically entitled to Swedish citizenship. Naturalization is possible after five years of residence in Sweden, and for refugees, after four years. Citizens from Nordic countries are exceptions to this rule and can obtain citizenship after two years of residence. In addition, applicants must be eighteen years of age or older and have no criminal record.[1]

Swedish citizenship legislation has been reformed over the past 40 years with respect to naturalization, civil and political rights of citizens and non-citizens, and dual citizenship. The waiting period for citizenship was shortened in 1976, and the subsistence requirement,[2] which had been relaxed during the 1950s and 1960s, was abolished, as was the language proficiency test. Despite a number of debates and proposals – most recently during the 2002 electoral campaign – about naturalization requirements, including language proficiency, no changes to legislation or policy have been made.

The relation between residence and citizenship is also important. Most of the rights given to citizens in Sweden are also granted to others residing in the country, with some exceptions such as the exclusive right to enter the country and voting rights in national elections. As well, legally speaking, it is easier to limit certain civil rights in respect to foreigners. The citizenship requirement for several government positions has been relaxed over time, and today only a few positions – including certain senior officials, judges and military personnel – are reserved for citizens.[3]

Canada's citizenship acquisition rules are based on a combination of *jus sanguinis* and *jus soli*. Thus, being born in Canada means automatically being granted citizenship, and being the offspring of a Canadian has until recently meant having automatic citizenship.[4] The basic requirements for citizenship acquisition for those 18 years and older include three years of residency over a four-year period, the ability to speak an official language, and an understanding of citizenship rights and responsibilities (as defined by a citizenship test) (CIC 2010). Dual citizenship has been allowed since 1977. The obvious advantages of Canadian citizenship are somewhat limited. Basically, non-citizens enjoy all the rights of citizens except for privileged access to federal public service jobs and the right to vote in federal elections.

CITIZENSHIP AND EMPLOYMENT

Although political and research interest in the topic has grown in recent years, there are few studies analyzing the socio-economic impacts of the citizenship ascension of immigrants. Internationally, it was Chiswick (1978) who did the first study tracing the economic performance of immigrants to the United States, including consideration of whether immigrants had become US citizens or not. Initially this study finds a positive effect of naturalization on earnings. When including years since migration, however, this initial effect of citizenship acquisition is insignificant.

Renewed interest in the socio-economic effects of naturalization can be observed in both North America and several European countries. Bratsberg, Ragan, and Nazir (2002), employing both cross-sectional and longitudinal data for the United States, showed a positive significant effect of naturalization on the earnings growth of immigrants, controlling for differences in unobserved individual characteristics. Using cross-sectional data, DeVoretz and Pivnenko (2006, 2008) showed for Canada that naturalized immigrants had higher earnings and consequently made larger contributions to the Canadian federal treasury than their non-naturalized counterparts. Similarly, Akbari (2008) used cross-sectional data for the year 2000 in the United States and found that naturalized immigrants have increased treasury payments as well as a higher rate of welfare participation. In addition, tax payments exceed transfer payments for naturalized immigrants after ten years of residence in the United States. Mazzolari (2007) found employment and earnings increased for naturalized Latin American immigrants to the United States when their home countries passed dual citizenship laws and granted expatriates the right to naturalize in the receiving country.

For Europe, Kogan (2003) analyzed the impact of naturalization policy on former Yugoslavian immigrants to Sweden and Austria and showed a positive effect of naturalization for Austria but not for Sweden, indicating that the institutional framework around citizenship is different in the two countries, consequently impacting the effects of naturalization. Bevelander and Veenman (2006) analyzed the naturalization effect on Turkish and Moroccan immigrants to the Netherlands with cross-sectional survey data. The results of the multivariate analyses indicate that naturalization of Turks and Moroccans in the Netherlands is not positively related to cultural integration or to employment integration. In their 2008 study, Bevelander and Veenman analyzed the effect of naturalization on refugee groups in the Netherlands and found naturalization to have a positive effect on the probability of obtaining employment. Moreover, this analysis indicates that so-called "naturalization classes" have no significant effect on the labour market participation of immigrants. For Norway, using longitudinal data, Hayfron (2008) showed that refugees in particular have higher earnings when naturalized relative to non-naturalized immigrants and confirmed that naturalization is positively related to economic integration. Similarly, in a study of Germany using panel data, Steinhardt (2008) found an immediate positive naturalization effect on wages as well as an accelerated wage growth in the years after the naturalization.

Using 1990 census data for Sweden, Bevelander (2000) found increased odds of obtaining employment for those naturalized compared to non-naturalized residents. Scott (2008), however, using longitudinal data for a number of immigrant countries, found only small "naturalization" effects on income. Moreover, Scott's study suggests that this citizenship effect is largely a selection effect and not a function of citizenship itself.

Summarizing the literature on citizenship and economic integration, and in line with Bevelander and DeVoretz (2008), studies for the United States and Canada seem to support the existence of a "citizenship premium," whereas European studies show only scattered support for this hypothesis. One reason for the difference in results may be the variance in data across countries. Another may be that citizenship effects could be mixed with other selection effects as well as issues of participation.

Ethnic Enclaves

In the context of labour markets, cultural communities may be closely connected to labour market enclaves for three reasons (see Bonacich and Modell 1980; Wilson and Portes 1980). First, labour market enclaves may offer a degree of social comfort through language and shared identity that is not available outside the enclave. Second, ethnically defined enclaves may buffer the effects of ethnically based discrimination on the part of mainstream society. Third, ethnic or cultural enclaves that are "institutionally complete" (see Breton 1974) offer a wide variety of services and employment opportunities to group members. Large enclaves are more likely to be institutionally complete than small enclaves. We may then expect workers in large enclaves to earn more than workers in small enclaves because of the greater degree of choice that exists. Pendakur and Pendakur (2002) assessed the labour market impact of three types of enclaves in Canada (ethnic, linguistic, and ethno-linguistic) and concluded that the size of the ethnic enclave is important in reducing earnings differentials across minority groups.

DATA, METHOD, AND MODEL

Our data are drawn from the 2006 Canadian Census and the 2006 Swedish register through STATIV, the statistical integration database held by Statistics Sweden. These data contain information for every legal resident, including age, sex, marital status, children in the household, educational level, employment status, country of birth, years since migration,[5] and citizenship status. We sample people aged 25-64 because we want to concentrate on people who have finished their studies and are likely to be active in the labour force.

As we limit our sample to people likely to be active in the labour force, this means that all immigrants are included for Canada but not necessarily for Sweden. In Sweden all working age Nordic and EU 25[6] immigrants on entry are eligible to be employed. However, nearly all non-Nordic/non-EU immigrants spend the first few years of residence in settlement training courses and therefore have limited possibilities to acquire gainful employment.[7] For this reason, we only include non-Nordic/non-EU immigrants who have been resident in Sweden for at least two years.

Our study has two main goals. First, we wish to understand how citizenship acquisition may be a factor in attaining employment. Second, we wish to understand the degree to which the presence of a co-ethnic population may contribute to patterns of employment across different immigrant groups. However, citizenship acquisition is heavily correlated with other variables related to general integration and employment such as time in the country, development of networks, etc. In order to measure the "clean" effect of citizenship, we run instrumental variable regressions in which we define citizenship to be a product of whether or not an immigrant is eligible to acquire citizenship.[8] Using this definition, we run IV regressions on the entire immigrant population to measure the impact of citizenship acquisition and the size of the immigrant population. We then run IV regressions for each of 11 places of birth, which is equivalent to a single model in which all variables are interacted with country of birth. Within these regressions, we include a variable that identifies the number of people in the municipality who share place of birth with the respondent. In this way we can see the impact of the size of the ethnic enclave in a given city on the employment prospects of co-ethnic members.

We understand both citizenship acquisition and working to be forms of participation in the larger society. Within this context, the impact of citizenship may be interpreted two ways: citizenship acquisition may be a sign of commitment, in that immigrants who acquire citizenship may be signalling their intentions to remain and participate in the host society; and, within the context of employment, citizenship acquisition may act as a signal to employers that the prospective employee is committed to remaining and is thus a better "risk." We instrument citizenship because we believe that citizenship acquisition is wrapped up with a host of other participatory factors, including whether or not a person is employed. If this assumption is the case, people who get a job are also likely to become citizens. In order to remove the bias caused by both actions being forms of participation, we use citizenship acquisition rules and the years since first eligibility for citizenship as an instrument for citizenship. The rules for Sweden are as follows:

1. Immigrants from Nordic countries who have lived in Sweden for two or more years are eligible for citizenship. For Nordic immigrants, the number of years in Sweden after two years of residence is assumed to be the number of years he or she has been eligible for citizenship.
2. Immigrants from other countries are eligible to apply for citizenship after five years. The number of years after this point is considered to be the number of years he or she has been eligible for citizenship.

For Canada, immigrants must be resident in Canada for a period of three years, over a four year period.[9] We operationalize these rules separately for Canada and Sweden. For Canada, we define eligibility for citizenship as having been in Canada for more than four years. For Sweden, eligibility is defined separately by place of birth and intake class. By "instrumenting" citizenship in this way, we interpret the coefficient for citizenship as the "clean" effect of citizenship on employment possibilities (without the impact of participation that is correlated with getting a job).

We include 14 variable types in our models. Contextual variables, drawn from the registry, include the log of the city population, the log of the immigrant population, and the local unemployment rate for the city labour market area. In order to define the size of the enclave population, we aggregated immigrant place of birth data from the Swedish registry to a municipal level and then merged this new dataset with our individual level dataset.

Demographic variables include age (four dummy variables), marital status (four dummy variables), presence of children in the household (four dummy variables), and whether the spouse is Swedish (one dummy variable).

Socio-economic variables include schooling (five dummy variables) and schooling interacted with whether the last level of schooling was outside Sweden (for a total of ten dummy variables). For regressions with all immigrants, we include country of origin (nine dummy variables), years since immigrating, and citizenship.[10]

Results

Descriptives

Table 1 provides information on the percentage of men and women who are employed by country of birth and citizenship status. The most important thing to note in this table is the substantial variance in employment probabilities across groups and citizenship. In general, it appears that the impact of citizenship on employment is lower in Canada than in Sweden; however, there are differences by place of birth.

Looking first at citizens, we see that amongst female immigrants in Sweden, the employment rate ranges from a high of 72 percent for women from East Asia, the United States, Australia, and New Zealand to a low of 48 percent for women from the Middle East. For women who are not Swedish citizens, the employment rates are considerably lower for most groups compared to their co-ethnics who are citizens. Among men with citizenship, over 70 percent of those from the Nordic countries, East Asia, and the Americas are employed. Around 70 percent of immigrant citizens from the EU and the rest of Europe as well men from South Asia are employed. However, for other groups, that proportion drops to about 60 percent. As was the case for women, men who are citizens are more likely to be employed than their co-ethnic non-citizens. Looking at Canada, we see a similar pattern. Women with citizenship from the United States, Australia, New Zealand, Latin America, and East Asia enjoy the highest employment rates (over 70 percent). As was seen in Sweden, their non-citizen counterparts generally have lower employment rates (with the exception of women from Scandinavia and Germany). Male immigrants who are citizens from all regions except Scandinavia and Germany have employment rates in excess of 80 percent. Non-citizens tend to have lower employment rates. However, immigrants from Scandinavia and Germany have higher employment rates than their co-ethnics with citizenship.[11]

Our examination of some fairly basic descriptives suggests that citizenship acquisition is correlated with higher employment integration in both the Canadian and Swedish labour market. However, citizenship is correlated with a number of attributes that are also correlated with employment probabilities, including time in the country. Our question is whether citizenship still has this impact when controlling for other variables and whether the size of the enclave acts to increase the employment rate.

TABLE 1
Citizenship and Percent Employed for Immigrants by Place of Birth for Canada and Sweden, 2006

Sex	Country of Birth	Canada Citizen Total	Canada Citizen % Employed	Canada Non-citizen Total	Canada Non-citizen % Employed	Sweden Citizen Total	Sweden Citizen % Employed	Sweden Non-citizen Total	Sweden Non-citizen % Employed
Females	Total	1,598,480	68	7,272,125	71	245,474	62	137,555	45
	Scandinavia	8,940	64	3,730	66	43,309	71	37,695	68
	Germany	35,215	64	17,025	71	3,682	69	5,967	59
	Rest of EU27	423,065	67	113,335	65	30,782	67	22,408	51
	OtherEur	77,235	71	23,225	58	49,748	62	15,981	37
	USAAustNZ	50,800	73	62,315	68	4,792	72	5,014	44
	Africa	91,095	69	42,125	49	15,383	59	8,454	21
	Latincarib	223,125	72	70,225	57	15,307	68	5,759	44
	MiddleEast	73,340	57	25,900	38	53,810	48	14,715	13
	S Asia	163,450	63	95,335	47	11,822	61	8,705	25
	China/HK	189,370	67	65,620	52	2,252	68	2,479	27
	E Asia	241,815	72	96,790	61	14,587	72	10,378	39
Males	Total	1,498,910	82	7,010,640	81	222,283	68	141,303	49
	Scandinavia	8,635	77	3,190	83	33,475	74	30,018	60
	Germany	34,630	76	14,695	85	3,875	72	6,810	66
	Rest of EU27	423,660	81	113,935	81	22,954	68	29,642	63
	OtherEur	73,795	84	19,830	79	43,734	71	14,324	47
	USAAustNZ	42,955	84	45,885	83	4,922	75	7,041	54
	Africa	98,920	83	48,210	69	18,104	64	12,149	32
	Latincarib	180,830	84	66,235	77	13,331	73	6,242	57
	MiddleEast	85,345	80	28,210	68	64,687	61	20,496	26
	S Asia	177,580	85	88,380	79	10,658	68	10,847	31
	China/HK	163,820	81	56,990	66	1,288	74	2,011	31
	E Asia	189,335	82	57,440	73	5,255	73	1,723	44

Source: 2006 Census of Canada and 2006 Swedish Registry.

Regressions

OLS regression results: Table 2 shows results from four instrumental variable (IV) regressions (two for each country, split by sex) where the dependent variable is whether the respondent is employed. In this analysis we instrument citizenship to be a product of whether or not a person is eligible for citizenship acquisition. This allows us to examine the degree to which effects attributed to socio-economic characteristics are actually a product of citizenship acquisition. The last two columns of Table 2 show the results of a t-test that measures the degree to which the coefficients for Canada and Sweden are significantly different from each other.[12]

Looking first at Sweden, we see that the impact of the contextual (city characteristics) variables all have significant and fairly strong effects. For men and women the coefficient for city size is –0.03, which means that for every unit increase in the log of city size (which varies from about 1 to 16), employment decreases by –0.03. However, this effect is largely negated by the impact of the size of the immigrant population. As is to be expected, having high employment benefits employment probabilities for immigrants.

Higher employment is also associated with demographic characteristics. Generally, being aged 25-34, being married, having higher levels of schooling, and having children are all associated with higher employment probabilities. The effect of obtaining schooling from outside Sweden is relatively small but significant.

The coefficients for our "clean" version of citizenship are 0.43 for women and 0.26 for men, suggesting that citizenship has a very strong impact on the probability of getting a job. Further, there are important differences that become evident by considering place of birth. As compared to women from Scandinavia, the coefficient for women born in Germany is –0.04 and for women from the rest of the EU –0.29. For women from the Middle East, the coefficient is –0.46. Among men, the impact of instrumenting citizenship is strong but not quite as stark. The coefficient for men from the Middle East is –0.27.

In Canada the effect of our control variables on being employed is generally smaller than in Sweden. Looking at contextual variables, it appears that the negative impact of city size is smaller in Canada (–0.01) than is the case in Sweden. However, the positive impact of the size of the immigrant population is about the same, which suggests that in Canada at least, a large immigrant population can undo the negative impact of a large population. The effect of naturalization is about one-third of that seen in Sweden (0.10 for men and 0.13 for women). Place of birth effects are generally small, with the exception of the Middle East, which is associated with a fairly strong negative effect (–0.17 for women and –0.10 for males).

TABLE 2
IV Regression Results on Full Employment for Immigrants, Sweden and Canada, 2006

Variable		Sweden				Canada				T-test of Dif. bet. 2 Countries	
		Female		Male		Female		Male		Females	Males
		Coef.	SE	Coef.	SE	Coef.	SE	Coef.	SE		
	Observations	336,689		314,050		362,260		322,820			
	R2	0.05		0.09		0.10		0.06			
	Prob>0	0.00		0.00		0.00		0.00			
	Log of city pop	-0.03	0.00	-0.03	0.00	-0.01	0.00	0.01	0.00		**
	Log of immigrant pop	0.02	0.00	0.02	0.00	0.02	0.00	-0.01	0.00		**
	City employment rate	0.94	0.04	1.36	0.04	1.44	0.05	0.82	0.02		**
Age (25-34)	Age 35-44	0.04	0.00	-0.03	0.00	0.05	0.00	-0.02	0.00		**
	Age 45-54	-0.01	0.00	-0.10	0.00	0.06	0.00	-0.04	0.00		**
	Age 55-64	-0.16	0.00	-0.24	0.00	-0.16	0.00	-0.19	0.00		**
Marital status	Married	0.02	0.00	0.08	0.00	-0.04	0.00	0.10	0.00		**
(single)	Divorced/separated	-0.04	0.00	0.00	0.00	0.01	0.00	0.08	0.00	**	**
	Widowed	-0.06	0.01	-0.03	0.01	-0.05	0.01	0.02	0.01		**
Children (non)	One child	0.04	0.00	0.10	0.00	0.00	0.00	0.02	0.00	**	**
	Two children	0.03	0.00	0.12	0.00	-0.01	0.00	0.04	0.00	**	**
	Three + children	-0.06	0.00	0.06	0.00	-0.07	0.00	0.02	0.00		**
Schooling	Highschool	0.18	0.01	0.14	0.01	0.14	0.01	0.02	0.01		**
(less than hs)	Vocational	0.33	0.01	0.24	0.01	0.17	0.01	0.06	0.01		**
	Lower university	0.16	0.01	0.13	0.01	0.21	0.01	0.06	0.01		**
	Upper university	0.35	0.01	0.26	0.01	0.23	0.01	0.09	0.01		**
	Schooled outside host country	0.04	0.01	0.09	0.01	-0.04	0.01	-0.02	0.01	**	**
	Highschool	-0.01	0.01	-0.04	0.01	-0.02	0.01	0.02	0.01		**
	Vocational	-0.03	0.01	-0.05	0.01	-0.01	0.01	0.01	0.01		**
	Lower university	0.02	0.01	-0.02	0.01	-0.02	0.01	0.02	0.01		**
	Upper university	-0.04	0.01	-0.05	0.01	-0.01	0.01	0.00	0.01	**	**

...continued

TABLE 2
(Continued)

Variable		Sweden				Canada				T-test of Dif. bet. 2 Countries	
		Female		Male		Female		Male		Females	Males
		Coef.	SE	Coef.	SE	Coef.	SE	Coef.	SE		
Place of birth	Germany	-0.04	0.01	0.02	0.01	-0.01	0.01	-0.02	0.01	**	**
(Scandinavia)	Other EU 27	-0.19	0.00	-0.05	0.00	-0.01	0.01	-0.02	0.01	**	**
	Other Europe	-0.29	0.01	-0.14	0.01	-0.03	0.01	-0.04	0.01	**	**
	USA Aust NZ	-0.19	0.01	-0.08	0.01	0.03	0.01	0.02	0.01	**	**
	Latin Amer Caribbean	-0.23	0.01	-0.08	0.01	-0.02	0.01	-0.04	0.01	**	**
	Africa	-0.32	0.01	-0.21	0.01	-0.07	0.01	-0.07	0.01	**	**
	Middle East	-0.46	0.01	-0.27	0.01	-0.17	0.01	-0.10	0.01		**
	S. Asia	-0.31	0.01	-0.19	0.01	-0.08	0.01	-0.05	0.01	**	**
	China	-0.28	0.01	-0.19	0.01	-0.07	0.01	-0.10	0.01	**	**
	E. Asia	-0.17	0.01	-0.13	0.01	-0.03	0.01	-0.07	0.01	**	**
	Years since migrating	0.01	0.00	0.01	0.00	0.01	0.00	0.00	0.00		
	Yrs since mig squared	0.00	0.00	0.00	0.00	0.00	0.00	0.00	0.00		
	Naturalized	0.43	0.01	0.26	0.01	0.13	0.01	0.10	0.01	**	**

Source: 2006 Census of Canada and 2006 Swedish Registry.

Looking at differences across countries, we see that for women, the impact of socio-economic factors are generally not significantly different from each other – in other words, it appears that the impact of age, marital status, and schooling are about the same in both Sweden and Canada. However, the effect of place of birth and naturalization are significantly different, the impact being generally smaller in Canada than in Sweden. For males, almost all the effects are significantly different from each other, suggesting that for males at least, there are real differences in the way in which socio-economic and ethnic markers play in the labour force across the two countries.

Differences by country of birth: Table 2 provides a bird's-eye view of the impact that different characteristics have on the probability of employment. This table allow us to understand the average degree to which the probability of employment differs across immigrant groups. However, it does not allow for the possibility that payoffs for different characteristics are different across immigrant groups. Results from Table 2, for example, do not allow us to see if Nordic women have a very different payoff to schooling as compared to women from the Middle East. Further, results at this level do not allow us to measure the impact of the co-ethnic population because all immigrant groups are rolled into the "log of immigrant population" variable. Table 3 resolves this situation by providing selected coefficients from a total of 44 separate regressions – a separate regression for each place of birth by gender by country group. The dependent variable remains employment status, and independent variables include all the variables from Table 2. Thus we allow each of the coefficients to vary independently for each place of birth group (equivalent to results from Table 2, but where each characteristic is interacted with place of birth).

Regression results shown in Table 3 include one additional independent variable. For each respondent we have added the log of the number of immigrants from the same group who live in their city. Thus, for example, in the case of a Nordic immigrant from Malmo, the "log of immigrant population" variable corresponds to the log of the number of Nordic immigrants living in Malmo.

As discussed, we include three variables that describe the size of the city – log of city size, log of immigrant population, and log of co-ethnic population. As can be seen, as city size increases, the probability of employment decreases. As the size of the immigrant population increases, employment probabilities also often decrease – this is the case for Nordic men and women, German females, North American immigrants, immigrants from the Middle East and Africa, South Asian females, and Chinese men. However, this negative effect is generally countered by a positive effect from the size of the co-ethnic population. In most cases, as the size of the co-ethnic population increases, the probability of employment also increases. Citizenship acquisition has a strong positive effect for all groups with the exception of Scandinavian immigrants.

TABLE 3
Results from 11 IV Regressions on Employment, Sweden and Canada, 2006

POB	Variable	Sweden				Canada				T-test of Dif. bet. 2 Countries	
		Female		Male		Female		Male		Females	Males
		Coef.	SE	Coef.	SE	Coef.	SE	Coef.	SE		
Nordic	Observations	79,277		60,494		2,025		1,825			
	R2	0.00		0.00		0.07		0.00			
	Prob>0	0.00		0.00		0.00		0.00			
	Log of city pop	0.04	0.02	0.04	0.01	0.00	0.03	-0.03	0.03	**	**
	Log of immigrant pop	-0.07	0.02	-0.05	0.01	0.00	0.02	0.04	0.02	**	**
	City employment rate	1.39	0.22	1.63	0.15	0.23	0.46	0.52	0.23	**	**
	Yrs since migrating	0.05	0.01	0.04	0.00	0.00	0.01	-0.01	0.01	**	**
	Yrs since mig. squared	0.00	0.00	0.00	0.00	0.00	0.00	0.00	0.00		**
	Naturalized	-2.90	0.40	-1.65	0.25	0.17	0.24	0.56	0.38	**	**
	Log co-immig pop	0.00	0.00	0.02	0.00	-0.01	0.02	-0.02	0.02	**	**
Germany	Observations	8,827		9,397		7,485		6,885			
	R2	0.00		0.00		0.00		0.09			
	Prob>0	0.00		0.00		0.00		0.00			
	Log of city pop	0.01	0.03	-0.04	0.02	-0.02	0.02	-0.01	0.01		
	Log of immigrant pop	-0.02	0.03	0.03	0.02	0.02	0.01	0.02	0.01		
	City employment rate	0.64	0.48	1.14	0.23	1.16	0.29	0.85	0.10		
	Yrs since migrating	-0.04	0.03	0.00	0.01	-0.01	0.01	-0.01	0.00		
	Yrs since mig. squared	0.00	0.00	0.00	0.00	0.00	0.00	0.00	0.00		
	Naturalized	2.72	1.23	0.74	0.27	0.57	0.23	0.23	0.12		
	Log co-immig pop	0.01	0.03	-0.01	0.01	0.00	0.01	-0.01	0.01		
Rest of EU	Observations	49,384		46,298		88,455		86,615			
	R2	0.00		0.00		0.11		0.07			
	Prob>0	0.00		0.00		0.00		0.00			
	Log of city pop	0.00	0.01	0.08	0.02	-0.01	0.00	0.01	0.00		**

Variable	Est (1)	SE (1)	Est (2)	SE (2)	Est (3)	SE (3)	Sig (3)	Est (4)	SE (4)	Sig (4)
Log of immigrant pop	0.01	0.01	0.01	0.02	0.02	0.00		0.01	0.00	**
City employment rate	0.99	0.11	1.40	0.19	1.13	0.09	**	0.74	0.03	**
Yrs since migrating	-0.01	0.00	-0.05	0.01	0.00	0.00	**	0.00	0.00	**
Yrs since mig. squared	0.00	0.00	0.00	0.00	0.00	0.00	**	0.00	0.00	**
Naturalized	0.63	0.05	1.66	0.36	0.17	0.02	**	0.16	0.01	**
Log co-immig pop	-0.02	0.01	-0.09	0.02	-0.02	0.00		-0.02	0.00	
Rest of Europe Observations	57,777		51,963		17,055			15,245		
R2	0.09		0.14		0.10			0.08		
Prob>0	0.00		0.00		0.00			0.00		
Log of city pop	-0.01	0.01	0.00	0.01	-0.02	0.01		0.00	0.01	
Log of immigrant pop	-0.01	0.01	-0.02	0.01	0.01	0.01		0.00	0.01	
City employment rate	0.52	0.08	0.98	0.07	1.42	0.22		0.74	0.09	
Yrs since migrating	0.00	0.00	0.00	0.00	0.01	0.00		0.01	0.00	
Yrs since mig. squared	0.00	0.00	0.00	0.00	0.00	0.00		0.00	0.00	
Naturalized	0.44	0.02	0.20	0.02	0.18	0.02		0.08	0.02	
Log co-immig pop	0.01	0.00	0.01	0.00	0.01	0.01		0.00	0.01	
N. America Observations	7,739		9,218		17,805			12,665		
R2	0.10		0.12		0.07			0.07		
Prob>0	0.00		0.00		0.00			0.00		
Log of city pop	0.00	0.02	-0.01	0.02	0.00	0.01		-0.01	0.01	
Log of immigrant pop	-0.01	0.02	0.00	0.01	0.00	0.01		0.01	0.01	
City employment rate	0.61	0.27	1.11	0.26	0.69	0.11		0.67	0.06	**
Yrs since migrating	0.02	0.00	0.01	0.00	0.01	0.00		0.00	0.00	
Yrs since mig. squared	0.00	0.00	0.00	0.00	0.00	0.00		0.00	0.00	
Naturalized	0.29	0.09	0.10	0.08	0.09	0.07	**	0.08	0.05	
Log co-immig pop	0.01	0.00	0.01	0.00	0.00	0.01		0.00	0.01	
Latin America Observations	18,723		17,713		46,120			35,970		
R2	0.00		0.02		0.08			0.05		
Prob>0	0.00		0.00		0.00			0.00		
Log of city pop	-0.01	0.01	-0.03	0.01	-0.03	0.01		0.00	0.01	**

... *continued*

TABLE 3
(Continued)

POB	Variable	Sweden				Canada				T-test of Dif. bet. 2 Countries	
		Female		Male		Female		Male		Females	Males
		Coef.	SE	Coef.	SE	Coef.	SE	Coef.	SE		
	Log of immigrant pop	0.00	0.01	0.02	0.01	0.05	0.01	0.02	0.01		
	City employment rate	0.94	0.19	1.19	0.18	2.02	0.17	0.87	0.06		
	Yrs since migrating	0.00	0.00	0.00	0.00	0.01	0.00	0.00	0.00		
	Yrs since mig. squared	0.00	0.00	0.00	0.00	0.00	0.00	0.00	0.00		
	Naturalized	0.50	0.07	0.34	0.10	0.17	0.02	0.12	0.02	**	**
	Log co-immig pop	0.02	0.00	0.01	0.00	-0.01	0.00	-0.01	0.00	**	**
Middle East	Observations	60,881		74,243		16,755		17,400			
	R2	0.18		0.11		0.14		0.07			
	Prob>0	0.00		0.00		0.00		0.00			
	Log of city pop	0.02	0.01	-0.02	0.01	-0.06	0.01	0.01	0.01		**
	Log of immigrant pop	-0.04	0.01	-0.01	0.01	0.07	0.01	0.00	0.01		
	City employment rate	0.93	0.11	1.39	0.10	1.43	0.27	0.80	0.09		**
	Yrs since migrating	0.04	0.00	0.02	0.00	0.02	0.00	0.01	0.00		**
	Yrs since mig. squared	0.00	0.00	0.00	0.00	0.00	0.00	0.00	0.00		**
	Naturalized	0.14	0.02	0.11	0.02	0.03	0.02	0.07	0.02	**	**
	Log co-immig pop	0.02	0.00	0.02	0.00	-0.02	0.01	-0.01	0.01		**
Africa	Observations	18,260		23,271		20,865		19,985			
	R2	0.10		0.10		0.14		0.08			
	Prob>0	0.00		0.00		0.00		0.00			
	Log of city pop	0.04	0.01	0.02	0.01	-0.04	0.01	-0.01	0.01		
	Log of immigrant pop	-0.07	0.01	-0.04	0.01	0.05	0.01	0.03	0.01	**	**
	City employment rate	0.93	0.22	1.10	0.20	1.72	0.23	0.73	0.07		
	Yrs since migrating	0.01	0.00	0.01	0.00	0.01	0.00	0.01	0.00		
	Yrs since mig. squared	0.00	0.00	0.00	0.00	0.00	0.00	0.00	0.00		
	Naturalized	0.33	0.05	0.14	0.07	0.13	0.02	0.11	0.02	**	**
	Log co-immig pop	0.03	0.00	0.02	0.00	-0.02	0.01	-0.03	0.01	**	**

S. Asia

	Model 1	sig	Model 2	sig	Model 3	sig	Model 4	sig
Observations	15,426		14,578		45,480		44,720	
R2	0.08		0.08		0.12		0.07	
Prob>0	0.00		0.00		0.00		0.00	
Log of city pop	0.02	0.01	-0.03	0.01	-0.03	0.01	0.01	0.01
Log of immigrant pop	-0.03	0.01	0.00	0.01	-0.01	0.01	-0.01	0.01
City employment rate	1.50	0.19	1.13	0.20	2.97	0.24	0.82	0.06 **
Yrs since migrating	0.01	0.00	0.00	0.01	0.02	0.00	0.01	0.00
Yrs since mig. squared	0.00	0.00	0.00	0.00	0.00	0.00	0.00	0.00
Naturalized	0.38	0.07	0.33	0.07	0.03	0.02 **	0.03	0.01 **
Log co-immig pop	0.02	0.00	0.02	0.00	0.04	0.00	0.00	0.00 **

China

	Model 1	sig	Model 2	sig	Model 3	sig	Model 4	sig
Observations	3,330		2,069		43,365		37,450	
R2	0.11		0.14		0.10		0.08	
Prob>0	0.00		0.00		0.00		0.00	
Log of city pop	-0.05	0.02	-0.04	0.03	0.02	0.01 **	0.04	0.01 **
Log of immigrant pop	0.03	0.03	-0.01	0.03	0.00	0.01	-0.04	0.01
City employment rate	1.90	0.43	0.43	0.64	1.24	0.18	0.72	0.07
Yrs since migrating	0.02	0.01	-0.01	0.01	0.01	0.00	0.01	0.00
Yrs since mig. squared	0.00	0.00	0.00	0.00	0.00	0.00	0.00	0.00
Naturalized	0.27	0.14	0.60	0.20	0.12	0.02	0.14	0.02 **
Log co-immig pop	0.01	0.02	0.03	0.02	-0.01	0.00	0.00	0.00

Rest of E. Asia

	Model 1	sig	Model 2	sig	Model 3	sig	Model 4	sig
Observations	19,391		6,078		51,935		39,715	
R2	0.00		0.08		0.06		0.05	
Prob>0	0.00		0.00		0.00		0.00	
Log of city pop	0.00	0.01	-0.07	0.02	0.04	0.01 **	0.04	0.01 **
Log of immigrant pop	0.03	0.01	0.06	0.02	-0.01	0.01	-0.02	0.01 **
City employment rate	1.41	0.16	1.59	0.25	1.74	0.17	0.75	0.06
Yrs since migrating	-0.01	0.00	0.00	0.01	0.02	0.00	0.01	0.00
Yrs since mig. squared	0.00	0.00	0.00	0.00	0.00	0.00	0.00	0.00
Naturalized	0.44	0.06	0.16	0.16	0.02	0.02 **	0.02	0.02 **
Log co-immig pop	-0.03	0.01	0.00	0.02	-0.01	0.01	-0.01	0.00

Source: 2006 Census of Canada and 2006 Swedish Registry.

Looking at Canada, we see similar but smaller effects. The effect of naturalization is positive for all countries but is smaller than is the case for Sweden. The impact of city size, immigrant population, and co-ethnic population is very mixed. For immigrants from Germany, as city size increases, employment probability decreases; however, as the immigrant population increases, employment increases for males but not females. The impact of the co-ethnic population is null for females and negative for males. For Chinese immigrants in Canada, the naturalization effect is relatively large (0.12 for women and 0.14 for men). However, as compared to most immigrant groups, as city size increases, employment probabilities for Chinese immigrants also increase. The size of the co-ethnic population has a positive impact for women but not for men.

An examination of the last two columns provides an understanding of the degree to which the effect of place of birth on employment differs between Canada and Sweden. As was seen in Table 2, there are more significant differences for men than for women. For women, the impact of naturalization is significantly higher for women from the Middle East, South Asia and from East Asia (outside China and Hong Kong). For women from Africa, the size of the co-ethnic population has a positive impact in Canada and a negative impact in Sweden (a difference that is statistically significant). As is to be expected, the effect of being Scandinavian is statistically different in Canada and in Sweden. In Sweden, attaining citizenship has a strong negative effect on employment for immigrants from other Scandinavian countries. In Canada the effect for this group is positive.

Amongst men, German and North American immigrants face about the same effects in both Canada and Sweden. However, immigrants from the Middle East, South Asia, and Europe face effects that are significantly different in Canada and Sweden, with the impact generally being lower in Canada.

Conclusion

The latter half of the twentieth century saw a liberalization in immigrant intake and citizenship acquisition regulations in many immigrant receiving countries. More recently, countries such as Denmark, the Netherlands, the United Kingsdom, and the United States have tightened citizenship acquisition rules and immigrant intake regulations and have witnessed declines in the employment probabilities for immigrants.[13] In contrast, Sweden has continued to liberalize citizenship acquisition regulations, most recently recognizing dual citizenship (2001), while at the same time seeing declining employment prospects for immigrants. Canada has a long-standing history of fairly liberal citizenship regulations, demanding a relatively short period of residency before citizenship acquisition is possible and recognizing dual citizenship.

Several scholars have argued that there is a link between citizenship acquisition and employment status – Devoretz and Pivenko (2008) in regards to Canada; Akbari (2008) in studies of the United States; and Steinhardt (2008) and Hayfron (2008) in European studies. These studies, however, are hampered by their inability to distinguish the effect of citizenship from the effect of integration processes (i.e., they cannot say whether the measured impact is a product of citizenship or some correlate of citizenship such as better integration).

In this chapter we have used instrumental variable regression to examine the "clean" impact of citizenship acquisition and the size of the co-immigrant population on the probability of being employed in Canada and Sweden. In contrast to Scott (2008), we find that citizenship acquisition has a positive impact for all immigrant groups with the exception of Scandinavian immigrants in Sweden. This positive impact is particularly the case for non-EU/non-North American immigrants in Sweden and for European, Latin American, and African and Chinese immigrants in Canada. The size of the co-ethnic population has a positive impact for many immigrant groups – as the co-ethnic population increases, the probability of being employed also increases. It appears to be particularly important for immigrants from Asia and Africa in Sweden and for immigrants from South Asia and Africa in Canada. For these groups, the co-immigrant population may serve as an employer of last resort, buffering the impact of possible discrimination by the majority population. It could also be an indicator of a lack of linguistic integration, which effectively locks immigrants out of the majority labour force (see, e.g., Pendakur and Pendakur 2002).

So, in a country where the barriers to non-citizens are relatively few (i.e., non-citizens have access to most of the jobs and most of the rights of citizens, both social and legal), why might citizenship help in employment prospects? Spence (1973) argues that observable characteristics act as signals to employers about the potential risk of hiring new employees. Within this context, citizenship may act as a signal to employers about an immigrant's commitment to remaining in the host country. Hiring a citizen thus reduces transaction and risk costs to employers because they can be more certain that the new employee will remain in the position.

Looking at citizenship and employment from a policy perspective, what are the implications of tightening citizenship acquisition requirements? Our contention is that given citizenship's apparent link to improved employment prospects, tightening citizenship regulations may result in decreased employment opportunities for immigrants in receiving countries. This means, in turn, that stricter citizenship regulations could have the effect of actually increasing social welfare costs – an effect neither intended nor desirable.

NOTES

The authors would like to acknowledge the NORFACE Research Progamme on Migration for generous funding for doing the research, and they wish to thank Jean-Michel Billette of the COOL-Research Data Centre for his logistical and analytical help.

1. In this case, the applicant has a waiting period before he or she can apply for Swedish citizenship. Acquiring citizenship by notification is also possible. This is basically a simplified juridical naturalization procedure that is mainly used by Nordic citizens. For notification, the applicant must be eighteen years of age or older and have five years of residence in Sweden, with no prison sentencing during this time.
2. The subsistence requirement relates to persons' ability to support themselves in terms of work or other income.
3. Obtaining a Swedish passport reduces barriers in certain jobs, such as those in the transport sector or cross-border service jobs.
4. Recent changes to citizenship legislation has meant that the ability to pass on citizenship to children is somewhat restricted. People who are not born in Canada but who acquire Canadian citizenship cannot automatically pass on citizenship if their children are born outside Canada.
5. Since Statistics Sweden has no individual information on year of immigration before 1968, we exclude immigrants arriving before that date from the analysis.
6. Member states as of May 2004.
7. This is largely true for immigrants from North America as well, and we therefore treat these immigrants as eligible for employment on entry.
8. We also test models in which the instrument for citizenship is both being eligible and the number of years since eligibility. Both models yield similar results, but the tests for the instrument are better for models using just eligibility for citizenship and not years since being eligible.
9. Candidates for citizenship can only apply after four years of residency. If an immigrant was in Canada prior to receiving landed status, each day before permanent residency counts as half a day. Time spent serving a sentence for an offence in Canada (e.g., prison, penitentiary, jail, reformatory, conditional sentence, probation, and/or parole) is generally not counted (CIC 2010).
10. We use the EU 25 definition for our EU (non-Nordic category).
11. The higher employment rate for German and Scandinavian non-citizens could be a generational effect. The bulk of Scandinavian and German immigrants with citizenship in Canada are likely to be older and therefore less likely to be active in the labour force.
12. We determine if there is a significant difference between the two variables by calculating the *t* value for independent samples:

$$t = \frac{coef_{Canada} - coef_{Netherlands}}{\sqrt{SE^2_{Canada} + SE^2_{Netherlands}}}$$

A *t* value greater than 1.96 is taken as significant.

13. The Canadian government under Stephen Harper tightened up citizenship acquisition rules in 2009. These rules relate to passing on Canadian citizenship to children for parents who are born outside Canada.

REFERENCES

Akbari, A.H. 2008. "Immigrant Naturalization and Its Impacts on Immigrant Labour Market Performance and Treasury." In *The Economics of Citizenship*, ed. P. Bevelander and D.J. DeVoretz. MIM/Malmö University. Malmö: Holmbergs.

Bevelander, P. 2000. *Immigrant Employment Integration and Structural Change in Sweden, 1970–1995*. Stockholm: Almqvist and Wiksell International.

—2009. "The Immigration and Integration Experience: The Case of Sweden." In *Immigration Worldwide*, ed. U.A. Segal, N.S. Mayadas, and D. Elliott. Oxford: Oxford University Press.

Bevelander, P. and D. DeVoretz, eds. 2008. *The Economics of Citizenship*. MIM/ Malmö University. Malmö: Holmbergs.

Bevelander, P. and J. Veenman. 2006. "Naturalization and Immigrants' Employment Integration in the Netherlands." *Journal of International Migration and Integration* 7(3):327-49.

—2008. "Naturalisation and Socioeconomic Integration: The Case of the Netherlands." RIIM and IZA discussion paper. In *The Economics of Citizenship*, ed. P. Bevelander and D.J. DeVoretz.

Bonacich, E. and J. Model. 1980. *The Economic Basic of Ethnic Solidarity*. Berkeley: University of California Press.

Bratsberg, B., J. F. Ragan, and Z.M. Nasir. 2002. "The Effect of Naturalization on Wage Growth: A Panel Study of Young Male Immigrants." *Journal of Labor Economics* 20:568-97.

Breton, R. 1974. "Ethnic Stratification Viewed from Three Theoretical Perspectives." In *Social Stratification: Canada*. 2nd ed., ed. J.E. Curtis and W. Scott. Toronto: Prentice-Hall.

Chiswick, B. 1978. "The Effect of Americanization on the Earnings of Foreign-Born Men." *Journal of Political Economy* 86:897-921.

Citizenship and Immigration (CIC). 2010. "Applying for Citizenship." At http://www.cic.gc.ca/english/citizenship/become-eligibility.asp

DeVoretz, D.J. and S. Pivnenko. 2006. "The Economic Causes and Consequences of Canadian Citizenship." *Journal of International Migration and Integration* 6:435-68.

—2008. The Economic Determinants and Consequences of Canadian Citizenship Ascension. In *The Economics of Citizenship*, ed. P. Bevelander and D.J. DeVoretz.

Galabuzi, G.E.. 2009. "The Just Society: Addressing Discrimination in Employment." NCVM 10th Anniversary Symposium and National General Meeting, 8–10 September 2009.

Hayfron J.E. 2008. "The Economics of Norwegian Citizenship." In *The Economics of Citizenship*, ed. P. Bevelander and D.J. DeVoretz.

HRSDC. 2010. "Indicators of Well-Being in Canada." At http://www4.hrsdc. gc.ca/.3ndic.1t.4r@-eng.jsp?iid=13

Kogan, I. 2003. "Ex-Yugoslavs in the Austrian and Swedish Labor Markets: The Significance of Period of Migration and the Effect of Citizenship Acquisition." *Journal of Ethnic and Migration Studies* 29:595-622.

Mazzolari, F. 2007. "Dual Citizenship Rights: Do They Make More and Better Citizens?" IZA Discussion Paper No. 3008. Institute for the Study of Labor, Bonn.

Pendakur, K. 2000. Immigrants and the Labour Force: Policy, Regulation and Impact. Montreal and Kingston: McGill-Queen's University Press.

Pendakur, K. and R. Pendakur. 2002. "Language Knowledge as Human Capital and Ethnicity." *International Migration Review* 36(1):147-77.

Scott, K. 2008. "The Economics of Citizenship: Is There a Naturalization Effect?" In *The Economics of Citizenship*, ed. P. Bevelander and D.J. DeVoretz.

Spence, M. 1973. "Job Market Signalling." *Quarterly Journal of Economics* 87(3):355-74.

Steinhardt, M. F. 2008. "Does Citizenship Matter? The Economic Impact of Naturalizations in Germany." Centro Studi Luca D'Agliano Development Studies Working Paper No. 266. Milan/Torino: Centro Studi Luca D'Agliano.

Wilson, K. and A. Portes. 1980. "Immigrant Enclaves: An Analysis of the Labor Market Experiences of Cubans in Miami." *American Journal of Sociology* 86:295-319.

CHAPTER 13

IDENTITIES, INTERESTS, AND IMMIGRANT INTEGRATION IN THE TWENTY-FIRST CENTURY: CONTRASTING PUBLIC OPINION IN CANADA, THE UNITED STATES, FRANCE, AND THE UNITED KINGDOM

JACK JEDWAB

The degree to which newcomers feel a sense of belonging to their adopted nation has been the object of ongoing debate in several immigrant-receiving countries. Measuring the population's sense of belonging to the nation is not simple. More attention seems directed at whether the general public believes that immigrants identify adequately with the nation than with the extent to which newcomers affirm such identification. The term "social integration" is used in part to refer to the immigrant's level of national identification. Public opinion surveys are widely employed in order to provide insight into the success of such social integration. Views on the level of immigration in a given country are believed to have much influence on the public perspective on social integration. Presumably, those who feel that there are too many immigrants are more likely to worry about newcomers' impact on the strength of national identity. Perceptions around the share of immigrants within the national population are also believed to have an important bearing on the economic impact of newcomers.

In an analysis of European public opinion on immigration, Sides and Citrin (2007) contend that interests (economic concerns) are less important to the public than identities (symbolic attitudes about the nation). In

International Perspectives: Integration and Inclusion, ed. J. Frideres and J. Biles. Montreal and Kingston: Queen's Policy Studies Series, McGill-Queen's University Press. © 2012 The School of Policy Studies, Queen's University at Kingston. All rights reserved.

both interest based and identity based theories, they contend that feeling threatened is a prior condition of hostility to immigration. What differs is the nature of the threat and whether its origins lie in objective social and economic conditions or in cultural and psychological predispositions.

This chapter focuses on public views on immigration and social integration in Canada, the United States, the United Kingdom, and France. Apart from these countries being amongst the most desired immigrant destinations in the world, they also share important historic ties. Great Britain was at one time the mother country for much of North America, and France was once the mother country for the French part of the continent whose majority today resides in the province of Quebec. We will look at the extent to which British and French views on immigration and integration diverge from those of Canadians and Americans and assess the respective importance of cultural and economic factors in explaining concerns around immigration. Insight will be offered into the degree to which the public believes that immigrant influence upon national identities in the four countries outweighs preoccupations around newcomer impact on their economies.

Certain experts have contended that the absence of a majority population that defines itself on the basis of a common ethnic identity makes for less anxiety about the presence of immigrants on national identity and this is reflected in discourse amongst opinion leaders that tends to look more favourably upon the contribution of immigrants. Wrench (2008) contends, "There are important differences in 'national myths' which have implications for the acceptability of polices relating to immigrant and ethnic minorities. In countries such as the USA, Canada and Australia, which have been built on immigrants, the idea of immigration has been a relatively positive theme in national development." In the case of European countries, Wrench maintains that they see their cohesion arising from nationality or ethnicity rather than the "strength through diversity" paradigm that is associated with countries that possess a substantial share of immigrants. On this point, Favell (2003) notes:

> In Europe we are talking about tightly bounded and culturally specific nation-states dealing in the post-war period with an unexpected – but still not very large – influx of highly diverse immigrant settlers, at a time when for other international reasons, their sense of nationhood is insecure or in decline. It is a problematic very different to those faced by the USA or Australia, whose histories and sense of nationhood have always been built on immigration. Europe, rather, faces a problematic, where the continuity of nation-building is perhaps a much more significant fact than the multicultural hybridity that is sometimes sought for in these other, newer "model" nations.

Another perspective is offered by Fetzer (2000), who has compared twentieth century public opinion on immigration in the United States,

France, and Germany. He contends that anti-immigrant attitudes are made of the same basic fabric in the United States, France, and Germany, despite significant differences in culture, history, and immigration patterns. Fetzer (2000) believes that the decisive factor is resentment against cultural outsiders.

In an essay contrasting views on immigration in the United Kingdom and the United States, Fisher (2010) argues that anxieties about immigration may be less about racism and xenophobia and more about the economy. He acknowledges that cultural anxieties persist in both countries but maintains that economic factors appear to be a more driving force in anti-immigration movements. If British anti-immigration sentiment were only rooted in xenophobia, then the 150,000-plus Pakistani migrants who arrived between 2004 and 2008 would have been the object of the same outrage as that which met the 400,000-plus Polish immigrants who entered over the same period. Fisher notes that Pakistani migrants look different from most Brits and practice Islam whereas Poles look similar and practice Christianity.

Fisher also refers to the legislation adopted in 2010 by the State of Arizona permitting law enforcement officials to detain those persons suspected of being in the country illegally unless they can prove otherwise. The law sparked protests in Arizona and other parts of the United States, and many observers insist that it specifically targets migrants from Mexico who represent an ever-growing share of the American population. Fisher is surprised by the severity of the Arizona legislation but less so by the rise of anti-immigrant sentiment, which he attributes to the difficult economic conditions of the period.

During the first decade of the twenty-first century, Britain, France, the United States, and Canada each experienced important debates over the impact of immigrants on national identity. In November 2009, the government of France launched a debate about national identity that involved a series of more than 100 town hall meetings across the country aimed at defining what it meant to be French in this century. Observers criticized the initiative as a "Machiavellian" way of casting immigrants, their French born children, and especially Muslims as a threat to France's national identity. Government officials defiantly took the initiative to term.

The first decade of the twenty-first century has not seen the government of Canada hold a formal national debate on the role of immigration in national identity, yet the issues have been the object of ongoing discussion in the national media. In Quebec, the government held province-wide consultations on accommodation practices related to cultural differences. Referred to as the "Reasonable Accommodation Commission," the iniative gave rise to much deliberation on the impact of newcomers on Quebec identity. While no such process was undertaken elsewhere in Canada, it was the object of much attention in the rest of the country.

IMMIGRANTS: TOO MUCH OF A "GOOD THING"?

Foreign born residents make up about 10 percent of the population in both France and the United Kingdom and 11.5 percent in the United States. In Canada, nearly one in five residents of the country is foreign born. It is worth noting, however, that more than one in four foreign born residents of the United States is estimated to be in the country illegally.

A 2009 Gallup poll estimated that some 700 million people (16 percent of the world's adults) worldwide would like to migrate permanently (Esipova and Ray 2009). Conducted in 135 countries, the survey revealed that the United States is the first choice of nearly one-quarter (24 percent) of these respondents – the equivalent of more than 165 million adults – followed by an estimated 45 million who say they would like to move to Canada. Other most desired destination countries are the United Kingdom and France, together preferred by some 45 million adults.

One of the main challenges encountered by those wishing to leave their countries of origin is that relatively few nations seem enthusiastic about receiving them. An International Social Survey Programme global survey of some 37,000 respondents in 35 countries (ISSP 2003) revealed that a majority preferred reductions in the number of newcomers. Public opinion surveys generally reveal that in only a few countries do the majority favour increases in immigration. It may seem paradoxical that countries admitting relatively significant numbers of immigrants seem consistently reluctant to do so, as reflected in public opinion surveys.

A May 2007 poll conducted by Harris revealed that some two-thirds (67 percent) of British adults believed there were too many legal immigrants in their country. A slightly lower number, one-third of adults in both France (32 percent) and the United States (35 percent), believed that their country had too many legal immigrants. The same survey revealed that 59 percent of Americans believed that immigration helped their country, a sentiment shared by 54 percent of the French population and 36 percent of the British population. Surveys conducted by Gallup in the United States (Esipova and Ray 2009) have shown fluctuations in the desire for reducing the numbers of immigrants to the country. In 2002 some 58 percent favoured reductions in immigrant intake, which dropped to 40 percent in 2007 and then rose to 50 percent in 2009 (July 10-12). Gallup analysts feel the shift toward a tougher stance reflects the country's economic situation, as Americans tend to become less pro-immigration during difficult economic times. A similar shift is evident when Americans were asked more broadly whether immigration was a good thing or a bad thing for the country. In 2009, 58 percent said it was a good thing – the lowest percentage saying so since 2003. The historical low for this measure, 52 percent, came in 2002, after the 9/11 attacks. Opinion around immigration levels in Canada has not evolved much in recent years. Both in 2004 and 2009, surveys done for Citizenship and

Immigration Canada revealed that about 50 percent of the population believed immigration levels were "about right" and 14 percent thought there were too few immigrants. In 2004 some 31 percent of Canadians felt that there were too many immigrants and in 2009, the figure dropped to 26 percent (CIC 2009)

DEFINING AND DEBATING SOCIAL INTEGRATION

The United Nations Research Institute for Social Development (UNRISD 1994) has suggested that there are several ways of understanding the concept of social integration. On the one hand, it can be equated with the goal of inclusion and therefore imply equal opportunities and rights. As such, greater social integration may target improved life chances. Some hold that the opposite of social integration is disintegration or exclusion. Others, however, attribute a negative connotation to social integration by suggesting that it seeks to impose uniformity. Yet others feel the notion is neither positive nor negative but merely describes established patterns of human relations in society.

For example, Reitz and Bannerjee (2007) define "social integration" as the extent to which individual members of a group form relationships with people outside the group – relationships that help them to achieve individual economic, social, or cultural goals. Social integration, in this sense, is relevant to the broader question of social cohesion, which they define as the capacity of society to set and implement collective goals. They consider in particular the impact of inequality and discrimination on minority social integration.

The UNRISD report (1994) points out that the meaning of social integration is frequently broad and ambiguous. It generally envisions heightened solidarity and common identity to deal with sharpening ethnic strife that persists globally. Although it is difficult to dismiss the importance of remedying intergroup tension and making an appeal for greater solidarity, the promotion of social integration invites questions around what such integration comprises. To the extent that social integration theorists believe that ethnic strife is a source of disintegration, does the pursuit of social integration thus undercut cultural diversity? The authors of the UNRISD report wonder whether "the excluded can be included in ways which attempt to promote an unacceptable degree of homogeneity; and, when this occurs, the search for social integration becomes synonymous with the imposition of uniformity" (1994).

Soroka, Johnston, and Banting (2007) point out that several analysts believe that a common sense of identity is critical to the capacity of a society to undertake collective action and prevent fragmentation by attaining social cohesion. Others place less emphasis on shared values and identities and argue that civic participation is the key to social integration.

Johnston and Banting note that contemporary societies are characterized by multiple identities and diverse values, and it may be illusory to find the wellspring of cohesion in common attitudes. Berger (1998) contends that society can function effectively as long as there is a general consensus on the institutions and procedures through which tensions can be mediated and conflicts adjudicated.

Appeals to cultural unity are powerful influences on attitudes towards immigration, despite elite endorsements of a multicultural society engendered by immigration. According to Soroka, Johnston, and Banting, "growing ethnic diversity has generated two intersecting policy agendas in Western democracies" (2007, 561). The first agenda celebrates diversity and challenges government to respect cultural difference and construct inclusive forms of citizenship. The other emphasizes social cohesion or social integration where the objective facing diverse societies is to strengthen a shared sense of community and construct a common national identity. As the authors rightly observe, there is no logical reason why both these agendas cannot be pursued simultaneously. They note that in general, policy orientation has shifted back and forth between these agendas.

QUESTION AND OPINION ON SOCIAL INTEGRATION

Researchers examining social integration generally employ qualitative or quantitative tests to understand the importance of national identities on the part of the population by looking specifically at levels of attachment, belonging, and/or pride in nation and/or ethnic community. Another facet of social integration involves the public's assessment of the extent to which they believe immigrants are successfully integrating into society. Establishing some empirical basis for views on social integration is no simple task. The view that identities are in competition often influences the manner in which survey questions on social integration are constructed. Underlying such questions is the presumption that there are inevitable contradictions between preserving minority cultures and the adaption of the majority culture.

Also underlying these approaches is the question of whether identities are inherently in conflict, or if they are complementary (notably as regards minority ethnic and national expressions of culture). By consequence, surveys that purportedly measure social integration frequently present respondents with sets of competing choices. In response to a question around whether immigrants are perceived to be a threat or an opportunity, some 37 percent of British respondents surveyed described immigrants as an opportunity and 28 percent described them as a threat. In the case of France, some 25 percent of respondents viewed immigration as an opportunity and 19 percent viewed them as a threat, with the rest choosing no response (Teinturier, Simon, and Bassett 2007; Simon and Bassett 2007).

The same survey asks the public to rank the extent to which immigration offers more cultural or economic opportunities. While 42 percent of the French population considers that immigration bolsters their national culture, some 30 percent value its economic benefit. The British (42 percent) see immigration as a chance to improve their country's economy, more so than its culture and identity. Unlike the French, a significant number of British respondents feel threatened by immigration affecting their culture and identity. Close to one in two agree that immigration is a threat to their culture (49 percent) and identity (52 percent). There again, the way the questions are ranked leaves little room for attributing equal importance to both options.

A survey done in Canada in 2008 asked whether new Canadians hold onto their customs and traditions for too long when they come to Canada (45 percent agree) or whether they integrate into Canadian life at a natural and acceptable pace (47 percent agree). The same survey invited a response to the statement that "accommodating so many new Canadians of such diverse ethnic and religious backgrounds means we have less in common as Canadians and that this weakens our sense of national identity"; 61 percent contended that "having all this diversity is actually a defining and enriching part of our Canadian identity and strengthens our sense of national identity." However, some 61 percent agreed that "we make too many accommodations to visible minorities in Canada" (Strategic Council 2008).

TESTING THE RELATIONSHIP BETWEEN INTERESTS AND IDENTITIES

To what extent do persons who believe that immigrants undercut national identity also think that they negatively influence the state of the economy? This section tests this relationship by using data from the 2003 International Social Survey Programme (ISSP) in Canada, the United States, the United Kingdom, and France. Insights relevant to the issues raised here are provided by comparing public perceptions around immigration and integration in the four countries. Also examined are views around the degree to which views on levels of immigration affect perceptions over immigrant integration, the degree to which national pride influences opinion on immigrant integration, and the perceived relationship between the economic contribution of immigrants and the prospects for successful social integration.

Around levels of immigration in the four countries, the 2003 ISSP finds that Canadians were, by far, the least likely to favour reductions in the numbers entering the country. As observed in Table 1, nearly three-quarters of respondents in the United Kingdom and some two-thirds in France favour reductions, as do approximately 55 percent of respondents in the United States.

TABLE 1
Opinion on Levels of Immigration in the United Kingdom, United States, Canada, and France, 2003

Number of Immigrants Coming to Country	United Kingdom (%)	United States (%)	Canada (%)	France (%)
Increase a lot	2.1	4.1	6.9	2.7
Increase a little	3.7	7.1	22.1	5.1
Remain the same	16.4	32.4	38.7	26.2
Reduced a little	24.1	30.9	20.8	25.0
Reduced a lot	53.7	25.4	11.4	41.1
Total	100.0	100.0	100.0	100.0

Source: ISSP (2003).

The pattern of responses to questions touching upon social integration is more complex. In the four countries examined here, a minority hold the view that ethnic groups should be given government assistance to preserve their customs and traditions. Important majorities in each country agree that it is important for immigrants to be able to speak the national language(s). As observed below, Americans are somewhat more likely to agree upon the importance of speaking the national language. Discrepancies across the four countries appear when it comes to perceptions of immigrant adjustment; French and British respondents are more likely than Canadians and Americans to think "it is impossible for people who do not share the country's customs and traditions to become full participants in the society." Canadians and Americans are also more likely than British and French respondents to think "immigrants improve society by bringing in new ideas and cultures."

TABLE 2
Responses to Selected Questions on Aspects of Social Integration in the United Kingdom, United States, Canada, and France, 2003

Strongly and somewhat agree that ... (%)	It is impossible for people who do not share country's customs and traditions to become full participants	Ethnic minorities should be given government assistance to preserve their customs and traditions	Help minorities to preserve traditions	Important to be able to speak [country language]	Immigrants improve society by bringing in new ideas and cultures
United Kingdom	54.2	17.5	24.7	65.1	33.6
United States	32.8	22.9	47.4	83.3	57.2
Canada	41.5	16.6	28.9	69.4	67.2
France	60.1	19.7	26.8	67.0	41.3
All other ISSP countries	54.7	52.7	49.4	57.0	46.9
Total ISSP	53.9	48.8	47.6	58.6	47.3

Source: ISSP (2003).

As to perceptions around the economic dimensions of immigration, the French and Canadian populations are less likely than American and British respondents to agree that immigrants take jobs away from people who were born in the country. Canadians are most likely to agree that immigrants are good for the economy, followed by Americans with minorities in France and the United Kingdom holding that view. It is worth noting that, taken together, just over one out of three persons in all the ISSP countries surveyed agree that immigrants are good for the country's economy. Two-thirds of British respondents believe that the government spends too much money assisting immigrants. This view is held by approximately half of the respondents in the United States, Canada, and France.

TABLE 3

Responses to Selected Questions on Economic Contribution of Immigrants and the Role of Government in the United Kingdom, United States, Canada, and France, 2003

Strongly agree and somewhat agree that ... (%)	Immigrants take jobs away from people who were born in the country	Immigrants are generally good for country's economy	Government spends too much money assisting immigrants
United Kingdom	34.8	21.6	67.0
United States	43.1	45.5	51.6
Canada	27.0	62.6	47.3
France	25.6	35.1	49.7
All other ISSP countries	43.4	37.3	46.6
Total ISSP	42.2	37.9	47.3

Source: ISSP (2003).

Sides and Citrin (2007) contend that immigrant integration cannot be separated from the perceived levels of immigration. In other words, those who believe that there are too many immigrants are more inclined to agree that it is impossible for people who do not share national customs and traditions to become fully integrated. It should not be presumed, however, that reducing levels of immigration will result in a change in views, as the social integration concern may exist independently of the perceived numbers of immigrants.

In Canada, France, and the United Kingdom, the more one prefers reductions in immigration, the more likely one is to believe that it is impossible for people who do not share the country's customs and traditions to be fully accepted. Yet the response pattern is somewhat less consistent in the United States, where the variation in opinion around levels of immigration has less impact on the degree to which it is felt that persons not sharing national customs are unlikely to gain acceptance.

TABLE 4
Opinion on Level of Immigrants Coming to the Country and Agreement over Whether "It Is Impossible for People Who Do Not Share Customs and Traditions to Become Fully [Country's Nationality]" in the United Kingdom, United States, Canada, and France, 2003

Strongly agree and somewhat agree that ... (%)	Number of Immigrants Coming to Country				
It is impossible for people who do not share [country's] customs and traditions to become fully [country's nationality]	Increase a lot	Increase a little	Remain the same	Reduce a little	Reduce a lot
United Kingdom	ns*	25.0	25.2	43.8	73.6
United States	40.9	32.9	22.2	32.2	49.5
Canada	29.7	33.2	35,4	50.2	73.0
France	27.0	32.9	40.4	69.2	83.6
All other ISSP countries	44.0	37.7	47.3	57.3	67.4

*ns = number of respondents is not sufficient.
Source: ISSP (2003).

Similarly across all four countries, those who favour reductions in immigration are less likely to agree that ethnic minorities should be given government assistance to preserve their customs and traditions.

TABLE 5
Opinion on Level of Immigrants Coming to the Country and Agreement over Whether "Ethnic Minorities Should Be Given Government Assistance to Preserve Their Customs and Traditions" in the United Kingdom, United States, Canada, and France, 2003

Strongly agree and somewhat agree that ... (%)	Number of Immigrants Coming to Country				
Ethnic minorities should be given government assistance to preserve their customs and traditions	Increase a lot	Increase a little	Remain the same	Reduce a little	Reduce a lot
United Kingdom	53.0	65.5	29.0	16.7	8.5
United States	38.7	37.7	25.1	19.0	18.1
Canada	43.1	23.0	15.9	9.1	4.1
France	45.9	48.5	27.0	15.1	8.5
All other ISSP countries	67.0	59.4	55.8	48.6	42.9

Source: ISSP (2003).

The relationship between opinion on immigration levels and the importance attributed to adaptation does not generate a linear response pattern in the United Kingdom and France. When asked to choose whether adaptation of immigrants is more important than immigrants maintaining their traditions, those favouring significant increases in immigration are more likely than those supporting some increases to prefer adaptation. Not surprisingly, those favouring reductions to immigration levels overwhelmingly favour adaptation, which is true in Canada as well as the United Kingdom and France. Canada's pattern of response to these questions is more linear, as the preference for immigrant adaptation varies with the level of immigration that is supported. In the United States, the preferred level of immigration has relatively little influence on the prioritizing of immigrant adaptation over maintaining tradition.

TABLE 6
Opinion on Level of Immigrants Coming to the Country and Agreement over Whether "Adapting into larger Society More Important Than Maintaining Traditions," United Kingdom, United States, Canada, and France, 2003

Strongly agree and somewhat agree that ... (%)	*Number of Immigrants Coming to Country*				
Adapting into larger society more important than maintaining traditions	*Increase a lot*	*Increase a little*	*Remain the same*	*Reduced a little*	*Reduced a lot*
United Kingdom	63.6	47.8	57.8	73.7	84.7
United States	51.2	48.7	49.1	53.5	58.3
Canada	53.7	69.8	65.7	77.5	95.2
France	57.7	41.3	61.7	79.5	86.1
All other ISSP countries	39.3	46.3	48.7	53.3	60.0

Source: ISSP (2003).

Correlating support for either increases or reductions in immigration levels with feelings of national pride also gives rise to unevenness in the response pattern. In the United Kingdom and France, those favouring significant increases in the numbers of immigrants are more likely to feel national pride than are those favouring a modest increase or no changes in numbers. Those favouring significant reductions in France, the United Kingdom, and the United States are somewhat more likely to feel strong national pride than those preferring the big increase. For their part, Canadians favouring significant increases in immigration levels are more likely to feel national pride than those in support of significant reductions.

TABLE 7
Opinion on Level of Immigrants Coming to the Country and Percentage of Respondents Who Are "Very Proud to Be Country National," United Kingdom, United States, Canada, and France, 2003

Very proud to be country national (%)	*Number of Immigrants Coming to Country*				
	Increase a lot	*Increase a little*	*Remain the same*	*Reduced a little*	*Reduced a lot*
United Kingdom	52.9	25.0	34.4	43.4	53.9
United States	77.5	65.3	74.1	83.4	86.3
Canada	71.0	67.4	72.0	72.6	65.8
France	29.4	23.7	23.6	32.2	39.7
All other ISSP countries	52.6	44.7	48.6	50.1	53.6

Source: ISSP (2003).

National Pride and Social Integration

It is widely contended that persons possessing strong national identities are more inclined to harbour anti-immigrant sentiments, and this is presumably the case where majorities define themselves on the basis of common ethnicity. The ISSP reveals little difference in overall rates of national pride between the United States and Canada on the one hand and between France and the United Kingdom on the other. However, looking at the percentages reporting they were "very proud," respondents in the United States, followed by Canada, were well ahead of persons in the United Kingdom and France. It seems apparent that national pride is not greater in countries that possess a higher share of "ethnic" majorities within the overall population.

TABLE 8
Pride in Being Country National, United Kingdom, United States, Canada, and France, 2003

How proud are you being country national? (%)	United Kingdom	United States	Canada	France	All other ISSP countries
Total pride	87.1	97.7	96.9	88.9	87.2
Very proud	45.9	79.8	69.8	31.4	50.4
Somewhat proud	41.2	17.9	27.1	57.5	36.8

Source: ISSP (2003).

As observed above, it is difficult to make firm conclusions on attitudes towards immigrants based on an analysis of the relationship between national pride and desired immigration levels. However, looking at the relationship between national pride and public views on integration provides clearer insights. In effect, those expressing stronger feelings of national pride are more likely to agree that it is impossible for people who do not share national customs and traditions to become fully part of the society. Amongst Canadians, the variation in the level of pride has only modest effects on views about the opportunity for societal participation amongst those not sharing national customs and traditions.

TABLE 9
Level of Pride in Being Country National and Agreement over Whether "It Is Impossible for People Who Do Not Share Country's Customs and Traditions to Become Fully [Country's Nationality]," United Kingdom, United States, Canada, and France, 2003

Strongly agree and somewhat agree that ... (%)	*How proud are you being country national?*		
It is impossible for people who do not share country's customs and traditions to become fully ...	*Very proud*	*Somewhat proud*	*Not very proud*
UK	64.8	50.8	33.8
USA	35.8	22.1	14.3
Canada	42.6	39.8	36.0
France	78.6	56.5	54.6
All other ISSP countries	59.3	53.3	46.6

Source: ISSP (2003).

With the exception of the United States, feelings of national pride have little influence on the extent to which immigrants are believed to improve society by bringing in new ideas and cultures. In the United States, respondents expressing less pride in the nation were somewhat more likely to value the cultural contribution of immigrants to society.

TABLE 10
Level of Pride in Being Country National and Agreement over Whether "Immigrants Improve Society by Bringing in New Ideas and Cultures," United Kingdom, United States, Canada, and France, 2003

Strongly agree and somewhat agree that ... (%)	*How proud are you being country national?*		
Immigrants improve society by bringing in new ideas and cultures	*Very proud*	*Somewhat proud*	*Not very proud*
UK	30.2	33.6	37.3
USA	54.6	64.2	77.3
Canada	68.4	63.2	65.2
France	32.1	43.1	34.3
All other ISSP countries	47.3	44.3	47.8

Source: ISSP (2003).

INTERESTS AND SOCIAL INTEGRATION

In this section we explore how perceptions around the economic contribution of immigrants affect views on social integration issues. Sides
and Citrin (2007) have described the scholarly literature as dominated
by the distinction between public concern over economy and identity. It
has been widely contended that difficult economic circumstances fuel
anti-immigrant sentiment and that therefore the concerns around immigrants' impact on identity cannot be disassociated from economic fears.
In general, those who feel that immigrants do not make a positive contribution to the economy are more likely to agree that immigrants should
abandon their customs and traditions. This response pattern is reflected
in the table below for the United Kingdom, Canada, and France, but it is
not the case for the United States where, regardless of how the economic
contribution of immigrants is perceived, there is no discernable impact
on whether they should maintain traditions.

TABLE 11
**Level of Agreement That "Immigrants Are Generally Good for Country's Economy" and
Percentage That Support Immigrants Maintaining Their Traditions, United Kingdom,
United States, Canada, and France, 2003**

Support immigrants maintaining their traditions, %	Immigrants are generally good for country's economy				
	Strongly agree	Agree	Neither agree nor disagree	Disagree	Disagree strongly
United Kingdom	50.0	29.2	26.9	18.5	20.0
United States	51.3	48.7	49.7	40.1	43.4
Canada	46.7	31.6	19.4	17.1	–
France	57.3	35.1	25.4	17.5	12.6
All other ISSP countries	56.9	48.8	48.4	48.2	38.8

Source: ISSP (2003).

But the United States is no exception in the response pattern on other
social integration questions. In all countries surveyed, those strongly
disagreeing that immigrants are good for the economy are more likely
to agree that it is impossible for people who do not share the country's
customs and traditions to become fully integrated.

If, however, those who disagree that immigrants are good for the
economy are very inclined to doubt the capacity for successful social
and cultural inclusion of persons who do not share national customs
and traditions, the inverse relationship is not always apparent. In other

words, those who feel that inclusion is a problem for persons who do not share national customs and traditions may still agree that newcomers are good for the economy. As revealed below, those Canadians who feel inclusion is impossible for people who do not share the national customs still widely agree that immigrants are good for the economy. More than one-third of Americans who agree that inclusion is difficult for those not sharing national customs nonetheless agree that there are benefits to the economy arising from immigration.

TABLE 12
Level of Agreement That "Immigrants Are Generally Good for Country's Economy" and Percentage That Agree with Statement That "It Is Impossible for People Who Do Not Share Country's Customs and Traditions to Become Fully [Country's Nationality]," United Kingdom, United States, Canada, and France, 2003

It is impossible for people who do not share country's customs and traditions to become fully [country's nationality]	*Immigrants are generally good for country's economy*				
Strongly agree and somewhat agree (%)	*Strongly agree*	*Agree*	*Neither agree nor disagree*	*Disagree*	*Disagree strongly*
United Kingdom	30.0	38.9	46.2	66.8	78.7
United States	32.9	27.3	27.9	41.8	63.0
Canada	29.7	38.1	44.7	61.0	85.7
France	29.4	43.6	59.0	74.5	86.6
All other ISSP countries	25.8	12.1	51.7	59.7	72.3

Source: ISSP (2003).

TABLE 13
Level of Agreement with That "It Is Impossible for People Who Do Not Share Country's Customs and Traditions to Become Fully [Country's Nationality]" and Agreement with the Statement That "Immigrants Are Generally Good for Country's Economy" in the United Kingdom, United States, Canada , and France, 2003

Immigrants are generally good for country's economy	*It is impossible for people who do not share country's customs and traditions to become fully [country's nationality]*				
Strongly agree and somewhat agree (%)	*Strongly agree*	*Agree*	*Neither agree nor disagree*	*Disagree*	*Disagree strongly*
United Kingdom	30.9	17.6	13.0	34.8	65.5
United States	34.2	41.4	29.9	53.1	71.1
Canada	48.7	59.0	53.0	71.5	76.8
France	18.0	31.6	38.5	55.5	66.9
All other ISSP countries	26.7	36.8	33.9	46.5	53.7

Source: ISSP (2003).

On a related question, those who agree that immigrants are good for the economy are far more likely to agree that immigrants improve society by bringing in new ideas and cultures. Nearly nine in ten respondents in the United Kingdom, United States, Canada, and France who agree that immigrants are good for the economy also agree that immigrants bring in new ideas. This confirms the strong tie between those who believe that immigrants contribute to economic well-being and those who feel that they make an important contribution to national culture. In effect, the data challenge the finding that one can clearly divide public opinion on immigration between those persons whose concerns are interest based and those whose concerns are identity based.

TABLE 14
Level of Agreement That "Immigrants Are Generally Good for Country's Economy" and Percentage That Agree with Statement That "Immigrants Improve Country Nationality by Bringing in New Ideas and Cultures," United Kingdom, United States, Canada, and France, 2003

Strongly agree and somewhat agree that ... (%)	Immigrants are generally good for country's economy				
Immigrants improve country nationality by bringing in new ideas and cultures	Strongly agree	Agree	Neither agree nor disagree	Disagree	Disagree strongly
United Kingdom	100.0	74.6	31.0	13.2	6.0
United States	93.7	82.1	43.0	28.4	11.1
Canada	89.3	82.7	43.9	30.3	21.4
France	85.0	72.0	35.9	16.4	6.1
All other ISSP countries	78.2	71.9	38.8	25.9	15.3

Source: ISSP (2003).

CONCLUSION

Is discussion over issues of immigration in the United Kingdom, France, the United States, and Canada dominated by concerns over economic well-being (interests) or rather, by fear that the national culture is threatened by the influx of immigrants (identities)? This dichotomy purportedly underlying twenty-first century immigration and integration debates is carefully articulated in the analysis on European public opinion by Sides and Citrin. The identity-based focus of recent public debates around immigrant integration in the four countries examined indeed appears to support their analysis. Their thesis does not undercut the view that where there is less economic concern over immigration, there will be less fear about newcomers negatively influencing national identities. The evidence provided here only partially supports that idea that concerns over the impact of immigration on national identities is rooted in economic anxieties. It seems true that the more individuals possess economic concerns about immigration, the more likely they feel that immigrants undercut national identity. But the survey evidence presented here suggests that the inverse does not always apply and that the feeling that social or cultural integration is a problem does not always result in feeling that newcomers adversely affect the economy. Many people in Canada and the United States who worry about such adaptation nonetheless believe that immigrants are good for the economy. It is also worth noting that many Americans surveyed who feel that immigrants do not contribute favourably to the economy also do not support the idea that newcomers should abandon their cultural heritage.

Our analysis does suggest that Canadians and Americans are generally less concerned with the social integration of immigrants than are the British and French. Affirming that identity is the principal element in European and North American immigration debates invites reflection over whether this perspective represents a break with earlier public discourse and whether economic concerns consistently underlie fears around immigrants' influence on national identities. The fact remains that in the case of Canada and the United States, economic downturns have not resulted in a growing outcry for curbing the levels of immigration.

NOTE

Special thanks to Siddharth Bannerjee, director of research at the Association for Canadian Studies, for editorial assistance.

REFERENCES

Berger, P. 1998. "Conclusion: General Observations on Normative Conflicts and Mediation." In *The Limits to Social Cohesion: Conflict and Mediation in Pluralist Societies: A Report of the Bertelsmann Foundation to the Club of Rome*, ed. P. Berger. Boulder, CO: Westview Press.

Citizenship and Immigration Canada (CIC). 2009. *Citizenship and Immigration Canada Tracking Survey 2008–2009*. Final report prepared for Citizenship and Immigration Canada by Phoenix Strategies (February). At http://epe.lac-bac.gc.ca/100/200/301/pwgsc-tpsgc/por-ef/citizenship_immigration/2009/030-08-e/index.html

Esipova, N. and J. Ray. 2009. "U.S. Tops Desired Destination Countries." Gallup Poll, 2 November. At http://www.gallup.com/poll/124028/700-million-worldwide-desire-migrate-permanently.aspx

Favell, A. 2003. "Integration Nations: The Nation-State and Research on Immigrants in Western Europe." In *The Multicultural Challenge: Comparative Social Research*, vol. 22, ed. G. Brochmann, 13-42. Amsterdam: Elsevier.

Fetzer, J.S. 2000. *Public Attitudes toward Immigration in the United States, France, and Germany.* Cambridge: Cambridge University Press.

Fisher, M. 2010. "In UK, an All-Too-Familiar Immigration Debate." *Atlantic,* 3 May 2010. At http://www.theatlantic.com/international/archive/2010/05/in-uk-an-all-too-familiar-immigration-debate/56100/

Harris Poll. 2007. "Majorities of British, Germans and Italians Believe There Are Too Many Legal Immigrants in Their Country." 29 May 2007. At http://www.harrisinteractive.com/vault/Harris-Interactive-Poll-Research-IHT-immigrants-2007-05.pdf

International Social Survey Programme (ISSP). 2003. "National Identity II." At http://www.gesis.org/en/services/data/survey-data/issp/modules-study-overview/national-identity/2003/

Reitz, J.G. and R. Banerjee. 2007. "Racial Inequality, Social Cohesion, and Policy Issues in Canada." In *Belonging? Diversity, Recognition and Shared Citizenship in Canada,* ed. K. Banting, T.J. Courchene, and F.L. Seidle, 489-545. Montreal: Institute for Research on Public Policy. At http://www.utoronto.ca/ethnicstudies/ReitzBanerjeeRev.pdf

Sides, J. and J. Citrin. 2007. "European Opinion about Immigration: The Role of Identities, Interests and Information." *British Journal of Political Science* 37:477-504.

Simon, F. and S. Bassett. 2007. "Les Français et l'immigration." Sondage réalisé pour France 24. September. TNS Sofres. At http://www.tns-sofres.com/_assets/files/151007_immigration-france.pdf

Soroka, S.R. Johnston, and K. Banting. 2007. "Ties That Bind: Social Cohesion and Diversity in Canada." In *The Art of the State III: Belonging? Diversity, Recognition and Shared Citizenship in Canada,* ed. K. Banting, T.J. Courchene, and F.L. Seidle.

Strategic Council. 2008. "Attitudes towards Canada's Growing Visible Minority Population." 2008. Report to the *Globe and Mail* and *CTV,* 14 April. At http://www.thestrategiccounsel.com/our_news/polls/2008-04-14%20GMCTV%20Visible%20Minority%20Population.pdf

Teinturier, B., F. Simon, and S. Bassett. 2007. "The British and Immigration, 21st September to 23rd September. TNS Sofres. At http://www.tns-sofres.com/_assets/files/081007_immigration-uk.pdf

United Nations Research Institute for Social Development (UNRISD). 1994. "Social Integration: Approaches and Issues." Briefing Paper No. 1, World Summit for Social Development, March. At www.unrisd.org/80256B3C005BCCF9

Wrench, J. 2007. *Diversity Management and Discrimination: Immigrants and Ethnic Minorities in the EU.* Hampton, England: Ashgate.

CONCLUSION

JOHN BILES* AND JAMES FRIDERES

Having reviewed the various policies of countries around the world, we now wish to provide the reader with a broad overview of the approaches to immigrant settlement and integration policy that countries included in this volume have pursued, to discuss what light can be shed on questions guiding strategic integration policy discussions, and to gaze into our crystal ball and suggest likely future trends in integration policy.

BROAD OVERVIEW COMPARISONS

Drawing upon the work of Schmidt (2007, 104) we begin with three important points of comparison for integration policies: 1) type and nature of policy utilized by the state; 2) the various aspects of immigrant integration; and 3) the manner in which policy expects immigrants to adapt to their new environment. To these we add three more dimensions: 4) the role of the "host society"[1] in facilitating immigrant integration; 5) the historical context in which the state finds itself; and 6) the breadth and depth of engagement of actors involved with immigration and integration policy.

Type and Nature of Policy

Schmidt (2007) suggests that governments use four major modes of policy intervention with regard to immigrant integration: *prescriptive*,

---

*The opinions expressed in this chapter are those of the authors and do not necessarily reflect those of Citizenship and Immigration Canada or the Government of Canada.

International Perspectives: Integration and Inclusion, ed. J. Frideres and J. Biles. Montreal and Kingston: Queen's Policy Studies Series, McGill-Queen's University Press. © 2012 The School of Policy Studies, Queen's University at Kingston. All rights reserved.

proscriptive, proactive, and *laissez-faire.* We employ those dimensions here using Canada as the referent to allow the reader to better understand the comparisons being made.

For example, Canada is most commonly characterized by its reliance on a series of *proactive* policies and programs implemented over the past two decades. Immigrant settlement, language training, host-immigrant mentorships, and refugee programs have been put in place to promote immigrant integration. By comparison, we find a *laissez-faire* approach in the United States, with virtually no formal policies and few programs established by the federal or state governments.[2]

"*Prescriptive* approaches" refers to policies that specify that immigrants must engage in specific behaviour(s) in order to be acceptable to the host society. For example, the receiving society may require that the immigrant learn the host language within a specified time or risk having his/her visa revoked and/or being deported; children must attend school until a certain age or laws must be followed. All immigrant-receiving societies have some prescriptive elements to their approach to integration. In this analysis, however, we are focusing only on the predominant component of the policy approach.

On the other hand, *proscriptive* policies are those that identify activities that immigrants must *not* engage in if they wish to continue to reside in the host society. Again, all immigrant-receiving societies have some proscriptive elements to their approach to integration, but we focus here on the principal policy orientation in which sanctions are imposed on those who engage in activities indentified as inappropriate. For example, proscriptive policies regarding immigrants might include not wearing a veil and not being convicted of a serious crime. Immigrants engaging in these proscribed behaviours will encounter negative sanctions and may lose their visa or be deported from the receiving society.

Aspects of Integration

A second dimension identified as important for assessing approaches to integration focuses on the various aspects of immigrant integration – social, cultural, economic, and civic – embedded in policy. These aspects may be exhibited in a number of ways, such as in cultural practices (e.g., language, food), social networking, economic integration, or linking with the host society's political structure through civic engagement.

Adaptation Expectations

A third dimension covers the explicit or implicit adaptation expectations embedded in policy. The best-known typology of these expectations was developed by Berry (1980; 2001) (see Figure 1) and has been adapted by others (e.g., Bourhis et al. 1997). Figure 1 illustrates that both immigrants and host societies have a range of adaptation strategies they can employ. Moreover, these strategies may change over time. For example, newcomers may at the time of their arrival choose to employ the strategy of segregation but over time may move to integration or assimilation. Clearly no immigrants are going to actively seek out marginalization – this is more likely the result of host adaptation policies, which may also promote one of the other strategies identified in Figure 1.

FIGURE 1
Modes of Immigrant Adaptation

		Cultural Maintenance	
		YES	NO
Contact/Participation	YES	Integration	Assimilation
	NO	Segregation	Marginalization

Role of Host Society

Central to this typology of adaptation expectations is whether or not policy includes reciprocal obligations between newcomers and the host populations. We believe that this variable is so crucial to the probability of integration success that we have separated it to bring to the foreground the question of privileges, responsibilities, and duties of both the host society and the immigrants. In short, is there a clear understanding with regard to policy that both have specific duties and responsibilities (two-way process), or do only immigrants have identified requirements (one-way process)?

Historical Context

Each approach undertaken by government is embedded in a specific historical context. This is often the point at which international comparisons flounder in complexity. Drawing from the literature, we have settled on four key aspects of context that we feel are operative here: existence of what Kymlicka describes as "national minorities" (1995), static or dynamic conceptions of national identity (Biles and Spoonley 2007), and longevity of immigration in-flows (Collett 2011), to which we have added the relative homogeneity of immigrant populations in the belief that the perceived "threat" of newcomers is highest in environments where a clear "us-them" dichotomy is sustainable (Kymlicka 2004). Naturally, there are many more contextual variables that could be utilized, but in the interests of clarity and simplicity, we feel these four are sufficient here.[3]

Breadth and Depth of Engagement

The breadth and depth of engagement in integration varies tremendously across jurisdictions. This commitment can be gauged via expenditures, full-time equivalent staff positions, and bureaucratic structures (Biles 2008), via the presence of an articulated strategy (Biles et al. 2011), and/or via the engagement of a wide range of ministries (IOM 2010). Unfortunately this information is extremely difficult to gather for international comparisons. Accordingly, we have simplified our measures here and simply gauged whether there is depth of engagement (as measured by dedicated bureaucratic structure, a plan, or significant expenditures) and breadth of engagement (indication that other governmental actors have also invested resources in the settlement and integration of newcomers).

Analysis

Using the framework described above and a close reading of the chapters of this volume, we have summarized the policies of the countries discussed here with regard to the various dimensions of immigrant integration policy. We wish to be clear that there are subtle variations in each country that we cannot account for here. It is worth reiterating that we are not describing "models"; our goal is to provide the reader with an over-arching portrayal of the policies enacted and implemented for each country. It should also be noted that this portrayal reflects the policies as described in the chapters. Many countries have since adjusted their policies in light of the economic downturn or for other reasons.

The results depicted in Table 1 show both similarities and differences among the various countries in terms of policies regarding immigrant integration. Only the United States has taken a laissez-faire approach, while all other countries have concluded that to obtain the results they wish, they must have active policy at various levels. Prescriptive and proscriptive approaches are the most widely employed. We also see that there are wide differences among the countries in terms of how long they have dealt with immigrants. Previous policies and historical events influence the trajectories of contemporary policies. We have also seen from the preceding chapters (particularly Jedwab's) that public opinion is critical and that the relative rate of politicization of immigration and integration seriously constrains the field of action available to the state.

TABLE 1
Comparative Framework of Immigrant Policy by Country

Nation	Policy Orientation	Historical Context	Dimensions	Expectations	Role of Host Society	Breadth and Depth of Engagement
Canada[a]	Proactive	i) National minorities ii) Dynamic national identity iii) Long experience with immigration iv) Heterogeneous immigrant flows	Economic Cultural (social and civic components weak)	Integration (multiculturalism)	Strong reciprocal obligation framing Weak implementation	Structure and expenditures Other actors investing resources
United States	Laissez-faire	i) National minorities ii) Static national identity iii) Long experience with immigration iv) Heterogeneous immigrant flows	No policy	Assimilation	Assimilate immigrants	Small structure and proportionately minimal funding at federal level Other actors investing resources
Spain	Prescriptive	i) National minorities ii) Static national identity iii) Short experience with immigration iv) Homogeneous immigrant flows	Civic Cultural Economic	Integration	Minimal	Structure and expenditures Autonomous regions and communities heavily invest resources
Australia	Prescriptive	i) National minorities ii) Dynamic national identity iii) Long experience with immigration iv) Heterogeneous immigrant flows	Economic Cultural Civic	Integration (multiculturalism)	Strong reciprocal obligation framing Weak implementation	Structure and expenditures Other actors investing resources
Finland	Proactive	i) National minorities ii) Static national identity iii) Short experience with immigration iv) Homogeneous immigrant flows?	Economic Cultural	Integration	Minimal	Legal structure and expenditures Regional and local authorities have responsibilities

... continued

TABLE 1
(Continued)

Nation	Policy Orientation	Historical Context	Dimensions	Expectations	Role of Host Society	Breadth and Depth of Engagement
Austria	Prescriptive Proscriptive	i) No national minorities ii) Static national identity iii) Short experience with immigration iv) Homogeneous immigrant flows?	Cultural	Segregation	None	Minimal and recent structure third party financing Minimal breadth (high anti-immigration environment)
Israel	Proactive	i) National minorities ii) Static national identity iii) Short experience with immigration iv) Homogeneous immigrant flows	Cultural	Integration	Minimal	Structure and expenditures Diverse series of organiza-tions, agencies to support integration)
China[b]	Prescriptive Proscriptive	i) National minorities ii) Static national identity iii) Short experience with immigration iv) Homogeneous migrant flows	None	None	None	Structure is legal with few expenditures Few actors investing resources
Japan	Prescriptive Proscriptive	i) National minorities ii) Static national identity iii) Short experience with immigration iv) Homogeneous migrant flows	Civic Cultural Economic	Integration (multi-culturalism)	Minimal	Structure and expenditures Other actors investing resources
United Kingdom	Prescriptive Proscriptive	i) National minorities ii) Static national identity iii) Medium experience with immigration iv) Homogeneous migrant flows?	Cultural	Integration (multi-culturalism)	Weak reciprocal obligations	Structure and expenditures Other actors investing resources

[a]Quebec's policy on immigrant integration is referred to as "Interculturalism."
[b]Policy implementation is directed toward internal migrants as international immigration is rigidly controlled.

However, at the same time, we find that the national context, such as the presence or absence of national minorities, and the static or dynamic nature of national identities do not appear to be correlated with a particular policy orientation or expected end result. Nevertheless, dynamic national identities appear to have a close connection with integration approaches that actively seek to engage host society members in the integration of newcomers.

In terms of policy focus, we also see that different nations focus on different indicators of integration. Some prefer to focus on economic integration, while others are more concerned with cultural (e.g., language) or civic/political elements in their quest for immigrant integration. In terms of the different policy objectives of the various nations, while the choices are limited, there is a clear preference for "integration," in whatever form it might take. Most countries around the world have given up focusing on "assimilation" and realize the pitfalls of such a position (Frideres 2010; Bertelsmann Stiftung and MPI 2010). Equally, it appears that the overwhelming trend across all the countries covered here is the increasing allocation of resources within and across levels of government and other actors to tackle integration and inclusion. We find that in most countries the overall expectation on the part of the host society is that newcomers will integrate in some way. We also find that generally little is expected in terms of the role of the host population, and although there is talk about integration as a two-way process, the evidence suggests that most countries focus on how immigrants can change in order to integrate.

Other structural factors not captured here also clearly impact upon integration policy. For example, Collett (2011) points out that both foreign and native born unemployment as well as debt-to-GDP ratios are important factors that will bring about policy changes as well as goals and objectives. Further factors such as the extent to which immigration and those policy areas most affected by immigration are the sole responsibility of the national state will have an immediate impact on the aims of policy. In some countries, the national government has sole responsibility for immigrant integration, whereas in others, provinces, municipalities, and/ or autonomous communities have now been given partial responsibility for immigrant integration as well as setting policy. We find that the extent of embeddedness of integration policies is an important factor in the rate and nature of change (Bonjour 2011). For example, we find that if integration policies and the institutions and infrastructure for their delivery are intertwined within other government policies, change is slow to take place. Of course, this change may well prove to be more sustainable and possibly effective than those systems where the ministry responsible for immigration is expected to address all challenges faced by migrants (Collett 2011; Biles et al. 2011). In addition, a horizontal approach may better guard against the vicissitudes of government funding for integration, particularly during economic downturns. For example, in Spain, integration policy is coordinated within the Ministry for Employment and Immigration but involves a wide range of government departments and autonomous communities (Collett 2011). With the recession, funding for integration for such activities as combating racism and xenophobia has been cut back. However, it is the responsibility for each region to determine how much will be spent on specific integration policies. Consequently, no one budget cut will completely imperil the Spanish approach to integrating newcomers.

In terms of depth of policies, we find that most countries have a national ministry that implements national integration policy, monitors it, and provides some funding for its enactment. However, the nature of that national policy varies considerably; some focus on legal elements of integration while others are more concerned with the social and civic dimensions of integration. We also see a wide range of expenditures allocated to integration programs. In terms of breadth of policies, again we find that while there are some differences, all of the countries under consideration reveal that they have involved other stakeholders to take on some responsibility in ensuring integration of newcomers. However, the extent of expenditures and the specific programs put in place by the regions and/or cities vary considerably.

STRATEGIC POLICY QUESTIONS

Policy-makers are not only interested in the comparative examination of integration policy frameworks of so much interest to researchers; neither are they only motivated by the exchange of best practices so characteristic of the international Metropolis conferences that are often a focus for practitioners. Moreover, they are not solely interested in the operationally minded policy-maker's focus on the micro-level of program details gleaned from conversations like those of the integration working group of the Intergovernmental Consultations on Asylum Refugee and Migration Policies.

While all of these components are critical in policy development and program management, those policy-makers tasked with strategic analysis often struggle with the similarities and differences across jurisdictions on a relatively finite range of higher level and deceptively simple questions: 1) What impact does/can selection have on the need for settlement and integration programs (e.g., who needs to be settled?); 2) How can the transaction costs incurred from immigration and settlement be minimized (e.g., who pays?); 3) What are the most effective (and efficient) governance and delivery mechanisms/vehicles for settlement services (e.g., who plays?); 4) What is the most effective array of settlement services required, and when should they be delivered on the immigration continuum to achieve optimal outcomes? (e.g., what settlement services should be offered and when?); and finally, 5) What kind of research/evaluations/performance measurement frameworks are likely to yield the most valuable information to answer these questions (e.g., how do we know if programs work?).

Answers to these questions have proven to be quite elusive, and in the present economic downturn and its aftermath where all governments are re-examining expenditures, this lacunae is especially acute. To further exacerbate the situation, some observers have noted that countries must confront two competing realities – increasing integration needs and vastly reduced spending capacity (Bertelsmann Stiftung and MPI 2010). In other words, too few resources were already dedicated to integration, and a significant financial contraction now seems probable, thus making the situation worse. As a result, the findings contained in this volume come at a critical moment as they may contribute to the decision-making processes that will prune and shape integration initiatives around the globe for the coming decade. We do not pretend that this collection provides definitive answers; rather, we believe that a close reading of it suggests some interesting similarities and differences as well as fruitful directions worthy of further exploration.

Who Needs to Be Settled?

The linkages between selection and settlement/integration have moved up the policy agenda in recent years. In particular, there has been recognition that the changing composition of newcomer populations has a direct impact on the necessity of settlement/integration programs and their concomitant costs, and most importantly, the long-held belief has been discounted that "if we only got selection right, we wouldn't need settlement/integration." However, as Hollifield (2000) and Guiraudon and Lahav (2000) amongst others observe, policy-makers have lost a significant part of their power to control immigration and integration policies since the vast majority of newcomers are not selected by the state but arrive through family reunification or humanitarian streams. This situation is exacerbated by the focus of selection regimes on individuals, despite the reality that most newcomers migrate as families. These disjunctures highlight the limitations of an excessive policy focus placed on selected economic migrants in order to minimize settlement/integration needs.[4] Of course, not all countries have pursued this policy chimera with equal vigour. Indeed, Austria, Finland, Sweden, and the United States have long placed the emphasis squarely on family reunification and humanitarian migration, and in almost all other countries covered in this volume these categories are important components of the mix of admitted newcomers. We return to questions of settlement costs below, although it is worth noting here that in almost all countries covered here there is support for resettling refugees as well as an expectation of family members supporting their sponsored relatives (the exception is Sweden, which is presently reconsidering this position as a result of sweeping review of its approach to settlement and integration).

Temporary foreign workers provide an interesting example as none of the countries covered here appear to consider them eligible for settlement services as they are not anticipated to become permanent residents or citizens. How accurate this expectation actually is remains open to debate. For example, in the Canadian context, many temporary foreign workers are converted to permanent residents through the Provincial Nominee programs. "Illegal" immigrants are another interesting category touched upon in only a few chapters, such as the one focused on the United States and, in a different fashion, the one focused on China. This whole question of pathways to permanence remains to be further explored.

Related to the "who needs to be settled" question is: Where do they need to be settled? The comfortable assumption that most newcomers will settle in major urban centres where settlement service provision can be almost exclusively urban and economies of scale can be brought to bear is increasingly being challenged. Unquestionably, the majority of newcomers are settling in large urban centres, but increasingly it is in the suburbs, and a sizable number of newcomers are now flowing to smaller communities, demanding a rethink of settlement/integration strategies (Wulff et al. 2008). In our analysis of the policies regarding settlement services, we find that in almost all of the 11 countries examined, regional and municipal governments play an important role in the delivery of those services, despite their often limited capacity.

Who Pays?

An implicit assumption surrounding the nexus of selection and settlement/integration is that costs can be minimized with the appropriate selection process. This claim is a dramatic over-simplification, and it would be more accurate to perceive the selection regimes as a means to minimize costs to the receiving society. Indeed, any additional selection criteria result in increased costs elsewhere. For example, requiring third-party language testing will shift an additional financial burden onto newcomers. Similarly, changes to requirements for naturalization have the effect of increasing costs to the migrants, their families, and communities if not accompanied by cost-free settlement services or citizenship preparation courses.[5]

In addition, as several researchers have noted, gathering evidence on integration expenditures is extremely challenging. Not only is there scant evidence on the public record but that evidence itself is scattered across several ministries and programs within those ministries; some programs are part of broader social inclusion strategies that include but are not limited to immigrants; and finally, the definition of "immigrant" also varies considerably from one country to the next (Biles et al. 2011; Collett 2011; Biles 2008).

We find some evidence that in the countries discussed in this text settlement/integration is more often than not funded by local or regional governments. Canada is a bit of an aberration, where the majority of funds are provided by the federal government (even in the cases of three provinces where the regional government delivers the program) and the municipal governments are generally involved financially in a somewhat peripheral manner (Andrew et al. 2011; Tolley and Young 2011; Good 2010). In Australia, Israel, and the United Kingdom, the bulk of settlement funds are also provided nationally, although a far higher degree of heavy-lifting than in the Canadian case also appears to be undertaken locally. Finland is another interesting example where the bulk of settlement/integration programs are funded either by the European Union or the Finnish lottery fund.

Israel and its "absorption basket" may be considered the Rolls-Royce of settlement programs, with a cash value of $10,000 per couple[6] in addition to other settlement programs such as language training and community absorption that focus on social and cultural integration. The next largest per capita expenditure for settlement programming for newcomers is in Canada which allocates roughly $3,000 per person or approximately $6,000 per couple (Standing Committee on Citizenship and Immigration 2003). It is perhaps no accident that these two states are often cited as those with the best settlement/integration outcomes. All other countries covered here expend significantly less on settlement services per newcomer.

Clearly the bulk of expenditures for migration are borne by sending societies in the case of the highly educated and skilled (e.g., the societal cost of educating a medical doctor is extremely high) and in all cases, by newcomers themselves and their families, friends, and communities. Interestingly, only the chapters on Australia and the United States address this phenomena. Policy-makers would be well advised to remember that no matter how large their financial envelope for settlement/integration, it represents only a portion of the overall cost.

Perhaps most surprising is the relative absence of discussion about the role of employers in providing settlement/integration services to newcomers, although the Israel chapter does refer to some services that employers have provided to temporary foreign workers. Given that employers are often the most vocal in terms of demanding higher levels of immigration and that the financial returns to these same companies are usually the highest, this area is certainly worthy of further exploration. Perhaps the German example in which employers were (until recently) more active than the government in integrating newcomers through initiatives like the "Charta for Diversity"[7] would be a useful starting point (Sussmuth and Morehouse 2009; Zambonini 2009).

Without question, shifting the cost structure of settlement and integration is likely to be increasingly at the centre of policy discussions around the world as countries seek to manage their debts and deficits. As we have stated earlier, we believe that, at best, policy can shift the balance of costs along a continuum running from the majority borne by sending countries to the majority borne by receiving countries. Several countries, most notably the United Kingdom and the Netherlands, have already dramatically shifted costs to newcomers. In an era when an increasing number of countries must rely on highly skilled immigrants to shore up their labour force, this seems like a particularly risky strategy. It may indeed facilitate control of overall numbers of newcomers and may function to exclude those deemed to be the least desirable, but in the long term we imagine this will cost more than it gains. Immigration is not a short-term phenomena nor one that can be contracted or expanded overnight. The data presented reveal that costs to the initial wave of newcomers for settlement are extremely high; exacerbating these costs will be unlikely to assist countries in attracting the best and the brightest. The strength of an immigration program and the most effective means to manage settlement costs lie in chain migration: second and subsequent waves of newcomers benefit extensively from the assistance of their predecessors (Statistics Canada 2005).

Nevertheless, there are examples where the benefits of immigration are highly concentrated while costs are dispersed. In these instances, pricing behaviour may not have detrimental effects in terms of attracting the highly skilled. For example, if post-secondary institutions derive significant financial benefit from international students, they can be expected to pay for the settlement assistance these students require – international student advisors are a modest form of this kind of investment. Similarly, employers who seek temporary foreign workers should be obliged to ensure the acquisition of sufficient language skills to maintain health and safety. If they seek to convert the employee from temporary to permanent, it seems odd that society should be expected to foot the bill for settlement costs while the majority of the benefits accrue to the employer. Far more controversially, it is possible to imagine that families who wish to sponsor relatives could be expected to ensure basic language acquisition to minimize risk of their isolation and exploitation, and that additional settlement costs would be borne by the family, particularly since we know that, along with refugees, family members are the largest users of settlement services. Once again, the benefits are quite concentrated within the family unit, begging the question of why costs should be borne by the community at large.

Who Is Involved in Decision Making?

As we have described above, in most of the countries covered here the municipal or regional governments are often the most active in settlement and integration programming. In part this pattern is no doubt related to where newcomers live and the wide array of local services upon which they rely in the initial settlement period. It may also be viewed as a kind of forced downloading onto this level of government. It is worth noting that of the 15 international Metropolis conferences, many, including those in Rotterdam, the Hague, Toronto, and Vienna, were hosted by municipal governments because the issues of immigration and settlement/integration were important to their jurisdictions. In addition, their motivations included pursuing a political agenda whereby the larger levels of government would be forced to consider the costs being forced onto municipal shoulders. This phenomenon has been noted by the International Organization for Migration in its most recent *World Migration Report* (IOM 2010), which observes that one obstacle to better integration is that in many countries there is a lack of centralized responsibility for integration and that policy in this area is driven by local and regional factors that often reflect the vision and limited capacity of local administrations.

The Canadian exception alluded to in Huddleston's chapter is worth noting. Canada is one of the very few countries where settlement services are primarily delivered by third party, principally non-governmental agencies, although Finland, Spain, and the United Kingdom do fund some NGOs on a project-by-project basis, and Australia also funds settlement via a small set of settlement agencies. Accordingly, in Canada, civil society organizations tend to have a far greater impact on policy and program development for settlement and integration than they do in European countries with more formal, and rigid, consultation bodies.[8]

In addition, across almost all countries covered in this volume, we see a compartmentalization of policy areas (often focused on the role of immigrants-specific ministries) and inadequate linkages with the full gamut of policies necessary to ensure settlement and integration success. This situation should be no surprise, as the international literature has increasingly pointed to the need for mainstreaming and horizontality of approach (Biles et al. 2011; Bertelsmann Stiftung and MPI 2010; IOM 2010). Many of the chapters here have highlighted the importance of labour market engagement, housing, education, health, and social services. In most cases these remain in the purview of ministries tasked with serving the entire population, not only migrants. There are few examples of national strategies for integration that seek to pull together the disparate programming of all relevant ministries, although Canada does have some governance infrastructure to connect officials of various ministries to discuss settlement and integration.[9] This governance challenge is identified most strongly in the Spanish chapter but resonates throughout the countries covered. A recent IOM report (2010) also suggests that coordinating efforts across governments is key to improving integration and that this coordinated effort needs to be supported by clearly defined integration goals and a coordination strategy. In short, countries need to define success and develop a game plan to achieve it that incorporates all of the actors necessary for success.

What Settlement Services Should Be Offered and When?

There is almost complete agreement across all chapters that language[10] and labour market attachment are vital to settlement and integration: foreign credential recognition is one of the most commonly referenced barriers to be overcome. Equally, almost all countries appear to consider that offering settlement programs to refugees should be a priority along with an enhanced citizenship hurdle for newcomers to clear.[11] How these services are offered varies considerably and provides ample food for thought for policy-makers. Interestingly, other aspects of settlement/integration programming, including information/orientation and welcoming communities/community connections, appear to be far more variable. The exceptions are Finland and Sweden, which support the creation of integration plans for newcomers. The silence on these areas in other countries may in part be explained by the extensive engagement of local governments in the funding and provision of settlement services. The proximity of these governments to communities may systematize community connections and orientation activities in particular more than in those countries where settlement/integration is delivered nationally or regionally.

The chapters are also relatively silent on the extent to which settlement services are offered prior to arrival. There is more detail on eligibility and timing after arrival, with a number of countries utilizing naturalization as a distant end point for some testing of the relative integration of newcomers. Others have concentrated their settlement programming in the early months/years of arrival. We must note our concern that the outcomes of 1.5 and second generation youth were not heavily featured in the chapters included here. Given that the majority of newcomers report that a principal motivation for migrating is a better future for their children, this measure seem particularly important for aligning newcomer expectations and the realities they experience, not to mention the potential social cohesion challenges that poor outcomes for these children and youth may pose (Statistics Canada 2005).

How Do We Know if Programs Work?

A robust performance measurement framework is clearly key to answering this most critical of questions. The framework must begin with a clear understanding of the population in question, what constitutes settlement/integration success, and what assistance newcomers need/ what societal structural barriers need to be overcome to achieve that success. It is somewhat discouraging to note that in many of the countries covered in this volume there is no consensus on what constitutes success. Countries such as Australia, Canada, and Israel that explicitly seek to create new citizens have at least implicit definitions of success, often grounded in the language of full participation. They are also the most likely to accept that success is premised upon both newcomers and the receiving society working towards that end. On the other hand, those states where the emphasis appears to be on upping the bar for naturalization seem much more focused on control than on ensuring that immigrants participate fully (Wallace-Goodman 2010).

Given that the majority of academic research focuses on problem identification (e.g., poverty rates of newcomers or returns to foreign education, credentials, and experience), there is very little to guide to policy-makers in terms of ascertaining what kinds of programming appear to have an impact. Researchers typically argue this is evaluation research and they can only undertake it if access to data is provided and if contracted to do so. As a result, little of this type of information is available in the public domain. The Government of Canada may be somewhat of an exception to the norm (New Zealand also posts many evaluations online[12]) as it evaluates all programs on a five-year cycle and is obliged to post results online.[13] Whatever the cause of this paucity of research, it negatively impacts the ability of governments and societies to gauge how newcomers are faring and whether settlement and integration programs and policies are effective.[14]

FUTURE TRENDS IN INTEGRATION POLICY

There is considerable agreement that immigrant integration is one of the major challenges facing immigrant receiving societies (Biles et. al. 2011; Wallace-Goodman 2010; Bertelsmann Stiftung and MPI 2010). In this volume we have seen an extraordinary breadth of approaches to integration, and some striking similarities. We believe that it is these similarities that suggest some key future trends in integration policy that we briefly explore below. These trends include more emphasis on a needs driven, outcome based approach to settlement programming; increased attention to either minimizing the need for settlement via selection policies or better preparatory work prior to migration; a rebalancing of who pays for settlement and integration; a broader societal approach to settlement and integration; and a shift from a nearly exclusive focus on short-term settlement to a longer-term eye on integration, including outcomes of the second generation.

Needs Driven and Outcome Based

Tough fiscal times reinforce the need to better tailor settlement programs to aid those most in need and to demonstrate that policies and programs are effective. This process will entail universal needs assessments of all newcomers and the development of tailored settlement and integration strategies for newcomers and their families. Scandinavian experiences with developing settlement plans may well be the best place to begin in the development of these kinds of strategies. Ironically, Denmark has come to be viewed as a bit of a settlement pariah over the last few decades because of its strong emphasis on control in place of inclusion. However, it has developed some extremely sophisticated measures of program success and has adapted its policies and programs as a result. Australia has also developed solid performance measurement framework structures and adapted its selection system accordingly. Other countries might well be recommended to consider developing similar performance frameworks.

Increased Attention on Overseas Strategies and Selection/ Integration Synergies

The bromides of perfect selection policies have been increasingly questioned in recent years. In part this has been because of their inability to deliver "ready-to-wear" immigrants who require no assistance to settle and integrate into a new society. Equally, it has become clear that even in the birthplace of the points system – Canada – relatively few people are actually accessed against the points system. Rather, the majority of newcomers arrive as family members, and very few countries "select" family members.

Thus, a fundamental reconsideration of what work can be legitimately undertaken via selection regimes, and for whom, and what the downstream costs will be for settlement and integration is likely to dominate immigration discourse in the coming years. A related consideration is pathways to permanent residence for temporary workers and international students. The numbers of both international students and temporary foreign workers have been growing rapidly. Some countries like Canada have already introduced limited pathways to permanent residence, and the pressure to continue enlarging these avenues is growing; newcomers who have already spent time in the country have largely tackled their settlement challenges and acquired the human and social (if not the financial) capital to participate fully, and so may yield potential citizens who are closer to the ideal "ready to wear" immigrants than other selection regimes. Of course, this situation raises questions about how far countries are prepared to out-source selection to post-secondary learning institutions and employers.

Alternatively, countries may consider exploring how successful overseas preparation of newcomers may be in order to manage expectations and minimize need for settlement and integration services (Salter and Mutlu 2010). Some hold out hope that this approach may both minimize expenses and, more importantly, improve settlement and integration outcomes for newcomers (Biles et al. 2011; Bertelsmann Stiftung and MPI 2010). Experiments undertaken by Australia on foreign credential recognition, by the Netherlands and Quebec on language acquisition, and by Canada on counselling for both government assisted refugees and highly skilled workers may be worth emulating.

Societal Strategies

Knowing why a particular mix of newcomers is admitted to a country is a necessary first step to determining who benefits and who should therefore pay. All too often immigration policy and regulations are accrued over time until the "framework" becomes self-evident and beyond critique (Duyvendak and Scholten 2011). This is not a well-thought-out strategy, since one galvanizing incident – a terrorist attack, riots, or a media spectacle like those surrounding the arrival of a shipload of refugee claimants – can quickly dominate public discourse and give rise to "knee-jerk" calls for tougher immigration policies to preserve the integrity of the border. The result is seldom carefully developed policy that balances access to those people the country needs, and security to exclude those people it legitimately fears.

Increasingly, governments at both the national and sub-national levels have sought to develop carefully articulated strategies that explicitly build the case for immigration, the appropriate mix of newcomers to meet needs, and the settlement and integration strategies required to maximize returns to this investment for both the receiving society and the newcomers. It is our expectation that countries will come under increasing pressure to develop public plans and strategies for why they need immigration and how they intend to attract and retain the newcomers they need to succeed (Bertelsmann Stiftung and MPI 2009).

These plans and strategies seem destined to encompass not only national level policy and programs responsible for immigration, settlement and integration but a far wider vertical and horizontal approach that actively engages all three levels of government and other critical local actors such as employers and post-secondary institutions. It seems unlikely that policies can continue to focus only on the attraction side of the equation. As secondary migration, return migration, and transnationalism continue to increase, a focus on retention will also become inevitable. This focus will in turn lead to increased emphasis on the role of the host societies and the attitudes that need to be tackled and the barriers that must be overcome to increase the probability of retention.

It is already evident that heavily tied to this two-way street approach to integration is the increasing realization that static national identities and citizenship regimes need to be re-examined. The evolution of national identities is extremely discomforting for many who cling to the belief that they are autochthonous and never changing rather than "invented," as Hobsbawn (1992) has suggested. As a result, in the current emphasis on citizenship regimes, we see some states open to the idea of evolution and change while others cling to static notions of national identity and citizenship (Wallace-Goodman 2010). It is our contention that we will continue to see countries shift away from this latter perspective toward a more flexible and inclusive notion of both concepts. Countries faced with this dilemma may well examine how Germany has shifted its approach in a very compressed time period (Klusmeyer and Papademetriou 2009). We also anticipate that countries will become far more preoccupied with civic integration and begin to invest far more in citizenship preparation. It may be possible to out-source selection of newcomers to other orders of government, post-secondary institutions, and employers, but it is far less probable that states will relinquish control over what it takes to be a citizen. Thus, we anticipate a more robust public discourse in most immigrant-receiving countries about what they wish to be as a society and how they are going to get there.

Integration and Social Cohesion

Finally, we see the ultimate arbiter of success shifting considerably from short-term settlement to longer-term integration outcomes. These measures will likely be twofold – first, the outcomes of the integration of newcomers themselves, and secondly, of their children.

If, as in the Canadian case, most social, economic, civic, and cultural outcomes continue to converge at approximately 10-15 years in country, this will likely be deemed a success by newcomers themselves and their receiving societies (Tunis 2010). However, increasingly it appears that economic outcomes for most immigrants never fully recover from the turmoil of migration. At a minimum, countries must address this disconnect between expectation and reality or face damaging reports through the word-of-mouth chains that characterize much migration.

We also know that a majority of immigrants migrate to better the life chances of their children (Statistics Canada 2005). Should this fail to materialize, not only will immigrants report failure to meet these expectations to their communities in countries of origin, but the exclusion of an increasingly disgruntled second generation will pose a significant challenge to social cohesion of the host society. Accordingly, we expect countries to be far more transparent in the information they make available to prospective migrants but also to anticipate that greater policy attention will be paid to the outcomes of the second generation.

NOTES

1. "Host society" is a term commonly used to denote the society that receives immigrants and into which those immigrants integrate. We prefer it to "receiving society," which is the other commonly used term, as "host" at least implies some level of hospitality and reciprocity. However, we feel it falls short of the mark in terms of the depth of reciprocity and power sharing necessary for integration to work effectively (Biles and Ibrahim 2005). Nevertheless, owing to its wide currency within the field of immigration studies, we have opted to use it as shorthand throughout this chapter.

2. Some state governments have done more recently, including Washington (2009), Virginia (2009), Maryland (2009), and Massachusetts (2009), which have all either struck governor's advisory councils or similar structures to develop state strategies to attract and retain newcomers.

3. For example, although the presence/absence and relative strength of right-wing political parties (as measured by votes received) is often posited as a major arbiter of public discourse on immigration, recent research suggests that there is little empirical evidence to support this position (Muddle 2010).

   Another possible example pertains to public opinion: experts on both sides of the Atlantic have concluded that governments must persuade their public that not only are they effectively managing borders but also that their proposed immigration and integration measures are solution focused and measurable. In the absence of this sense of control and progress, support for immigration itself and expenditures on integration will likely remain tepid at best (Bertelsmann Stiftung and MPI 2009).

4. It is interesting to note that recent research has ascertained that economic migrants (e.g., those selected by the state, or by employers on behalf of the state) are the least likely to seek naturalization and to demonstrate attachment to the host society. Rather, it is the importance of kinship ties that predict this commitment to host societies (Massey and Redstone Akresh 2006; Khoo 2003).

5. While an in-depth exploration of citizenship regime changes falls outside of the scope of this volume, it is important to flag that this is an area of integration policy development where most immigrant-receiving states have been particularly active (Wallace-Goodman 2010; Etzioni 2007; Odmalm 2007). It is also worth flagging that policy-makers must carefully weigh whether raising the naturalization bar actually results in more immigrants investing more to integrate, or in more immigrants choosing the opposite path—resistance to integration.

6. The value of the absorption basket varies depending upon family situation. Specifics can be found at http://www.moia.gov.il/Moia_en/FinancialAssistance/TableAmountsBasket.htm.

7. The Charta for Diversity, launched in 2006, is a voluntary code of conduct for large German companies to create open-minded workplaces free of prejudice.

8. Despite this elevated level of involvement of civil society organizations in the Canadian context, on the MIPEX index the privileged role of formal

consultative bodies actually results in a misleadingly low score for Canada on this measure. For example, Canadian governments provide extensive support to various umbrella organizations for immigrant service provider organizations.

9. A director-general level committee meets annually to discuss integration issues. See also Biles (2008), note 4.

10. The infrastructure and provision for language classes in the various countries identified in the present volume are revealed as either extremely limited or insufficient (e.g., Spain, UK). In other countries, language policies are either reinforced for newcomers, restricted to specific categories of immigrants, or directed toward immigrants who have a low level of the host language (e.g., Austria, Finland).

11. In terms of granting citizenship as a measure of political integration, we find that some countries prioritize the *ius sanguinis* principle (blood relation where citizenship is based on ancestry) while others stress the importance of birthplace (*ius soli* principle). Yet others invoke the *ius doomicili* principle that pertains to rights based on residence. Nevertheless, with the exception of immigrants in North America, the naturalization process is long and compli-cated, and migrants are required to present a substantial number of formal, translated documents as well as to pass various citizenship tests in order to become eligible for naturalization (Kontos et al. 2009; Wallace-Goodman 2010).

12. Evaluations of the New Zealand Department of Labour can be found at http://www.dol.govt.nz/publications-browse.asp?BrowseBy=Subject&Su bject=40&Name=Immigration+-+Settlement.

13. All Citizenship and Immigration Canada evaluations are posted at http:// www.cic.gc.ca/english/resources/evaluation/index.asp.

14. Public opinion experts suggest that a necessary condition for increased sup-port of immigration and funding for integration is a public perception that the government is effectively managing the border (Bertelsmann Stiftung and MPI 2009).

References

Andrew, C., J. Biles, M. Burstein, V. Esses, and E. Tolley, eds. 2011. *Integration and Inclusion in Ontario Cities*. Kingston and Montreal: McGill-Queen's University Press.

Berry, J.W. 1980. "Social and Cultural Change." In *Handbook of Cross-Cultural Psychology: Social Psychology*, ed. H.C. Triandis and R.W. Brislin, vol. 5, 211-79. Boston: Allyn and Bacon.

—2001. "A Psychology of Immigration." *Journal of Social Issues* 57:615-31.

Bertelsmann Stiftung and Migration Policy Institute, ed. 2009. *Migration, Public Opinion and Politics*. Gütersloh, Germany: Verlag Bertelsmann Stiftung.

—2010. *Prioritizing Integration*. Gütersloh, Germany: Verlag Bertelsmann Stiftung.

Biles, J. 2008. "Integration Policies in English-Speaking Canada." In *Immigration and Integration in Canada in the Twenty-First Century*, ed. J. Biles, M. Burstein, and J. Frideres, 139-86. Kingston and Montreal: McGill-Queen's University Press.

Biles, J. and H. Ibrahim. 2005. "Religion and Public Policy: Immigration, Citizenship, and Multiculturalism – Guess Who's Coming to Dinner?" In *Religion and Ethnicity in Canada*, ed. P. Bramdat and D. Seljak, 154-77. Toronto: Pearson Longman.

Biles, J. and P. Spoonley. 2007. "National Identity: What Can It Tell Us about Inclusion and Exclusion?" *National Identities* 9(3):191-5.

Biles, J., M. Burstein, J. Frideres, E. Tolley, and R. Vineberg. 2011. Conclusion to *Integration and Inclusion of Newcomers and Minorities across Canada*, ed. J. Biles, M. Burstein, J. Frideres, E. Tolley, and R. Vineberg. Montreal and Kingston: McGill-Queen's University Press.

Bonjour, S. 2011. "The Power and Morals of Policy Makers: Reassessing the Control Gap Debate." *International Migration Review* 45:89-122.

Bourhis, R., L. Moise, S. Perreault, and S. Senecal. 1997. "Toward an Interactive Acculturation Model: A Social Psychological Approach." *International Journal of Psychology* 32:369-86.

Collett, E. 2011. "Immigrant Integration in Europe in a Time of Austerity." Migration Policy Institute. At http://www.migrationpolicy.org/pubs/TCM-integration.pdf (accessed 9 May 2011).

Duyvendak, J.W. and P.W.A. Scholten. 2011. "Beyond the Dutch 'Multicultural Model': The Coproduction of Integration Policy Frames in the Netherlands." *International Migration and* Integration 12:331-48.

Etzioni, A. 2007. "Citizenship Tests: A Comparative, Communitarian Perspective." *Political Quarterly* 78(3):353-63.

Frideres, J. 2010. "Conflict, Cohesion and Assimilation: The Value of Multi culturalism." Presentation at the Canadian Embassy, The Hague, 6 October.

Good, K.R. 2010. *Municipalities and Multiculturalism: The Politics of Immigration in Toronto and Vancouver*. Toronto: University of Toronto Press.

Guiraudon, V. and G. Lahav. 2000. "A Reappraisal of the State Sovereignty Debate: The Case of Migration Control." *Comparative Political Studies* 33:163-95.

Hobsbawn, E. 1992. *The Invention of Tradition*. Cambridge: Cambridge University Press.

Hollifield, J. 2000. "The Politics of International Migration. How Can We 'Bring the State Back In'?" In *Migration Theory: Talking across Disciplines*, ed. C. Brettell and J. Hollifield, 137-86. New York: Routledge.

International Organization for Migration (IOM). 2010. *World Migration Report: The Future of Migration, Building Capacities for Change*. Geneva: IOM.

Khoo, S.-E. 2003. "Sponsorship of Relatives for Migration and Immigrant Settlement Intention." *International Migration* 41(5):176-98.

Klusmeyer, D.B. and D.G. Papademetriou. 2009. *Immigration Policy in the Federal Republic of Germany: Negotiating Membership and Remaking the Nation*. New York: Berghahn Books.

Kontos, M., F. Anthias, M. Morokvasic-Muller, G. Campani, M. Pajnik, K. Slany, M. Liapi, and N. Trimikliniotis. 2009. *Integration of Female Immigrants in Labour Market and Society*. Frankfurt Am Main: Institute of Social Research, Goethe University.

Kymlicka, W. 1995. *Multicultural Citizenship*. Oxford: Oxford University Press.

—2004. "Marketing Canadian Pluralism in the International Arena." *International Journal* 59(4):829-52.

Massey, D.S. and I. Redstone Akresh. 2006. "Immigrant Intentions and Mobility in a Global Economy: The Attitudes and Behaviour of Recently Arrived U.S. Immigrants." *Social Science Quarterly* 87(5):54-71.

Muddle, C. 2010. "The Relationship between Immigration and Nativism in Europe and North America." In *Prioritizing Integration*, ed. Bertelsmann Stiftung and Migration Policy Institute, 299-348.

Odmalm, P. 2007. "One Size Fits All? European Citizenship, National Citizenship Policies, and Integration Requirements." *Representation* 43(1):19-34.

Salter, M. and C. Mutlu. 2010. *Asymmetric Borders; The Canada-Czech Republic Visa War and the Question of Rights.* Centre for European Policy Studies Working Paper Series.

Schmidt, R. 2007. "Comparing Federal Government Immigrant Settlement Policies in Canada and the United States." *American Review of Canadian Studies* 37:103-22.

Standing Committee on Citizenship and Immigration. 2003. "Settlement and Integration: A Sense of Belonging, 'Feeling at Home.'" June.

Statistics Canada. 2005. "Longitudinal Survey of Immigrants to Canada: A Portrait of Early Settlement Experiences." At http://www.statcan.gc.ca/pub/89-614-x/89-614-x2005001-eng.pdf (accessed 4 April 2011).

Sussmuth, R. and C. Morehouse. 2009. "The Future of Migration and Integration Policy in Germany." In *Migration, Public Opinion and Politics*, ed. Bertelsmann Stiftung and Migration Policy Institute, 263-90.

Tolley, E., and R. Young . 2011. *Immigrant Settlement Policy in Canadian Municipalities.* Kingston and Montreal: McGill-Queen's University Press.

Tunis, D. 2010. "Fostering an Integrated Society – An Aspiration or Reality?" Harold Crabtree Foundation Award in Public Policy Lecture, University of Western Ontario, 21 October. At http://ir.lib.uwo.ca/cgi/viewcontent.cgi?article=1017&context=mer&sei-redir=1#search=%22tunis%20uwo%20integration%20Fostering%20an%20Integrated%20Society%20-%20An%20Aspiration%20or%20Reality%3F%22 (accessed 7 July 2011).

Wallace-Goodman, S. 2010. "Integration Requirements for Integration's Sake? Identifying, Categorising and Comparing Civic Integration Policies." *Journal of Ethnic and Migration Studies* 36(5):753-72.

Wulff, M.A., T. Carter, R. Vineberg, and S. Ward, eds. 2008. "Attracting New Arrivals to Smaller Cities and Rural Communities: Findings from Australia, Canada and New Zealand." Special issue, *Journal of International Migration and Integration* 9(2):119-24.

Zambonini, G. 2009. "The Evolution of German Media Coverage of Migration." In *Migration, Public Opinion and Politics*, ed. Bertelsmann Stiftung and Migration Policy, 169-84.

CONTRIBUTORS

PIETER BEVELANDER, Malmo University

JOHN BILES, Citizenship and Immigration Canada

IRENE BLOEMRAAD, UC-Berkeley

ANNIE CARROLL, Citizenship and Immigration Canada

JOCK COLLINS, University of Technology, Sydney

ELS DE GRAAUW, Baruch College, CUNY

JAMES FRIDERES, University of Calgary

ANASTASIA GORODZEISKY, Ben Gurion University of the Negev/
Juan March Institute, Spain

THOMAS HUDDLESTON, Migration Policy Group

JACK JEDWAB, Association for Canadian Studies

EVA XIAOLING LI, University of Saskatchewan

PETER S. LI, University of Saskatchewan

TUOMAS MARTIKAINEN, University of Helsinki

DEREK MCGHEE, University of Southampton

JULIA MOURÃO PERMOSER, University of Vienna

NANA OISHI, Sophia University

RADOSTINA PAVLOVA, Citizenship and Immigration Canada

RAVI PENDAKUR, University of Ottawa

SIEGLINDE ROSENBERGER, University of Vienna

MOSHE SEMYONOV, Tel Aviv University/University of Illinois at Chicago

MARGARET SOKOL, Citizenship and Immigration Canada

VARUN UBEROI, Brunel University

KATHLEEN VALTONEN, University of Helsinki

ÖSTEN WAHLBECK, University of Helsinki

RICARD ZAPATA-BARRERO, Universitat Pompeu Fabra

Queen's Policy Studies
Recent Publications

The Queen's Policy Studies Series is dedicated to the exploration of major public policy issues that confront governments and society in Canada and other nations.

Manuscript submission. We are pleased to consider new book proposals and manuscripts. Preliminary enquiries are welcome. A subvention is normally required for the publication of an academic book. Please direct questions or proposals to the Publications Unit by email at spspress@queensu.ca, or visit our website at: www.queensu.ca/sps/books, or contact us by phone at (613) 533-2192.

Our books are available from good bookstores everywhere, including the Queen's University bookstore (http://www.campusbookstore.com/). McGill-Queen's University Press is the exclusive world representative and distributor of books in the series. A full catalogue and ordering information may be found on their web site (http://mqup.mcgill.ca/).

School of Policy Studies

Dynamic Negotiations: Teacher Labour Relations in Canadian Elementary and Secondary Education, Sara Slinn and Arthur Sweetman (eds.) 2012. ISBN 978-1-55339-304-7

Where to from Here? Keeping Medicare Sustainable, Stephen Duckett 2012. ISBN 978-1-55339-318-4

International Migration in Uncertain Times, John Nieuwenhuysen, Howard Duncan, and Stine Neerup (eds.) 2012. ISBN 978-1-55339-308-5

Life After Forty: Official Languages Policy in Canada/Après quarante ans, les politiques de langue officielle au Canada, Jack Jedwab and Rodrigue Landry (eds.) 2011. ISBN 978-1-55339-279-8

From Innovation to Transformation: Moving up the Curve in Ontario Healthcare, Hon. Elinor Caplan, Dr. Tom Bigda-Peyton, Maia MacNiven, and Sandy Sheahan 2011. ISBN 978-1-55339-315-3

Academic Reform: Policy Options for Improving the Quality and Cost-Effectiveness of Undergraduate Education in Ontario, Ian D. Clark, David Trick, and Richard Van Loon 2011. ISBN 978-1-55339-310-8

Integration and Inclusion of Newcomers and Minorities across Canada, John Biles, Meyer Burstein, James Frideres, Erin Tolley, and Robert Vineberg (eds.) 2011. ISBN 978-1-55339-290-3

A New Synthesis of Public Administration: Serving in the 21st Century, Jocelyne Bourgon, 2011. Paper ISBN 978-1-55339-312-2 Cloth ISBN 978-1-55339-313-9

Recreating Canada: Essays in Honour of Paul Weiler, Randall Morck (ed.), 2011. ISBN 978-1-55339-273-6

Data Data Everywhere: Access and Accountability? Colleen M. Flood (ed.), 2011. ISBN 978-1-55339-236-1

Making the Case: Using Case Studies for Teaching and Knowledge Management in Public Administration, Andrew Graham, 2011. ISBN 978-1-55339-302-3

Canada's Isotope Crisis: What Next? Jatin Nathwani and Donald Wallace (eds.), 2010. Paper ISBN 978-1-55339-283-5 Cloth ISBN 978-1-55339-284-2

Pursuing Higher Education in Canada: Economic, Social, and Policy Dimensions, Ross Finnie, Marc Frenette, Richard E. Mueller, and Arthur Sweetman (eds.), 2010. Paper ISBN 978-1-55339-277-4 Cloth ISBN 978-1-55339-278-1

Canadian Immigration: Economic Evidence for a Dynamic Policy Environment,
Ted McDonald, Elizabeth Ruddick, Arthur Sweetman, and Christopher Worswick
(eds.), 2010. Paper ISBN 978-1-55339-281-1 Cloth ISBN 978-1-55339-282-8

Taking Stock: Research on Teaching and Learning in Higher Education, Julia Christensen
Hughes and Joy Mighty (eds.), 2010. Paper ISBN 978-1-55339-271-2
Cloth ISBN 978-1-55339-272-9

Centre for the Study of Democracy

Jimmy and Rosalynn Carter: A Canadian Tribute, Arthur Milnes (ed.), 2011.
Paper ISBN 978-1-55339-300-9 Cloth ISBN 978-1-55339-301-6

*Unrevised and Unrepented II: Debating Speeches and Others By the Right Honourable Arthur
Meighen,* Arthur Milnes (ed.), 2011. Paper ISBN 978-1-55339-296-5
Cloth ISBN 978-1-55339-297-2

Centre for International and Defence Policy

*Security Operations in the 21st Century: Canadian Perspectives on the Comprehensive
Approach,* Michael Rostek and Peter Gizewski (eds.), 2011. ISBN 978-1-55339-351-1

Europe Without Soldiers? Recruitment and Retention across the Armed Forces of Europe,
Tibor Szvircsev Tresch and Christian Leuprecht (eds.), 2010.
Paper ISBN 978-1-55339-246-0 Cloth ISBN 978-1-55339-247-7

Mission Critical: Smaller Democracies' Role in Global Stability Operations,
Christian Leuprecht, Jodok Troy, and David Last (eds.), 2010. ISBN 978-1-55339-244-6

John Deutsch Institute for the Study of Economic Policy

The 2009 Federal Budget: Challenge, Response and Retrospect, Charles M. Beach,
Bev Dahlby and Paul A.R. Hobson (eds.), 2010. Paper ISBN 978-1-55339-165-4
Cloth ISBN 978-1-55339-166-1

Discount Rates for the Evaluation of Public Private Partnerships, David F. Burgess and
Glenn P. Jenkins (eds.), 2010. Paper ISBN 978-1-55339-163-0 Cloth ISBN 978-1-55339-164-7

Institute of Intergovernmental Relations

The Evolving Canadian Crown, Jennifer Smith and D. Michael Jackson (eds.), 2011.
ISBN 978-1-55339-202-6

The Federal Idea: Essays in Honour of Ronald L. Watts, Thomas J. Courchene, John R. Allan,
Christian Leuprecht, and Nadia Verrelli (eds.), 2011. Paper ISBN 978-1-55339-198-2
Cloth ISBN 978-1-55339-199-9

Canada: The State of the Federation 2009, vol. 22, *Carbon Pricing and Environmental
Federalism,* Thomas J. Courchene and John R. Allan (eds.), 2010.
Paper ISBN 978-1-55339-196-8 Cloth ISBN 978-1-55339-197-5

Our publications may be purchased at leading bookstores, including the Queen's University Bookstore (http://www.campusbookstore.com/) or can be ordered online from:
McGill-Queen's University Press, at **http://mqup.mcgill.ca/ordering.php**

For more information about new and backlist titles from Queen's Policy Studies, visit
http://www.queensu.ca/sps/books or visit the McGill-Queen's University Press
web site at: **http://mqup.mcgill.ca/**